The Industrial Organization and Regulation of the Securities Industry

A National Bureau
of Economic Research
Conference Report

The Industrial Organization and Regulation of the Securities Industry

Edited by Andrew W. Lo

1996

 The University of Chicago Press

Chicago and London

ANDREW W. LO is the Harris & Harris Group Professor of Finance at the Massachusetts Institute of Technology and a research associate of the National Bureau of Economic Research.

The University of Chicago Press, Chicago 60637
The University of Chicago Press, Ltd., London
© 1996 by the National Bureau of Economic Research
All rights reserved. Published 1996
Printed in the United States of America
05 04 03 02 01 00 99 98 97 96   1 2 3 4 5
ISBN: 0-226-48847-0 (cloth)

Library of Congress Cataloging-in-Publication Data

The industrial organization and regulation of the securities industry / edited by Andrew W. Lo.
    p.   cm.—(A National Bureau of Economic Research Conference report)
    Papers of a conference held Jan. 20–22, 1994, in Key Largo, Fla.
    Includes bibliographical references and index.
    1. Securities industry—Congresses. 2. Securities industry—State supervision—Congresses. I. Lo, Andrew W. (Andrew Wen-Chuan)
II. Series: Conference report (National Bureau of Economic Research)
HG4515.I53 1996
332.63'2—dc20   95-18033
                                               CIP

Contents

Acknowledgments

This conference was generously supported by a grant from the New York Stock Exchange to the National Bureau of Economic Research. Throughout the conference's two-year planning phase and over the past twelve months when the conference volume was being assembled, I have benefited enormously from the advice and help of many individuals.

Jim Shapiro was a tremendous resource on whom I drew frequently, and was among the few believers who shared my ambitious vision for this conference right from the very start. He and his colleagues at the NYSE, especially Jim Cochrane and George Sofianos, gave generously of their time and energy at every stage, providing historical data, industry contacts, and other resources to many of the conference participants. Without their enthusiasm and tireless efforts, this conference would not have been the success that it was.

I am also grateful to Bob Merton, whose research on the functional approach to financial regulation first sparked my interest in this area, and with whom I discussed many aspects of this conference over countless lunches at his expense.

The NBER has been an ideal forum for promoting interest in this new and exciting research area, and Geoff Carliner and Marty Feldstein have been invaluable sources of support and encouragement at every turn.

And as usual, Kirsten Foss Davis, Lauren Lariviere, and the other members of the NBER conference department must be congratulated for planning and executing yet another flawless conference—they made my job so easy, I wonder if my title of "conference organizer" isn't a misnomer.

Deborah Kiernan, Marc London, and Cristina McFadden of the NBER publications department and Anita Samen of the University of Chicago Press provided excellent support in turning ten manuscripts and twenty discussants' comments into this wonderful conference volume.

Finally, I would like to thank all the preconference and conference participants for taking time from their very busy schedules to take part in this unprecedented gathering of economists, regulators, lawyers, and practitioners. While academics think nothing of sequestering themselves for days on end to deliberate on issues large and small, those from other walks of life are usually not so inclined. That almost all of the conference participants attended the full three days of sessions (I did take attendance)—in a conference room with no windows—is a testament to the intense interest and excitement that they themselves have generated. This book is a worthy tribute to their contributions.

Introduction

Andrew W. Lo

On January 1, 1989, the Swedish government implemented a transactions tax on fixed-income securities and associated derivatives. In comparison to its equity counterparts, the fixed-income tax was rather small, reaching a maximum of only fifteen basis points of the notional amount traded. Nevertheless, during the first week of the tax, trading volume for bonds dropped by 85 percent, trading volume for futures on bonds and bills dropped by 98 percent, and trading in fixed-income derivatives all but disappeared (see Campbell and Froot 1994). This was accompanied by an *increase* in the variety and trading volume of nontaxable substitute securities, securities with almost identical risk/return profiles to their taxable counterparts, for example, Swedish debentures, variable-rate notes, forward-rate agreements, and swaps. On April 15, 1990, the tax was abolished, and trading volume quickly returned to pre-1989 levels.

The Swedish experience is only one of many recent examples that illustrate the flexibility and creativity with which financial systems adapt to changes in their operating environments, sometimes with unanticipated and unintended consequences. It also illustrates the complexities that face regulators in their attempts to correct market failures and improve social welfare. Regulating financial markets is not unlike managing an artificial ecology: in both cases, the goals are multifaceted and not always mutually consistent, the regulatory instruments are relatively few and blunt, and the agents react and adapt to changes in their environment in sophisticated ways that are not entirely understood or predictable. Moreover, the principles governing economic systems are considerably more fickle than those governing biological and physical systems.

Andrew W. Lo is the Harris & Harris Group Professor of Finance at the Sloan School of Management at the Massachusetts Institute of Technology and a research associate of the National Bureau of Economic Research.

1

These challenges provided the motivation for the NBER's conference "The Industrial Organization and Regulation of the Securities Industry," held January 20–22, 1994, in Key Largo, Florida. A smaller preconference planning meeting was held in Cambridge on July 17, 1992, to solicit ideas for the scope and organization of the conference.

Although the study of regulation has become an important part of the industrial organization literature, and although it has played a tremendous role in determining the fate of the airlines, telecommunications, transportation, and public utilities industries, relatively little attention has been paid to the industrial organization and regulation of the securities industry.

Of course, this is not to say that financial market regulation is new—indeed, regulations covering financial transactions can be found in the recorded histories of even the most ancient civilizations. But the notion that economic principles can be successfully applied to the design and implementation of regulatory structures is a relatively modern one. And while economists have figured prominently in many regulatory debates—Ronald Coase, Alfred Kahn, and George Stigler, to name just a few—their domain has not yet broadened to include financial market regulation, which has been dominated historically by lawyers, legislators, lobbyists, and an occasional practitioner or two. It is only very recently, and most visibly at this NBER conference, that financial regulation has begun to be discussed and debated in the jargon of traditional regulation economics: market failure, monopoly power, price discrimination, externalities, barriers to entry, and so forth.

The series of breakthroughs in our understanding of financial market risks and returns that economists have achieved over the past thirty years, coupled with the recent explosion of financial innovation in the securities industry, suggests that the time is ripe for economists to turn their attention to the securities industry. Contributions by Merton (1993) and Ross (1989) and those in Lehn and Kamphuis (1993) may signal the start of such a trend.

To encourage and support this trend, the NBER held a preconference meeting to engage industrial organization economists, financial economists, and practitioners in a dialogue about the most pressing issues facing financial market participants and regulators today. This dialogue grew quickly in scope and depth, and this conference volume is the culmination of the many ideas and issues that surfaced at that initial meeting.

Like many other NBER conferences, this conference was organized around the ten papers selected for presentation, with two discussants assigned to each paper. However, there was one very important difference. Because of the novelty of the conference topic, and because there was an underlying intention to spark research collaboration among three well-developed but rather insular academic disciplines—industrial organization, finance, and law—the conference participants were carefully selected to represent all three disciplines, with additional representation from regulatory agencies and the securities industry. In addition to the usual complement of economists from academia, the audience and discussants included practicing lawyers and legal scholars of securities law, portfolio managers, brokers and market makers, stock exchange officials, several former and current commissioners of the Commodity Futures Trading Commission and the Securities and Exchange Commission, the chief economist of the SEC, and the supreme court justice of the state of Delaware. The papers and the discussants' comments contained in this volume will provide readers with only a small glimpse of the exhilarating and dynamic exchanges among speakers, discussants, and the audience.

In chapter 1, William Albrecht, Corinne Bronfman, and Harold Messenheimer develop a framework for analyzing the efficiency of various regulatory structures. They begin with the premise that there are three goals of efficient financial regulation: (1) customer protection; (2) financial system integrity; and (3) market price integrity. However, typical regulatory incentives are not always consistent with these goals; hence some changes in the structure of financial services regulation may improve efficiency. For example, they find that increasing competition among regulatory agencies of substitute markets increases efficiency, but increasing competition among regulatory agencies of complement markets decreases efficiency. They conclude that the construction of efficient regulatory structures must include a careful analysis of the incentives facing regulators and the degree of complementarity or substitutability of the products to be regulated.

In chapter 2, Kathleen Hagerty and Robert McDonald focus on market fragmentation, an issue of increasing importance as financial markets become more highly computerized and payment for order flow becomes more prevalent. Market fragmentation refers to the splintering of securities trading across many different markets and dealers, resulting in less liquidity than if the trading were centralized. Hagerty and McDonald propose a model of market fragmentation in which some investors have valuable private information and others do not, and the efficient economic response to this asymmetry of information is what we perceive as fragmentation. They show that fragmentation may be a reflection of increased price competition among dealers, and that a fragmented market may provide better prices for customers than a less fragmented monopolistic dealer market. While their model does not capture every aspect of the market fragmentation issue, it does provide an important insight: central markets and brokerage markets serve different needs for different investors; hence reducing fragmentation may not necessarily improve market efficiency.

To complement Hagerty and McDonald's theoretical analysis, in chapter 3 Thomas McInish and Robert Wood provide an empirical analysis of fragmentation in which they use bid-ask spreads and other price data to measure the potential costs of dispersing orders among multiple market centers. Using transaction data from 1991, they form five equity portfolios that are nearly identical in those attributes that should affect their spreads, premiums (the difference between the transactions prices and the midpoint of their corresponding bid-ask spreads), and volatility, but as different as possible in the fragmentation of their orders. By comparing the properties of these portfolios, one can better observe the effects of fragmentation while controlling for economic factors that might otherwise confound the comparison. McInish and Wood find that bid-ask spreads and premiums are reduced by a decrease in fragmentation, while volatility seems unaffected. However, while the reduction in spreads is statistically significant, the range of the spread across the five portfolios is only 0.6 cent.

The impact of technology on financial markets is further underscored by Ian Domowitz's study on computer-automated equity trading systems in chapter 4. Trading systems such as Instinet, POSIT, and the Arizona Stock Exchange have stretched the limits of existing securities regulation, much of which was drafted before the personal computer and workstation revolution. Domowitz begins with a brief historical review of such trading systems and then turns his attention to how they are classified in the current regulatory environment, no small matter, since the classification of an automated trading system determines how it is to be regulated. The classification problem calls into question the very definition of a securities exchange, and Domowitz develops a more complete definition, distilled from legislative, legal, and SEC decisions, that identifies trade execution, price quotes, price discovery, and liquidity as key characteristics. While such a definition blurs the exchange/nonexchange distinction, it suggests that Merton's (1993) "functional" approach to designing securities regulation may be more effective than current practice.

Another example of the impact of technology on the securities industry is provided by Peter Reiss and Ingrid Werner's study of trading costs on the London Stock Exchange (LSE) in chapter 5. In 1986, the LSE switched from a closed, floor-based broker-dealer market to an open electronic quotation system called SEAQ. This system operates much like the National Association of Securities Dealers' Nasdaq dealer system: competing market makers post bid and ask prices and guaranteed trading volumes, but while SEAQ also displays trade information, brokers and dealers still negotiate trades by phone. The introduction of SEAQ coincided with the LSE's adoption of best execution rules and elimination of fixed commissions.

Reiss and Werner present a thorough empirical analysis of these liquidity-enhancing innovations of the LSE, using newly available 1991 SEAQ intraday quotation and transaction data. They develop a new measure of transaction costs that incorporates information on dealers' quotes and investors' transactions to capture the hypothetical cost of an immediate round-trip transaction. Using this measure, they find that medium and large trades often receive a discount off the best or "touch" bid-offer spread, whereas small and very large trades pay the touch or more. For wider touches, the discounts are larger. And finally, dealers and market makers treat customer trades differently: dealers tend to discount medium and large trades routinely, whereas market makers discount only very large trades. These patterns raise several interesting issues for further study, particularly in the context of information- or inventory-based theories of marketing making in which discounts have not yet played a role.

In chapter 6, Robert Neal and David Reiffen present an empirical analysis of the potential impact of the vertical integration of broker-dealers with specialists on trading costs. Although changes in the degree of vertical integration within a firm are rare and often triggered by unobserved events, in 1986 the New York Stock Exchange and American Stock Exchange relaxed their rules concerning the relationship between brokerage firms and specialists. Neal and Reiffen take advantage of this structural change in exchange policy by examining data on combinations of broker-dealer and specialist units on the New York, American, and Philadelphia Stock Exchanges between 1987 and 1993. Common objections to this type of vertical integration center on the possibility of increased trading costs for investors, due to moral hazard (brokers directing order to their own specialists rather than searching for the best price), or because integration "forecloses" a share of the market otherwise open to competition. Neal and Reiffen find that neither of these theories is supported by post-integration transaction data. Average trade sizes decline on the integrated exchanges, and there is some evidence for a divergence of order flow, but there is little evidence of a statistically significant increase in trading costs subsequent to integration.

Defining the regulatory environment of the securities industry is a nontrivial endeavor because of the industry's global reach. Each sovereign nation has its own regulatory agencies, with unique charters, incentives, and organizational structures, and these agencies must often operate across geopolitical boundaries. In chapter 7, Lawrence White addresses these issues by asking whether regulatory regimes should be harmonized internationally or be allowed to compete—harmonization can create a "level playing field," but competition may enhance the efficiency of capital flows. Using the concepts of market failure (externalities, market power, asymmetric information, etc.) and government failure (rent-seeking behavior, rent-creating capture, weak incentives, etc.), White argues that competition should be a "default": in the absence of substantial market and government failures, competition among regulatory regimes will lead to more efficient outcomes. But when market and government failures do exist, harmonization can be critical to correcting these failures.

Another important factor that governs and sometimes restricts the coordination of regulatory regimes across countries is the indigenous institutional environment of each country, which often changes slowly through time. Kenneth Singleton's study in chapter 8 highlights this factor by comparing the behavior of cash and futures prices for government bonds in Germany, Japan, and the United States. These three countries are at different stages of the financial liberalization process, and have different market structures, market-making costs, and liquidity. Singleton uses the joint distribution of cash and futures prices as a yardstick to measure the differences across these three countries. Using daily and weekly bond data from October 1, 1991, to November 30, 1993, he finds that the institutional settings in Germany and Japan, which contain considerably more frictions, are reflected in fatter-tailed distributions and, in the case of Japan, higher serial correlation for changes in bond yields. The presence of frictions in the cash market also imply a much more important price discovery role for the more liquid futures market, with Japan providing the extreme example where cash prices are priced almost exactly off the futures price. These patterns underscore the important link between the institutional environment in which price discovery occurs and the time-series properties of fixed-income yields.

The fact that institutional differences can be very significant indeed is also highlighted by Bruce Lehmann and David Modest's detailed analysis of liquidity on the Tokyo Stock Exchange (TSE) in chapter 9. Contrary to most organized equity exchanges in which designated market makers provide liquidity continuously, the TSE has a public limit order book in which incoming orders are matched according to strict priority rules based on price, time, and size. Therefore, it is the investor public that absorbs temporary imbalances between supply and demand, not designated market makers. When order imbalances are too large in either direction, the TSE provides warning and special quote (*chui* and *tokubetsu kehai*) mechanisms to flag such imbalances and to halt trading to attract orders to correct the imbalance. Using TSE transactions data from January 1, 1991, to November 30, 1991, and February 1, 1992, to April 30, 1993—yielding a staggering 25,863,726 transactions—Lehmann and Modest conclude that trading halts are seldom triggered by investors, and when they are, the investors usually execute all or part of their order at the warning quote, a price known in advance. Moreover, trading volume is similar when orders do and do not result in trading halts. Although it is tempting to infer from this that designated market makers may not provide as much liquidity as we thought, Lehmann and Modest are quick to point out that it is impossible to distinguish between the success of the TSE market mechanisms and investors who have learned to put up with their idiosyncrasies.

In chapter 10, Stephen Pruitt and Maurice Tse revisit the controversial debate concerning the effects of changes in Federal Reserve margin requirements on stock prices, volatility, and liquidity. Recent studies have focused on the behavior of the S&P Composite index in response to changes in margin levels, but since all securities in this index were listed on either the New York or American Stock Exchange over the 1937 to 1974 interval, they all faced the same margin constraints at all times. In particular, the extent to which changes in margin levels affect marginable stocks relative to their nonmarginable counterparts—a statement about cross-sectional differences—cannot be answered by comparing the performance of the same market index over different intervals of calendar time—a statement about time-series differences.

To perform the cross-sectional comparison, Pruitt and Tse exploit a 1969 amendment to the Securities Exchange Act of 1934, which allows securities dealers and brokers to extend margin credit on certain unlisted (OTC) equity securities. They collect daily price data for twenty marginable OTC securities, and for twenty matching nonmarginable OTC securities during each of the four post-1969 amendment margin changes (matched by industry, market capitalization, and debt/equity ratio), yielding 160 firms in their sample. By comparing the properties of portfolios of marginable and nonmarginable securities before and after margin changes, Pruitt and Tse conclude that prices, volatility, and liquidity are generally unaffected by margin changes, and any reactions to such changes are due to information effects only, and not to changes in investors' margin-imposed binding constraints.

As with most successful conferences, this conference concluded with many more new questions than new answers. The unprecedented breadth of interest in the issues surrounding the industrial organization and regulation of the securities industry, from such a diverse group of participants, may foreshadow the beginnings of a new discipline that, while truly interdisciplinary by its nature, has as its main focus the application of economic principles to policy issues in the securities industry. It has been my privilege to witness what may have been the birth of such a discipline at this NBER conference, and I hope this volume will encourage others to participate in this most exciting new venture.

References

Campbell, J., and K. Froot. 1994. International Experiences with Securities Transaction Taxes. In J. Frankel, ed., *The Internationalization of Equity Markets.* Chicago: University of Chicago Press.

Lehn, K., and R. Kamphius, eds. 1993. *Modernizing U.S. Securities Regulations: Economic and Legal Perspectives.* Burr Ridge, IL: Irwin Professional Publishing.

Merton, R. 1993. Operation and Regulation in Financial Intermediation: A Functional Perspective. In P. Englund, ed., *Operation and Regulation of Financial Markets.* Stockholm: Economic Council.

Ross, S. 1989. Commentary: Using Tax Policy to Curb Speculative Short-Term Trading. *Journal of Financial Services Research* 3:117–20.

1   Regulatory Regimes: The Interdependence of Rules and Regulatory Structure

William P. Albrecht, Corinne Bronfman, and
Harold C. Messenheimer

We consider the regulatory structure of the U.S. securities, futures, and options markets. Much of this regulatory structure has been in place for some time. The Securities and Exchange Commission (SEC), which oversees the securities markets, was established in 1934. The Grain Futures Act of 1922 and the Commodity Exchange Act of 1936 form the underpinnings of the 1975 statute establishing the Commodity Futures Trading Commission (CFTC) to oversee trading in futures and options on futures.

Many of the regulations that the CFTC and the SEC enforce are as old or older than the agencies themselves. One does not have to be a zealous deregulator to recognize that at least some of them are outdated and that at least some of the complaints about them are justified. These complaints generally fall into four broad areas: (1) the requirements imposed by the CFTC and the SEC entail unnecessary duplication and inconsistencies; (2) the level or type of regulation is inefficient (costs are greater than benefits); (3) regulation or the review procedures of a regulatory authority are an impediment to innovation; and (4) differential regulation of similar entities has resulted in an "unlevel" playing field.

In recent years, unhappiness about financial regulation has led more than one critic to call for a merger of the CFTC and the SEC. Recently there has

William P. Albrecht is professor of economics at the University of Iowa. Corinne Bronfman is assistant professor of finance at the University of Arizona. From 1991 to 1993, she was on leave from the university and worked in the Research Section of the Division of Economic Analysis at the Commodity Futures Trading Commission. Harold C. Messenheimer is an independent writer/ consultant and a research associate at the Center for Study of Public Choice at George Mason University. From 1991 to 1993, he served as economic adviser to Commissioner William Albrecht at the Commodity Futures Trading Commission.

The authors have been employed recently by the Commodity Futures Trading Commission. The views expressed in this paper are their own and do not necessarily reflect those of the commission or of its staff.

even been a call for consolidation of all agencies concerned with federal financial regulation in a single cabinet-level department.[1] The result of the political debate on the issue of consolidation has been preservation of the status quo. The academic debate has noted that, while dual regulation may impose costs, competition between or among regulators may also benefit market participants by providing them with a choice.[2]

In this paper, we focus specifically on the question of efficient regulation and how the regulatory structure affects regulators' incentives to act efficiently or inefficiently. To analyze the issues, we develop a model of regulation that describes the scope and the goals of an efficiency-seeking regulator with perfect information. We then relax the assumption of efficiency seeking and characterize the behavior of a regulator who has additional arguments in his or her utility function. We extend the model to this more realistic regulator and examine the constraints and incentives that affect that agency's behavior. We use the model to analyze the impact of different regulatory structures on the extent and scope of regulation. In particular, we examine the effect of the number of regulators on the level of regulation. We conclude that regulatory competition is likely to lead to a more efficient level of regulation than will occur with a single regulator when substitute products are involved. We find that the opposite holds in the case of complements. This leads to the conclusion that the desirability of combining the CFTC and SEC depends in part upon whether the products they regulate are substitutes or complements.

We begin by providing a background for our model with a brief discussion of the rationale of regulation, the structure and function of a regulatory agency, and regulatory incentives.

1.1   Background

1.1.1   The Rationale of Regulation

The goals of efficient regulation of securities and futures markets may be summarized under the following three headings: (1) customer protection, (2) financial system integrity, and (3) market price integrity. Customer protection includes protection from fraud and default. The potential for fraud and default raises investors' perceived costs of transacting much like a tax on trading would increase the cost of transacting. Regulation seeks to reduce those costs through a system of rules and regulations, governing, for example, registration,

---

1. Sandner, (1993). Under the proposal, the following federal agencies would be consolidated: Office of the Comptroller of the Currency, Office of Thrift Supervision, the Federal Deposit Insurance Corporation, the CFTC, the SEC, the Securities Investor Protection Corporation, the Pension Benefit Guaranty Corporation, and certain regulatory functions nonessential to their primary operations performed by the Federal Reserve Board and the Department of Labor.

2. Ed Kane has been the most prolific and articulate proponent of this view. See, for example, Kane (1984, 1988).

record keeping, and disclosure. Of course, by prescribing and proscribing specific behaviors, such regulations impose their own costs on market participants.

The second goal of regulation is financial system integrity. The possibility of a systemic problem, such as a bankruptcy of one brokerage house with a domino effect on other market participants, imposes a taxlike cost on market participants that can be thought of as an additional cost of transacting. Regulators attempt to reduce this taxlike cost by imposing, for example, capital requirements and minimum margins.[3]

The third goal is market price integrity. Market participants enjoy timely information about price relationships in futures and cash markets. And they use this information to make their plans. Consequently, "wrong" price signals, resulting from, say, manipulation or market fragmentation, harm market participants by misinforming them about market fundamentals. As with the other goals of regulation, this potential harm imposes a taxlike cost on market participants. Regulations that prescribe or proscribe certain behaviors to reduce this harm include position limits, position reporting, and trade practice restrictions.

Regulation will be efficient with respect to each of these goals when the marginal reduction in the anticipated cost from the various harms discussed above just equals the marginal cost imposed by the regulation. While our analysis is generalizable to all the harms discussed above, we simplify by focusing on a single aspect of regulatory concern: fraud. Much of our financial regulatory system is intended to protect against fraud. But why are specialized regulations and a specialized agency necessary for financial services? For most crimes such as robbery and murder, a general statutory prohibition suffices—as it does for fraud in the sale of many goods and services.

Fraud, especially in financial services, is often difficult to detect.[4] When one customer's order is filled at a worse price than that of another customer, it may or may not be fraud. When a broker takes the other side of his customer's order, it may or may not be fraud. When an agent loses money when trading a client's account over which she has discretionary power, it may or may not be fraud. In short, financial fraud is harder to detect than crimes such as robbery or murder. It is also harder to detect than some other types of fraud. When, for example, something advertised as peanut butter turns out to be guano, there is no problem in detecting the fraud.

Because of the difficulty of knowing when certain types of financial fraud have occurred, regulators have prescribed and proscribed various activities by those who engage in financial transactions on behalf of others. These prescriptions and proscriptions are designed to increase the costs of committing fraud and to make it easier to detect. Requiring floor brokers to execute orders in the order in which they are received makes it less likely that one customer will be

---

3. Ensuring the survival of weak firms is not the purpose of regulation addressing financial system integrity.

4. For a more complete analysis, see Albrecht and Messenheimer (1993).

favored over another. Requiring an audit trail for trades makes it easier to catch those who violate the rule concerning the order of execution. And, since market participants realize that detection is more likely because of the rule, it serves also to deter fraud. Presumably, then, the peculiar nature of financial fraud justifies the existence of independent regulatory agencies such as the CFTC and the SEC.

In actual practice, three functions of the CFTC and the SEC have evolved. One is to write specific regulations to supplement the various provisions of the statute(s) each agency is charged with implementing. A second function is to monitor or audit compliance with these regulations by the exchanges and regulated firms. A third function is to enforce compliance with both the statute and the commission's regulations. These three functions are the means by which a specialized financial regulatory agency actually goes about deterring fraud.

1.1.2   Regulatory Incentives

Writing an efficient set of regulations, given the imperfect information available to the agency, would be difficult even if there were strong incentives to adopt such a set of rules. The real incentives, however, are quite different. In large measure, this is because those who enact the legislation the agency implements and who oversee the agency's performance are often much less interested in economic efficiency than in their own political well-being.

One result of this interest in their own political well-being is to give regulators an incentive to protect the agency from blame if something goes wrong. They do not want to have to explain such an event to Congress. The preferred way of protecting the agency is to have enough regulations in place to cover every conceivable form of fraud or other undesirable behavior. Thus, even if something does go wrong, the agency can point out that one of its regulations has been violated and that it should not be blamed for what has happened. This point of view is particularly strong among staff members who are responsible for writing rules.

Another very strong incentive is to make it easy to catch violators by requiring many records to be kept and by prohibiting any behavior that might conceivably facilitate fraud—without paying much attention to cost. This incentive is particularly strong among staff members who are responsible for enforcing rules.

For the purpose of establishing a useful benchmark, we initially assume that regulators, irrespective of the regulatory structure, are motivated solely by efficiency.[5] The benchmark so established will be used to evaluate how closely real regulatory structures containing real regulators are able to approach it.

---

5. This benchmark is relevant to the extent one feels that efficiency *should* be the regulatory objective. Other regulatory objectives might be equity (or fairness). To enforce equity in order that the unsophisticated have access to capital and futures markets, while being protected from possible abuses, SEC and CFTC regulators emphasize protection of the small investor and customer in their rule making. Our focus on efficiency is intended to encourage advocates of equity and fairness to consider trade-offs with efficiency.

1.2 A Model of Regulation

We develop the benchmark diagrammatically in figures 1.1 and 1.2. Firms organize to facilitate transacting. We call this facilitation "transaction services," the quantity of which we represent by Q. Q, for example, could be thought of as containing the qualities of immediacy, standardization of contract terms, and guarantee of performance provided by futures exchanges. Assume initially that there is no regulation of Q. For simplicity, assume also that the per unit cost of providing Q is constant as indicated by the horizontal supply curve S.

The demand curve D for transaction services has the usual properties. It is downward sloping with respect to price. Again, if we think of Q as having the qualities of immediacy, standardization of contract terms, and guarantee of performance, then price can be thought of as the sum of the bid-ask spread, the exchange fee, and the clearing fee. The lower this price, everything else being equal, the greater is the quantity of Q demanded. The demand curve's location and slope depend on the prices of substitutes and complements as well as other relevant states of nature. For example, the demand for transaction services provided by exchanges depends, in part, on the price of the over-the-counter transaction services. And the demand for transaction services provided for risk-shifting products depends on the price of transaction services in capital markets.

Demanders know they face some prospect of fraud when purchasing Q. For example, in an exchange-type market, immediacy is provided by liquidity suppliers who stand ready to buy or to sell from the other market participants. While serving as an intermediary, the immediacy provider has ample opportunity to commit fraud through dishonest sales or trade practices (say by trading at the same time as a customer's order and taking the best fill). Whatever the particular source of the prospective fraud, demanders' behavior is altered *relative to no fraud* because their expected return is reduced and uncertainty increased. Their valuation of prospective fraud imposes a taxlike increase in the price paid for Q, which for simplicity we treat as a constant, per-unit tax. This unit taxlike valuation of prospective fraud by demanders is denoted by T_F, which serves to shift the demand curve faced by suppliers from D to $D - T_F$ in figure 1.1. Instead of the honest amount of equilibrium transaction services Q_u, Q_0 emerges in the presence of fraud.

Referring to figure 1.1, we see that regulation has the potential to reduce two losses that exist relative to "no threat of fraud." First, there are losses represented in the lightly shaded Harberger triangle.[6] The triangle represents the potential gains from trade that are forgone because of the taxlike wedge im-

---

6. Harberger (1959). Harberger measured the welfare cost of monopoly as the loss in consumer surplus because of the restriction on output and the higher price at which the reduced output was sold. His approach was subsequently applied to the analysis of tariffs. The Harberger triangle in this study arises through the distortion in trading behavior because of the presence of fraud, which has an impact on behavior similar to that of a tax.

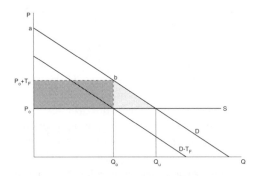

Fig. 1.1   Prospective valuation of fraud (T_F) modifies behavior like a tax

posed between demanders and suppliers of Q. The other loss associated with T_F is represented by the darkly shaded Tullock rectangle.[7] This economic loss arises because resources devoted to deception are diverted from potentially productive uses. For example, resources devoted to trade practice fraud could be diverted to providing improved transaction services, say by providing increased liquidity. Resources devoted to sales practice fraud could be diverted to the provision of honest Q (or some other honest endeavor that promotes gains from trade). Therefore, the Tullock rectangle is recognized as being, not a mere transfer from demanders to crooks, but a real economic loss in terms of wasted resources.[8]

Thus, we see that the total of the economic losses caused by fraud are the sum of the areas of the shaded triangle and rectangle. Looked at differently, the remaining gains from trade, in the presence of fraud and absent regulation, are the consumer surplus triangle $a(P_0 + T_F)b$ in figure 1.1. The potential role for regulators to improve efficiency is clear from the figure. They can simply impose rules that reduce the threat of fraud and so reduce the demanders' prospective valuation of it. By imposing and enforcing a set of rules, they shift the demand curve ($D - T_F$) toward the demand curve D; that is, by reducing the taxlike fraud premium, they reduce the losses represented by the Harberger triangle and Tullock rectangle. Looked at differently, by reducing the taxlike fraud premium, they increase the gains from trade represented by the consumer surplus triangle.

---

7. The extensive literature on rent seeking as an economic loss began with Gordon Tullock's article "The Welfare Costs of Tariffs, Monopolies, and Theft," first published in the *Western Economic Journal* in June 1967. That essay and many of the important contributions since are collected in Buchanan, Tollison, and Tullock (1980) and Rowley, Tollison, and Tullock (1987).

8. The rent-seeking literature is divided on the proportion of the rectangle that is an economic loss (Tullock 1980). The opportunity cost of resources devoted to fraud could be greater than, less than, or equal to this rectangle. The exact proportion is not relevant to our analysis, but for simplicity we will follow Posner (1975) and assume that the rent-seeking loss from fraud is equal to the area of the rectangle.

1.2.1   The Impact of Costs on Regulatory Initiatives

Regulation, of course, is not costless, and efficiency-seeking regulators would take into account both the direct and the indirect costs imposed. *Direct costs* are imposed by regulators when rules designed to reduce the fraud premium prescribe or proscribe certain behaviors. For example, regulators may prescribe record-keeping rules that increase the probability of detecting fraud, or they may proscribe certain trade practices to increase the cost of committing fraud; in so doing, they also increase the cost of providing immediacy. *Indirect costs* are the rent-seeking activity that is generated because of the potential to influence regulation. Once an agency is charged with writing rules, interest groups will spend considerable resources to influence the writing of the statute that is to govern the rule writing. And once the statute is enacted, further resources will be spent to influence the rule writers. Inasmuch as interest groups seek to obtain differential advantage via the political-regulatory process, these resources are wasted.[9]

The overall effect of the reduction in fraud and increase in costs is shown by the example in figure 1.2. The figure illustrates a case where regulation reduces the prospective valuation of fraud to T_R, and simultaneously increases the unit cost of providing Q by T_C. T_C is a per-unit taxlike cost imposed on suppliers. It includes direct costs of regulation as well as additional rent-seeking costs. Since T_C is less than $(T_F - T_R)$, Q will increase to Q_R, and consumer surplus will increase to triangle $a(P_R + T_R)b_R$.

It is obvious that, in the case where potential regulation would increase T_C more than T_F would be reduced, there is no set of regulations that will produce a triangle larger than $a(P_0 + T_F)b$ in figure 1.1. In that case, any existing (efficiency-seeking) regulators of Q would simply choose the null set of regulations. There would be no need for a specialized regulatory agency.

Recall that we sought in this section to establish an efficiency benchmark. We have now done so. The goal of efficiency-seeking regulators is clear from figure 1.2: they should choose the set of regulations that maximizes the consumer surplus triangle. Put differently, they should minimize the combined losses associated with prospective fraud and regulatory costs, that is, minimize the sum $(T_R + T_C)$ in figure 1.2. Put still differently, they should choose the set of regulations that maximizes equilibrium Q. By maximizing Q, the regulators will maximize gains from trade enjoyed by market users.

What if the regulator does not choose the efficient set of regulations? How can outcomes be characterized when the regulator over- or underregulates? After all, regulation cannot be defined in homogeneous units. Consider regulations, for example, that prescribe certain behaviors such as registration and record keeping. Even something as simple as registration cannot be defined in

---

9. Again the reader is referred to the rent-seeking literature, much of which is contained in Buchanan, Tollison, and Tullock (1980) and Rowley, Tollison, and Tullock (1987).

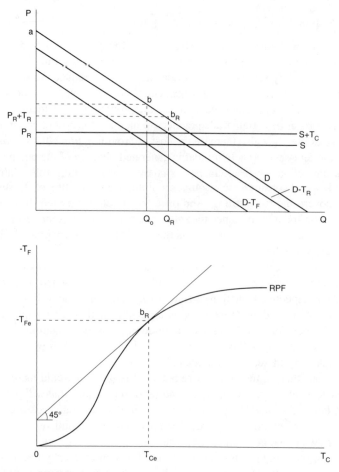

Fig. 1.2   Efficient regulation: *top,* **supply and demand;** *bottom,* **cost of regulation and cost of fraud**

homogeneous units. Who is to be registered? What are the criteria for acceptance of a potential registrant? How much information is required of a registrant? How often, and to what extent, will the information be updated and reviewed subsequent to registration? Similar remarks apply to various regulations that proscribe certain behaviors. In what sense, then, may we think of there being more (or less) regulation if we cannot measure it?

We assume that the regulator will attempt to choose the least costly set of regulations for each quantity of prospective fraud reduced.[10] We call this the *correct approach.* By this assumption, each incremental regulatory action,

10. We justify this assumption when we evaluate the incentives of regulators in section 1.2.2.

which further circumscribes or frees behavior in some fashion, changes prospective fraud (ΔT_F) and the unit cost (ΔT_C) of providing transaction services such that the ratio $(-\Delta T_F)/(\Delta T_C)$ is maximized among the remaining regulations. For example, a new registration requirement reduces prospective fraud, say by reducing the likelihood that crooks will enter, but it does so only by increasing the unit cost of transaction services. And it is the most effective possible change in regulation as long as the ratio is maximized and the regulator is using the correct approach. This is illustrated by the regulatory production frontier in the lower half of figure 1.2. When the marginal unit cost of regulation T_C and the marginal amount of fraud reduced are equivalent, the regulator achieves efficiency. The efficient set of regulations R imposes cost T_{Ce}. Points labeled b_R in the upper and lower halves of figure 1.2 are equivalent.

Assuming that the regulator follows the correct approach, we can derive possible equilibria for different levels of regulation. These are shown graphically along the locus in figure 1.3. These equilibria reflect market adjustments to the two unit taxlike effects of changing regulation: the change in the prospective valuation of fraud by demanders, and the change in the unit cost of providing Q. Q_0 and P_0 are the market price and quantity when regulation is zero. Q_R and P_R are the market price and quantity when regulation is R. The locus of regulatory equilibria (LORE) is the schedule of market price and quantity for each level of regulation. Between points 0 and e, as the level of regulation is increased from zero to R, the prospective valuation of fraud is being reduced faster than the unit cost of providing that level of regulation increases. Thus, Q and consumer surplus are increasing over that range. As the level of regulation increases above R, the unit cost of providing Q increases faster than the prospective valuation of fraud is reduced. Thus, Q and consumer surplus are decreasing. The efficiency-seeking regulator (with perfect information) will choose level of regulation R. Market participants adjust to point e in figure 1.3. At this point, consumer surplus and Q are maximized.

Underlying LORE are the demand and supply curves that reflect the trading

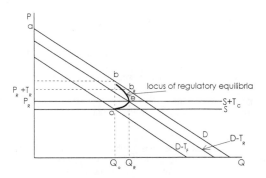

Fig. 1.3   Locus of regulatory equilibria (LORE)

public and the trading technology. It follows that LORE will differ according to the structure of the particular market being regulated, as the point at which costs increase more rapidly than benefits will not occur at the same point in all markets. This suggests that arguments to "level the playing field" across different markets, by making the regulatory approach and magnitude consistent, are not arguments for efficiency.[11]

1.2.2   The Incentives of Regulators

Even well-intentioned regulators are not generally motivated solely by efficiency. They may believe that reducing fraud always enhances efficiency; or, in a world of imperfect information, they may not know whether their regulations are overly burdensome. They may also enjoy the power and perks of their position. Therefore, we now consider the arguments that may plausibly enter a regulator's utility function and how they affect the level of regulation. We model the regulator of market i as having a utility function of the form

$$(1) \qquad\qquad U^{R_i} = U(\overset{+}{Q_i}, \overset{+}{R_i}, \overset{-}{T_{F_i}}),$$

where the signs over the arguments indicate the signs of the first partial derivatives. We can write the utility function in this form because each of the arguments is a function of the amount of regulation chosen by the regulator.[12] Q, the volume of trade, is a good proxy for the present value of the regulators' money income and prestige.[13] R, the number and the comprehensiveness of the regulations enacted by the regulator, is a good proxy for the regulator's power and perks. T_F is the per-unit fraud tax, the public "bad" that the regulator would like to reduce. The regulator's marginal utility decreases as Q increases ($U_{QQ} < 0$), decreases as R increases ($U_{RR} < 0$), and decreases as fraud increases ($U_{TT} > 0$).

While the costs of regulation are not included explicitly in the formulation above, they do enter into the demand and supply equilibrium constraints that are embedded in it. Q_1 is determined in equilibrium by demanders and suppliers in market 1 and substitute/complement markets. dQ_1/dR_1 is determined by the change in the valuation of prospective fraud, the change in costs imposed in market 1, and relevant feedback effects among other markets. The regulator chooses R_1 to maximize his or her utility, taking into account the expected

---

11. Stephen Schaefer (1992) reaches a similar conclusion in his analysis of capital requirements and arguments in support of "functional" regulation to ensure that banks and securities firms are regulated equally. He demonstrates that there may well be valid reasons for higher capital requirements on banks.

12. The particular specification has the advantage of being simple. More important, by focusing attention on the incentives of regulators, it provides a framework for an analysis of regulatory structure.

13. In general, the prestige of an agency is directly related to its size, the size of its budget, and the number of high-salary positions in the agency, which, in turn, are a function of the size and importance of the industry it regulates. Furthermore, the expected value of a regulator's postregulatory income is also a function of the size of the regulated industry.

adjustment of participants in market 1 and all related markets. The question is whether a utility-maximizing regulator will have a tendency to overregulate, underregulate, or (as if led by an invisible hand) to seek efficiency.

The first-order condition for the regulator's utility maximum is

$$
(2) \qquad U_{Q_1}\frac{dQ_1}{dR_1} + U_{R_1} + U_{T_{F_1}}\frac{dT_{F_1}}{dR_1} = 0.
$$

Assume that $(dQ_1/dR_1) > 0$, so that the regulator has the potential to increase efficiency with more regulation. Will it be in her self-interest to do so? Consider the signs of each of the terms in the marginal-utility expression for the regulator:

$$
(3) \qquad \overset{+}{U_{Q_1}}\frac{dQ_1}{dR_1} + \overset{+}{U_{R_1}} + \overset{-}{U_{T_{F_1}}}\frac{\overset{-}{dT_{F_1}}}{dR_1} = MU_R.
$$

The terms on the left of equation (3) all tend to increase the regulator's utility as she increases R_1, which suggests that regulators have very little incentive to underregulate. And if, by some fortuitous circumstance, a regulator stumbled onto the efficient point $((dQ_1/dR_1) = 0)$, that agent would be motivated to keep increasing regulation, since

$$
(4) \qquad \overset{0}{U_{Q_1}}\frac{dQ_1}{dR_1} + \overset{+}{U_{R_1}} + \overset{-}{U_{T_{F_1}}}\frac{\overset{-}{dT_{F_1}}}{dR_1} > 0.
$$

This is demonstrated in figure 1.4, where the LORE derived in figure 1.3 is replotted in Q_1, R_1 space. The regulator has the utility function posited above, and chooses level of regulation R_0 where the marginal rate of substitution of Q_1 for R_1 along indifference curve U_0 is tangent to the locus of regulatory equilibria. Contrast indifference curve U_0 with the indifference curve of an efficiency-seeking regulator. Recall that the efficiency-seeking regulator does not have R as a direct argument in her utility function, and neither does R enter it indirectly through prospective fraud. Therefore, the efficiency-seeking regulator will have horizontal indifference curves and choose the efficient quantity of regulation R_e where indifference curve U_e is tangent to the LORE. We see that more realistic regulators will have a natural tendency to overregulate, for example, by the amount $R_0 - R_e$ in figure 1.4.

1.3 Regulatory Competition and Its Implications for Regulatory Structure

If there were only a single market, a regulator would need to consider only the impact of the regulation on market 1. For this regulator, the marginal rate of substitution (*MRS*) between Q_1 and R_1 is

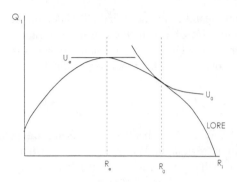

Fig. 1.4   Incentives of regulators and regulatory outcomes

$$(5) \qquad \frac{dQ_1}{dR_1} = MRS_{RQ} = - \frac{U_{R_1} + U_{T_1}\dfrac{dT_{F_1}}{dR_1}}{U_{Q_1}}.$$

The first-order condition for an efficiency-seeking regulator is defined by the condition that $dQ_1/dR_1 = 0$ at the utility maximizing point. Thus, in the case where the regulator does not derive utility from reduced fraud or increased regulation, the numerator of MRS would be zero. In terms of figure 1.4, the regulator would have horizontal indifference curves such as U_e, and choose regulatory vector R_e where Q_1 would be maximized and efficiency attained. More generally, however, equation (5) shows that a regulator will trade off more regulation for a reduced level of transaction services. The regulator who gets utility from regulation and from decreasing fraud will increase regulation beyond the efficient point, that is, beyond where $dQ_1/dR_1 = 0.$[14] As the level of regulation is increased, $dQ_1/dR_1 < 0$, until, at some point, the extra utility gained from a small increase in regulation and reduction in fraud is offset by the extra utility lost from decreasing transaction services.

Now suppose that there is another market where the products traded are reasonably close substitutes (complements) with those traded on market 1. With substitute (complement) markets, a change in regulation in market 1 will affect the demand for transaction services in market 2. And a change in regulation in the substitute market 2 will affect the utility of the regulator of market 1. Holding R_1 constant, we differentiate regulator 1's marginal rate of substitution of R_1 for Q_1 with respect to a change in R_2.

---

14. We note additionally that a very zealous regulator could be characterized by a first-order condition > 0 even at the point where $dQ_1/dR_1 < 0$ so long as $U_{R_1} >> 0$ (large) and $dT_F/dR_1 <<$ 0 (that is, changing by a lot). These results show that, under plausible assumptions about regulatory behavior, regulators will have an incentive to choose more than the efficient amount of regulation.

(6)
$$\frac{d\left(\dfrac{dQ_1}{dR_1}\right)}{dR_2} = \frac{\left(U_{R_1} + U_{T_{F_1}}\dfrac{dT_{F_1}}{dR_1}\right)U_{QQ}\left(\dfrac{dQ_1}{dR_2}\right)}{U_{Q_1}^2}$$

Notice that the marginal rate of substitution will decrease or increase depending on whether markets 1 and 2 are substitutes or complements. We know that the two terms in parentheses in the numerator are positive, the denominator is positive, and U_{QQ} is negative (by assumption). Our characterization of regulatory behavior, that is, that regulators tend to overregulate, means that dQ_1/dR_2 is positive when markets 1 and 2 are substitutes and negative when they are complements. An increase in R_2 raises the fraud-adjusted price of transaction services in that market. Therefore, some demanders will shift to market 1 when they are substitutes, implying that $dQ_1/dR_2 > 0$. We illustrate this effect in figure 1.5.

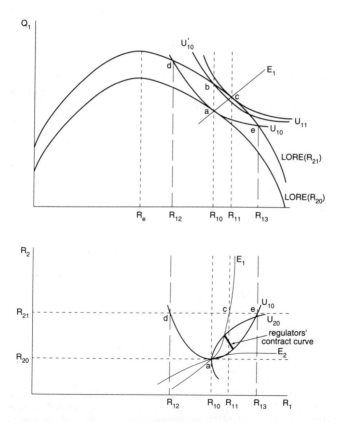

Fig. 1.5 Substitute markets: *top,* LORE shifts outward when the other regulator increases regulation; *bottom,* the potential gain to the regulator from overregulation

In the top panel, the regulator chooses R_{10} so as to maximize utility given LORE as a constraint. Initially, regulator 1 is at point a on indifference curve U_{10}. When the regulator in the substitute market increases R_2 from R_{20} to R_{21}, LORE in market 1 shifts upward ($dQ_1/dR_2 > 0$), and regulator 1 will find increased utility U'_{10} at point b. Because the markets are substitutes, if increased regulation in market 2 has the effect of decreasing Q_2, there will be an increase in Q_1, and regulator 1's marginal rate of substitution will decrease (increase in absolute value). We can also demonstrate diagrammatically these interactions between the two regulators.

Refer again to the top panel of figure 1.5. After the increase in regulation in market 2, the regulator of market 1 will increase regulation from R_{10} to R_{11} so as to put herself on indifference curve U_{11} at point c. These responses of regulator 1 are replotted in R_2, R_1 space in the lower panel of figure 1.5.[15]

In the lower panel, E_1 is regulator 1's independent adjustment response to the quantities of regulation chosen by regulator 2. Similarly, E_2 is the independent adjustment response of regulator 2 to quantities of regulation chosen by regulator 1. If the two regulators exhibit Cournot-Nash behavior, they will be in equilibrium at point a. Notice that indifference curve U_{10} in the upper panel through points a, d, and e is redrawn in the lower panel of figure 1.5. Similarly we draw an indifference curve for regulator 2 through point a. If the regulators recognize their interdependence, they will have an incentive to engage in cartellike behavior so as to move to the regulators' contract curve. Because movement toward the curve results in increased regulation and decreased Q in both markets, market participants are worse off relative to the independent adjustment equilibrium.[16]

To derive algebraically the slopes of the regulators' response curves shown in figure 1.5, we totally differentiate the first-order condition (equation [2]) for the regulator of market 1 (R_1 can be thought of as an implicit function of R_2).

$$(7) \left[U_{1Q_1Q_1} \left[\frac{dQ_1}{dR_1}\right]^2 + U_{1Q_1} \frac{d^2Q_1}{dR_1^2} + U_{1R_1R_1} + \left[\frac{dT_{F_1}}{dR_1}\right]^2 U_{1T_{F_1}T_{F_1}} + \frac{d^2T_{F_1}}{dR_1^2} U_{1T_{F_1}} \right] dR_1$$

$$+ U_{1Q_1Q_1} \frac{dQ_1}{dR_1} \frac{dQ_1}{dR_2} dR_2 = 0$$

15. We note that, since information is imperfect, shifts in the pattern of trade between markets are a noisy signal. An increase in volume could represent a vote of confidence in the regulatory environment, or a flight from a less-efficient regulatory regime.

16. However, over-regulation may serve as an incentive to innovation elsewhere. The futures markets have seen a huge growth in the cash foreign exchange market and a far lower growth in their markets. Some of the rules of trading on a contract market make it difficult for large institutional traders to accomplish their trades at minimum price impact. They find it more cost-effective to use a market where private negotiation of trades is not prohibited, as it is under the open and competitive requirements of the Commodity Exchange Act.

Assuming that regulators exhibit Cournot-Nash behavior, the slope of the regulator of market 1's response curve is given by

(8) $$\frac{dR_2}{dR_1} = -\left[U_{1Q_1Q_1}\left[\frac{dQ_1}{dR_1}\right]^2 + U_{Q_1}\frac{d^2Q_1}{dR_1^2} + U_{R_1R_1} + \left[\frac{dT_{F_1}}{dR_1}\right]^2 U_{1T_1T_1}\right.$$
$$\left. + \frac{d^2T_{F_1}}{dR_1^2}U_{1T_1}\right] \div \left[U_{1Q_1Q_1}\frac{dQ_1}{dR_1}\frac{dQ_1}{dR_2}\right] > 0.$$

Similarly, the slope of the response curve of the regulator of market 2 is

(9) $$\frac{dR_2}{dR_1} = -\left[U_{2Q_2Q_2}\frac{dQ_2}{dR_2}\frac{dQ_2}{dR_1}\right] \div \left[U_{2Q_2Q_2}\left[\frac{dQ_2}{dR_2}\right]^2 + U_{Q_2}\frac{d^2Q_2}{dR_2^2}\right.$$
$$\left. + U_{2R_2R_2} + \left[\frac{dT_{F_2}}{dR_2}\right]^2 U_{2T_2T_2} + \frac{d^2T_{F_1}}{dR_2^2}U_{2T_2}\right] > 0.$$

We can now see that regulator 1's response curve (E_1) would be vertical if she were efficiency seeking, since in that case $dQ_1/dR_1 = 0$. By similar reasoning, regulator 2's response curve (E_2) would be horizontal if he were efficiency seeking ($dQ_2/dR_2 = 0$). Notice also that the slope of regulator 1's (2's) response curve will be less (greater), the greater is the change in her marginal utility directly via R (the level of regulation) and T_F (the amount of fraud) from changing regulation.

Interactions between the two regulators occur when at least one of them is not efficiency seeking, that is, when writing regulations or reducing fraud are arguments in at least one regulator's utility function. As the quantity of transaction services in market i changes because of a change in the level of regulation in market j, the behavior of an efficiency-seeking regulator will not change. Formally, $dR_i/dR_j = 0$ holds so long as $dQ_i/dR_i = 0$. As we saw in figure 1.5, however, the situation is quite different when we have a regulator who values fraud reduction and the articulation of rules in and of themselves. In the case of substitute markets, this kind of regulator will face a relaxed constraint when the other regulator increases regulation. She will enjoy a positive externality (her LORE in figure 1.5 shifts upward) and increase regulation in her own market. Similarly, if the other regulator reduces regulation, she will be further constrained and decrease regulation in her own market.

The direction of the interactions is just the opposite in complement markets, as is illustrated in figure 1.6. In the top panel, the regulator chooses R_{10} so as to maximize utility, given LORE as a constraint. Initially, the regulator is at point a on indifference curve U_{11}. When the regulator in the complement market increases R_2 from R_{20} to R_{21}, LORE shifts downward, and regulator 1 finds herself with reduced utility U'_{10} at point b. Because the markets are complements, if increased regulation in market 2 results in a decrease in Q_2, Q_1 will also decrease. Because regulator 1's marginal rate of substitution will, therefore, have increased (decreased in absolute value), she responds by decreasing regulation from R_{11} to R_{10} to put herself on indifference curve U_{10} at point c. The corresponding responses of regulator 1 are replotted in R_2, R_1 space in the lower panel of figure 1.6.

As in figure 1.5, E_1 is regulator 1's independent adjustment response to the quantities of regulation chosen by regulator 2. Similarly, E_2 is the independent adjustment response of regulator 2 to quantities of regulation chosen by regulator 1. If the two regulators exhibit Cournot-Nash behavior, they will be in equilibrium at point c. Indifference curve U_{10} through points d, c, and e is redrawn in the lower half of the figure. Similarly, we draw an indifference curve for regulator 2 through point c. If the regulators recognize their interdependence, then they will have an incentive to engage in cartellike behavior so as to move to the regulators' contract curve. But by so doing, they actually make market

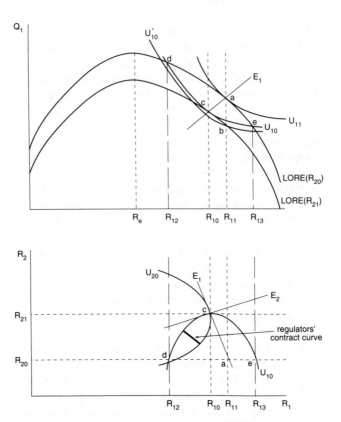

Fig. 1.6   Complementary markets: *top,* **LORE shifts inward when the other regulator increases regulation;** *bottom,* **the potential gain to the regulator from underregulation**

Table 1.1   **Taxonomy of Regulatory Collusion Relative to Cournot-Nash Equilibrium**

When the Markets Are Substitutes

	Regulator 1	
	Enjoys regulating and reducing fraud, $U_1 = U_1(Q_1,R_1,T_{f1})$	Only enjoys increasing Q, does not regulate for any other reason, $U_1 = U_1(Q_1)$
Regulator 2		
Enjoys regulating and reducing fraud, $U_2 = U_2(Q_2, R_2, T_{f2})$	both move further from efficiency	regulator 1 efficient, regulator 2 constrained from moving further from efficiency
Only enjoys increasing Q, does not regulate for any other reason, $U_2 = U_2(Q_2)$	regulator 2 efficient, regulator 1 constrained from moving further from efficiency	both regulators are efficient

When the Markets Are Complements

	Regulator 1	
	Enjoys regulating and reducing fraud, $U_1 = U_1(Q_1,R_1,T_{f1})$	Only enjoys increasing Q, does not regulate for any other reason, $U = U_1(Q_1)$
Regulator 2		
Enjoys regulating and reducing fraud, $U_2 = U_2(Q_2,R_2,T_{f2})$	both move closer to efficiency	regulator 1 efficient, regulator 2 constrained from moving further from efficiency
Only enjoys increasing Q, does not regulate for any other reason, $U_2 = U_2(Q_2)$	regulator 2 efficient, regulator 1 constrained from moving further from efficiency	both regulators are efficient

Note: The cells in the matrices represent predicted departures from/moves toward efficiency when the regulators collude.

participants better off relative to the independent adjustment equilibrium. So we see opposite effects when regulators collude, depending on whether the markets regulated are substitutes or complements.

We now summarize our results and apply them to the question of whether there is a regulatory structure that will encourage efficiency-seeking regulation. As mentioned in the introduction, various proposals to consolidate financial regulation in one agency have recently been advanced. Because a merger greatly decreases the costs of collusion, we have summarized the different collusive outcomes in table 1.1 for both substitute and complement markets for the case where the regulators are efficiency seeking and for the case where they have more of a tendency to overregulate.

The table provides a taxonomy of the effects of regulatory collusion relative to the Cournot-Nash duopoly equilibrium. The upper panel shows the results for substitute markets, the lower for complement markets. We see that only in the case of substitute markets does collusion lead to a worse outcome. But casual empiricism would suggest that this is the situation relevant to regulatory structure. Inasmuch as consolidation of the CFTC and SEC into one agency reduces the cost of collusion, it increases the departure from efficiency. Rules are not independent of the regulatory structure.

One other aspect of regulatory competition that cannot be captured in our static model deserves mention. Financial markets are highly innovative, in terms of the development of new products and new trading structures. This innovation poses a problem for a regulator concerned with the appropriate level of regulation (and this is true whether the regulator is efficiency seeking or departs from efficiency). As markets evolve, the appropriate level of regulation is likely to evolve as well. To fine-tune regulation, however, the regulator must maintain accurate information about the workings of the market it regulates. It is almost taken as axiomatic that the regulator's information lags market practice (see, e.g., Hu 1993). The magnitude of this lag will depend on the ability of the regulator to acquire information from market participants.

It is also possible that regulatory competition could result in an increase in the decentralized production of information in a Hayekian sense. Say, for example, in seeking to avoid a "crisis" the CFTC imposed regulations that were overly burdensome relative to efficiency and to SEC regulations. The resulting out-migration of business and decline in innovation would serve as a signal to the CFTC to reevaluate its regulations with respect to that "crisis." Separate regulators will react to the unique circumstances of their own markets. On the other hand, a consolidated regulatory authority will likely result in a more generalized approach, and it might be less responsive to changes in one market's circumstances. On this, Fischel (1989) has said:

> [R]egulatory bodies, like the organized exchanges they regulate, compete to supply rules and regulations that facilitate the provision of transaction services. To the extent that one regulatory body does a poor job in providing such rules and regulations, investors will shift to other exchanges governed by different and superior rules where substitute financial products are traded. Thus, competition among regulatory agencies creates an incentive to provide rules and regulations that benefit investors and at the same time limits the size of the regulatory tax that any agency can impose. (118)

Kane (1984) best sums up the view that the process of regulatory competition itself overwhelms any short-run losses reflected in criticisms of existing regulatory structure.

> [I]n the long run, competition among financial regulators lowers the level of the regulatory tax by fostering efficiency in the production of regulatory services. Much as in other kinds of competition, regulatory competition is

guided by an invisible hand to produce subtle and long-run benefits that are imperceptible to uncritical observers. Even though regulatory overlaps impose avoidable short-run costs, they facilitate a generalized form of market entry and exit that promotes dynamic or evolutionary optimality. Duplicate regulatory function and overlapping administrative boundaries provide opportunities for the entry and exit of regulatees. Regulated firms (especially new entrants into regulated and substitute markets) shrink the domains (and therefore the budget resources) of regulators whose response to the evolving needs of the marketplace proves short-sighted or inflexible. (369)

1.4 Conclusion

Our analysis is based on the belief that the goal of regulation should be efficiency. First, we provided a framework that characterizes efficient regulation in financial markets. Second, we formulated a model of regulatory behavior that takes into account the incentives of regulators. We focused particularly on these incentives because we believe they are central to the regulatory outcome, whereas much of the current discussion of regulatory reform seems to assume implicitly that significant changes in this outcome can be achieved without regard to these incentives. Last, we developed a framework for predicting the impact of regulatory structure on efficiency.

Our results suggest the following general principles about regulatory structure and regulatory competition. A change in the structure of financial services regulation would reduce some costs, such as those associated with duplicative or inconsistent regulations. It may also increase other costs due to (increased) overregulation. Competition between regulators of substitute markets increases efficiency, whereas such competition decreases efficiency in the case of complementary markets. Collusion between regulators of complement markets increases efficiency, whereas such competition decreases efficiency when the markets are substitutes. The question of optimal regulatory structure, therefore, depends on the incentives facing regulators, and the degree of complementarity or substitutability of the products to be regulated. In any event, rules are not independent of the regulatory structure.

Our analysis does not automatically lead to the conclusion that a merger of the CFTC and the SEC would be beneficial or detrimental to the cause of efficiency. There is first of all the question of whether the markets the two agencies regulate are primarily substitutes or primarily complements. Even if they are substitutes, the case where regulatory competition can lead to greater efficiency, the savings from reducing duplication and inconsistency may be greater than the risks of overregulation brought about by elimination of competition through the merger. Then there is the question of the production of knowledge under alternative regulatory regimes. If the "regulatory net burden" can perform the function of a price faced by regulators, will the reactions of market participants result in the production of information in a Hayekian, decentralized sense? Or are we extending the knowledge argument too far? Thus, even if one were to accept our model and believe that the markets are primarily substitutes, one would still need to know the relative costs and benefits of alternative regulatory structures.

Our own view is that the markets are substitutes and that the costs of merger would be high and the benefits low relative to the current structure and relative to alternative reforms. If we were to array the possible number of regulators along the real number line from zero to plus infinity, one regulator would probably be the number we would be least likely to choose, at least from the perspective of prospective efficiency. That, however, is at least another paper.

Other proposals for reform of the regulatory structure have been made, such as the proposed merger of all financial regulatory agencies under a cabinet-level superregulator, mentioned in footnote 1. While duplicative and inconsistent regulation might be eliminated, it is not clear that this new regulatory structure is necessary to accomplish that goal. The framework developed herein can be readily extended to analyze this proposal. The authors of the proposal maintain that the new structure will lead to "consistent" regulation across market centers; however, our analysis has suggested that a level playing field will not result in an efficient level of regulation across markets that differ in their principal users and in their structure. More important, this paper has demonstrated that the incentives of regulators are the principal determinant of the rules that are enacted. How would the incentives of the superregulator be different than those of an individual agency head? Would the merger lead to a more efficient level of regulation across all markets, or would it increase logrolling and other voting inefficiencies within the superagency? Any proposed change in regulatory structure should first and foremost be evaluated in terms of its impact on regulatory incentives.

References

Albrecht, William P., and Harold C. Messenheimer. 1993. Financial Fraud. Working paper.
Buchanan, James M., Gordon Tullock, and R. D. Tollison, eds. 1980. *Toward a Theory of the Rent-Seeking Society.* College Station: Texas A&M Press.
Fischel, Daniel R. 1989. Should One Agency Regulate Financial Markets? In Robert W. Kamphuis, Jr., Roger C. Kormendi, and J. W. Henry Watson, eds., *Black Monday and the Future of Financial Markets,* 113–20. Homewood, IL: Dow-Jones Irwin.
Harberger, A. C. 1959. Using the Resources at Hand More Effectively. *American Economic Review* 49 (May): 134–46.
Hu, H. 1993. Misunderstood Derivatives: The Causes of Informational Failure and the Promise of Regulatory Incrementalism. *Yale Law Journal* 102 (April): 1457–1513.
Kane, Edward J. 1984. Regulatory Structure in Futures Markets: Jurisdictional Compe-

tition between the SEC, the CFTC, and Other Agencies. *Journal of Futures Markets* 4, no. 3: 367–84.

———. 1988. How Market Forces Influence the Structure of Financial Regulation. In William S. Haraf and Rose Marie Kushmeider, eds., *Restructuring Banking and Financial Services in America.* Washington, DC: American Enterprise Institute for Public Policy Research.

Posner, Richard A. 1975. The Social Costs of Monopoly and Regulation. *Journal of Political Economy* 85 (August): 807–27.

Rowley, Charles K., R. D. Tollison, and Gordon Tullock. 1987. *The Political Economy of Rent-Seeking.* Boston: Kluwer.

Sandner, Jack. 1993. Model for Federal Financial Regulation. Chicago Mercantile Exchange.

Schaefer, Stephen M. 1992. Financial Regulation: The Contribution of the Theory of Finance. In John Fingleton, ed., *The Internationalization of Capital Markets and the Regulatory Response.* London: Graham and Trotman.

Tullock, Gordon. 1967. The Welfare Costs of Tariffs, Monopolies, and Theft. *Western Economic Journal* 5 (June): 224–32.

———. 1980. Efficient Rent Seeking. In James M. Buchanan, Gordon Tullock, and R. D. Tollison, eds., *Toward a Theory of the Rent-Seeking Society.* College Station: Texas A&M Press.

Comment   Edward H. Fleischman

In his paper (chap. 7 in this volume), relating to the likely more important obverse of our present topic—competition and collusion of regulatory regimes in the transnational sphere—Lawrence J. White concludes one section with the statement that "the real-world imperfections of government have yielded numerous instances of the regulatory process's being used for abusive purposes and reaching inefficient outcomes. . . . These abuses . . . point toward . . . the value of frequent reassessments of the motives, methods and outcomes of existing regulatory regimes." Proceeding from an awareness born of experience as well as academic study, I think that the paper by Albrecht, Bronfman, and Messenheimer can be seen—and should be received gratefully—as just such a reassessment.

The heart of the proposition presented to us is that "the question of optimal regulatory structure . . . depends on the incentives facing regulators, and the degree of complementarity or substitutability of the products to be regulated. In any event, rules are not independent of the regulatory structure."

That rules are not independent of regulatory structure I accept and agree. Laying incentives aside for a moment, I think it fair to summarize the paper as suggesting that it is the degree of complementarity or substitutability of the

Edward H. Fleischman is a former commissioner of the Securities and Exchange Commission. He is a consultant to Linklaters & Paines.

products and services regulated by financial regulators that is crucial to utilization of the framework put forward in the paper for predicting the impact of regulatory structure on efficiency.

That the paper's model speaks in terms of a single or a unitary good produced and regulated in each of two markets, while in fact the products and services produced in the financial markets and regulated by the financial regulators are in each market multiple and often distinct from one another, should not derogate from the validity of the paper's conclusion—*except* that that very multiplicity and differentiatedness shreds the key distinction between substitute and complementary markets.

The domestic financial markets are neither wholly or distinguishably substitutable nor wholly or distinguishably complementary; rather, they partake of complementarity and substitutability in varying and ever-changing degrees, as product and service mix in either (assuming that there are only two) reacts on and affects product and service mix in the other—in part, I understand, reflecting internal and external marketplace constraints and regulatory constraints—but the very complexity of the mix fractionalizes the impact of either competition or collusion among regulators on efficiency. Again, the inquiry into what he calls "government failure" (i.e., regulatory inability to effect [or affect] efficiency) is part of White's presentation.

My mention of the possibility of multiple (i.e., more than two) markets and my references to White's presentation on the transnational issues suggest not only the existence of other financial markets and other financial regulators in the *domestic* economy, but more important, of course, also the existence of markets abroad, which are increasingly easily substitutable and which tend to be much less regulated than their analogs here. If the thesis of the present paper proves itself by its applicability in the international sphere, I question whether the implications of that proof strengthen or weaken the robustness of its applicability to the activities of individual regulatory regimes here at home.

Well, I do want to return to incentives. The paper assumes regulators motivated solely by efficiency, although extending somewhat to take into account the regulators' own view of their utility function. I suggest, respectfully, that that assumption is simply too thin.

In a recent book focusing on the SEC, the author seeks to apply rational choice theory to the dynamics of SEC policymaking, that is, to regulatory incentives in one financial regulatory agency. In that author's words, "The formal and informal structures and procedural rules that guide bureaucratic behavior are critical to policy outcomes because they create incentives for action."

That author selects from the rational-choice literature the approaches to studying regulatory incentives that focus on the relationships between the regulator and its oversight, enabling, appointing and auditing institutions: the Congress, the president, the General Accounting Office. I would suggest looking in another direction as well. Regulators are institutions, but they are institutions comprising individual people—people who care not only for their respective institutions but for themselves. Career safety and enhancement are even stronger incentives than institutional policy preservation and enhancement, and often those incentives are intertwined.

I once spoke of the principal commandment for government regulators (omitted from the decalogue only by an unnoticed and erroneous touch on the delete key): Thou shalt expand thy jurisdiction with all thy heart, with all thy soul, and with all thy might. That commandment is not only institution-directed; it reflects the psychology of personal incentive: "My agency is growing; I am more important." "My division is getting new powers/new funds/new programs; I am advancing in stature." "The markets we regulate are increasing in volume and importance; I have prospects for more career satisfaction as well as more career advancement." And, negatively, as the present paper points out in the context of the self-protection of regulators in having enough regulations in place to cover every conceivable form of fraud or other undesirable behavior: "Although I may get no gold stars and no promotions for efficiency, my agency will be tarred and feathered in Congress and the press, and I will be subject to career termination or its equivalent in civil service or political exile, if any form of fraud or other undesirable behavior [which may include merely behavior resulting in market volatility—as though volatility were not inherent in markets] actually slips through the net of agency prohibitions."

In my experience, personal incentives are key to regulators' construction and implementation of policy, and self-protection is usually a stronger incentive than efficiency promotion.

So I take the present paper's thesis warily, and with deep-seated reservations, though with sufficient respect for all three of its authors to know that it merits further consideration.

In an interview last August, Albrecht put some of his thoughts underlying the present paper into layman's language. He was quoted as saying "Regulatory structure is not an end in itself, but only a means of arriving at a sensible system of rules. The best structure is that which gives regulators the ability and the incentives to create appropriate rules. . . . What regulators *do* is a lot more important than *how many* agencies there are." To that, we can all say amen.

Authors' Reply

Economists and attorneys all too often appear to operate on separate planets. Not only do they speak different languages, but they observe different realities. One of the great pleasures we get in dealing with Ed Fleischman is that he lives on the same planet we do. He is an attorney who not only understands economics but also listens to economists and is listened to by economists. We can only wish that some of his fellow attorneys at the SEC had listened to him more carefully.

Unfortunately (or perhaps fortunately), understanding economics is not always the same as understanding economists. We economists spend a lot of time constructing our own planet with its own language, which only we understand. We oversimplify reality in order to be able to construct abstract and internally consistent models. But there is a method to our madness. In oversimplifying reality, we try to gain insight into the real world.

Fleischman has reacted, we believe, to our simplifying assumptions in the way that most noneconomists would. In so doing, he appears to have missed the purpose of these assumptions, and, thus, he appears not to realize that our insight into the real world is actually quite similar to the substance of his comments. But even absent that realization, we think (as usual) that he has made some points worth considering.

We turn first to what we think he has missed. Our simplification of reality involved three abstractions. Our first abstraction established an efficiency benchmark by which we judge how well regulators are doing. The source of Fleischman's concern seems to lie in our second abstraction regarding the incentives of regulators. He says that "laying incentives aside . . . , it is the degree of complementarity or substitutability of the products . . . regulated . . . that is crucial to . . . predicting the impact of regulatory structure on efficiency." He misses our main point, which is that first and foremost regulators' incentives matter. Not only do they matter, but we characterize these incentives exactly the way Fleischman does. Their natural tendencies are to expand their turf and to be risk averse. This is the essence of our second abstraction from reality: that regulators act as if they have a utility function encompassing these tendencies.

Our third abstraction from reality is intended to gain insight into what regulators' incentives imply for efficiency over alternative regulatory structures. We assume that there are just two financial products being regulated, each one under the jurisdiction of its own regulator and, alternatively, both products under the jurisdiction of a single regulator. Fleischman critiques that this is not representative of the real world. We agree. But that is not our point. Our point is that *the incentives of regulators are relevant to efficiency*. This relevance means that, if the regulated products are substitutes, then regulatory collusion will increase harm to market users of those products. And if the regulated products are complements, regulatory collusion will actually increase the welfare of these market users.[1]

To us, this story seems to be quite rich in its implications for the design of regulatory structure that seeks to maximize the welfare of market users. This richness is not diminished by the fact that the real world is much more complex than that in our story. By emphasizing regulatory incentives in our route to regulatory reform, we can reduce the abilities of regulators to impose excessive regulatory net burdens. We can reduce government failure.

1. This result in the context of firms was analyzed years ago by Cournot ([1838] 1897) and by Allen (1938). We thank Lawrence White for calling these cites to our attention.

This, of course, is easier said than done. And in criticizing our third abstraction, Fleischman has raised some interesting empirical issues. "Domestic financial markets . . . partake of complementarity and substitutability in varying and ever-changing degrees, . . . reflecting internal and external marketplace constraints and *regulatory constraints*" (emphasis added). We agree. But we do not believe that this detracts from our conclusion. Clearly, financial innovation is not independent of regulatory structure; it is endogenous to a large extent. If regulators have an incentive to approach efficiency (say because existing substitute products are under separate jurisdictions), then individuals in the market will enjoy an incentive to create complementary instruments. On the other hand, if a monopoly regulator has an incentive to depart from efficiency (say because substitute products are under its jurisdiction), then individuals in the market will have an incentive to avoid excessive regulatory net burdens. Innovation will seek substitute products beyond the reach of the regulator. Of course, these substitutes may include those beyond domestic borders.

Fleischman thoughtfully questions the robustness of our conclusions to "the existence of markets abroad, which are increasingly easily substitutable and which do tend to be much less regulated than their analogs here." Our view is that foreign competition is indeed beneficial. Since regulatory incentives matter, foreign competition tends to reduce the ability of domestic regulators to depart from efficiency.

Rules, nonetheless, are not independent of regulatory structure. Regulators internationally have the same tendencies as our own: to expand their turn and to be risk averse. In other words, they act as if they have a utility function encompassing these tendencies. If regulated products tend to be substitutes internationally, then, internationally, regulators would like to collude to increase their power. But in so doing, they would increase government failure. Domestic regulatory competition raises the cost to regulators of forming such an international cartel of regulators. A domestic regulatory monopoly, on the other hand, would lower that cost. Our monopoly regulator would be like a dominant "regulatory firm" in an international cartel of regulators, increasing their potential to reduce the efficiency of regulation worldwide.

References

Allen, R. G. D. 1938. *Mathematical Analysis for Economists.* London: Macmillan.
Cournot, A. [1838] 1897. *Researches into the Mathematical Principles of the Theory of Wealth.* First published in French. Translated by Nathaniel Bacon. New York: Macmillan.

2   Brokerage, Market Fragmentation, and Securities Market Regulation

Kathleen Hagerty and Robert L. McDonald

2.1   Introduction

A striking fact about the organization of modern financial markets—and one of the great interest to market regulators and exchanges—is the prevalence of market fragmentation, that is, multiple mechanisms or locations for trading a security. A share of common stock, for example, may be traded on one of many organized exchanges, through dealers away from an exchange, in another country, or indirectly through a derivative financial contract, which in turn may be traded on an exchange or through a dealer.

To the extent that securities markets provide a central trading location serving to minimize the search cost of finding a counterparty, fragmentation is a puzzle. On the other hand, market participants often have private information, either about the "true value" of the traded security, or about their trading motives.[1] In markets with asymmetric information, informed traders earn a profit at the expense of the uninformed traders.[2] Therefore there is clearly an incentive to create mechanisms that mitigate (for at least some subset of participants) costs created by the existence of private information. One obvious way for uninformed traders to minimize these costs is to trade in a nonanonymous

Kathleen Hagerty is associate professor of finance at the Kellogg Graduate School of Management at Northwestern University. Robert L. McDonald is the Erwin P. Nemmers Distinguished Professor of Finance at the Kellogg Graduate School of Management at Northwestern University and a research associate of the National Bureau of Economic Research.

The authors are grateful for comments from Larry Harris, Geoffrey Miller, seminar participants at the University of Houston and Massachusetts Institute of Technology, and participants at the NBER conference.

1. As Fischer Black (1990) has observed, having no information and knowing you have no information can be valuable private information.

2. Kyle (1985), Glosten and Milgrom (1985), and Admati and Pfleiderer (1988) are examples of models like this.

market. Nonanonymous arrangements often have the appearance of a fragmented market.

Although forms of fragmentation have changed over time with technological and new product developments, fragmentation has been a perennial issue of interest to regulators and market participants. There have been a number of academic papers on topics related to fragmentation (see, for example, Chowdhry and Nanda [1991]; Madhavan [1993]; Pagano [1989]; and Röell [1990]). Harris (1992) in particular discusses fragmentation in detail and argues that it is an outgrowth of different traders' having different trading needs (for example, immediacy versus price improvement).

This paper discusses fragmentation in the context of two observations: first, brokers expend resources inducing investors to trade; second, most securities markets are replete with mechanisms permitting firms to capture order flow, including both implicit and explicit payments for order flow. We argue that these observations together suggest a reason for persistent fragmentation: when order flow arises from brokerage activity, the information characteristics of that order flow are known to the broker, or at least better known to the broker than to an average market maker. There is then an incentive for the broker to serve as a counterparty to the trade rather than just as a brokerage conduit. In order to avoid issues related to dual trading and front running, we assume that the brokers do not trade for their own account on information extracted from the customer order flow nor do they hold any uncrossed trades in their portfolio. This differs from the focus of papers such as Fishman and Longstaff (1992), Roell (1990), and Grossman (1992).

We assume that there exist both perfectly informed and uninformed traders, who have a choice of two ways to trade: with a broker who knows the trader's informedness, or anonymously with a market maker. We model market makers as in Easley and O'Hara (1987)—they are risk-neutral competitive agents who set a bid and ask price and accept all one-share orders at those prices. Brokers, however, serve a quite different function. They accept orders from traders, charging a bid-ask spread that is possibly type-dependent, cross buys against sells, and then export to a market maker any remaining order flow, paying the market bid-ask spread. Unlike market makers, brokers in our model face no price risk. And since brokers do not retain shares, they risklessly earn the bid-ask spread on any orders they net against one another.

In this setting, we compare monopolist and competitive brokers. In all cases, this kind of brokerage activity increases the bid-ask spread charged by market makers. The two kinds of broker treat their customers quite differently, however. The monopolist broker simply charges customers the market bid-ask spread. Competitive brokers, on the other hand, charge different spreads to the two types of customers, and in general *both* kinds of customers will be charged a lower spread than that set by the market maker. The ability of the broker to net orders, coupled with competition, forces the broker to charge each type of customer a price reflecting the contribution of that kind of order to the expected net order export. Perhaps surprisingly, perfectly informed investors will in general be charged a price less than the full bid-ask spread.

We find that fragmentation may be a reflection of increased price competition, and that the fragmented and competitive system provides better prices for customers than the less-fragmented monopolistic broker case. Order flow intermediaries in this setting foster competition at the brokerage level but raise the bid-ask spread in the central market.

As an example, consider a corporation that receives advice from trading firms and then undertakes a hedging transaction in the over-the-counter (OTC) derivatives market. By virtue of understanding the customer's trading motives, the brokers understand the information content of the order. When the customer obtains quotes on the deal, brokers will bid in a way that reflects their expected cost of hedging (or "exporting") the trade. Obviously this expected cost will be greater if the broker expects other orders in the same direction.

The perspective on fragmentation in this paper can be contrasted with the view that fragmentation reflects skimming the best customers from existing markets. First, brokers in this paper optimally accept all customers, informed and uninformed. Second, while we do not model the market participation decision of potential traders, our model is consistent with a world in which brokers can increase order flow by expending resources. The mechanisms that result in fragmented markets are also the mechanisms that give brokers the incentive to generate business. This view suggests that there is no "silver bullet" trading system that, if implemented, would attract all order flow. Rather, it suggests that central markets and brokerage markets serve different needs for different investors. This argument is very similar to aspects of Merton (1992) and Harris (1992).

Obviously, there are dimensions to fragmentation other than those we emphasize. In particular, agency problems—which we ignore—may be severe in practice. Our goal in this paper is not to exhaustively explore legal, regulatory, and practical issues associated with fragmentation, but rather to provide a framework for thinking about the link between fragmentation and market liquidity.

Section 2.2 introduces the model of the security market, and sections 2.3 and 2.4 look at the equilibrium bid-ask spreads and distributions of traders across brokerage firms and the central market in monopoly and perfectly competitive environments, respectively. Section 2.5 discusses policy implications. Proofs of the lemmas and propositions are in the appendix.

2.2   The Model

In this section, we describe the trading environment for a single risky asset. The assumptions and analysis are most similar to Easley and O'Hara (1987). The value of the risky asset is given by $\theta = \theta_H$ with probability .5 or θ_L with probability .5.

2.2.1   Traders

All traders are constrained to buy one unit or sell one unit of the asset. There are two types of traders, traders who are perfectly informed, of whom there are N_1, and traders who are uninformed, of whom there are N_0. When a trader is perfectly informed, he buys if $\theta = \theta_H$ and sells if $\theta = \theta_L$ with probability 1. An uninformed trader buys one unit with probability .5 and sells one unit with probability .5. A fraction ρ of uninformed traders are discretionary; the rest are nondiscretionary. The discretionary uninformed traders, of whom there are ρN_0, can choose where to trade. The nondiscretionary traders, of whom there are $(1 - \rho)N_0$, must trade in the central market. Fully informed traders can trade wherever they choose.

2.2.2   Market Makers

The central market can be thought of as the floor of an exchange or as a dealer market. In this market, trades are submitted simultaneously and anonymously to a risk-neutral market maker. Prior to observing order flow, the market maker posts a bid, b, and an ask, a, at which he will satisfy all orders.

The bid and ask prices are set so that the market maker earns zero expected profits. Let B_H equal the expected number of buys in the market if $\theta = \theta_H$ and let B_L be the expected number of buys in the market if $\theta = \theta_L$. In order for the market maker to earn zero expected profits, the ask must satisfy

$$0 = .5B_H(a - \theta_H) + .5B_L(a - \theta_L).$$

Solving for a, we get

(1)
$$a = \frac{B_H\theta_H + B_L\theta_L}{B_H + B_L}.$$

The bid, which is derived in an analogous way, is equal to

(2)
$$b = \frac{S_H\theta_H + S_L\theta_L}{S_H + S_L},$$

where S_L and S_H are the expected number of sell orders if $\theta = \theta_L$ and $\theta = \theta_H$, respectively. The number of buys and sells in the market is affected by both the traders who trade directly in the central market and the net exports of the brokerage firms. Given symmetry between good and bad information states and the symmetry between uninformed traders' propensity to buy or sell, it follows that $B_H = S_L$ and $B_L = S_H$. Therefore, the bid-ask spread can be written as

(3)
$$a - b = \frac{(B_H - B_L)(\theta_H - \theta_L)}{B_H + B_L}.$$

2.2.3   Brokers

A brokerage firm is a profit-maximizing trading firm. By assumption, brokers know a customer's type. In general, we can imagine that brokers learn a customer's type as part of marketing brokerage services. For example, a customer could be a firm with hedgeable exposure (e.g., currencies, interest rates, commodity prices), but where management lacks knowledge of financial hedging products, and is uncertain how to measure its own exposure. Because of correlations among input and output prices, it is often not obvious what derivatives position would constitute a hedge. While helping the firm determine the appropriate hedge, the broker learns the motives for the trade and the market views of the customer.

The broker is assumed not to invest for its own account. Brokers are able to immediately and frictionlessly export net order flow to the central market; thus brokers never bear inventory price risk. Obviously, in practice, broker-dealers will hold some inventory since, although they may provide immediate execution to customers, they will not be able to export large net order flow immediately without a price penalty. This in turn will make them sensitive to the information of customers: other things equal, an order from a more informed customer is costlier to accept.

As in the central market, the customers of a brokerage firm either buy one unit or sell one unit. After the buys and the sells are netted, the firm exports the unmatched buys or sells to the market. Note that, whereas individual traders trade only one share, the broker is able to anonymously trade many shares at once. This means that the brokerage firms earn a spread on any matched orders and must pay a spread on any unmatched orders.

The requirement that net order flow be exported to the central market can be motivated by the assumption that brokers face capital requirements and have limited capital. In this case, they would be forced to export net order flow or, similarly, run a hedged book. Many broker-dealers do in fact operate this way. For example, if a broker-dealer serves as counterparty in long-lived transactions involving OTC derivatives, customers will be concerned about broker-dealer credit ratings and long-term viability; hedging the book thus enhances the ability of the firm to engage in these transactions. The requirement that brokers not hold shares means that they are unable to trade on information they may glean from customer order flow.

Let n_0, $n_0 \leq \rho N_0$, and n_1, $n_1 \leq N_1$, denote the number of uninformed and informed customers, respectively, of a brokerage firm. Let S_0 and S_1 denote the number of sell orders by uninformed and informed customers, respectively, and let B_0 and B_1 denote the number of buy orders by uninformed and informed customers, respectively, where $B_0 + S_0 = n_0$ and $B_1 + S_1 = n_1$. Let $B = B_0 + B_1$ and $S = S_0 + S_1$. The ask and bid prices, a_i and b_i, are charged by a brokerage firm to customers of type i, $i = 0, 1$. The profit of a brokerage firm is given by

$$\tilde{\pi} = a_0 B_0 - b_0 S_0 + a_1 B_1 - b_1 S_1 - \begin{cases} -a(B - S) & \text{if } B - S > 0, \\ +b(S - B) & \text{if } S - B > 0, \end{cases}$$

and expected profits are therefore

$$\pi(n_0, n_1) = E(\tilde{\pi}) = \tfrac{1}{2}(a_0 - b_0)n_0 + \tfrac{1}{2}(a_1 - b_1)n_1 - aE(B - S \mid B - S > 0)$$
$$\text{Prob}(B - S > 0) + bE(S - B \mid S - B > 0)\text{Prob}(S - B > 0)$$

Since $E(B - S \mid B - S > 0)\text{Prob}(B - S > 0) = E(S - B \mid S - B > 0)\text{Prob}(S - B > 0)$, we can rewrite the expected broker profit as

(4) $$\pi(n_0, n_1) = \tfrac{1}{2}(a - b)[\lambda_0 n_0 + \lambda_1 n_1 - \phi(n_0, n_1)],$$

where

$$\lambda_i = (a_i - b_i)/(a - b),$$

and

(5) $$\phi(n_0, n_1) = 2E(B - S \mid B - S > 0)\text{Prob}(B - S > 0).$$

λ_i is the fraction of the market bid-ask spread that the broker charges to a customer, and $.5\phi$ is the expected number of trades exported to the market by the brokerage firm. Note that the expected broker profit is proportional to the market bid-ask spread, and is decreasing in the number of orders exported to the central market.

In the following sections, we first look at the mathematics of the net exports and then at the effect of the broker market on the distribution of traders across the central market and brokerage firms and the effect on the spreads that traders must pay. Two market structures are considered, a monopoly brokerage firm and perfectly competitive brokerage firms.

2.2.4   Understanding Net Order Exports

Since the focus of the paper is on order netting at the broker level, it is crucial to understand the behavior of $\phi(n_0, n_1)$, the expected order export. We are interested in two properties of ϕ: (1) how does the expected order export change when new customers are added, and (2) how does the expected order export change when one type of customer is replaced by the other. Let W denote the total number of customers, that is, $W = n_0 + n_1$; when there is no possibility of confusion, we will write $\phi(n_0)$, suppressing the argument $n_1 \equiv W - n_0$. For future reference, we now state some facts about ϕ.

LEMMA 1. (1) The expected net order flow is nondecreasing if one customer of either type is added, that is,

$$\phi(n_0, W - n_0) \geq \phi(n_0, W - n_0 - 1),$$

$$\phi(n_0, W - n_0) \geq \phi(n_0 - 1, W - n_0).$$

(2) If an uninformed customer is added, the expected net order flow per customer is nonincreasing:

$$\frac{\phi(n_0, W - n_0)}{W} \le \frac{\phi(n_0 - 1, W - n_0)}{W - 1}.$$

(3) If an informed customer is added, the expected net order flow per informed customer is nonincreasing:

$$\frac{\phi(n_0, W - n_0)}{W - n_0} \le \frac{\phi(n_0, W - n_0 - 1)}{W - n_0 - 1}.$$

For a given mix of customers, adding customers increases the expected net order export but at a decreasing rate, in a sense lemma 1 makes precise. It may be surprising that adding perfectly informed investors does not always increase net order flow by one. To see this, consider the case where $n_0 > 0$ and $n_1 = 0$. At this point, adding a single informed investor is exactly like adding an uninformed investor because the informed investor's trade is uncorrelated with the net trade of the uninformed investors. Adding a second informed investor contributes to net order flow by more than an uninformed investor since the informed trader's trade is partially correlated with the trades of the n_0 uninformed investors and the one informed investor. As we add informed investors, the marginal contribution to order flow increases. At the point where $n_1 \ge n_0$, additional informed investors increase net order flow one for one. This provides intuition for the second result:

LEMMA 2. $\phi(n_0, W - n_0)$ is decreasing and convex in n_0.

The intuition for both properties is straightforward. Increasing n_0 by 1 substitutes an uninformed customers for an informed customer. Conditional on net order flow being positive, the magnitude of the net order flow is smaller, the smaller the informed (and hence positively correlated) component of order flow.

Convexity implies that substituting informed for uninformed order flow increases the conditional expectation at an increasing rate. Substituting a single informed order for one uninformed order adds an order that is uncorrelated. Substituting an informed order for an uninformed order when there is a mix of informed and uninformed orders replaces an uncorrelated order with a partially correlated order and thus increases the conditional expectation.

2.3   Monopoly Brokerage Market

2.3.1   The Profit of the Monopoly Firm

Consider a market with a single brokerage firm. Traders are willing to trade with the brokerage firm as long as the firm matches the market spread. (This implies that the traders do not take into account the effect that their choice has on the equilibrium spread.) From examination of the profit function, (4), it is obvious that the monopoly broker sets $\lambda_0 = \lambda_1 = 1$; that is, he charges customers the full market spread. No customers would be attracted at a higher price, and the broker would needlessly give up profits at a lower spread. The brokerage firm chooses the number of informed and uninformed customers it wishes to have. From (4), therefore, the broker's maximization problem is to choose n_0 and n_1 so as to maximize

(6) $\pi(n_0, n_1) = \frac{1}{2}[a(n_0, n_1) - b(n_0, n_1)][n_0 + n_1 - \phi(n_0, n_1)]$.

The choice of n_0 and n_1 affects the brokerage firm's profits in two ways. First, it affects how well matched are the buys and the sells. Other things equal, the greater the matching of trades, the more profitable the brokerage firm. Second, the choice of n_0 and n_1 affects the ratio of informed to uninformed in the central market, which in turn affects the size of the market bid-ask spread. The monopolistic broker takes this into account in selecting customers.

2.3.2   Determination of the Market Bid-Ask Spread

The market bid-ask spread for a given customer mix, (n_0, n_1), is given in the following proposition.

PROPOSITION 1. For a given customer mix (n_0, n_1), the market bid-ask spread is given by

$$a(n_0, n_1) - b(n_0, n_1) = \frac{N_1(\theta_H - \theta_L)}{(N_0 + N_1) - n_0 - n_1 + \phi(n_0, n_1)}.$$

If $n_0 \leq n_1$, the spread simplifies to

$$a(n_0, n_1) - b(n_0, n_1) = \frac{N_1(\theta_H - \theta_L)}{(N_0 + N_1) - n_0}.$$

COROLLARY 1. The market spread is increasing in n_0 and nondecreasing in n_1.

The number of buys and sells in the market is affected by the net exports of the brokerage firm. As the number of uninformed customers increases, more uninformed trades are absorbed and crossed internally by the broker, which means they are never seen by the market maker. With effectively fewer uninformed traders, the market maker will raise the bid-ask spread. When the broker accepts a perfectly informed trade, the bid-ask spread either increases (if $n_0 > n_1$) or remains unchanged. If $n_0 > n_1$, an informed trader switching from the market maker to the broker does not change the expected difference in the number of "correct" and "incorrect" trades (e.g., $B_H - B_L$), but there is a decrease in the total number of trades the market maker sees (because the broker absorbs some trades). When $n_0 \leq n_1$, an additional informed trade switching from the market to the broker does not affect the expected number of trades in any state.

Substituting the bid-ask spread into (6) yields the broker's expected profit for a given customer mix (n_0, n_1):

$$\pi(n_0, n_1) = .5 \frac{N_1(\theta_H - \theta_L)(n_0 + n_1 - \phi(n_0, n_1))}{(N_0 + N_1) - n_0 - n_1 + \phi(n_0, n_1)}$$

2.3.3 Equilibrium in the Market with a Monopoly Brokerage Firm

Brokers in general want more orders, since both the bid-ask spread and the expected number of crossed orders are increasing in $n_0 + n_1 - \phi(n_0, n_1)$, and $n_0 + n_1 - \phi(n_0, n_1)$ is nondecreasing in scale. Thus, brokers accept as many orders as possible, up to the point where $n_0 = n_1$. This is summarized in the following proposition:

PROPOSITION 2. (1) The broker sets $n_0 = \rho N_0$. (2) The broker accepts informed trades up to the point where $n_1 = n_0 = \rho N_0$ and is indifferent about accepting further trades. (3) The expected profit is equal to

$$\pi(n_0, n_1) = .5 \frac{N_1(\theta_H - \theta_L)(\rho N_0)}{(N_0 + N_1) - \rho N_0}.$$

The equilibrium spread is maximized since the discretionary uninformed traders have been absorbed by the broker and the number of informed traders is unaffected by the presence of the broker. All traders, whether they trade with the broker or in the central market, are worse off relative to a setting where there is only a central market due to the higher spread. It is also interesting to note that, unlike many microstructure models, profits are nondecreasing in the number of informed traders. This is because unmatched informed trades are not held in inventory and hence do not impose any cost on the broker.

Note that the broker earns positive profits from uninformed customers. Thus, it is in the broker's interest to induce uninformed traders to trade. While outside the model, suppose that the brokerage firm could attract uninformed traders who were not participating in the market. These traders could be thought of as people who can be induced to trade if the brokerage firm makes some kind of marketing effort. In this case, the firm would not just be skimming from the central market but increasing the participation in the market as a whole. The addition of new customers lowers the spread, but the effect of netting is such that many new customers would be required for the spread to be as low as it would have been had there been no brokerage firm. With endogenous order flow (which we do not model), there is an ambiguous effect on the market spread of broker crossing of customer orders.

2.4 Competitive Brokers

In the competitive case, we assume that the composition of orders between uninformed and informed investors is selected by the broker; however, brokers are exogenously constrained to not accept more than W orders each. Generally speaking, the larger the scale of the broker, the more netting is achieved on a per-customer basis, and a larger broker could therefore charge customers lower prices. The restriction on firm size is necessary to ensure a competitive outcome, and it could reflect diseconomies of scale to brokerage activities. However, we show later that, in the presence of what we term "order flow intermediaries," the limit on firm scale is moot. We also assume that there is free entry into brokerage and to simplify the solution (i.e., to avoid an integer problem), we assume there are Mn_0^* uninformed customers in the pool available to brokers, and $M(W - n_0^*)$ informed customers.

2.4.1   Analysis of Equilibrium

Unlike in the monopoly case, where all customers pay the same price, in the competitive case we model the broker as posting a type-specific price for customers, and brokers are permitted to choose the fraction of informed and uninformed customers. Customers either accept or reject the posted price. Clearly, given the free-entry condition, in equilibrium all brokers must post the same type-specific price. The complication associated with type-specific prices is that customers with different information contribute differently to netting of orders. Further, the contribution to netting depends on both the size of the firm and the customer composition. Since the broker does not actually hold the order, however, the information content of a particular order does not affect the broker *except* as it affects netting. This differs from standard microstructure models such as Kyle (1985), where risk arising from holding the order flow is the reason prices depend on the information content of the order flow.

Unlike in the monopolistic case, we assume that the number of customers and brokerage firms is sufficiently large that, in setting prices, brokers do not take into account their effect on the market bid-ask spread. The problem for the brokerage firm is to set prices for customers that take account of the effect on order flow export. As noted above, λ_i in general depends on both the scale and customer composition of the firm. For example, suppose the firm has only uninformed customers. Clearly, the more such customers, the lower the cost per customer of order flow exports, and the lower the average competitive charge to a customer.

From (4), we can see that if brokers earn zero profits, we have

(7) $\phi(n_0, W - n_0) = n_0\lambda_0(n_0, W - n_0) + (W - n_0)\lambda_p(n_0, W - n_0).$

We now have the apparatus necessary to define an equilibrium. Recall that, by assumption, competitive brokerage firms can have only W customers. Brokers announce type-specific prices for orders, and customers give their order to the broker with the lowest price. Therefore, given the free-entry condition, all brokers with a positive order flow from a given type charge the same price for a given type. We use the Nash equilibrium concept, in that brokers take as given the prices of other brokers.

DEFINITION 1. An equilibrium is a type-specific price schedule $\{\lambda_0, \lambda_1\}$ such that (1) brokers earn nonnegative expected profits, taking as given prices of other brokers; (2) newly entering brokers earn nonpositive expected profits; (3) customers are no worse off dealing with brokers than transacting directly at the market bid-ask spread.

The next proposition is a direct consequence of the convexity of ϕ.

PROPOSITION 3. All brokers select the same mix of informed and uninformed customers.[3]

Note that in no case can the equilibrium price for a given type exceed the zero-profit price for a broker that accepted customers only of that type. Otherwise, it would be profitable for a broker to specialize in customers of that type. Thus, we have

PROPOSITION 4. Type-specific prices can never be greater than the prices charged by a firm specializing in customers of a given type: $\lambda_0(n_0) \leq \lambda_0(0)$; $\lambda_1(n_0) \leq \lambda_1(W)$.

Convexity of ϕ implies that, given equilibrium prices, all brokers seek to have the same mix of informed and uninformed customers. Given a potential equilibrium, however, we must verify that at the posited prices it does not pay for the broker to accept a different mix of customers. In particular, if n_0 is the equilibrium customer mix, it must be the case that profits are nonpositive at the same prices but with a different customer mix, that is,

$$(8) \quad (n_0 + j)\lambda_0(n_0) + (W - (n_0 + j))\lambda_1(n_0) \leq \phi(n_0 + j) \qquad -n_0 \leq j \leq W - n_0.$$

Because ϕ is convex, an equilibrium price schedule exists, and we present an example price schedule below. The proof of existence involves showing the following:

LEMMA 3.1. At an equilibrium price schedule, if it is not optimal to switch the customer mix for $j = \pm 1$, then it is not optimal to switch for any larger j. Thus, in verifying that (8) is satisfied for a given n_0, it suffices to check the cases $j = \pm 1$.

LEMMA 3.2. Convexity of ϕ is a necessary condition for the existence of an equilibrium price schedule.

LEMMA 3.3. Equilibrium $\lambda_0(n_0, n_1)$ and $\lambda_1(n_0, n_1)$ schedules are given by

$$\lambda_0(W, 0) = \phi(W, 0)/W; \lambda_1(0, W) = \phi(0, W)/W;$$

$$(9) \quad \lambda_1(n_0, W - n_0) = \frac{\phi(n_0, W - n_0)}{W} + \frac{n_0}{W}[\phi(n_0 - 1, W - n_0)$$

$$- \phi(n_0, W - n_0 - 1)];$$

3. Note that, because of the assumption that there are MW brokerage customers, the only way there can be two different customer mixes is if n_0^1 and n_0^2 differ by more than one.

$$(10) \quad \lambda_0(n_0, W - n_0) = \frac{\phi(n_0, W - n_0)}{W} + \frac{W - n_0}{W}[\phi(n_0, W - n_0 - 1)$$

$$- \phi(n_0 - 1, W - n_0)].$$

Since the convexity of ϕ is used to construct a price schedule, and since convexity is necessary for an equilibrium to exist, we have

PROPOSITION 5. There exists an equilibrium price schedule if and only if ϕ is convex.

From lemma 2, ϕ is convex. Since we have assumed that the numbers of traders accessible to brokers is a multiple of W, we have

COROLLARY 2. It is an equilibrium for there to be M brokerage firms, each with n_0^* uninformed and $W - n_0^*$ informed customers.

There are several interesting features of the equilibrium. First, if a mix of customers exists, then it is optimal for all firms to have a mix of customers. It would not be optimal, for example, to specialize in uninformed customers if other firms had a mix of informed and uninformed customers. The intuition for this follows from the properties of an equilibrium price schedule: for a fixed number of total customers, as brokers choose to trade with fewer customers of a given type, the price charged customers of that type declines. For example, the marginal value of an uninformed customer is greater, the smaller the number of uninformed customers (and hence the greater the number of informed customers). Similarly, adding an informed customer to a group of uninformed customers is not costly because the informed customer is uncorrelated with existing order flow. However, adding an informed customer to a large number of informed customers is more expensive.

The value of having uninformed customers is greater for a broker who also has informed customers, so firms that have both types would be able to undercut the price of firms that had only uninformed customers. Effectively, customers of different types cross-subsidize one another.

If all customers who can deal with brokers do so, and if brokers charge equilibrium fees as outlined above, then customers are at least as well off dealing with brokers as with market makers, and brokers have no incentive to attract a different mix of customers, given prices charged by other brokers.

It is worth emphasizing that, since customers end up receiving a better bid-ask spread from the broker than from the market maker, equilibrium requires that all customers who can use a competitive broker, do use a competitive broker. Otherwise, customers of the same type would pay different prices for the same order.

2.4.2   Example

Figures 2.1 and 2.2 present a numerical example, with the competitive brokerage firm having a scale of ten customers (i.e., $W = 10$). This example dem-

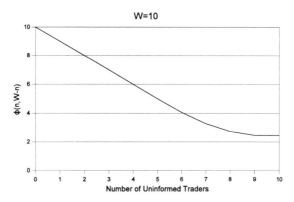

Fig. 2.1   Change in expected net order export, $\phi(n, W - n)$, as fraction of uninformed customers increases

Note: Assumes ten customers.

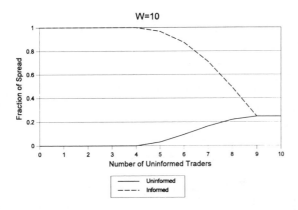

Fig. 2.2   Fraction of market spread charged to each type of customer, $\lambda_0(n, W - n)$ and $\lambda_1(n, W - n)$, as fraction of uninformed customers increases

Note: Assumes ten customers.

onstrates how customers of different types effectively cross-subsidize each other in the competitive equilibrium. Figure 2.1 displays $\phi(n_0, n_1)$ for all different possible mixes of customer types. Figure 2.2 displays the competitive spreads charged to each type of customer, computed using the schedule derived in the appendix in the proof of lemma 3. The cross-subsidization is evident in the first informed customer being charged the same spread as uninformed customers. As the customer mix moves from uninformed to informed, the spread charged the informed rises and that charged the uninformed falls. Once there are more informed than uninformed customers, the uninformed are charged a zero spread since *ex ante* the contribute nothing to the firm's net order exports.

2.4.3   Effect on the Market Bid-Ask Spread

As in the monopolistic case, $\phi(n_0, W - n_0)$ becomes linear when $n_0 < W/2$, with the result that the broker is indifferent about accepting additional uninformed traders. Thus, as in the monopolistic case, there is a corner solution at $n_0 = W/2$. Although the maximization problems faced by the monopolist and the competitive brokers are different, the implications for the market bid-ask spread are similar. Since both kinds of brokers net orders and export the residual, exported order flow represents more information than the original order flow.

The difference between the monopolist and the competitive broker stems from the fact that competitive order flow exports are greater by

$$\sum_{i=1}^{M} \phi_i(n_0^*, W - n_0^*) - \phi(Mn_0^*, M(W - n_0^*)).$$

Thus, the increase in the spread is smaller in the competitive case. Notice, however, that this implies that, for a given spread, brokerage customers do not pay the lowest possible fees because there is less than full netting at the broker level. This suggests that it would be profitable for a broker to enter as a "broker's broker," crossing broker net order flow.

2.4.4   Competitive Order Flow Intermediaries

Because the expected order export per customer declines with the number of customers, there is a natural economy to scale for brokers. If there are competitive order flow intermediaries, however, scale economies can be achieved through the purchase and sale of order flow. For example, suppose there are M retail brokers who on average export $\phi(n_0, W - n_0)$ shares each. Unconditionally, this export has a 50 percent chance of being either a buy or a sell. Assuming that the order flow broker knows the customer characteristics of the retail broker, expected profits are

$$M[.5a\phi(n_0, W - n_0) - .5b\phi(n_0, W - n_0)] - .5(a - b)\phi(Mn_0, M(W - n_0)).$$

With entry, the order flow broker's expected profits must be zero. This means that in order to attract business the order flow broker charges the retail broker a discount from the market spread. On a per-firm basis, this discount is

$$.5(a - b)[\phi(n_0, W - n_0) - \phi(Mn_0, M(W - n_0))/M].$$

Since $\phi(Mn_0, M(W - n_0))/M$ is decreasing in M, the order flow broker provides a bigger discount the greater the number of customers.

Notice that with this discount added to the broker profit function (4), the broker sets a spread for customer orders that is equivalent to having MW customers. As long as there are no transaction costs or frictions, there can be many layers of order flow brokers, each buying order flow, aggregating it, and giving to the preceding broker a discount reflecting the benefits of aggregation.

In comparing the monopolistic equilibrium and competitive equilibrium where there are order flow intermediaries, we find that both produce the same effect on the spread, but customers receive better prices in the competitive case because brokers bid for orders and pass along any cost advantages. The interesting point is that the competitive case is more "fragmented," in the sense that there are many more separate mechanisms by which shares are exchanged. In this setting, however, fragmentation is associated with benefits for customers because it reflects increased competition for orders.

2.5   Discussion and Policy Implications

In this section, we discuss some policy implications of the model, as well as its robustness.

2.5.1   OTC versus Exchange-Oriented Markets

We have focused on the implications of order netting for market spreads. A natural question is, to what kind of market does this model apply? One interpretation of the model is that brokers are also serving as principals in a trade, and customer prices and orders are determined individually in negotiations with the broker without any requirement that they be exposed to the central market. This description is suggestive of the OTC market for custom financial products, in which broker-dealers originate the trade, serve as counterparty, and generally hedge the transaction in some related central market.

The model also has applicability for thinking about equity markets, however. A common description of trade in listed equities in the United States characterizes stock trading as involving the submission of an order to a central exchange, where it is bid for by a variety of market participants. While this does appear to describe how a significant fraction of orders are handled, the National Association of Securities Dealers (1991) report on order flow inducement practices makes clear that there are many ways for firms to acquire order flow.

- *Explicit payment for orders.*
- *Agreements for exchange of order flow.* For example, on Nasdaq, broker A may direct orders for stock X to broker B, who in turn directs orders for stock Y to broker A. Such order-preferencing arrangements are often explicit.
- *Vertical integration of brokers and specialists.* For a given stock, the Intermarket Trading System reports posted bids and asks from a variety of locations. However, any market maker can take an order for his own account by matching the best quoted price. Thus, a broker for securities firm XYZ can send orders to market maker A, who is owned by XYZ. The market maker can then accept the order on behalf of the brokerage firm by matching the best current price.

All of these practices effectively provide ways for brokers to selectively choose to be counterparty to an order.

In addition, Angel (1994), using data from the New York Stock Exchange (NYSE), shows that different kinds of order flow (e.g., retail versus proprietary trades) systematically receive different amounts of price improvement over the spread, as would be suggested by our model. We conclude that the model is at least partially descriptive of both exchange-centered and OTC markets.

2.5.2   Policy Implications

The interesting policy implication is that increased fragmentation reflects increased competition for orders, generating better prices for customers and no worse prices in the central market. Of course, this results from a comparison of central market prices between two settings with broker-dealers. Since we do not model the decisions of customers to trade in the first place, welfare comparisons with just a central market (which typically will yield a lower spread) are not possible. It seems safe to speculate, however, that in general there will always exist parameters where such comparisons are ambiguous, and the purpose of analysis such as this is to point out sources of costs and benefits.

Although we do not model the generation of order flow, it is obvious that once a broker is permitted to also serve as market maker, the incentives to generate order flow are increased: in addition to generating commissions, the broker can earn some portion of the spread as well. This raises the issue of endogenous order flow generation, or "order flow discovery." In order to capture order flow, broker marketing efforts may include customer education about markets and about personal or corporate financial issues. The result may be increased trading and a welfare improvement for customers. The offsetting effect, of course, is that liquidity is typically reduced for traders who use the central market.

This view of fragmentation also has implications for the empirical literature on trade execution quality. It is well-documented (e.g., Lee [1993]; Petersen and Fialkowski [1992]) that execution quality for a given stock differs among stock exchanges in the United States with the NYSE typically providing execution at least as good as regional exchanges. One common interpretation of poorer performance on regional exchanges is that it reflects an agency problem resulting from vertical integration of brokers and market makers; the incentive of the broker to seek the best price is compromised. However, it could also reflect a payment to the broker in exchange for marketing services that would not have been performed in the first place had the broker not been able to route the trade to a particular market maker.[4]

There are several implications for policy. First, given the existence of asymmetric information and the broker's superior knowledge about the quality of order flow, it is inevitable that brokers will try to capture order flow. Preventing

---

4. This discussion ignores other dimensions of trade execution, such as immediacy and depth.

capture of order flow would not be unambiguously beneficial. Even mechanisms designed to ensure the best execution price, such as a consolidated limit order book (CLOB), may not guarantee best execution in a broad sense (by reducing the ability to capture order flow, the CLOB reduces the incentive by brokers to provide marketing services). In addition, the creation of derivative securities and offshore trading provide ways to bypass a CLOB.

From a regulatory perspective, it is desirable to increase competition among brokers, and a key to doing this is making sure that customers have enough information to make an informed choice among different brokerage and trade execution practices. Since marketing services most benefit precisely those customers least able to make an informed choice, this is likely to be difficult.

Appendix

Using assumptions from the text, the explicit expression for ϕ (the expected number of net buy orders conditional on buy orders exceeding sell orders) is

$$
\phi(n_0, n_1) = 2\left[\sum_{i=ceil[W/2-n_1]}^{n_0} \left(i + n_1 - \frac{W}{2}\right)\binom{n_0}{i}(.5)^{n_0} \right.
$$

(A1)
$$
\left. + \sum_{i=ceil[W/2]}^{n_0} \left(i - \frac{W}{2}\right)\binom{n_0}{i}(.5)^{n_0}\right], \qquad \text{if } n_0 > n_1;
$$

$$
\phi(n_0, n_1) = n_1, \qquad \text{if } n_0 \le n_1,
$$

where $ceil(x)$ is the smallest integer greater than or equal to x and $W = n_0 + n_1$. Since informed orders can be either buys or sells, there are different terms in the first expression accounting for these two cases.

The following recursive relationships may be verified by direct calculation:

(A2) $\phi(n_0, n_1) = \phi(n_0 - 1, n_1) + \tfrac{1}{2}\eta(n_0 - 1, n_1);$

(A3) $\phi(n_0, n_1 + 1) = \phi(n_0, n_1) + \sum_{i=ceil(W/2)-n_1}^{floor(W/2)} \binom{n_0}{i}.5^{n_0};$

where

$$
\eta(n_0, n_1) = .5^{n_0}\left[\binom{n_0}{\frac{W}{2} - n_1} + \binom{n_0}{\frac{W}{2}}\right], \qquad W \text{ even,}
$$

$$
= 0, \qquad\qquad\qquad\qquad\qquad W \text{ odd,}
$$

is the probability of exactly zero buy orders with x uninformed and y informed customers. Note that when W is even, removing one uninformed customer leaves ϕ unchanged.

PROOF OF LEMMA 1. (1) From equations (A2) and (A3), ϕ is increasing in both n_0 and n_1. (2) From (A2), $\phi/(n_0 + n_1)$ is obviously decreasing in n_0 when $n_0 + n_1$ is even. For odd values, $\phi/(n_0 + n_1) = \phi/W$ is nonincreasing in n_0 if and only if $\frac{1}{2}W\eta(n_0, n_1) < \phi(n_0, n_1)$. For given W, ϕ is decreasing and η is increasing in n_0, so it is sufficient to consider the case $n_1 = 0$. It is straightforward to show that $n_0\eta(n_0, 0) > (n_0 + 2)\eta(n_0 + 2, 0)$, which implies that $n_0\eta(n_0, 0)$ is decreasing in n_0. Considering $n_0 = 3$ as a base case, $\phi(3, 0) = 1.5$ and $.5 \times 3\eta(3, 0) = .75$. Thus, the condition holds for all greater n_0. (3) The claim is that $(n_1 - 1)\phi(n_0, n_1) \le n_1\phi(n_0, n_1 - 1)$. Using (A3), this can be rewritten as

$$\phi(n_0, W - n_0) \ge (W - n_0) \sum_{W/2-n_1}^{W/2-1} \binom{n_0}{i}.$$

Using equation (A1), this inequality holds if

$$\sum_{W/2}^{n_0}\left(i + \frac{W}{2} - n_0\right)\binom{n_0}{i} + \sum_{n_0-W/2}^{W/2-1}\left(i - \frac{n_0}{2}\right)\binom{n_0}{i} > 0.$$

Using the fact that

$$\binom{n_0}{x} = \binom{n_0}{n_0 - x}$$

and comparing terms for a given combinatorial factor shows that the inequality is satisfied.

PROOF OF LEMMA 2. To demonstrate convexity of ϕ, we need to show that

$$\phi(n_0 - 1, W - (n_0 - 1)) + \phi(n_0 + 1, W - (n_0 + 1)) - 2\phi(n_0, W - n_0) > 0.$$

Consider the case where W is odd (the case where W is even is similar and easier). Using the recursion relationships (A2) and (A3) we can reduce this inequality to

$$.5^{n_0-1}\sum_{i=W/2-n_1}^{W/2-1}\binom{n_0-1}{i} + .5^{n_0}\sum_{i=W/2-(n_1-1)}^{W/2-1}\binom{n_0}{i} > \eta(n_0 - 1, n_1) - \eta(n_0, n_1 - 1).$$

Using the fact that

$$\binom{N}{j} = \binom{N-1}{j} + \binom{N-1}{j-1}; \quad \binom{N}{N} = \binom{N-1}{N-1}; \quad \binom{N}{0} = \binom{N-1}{0},$$

the inequality can be shown to hold.

PROOF OF PROPOSITION 1.

$$B_H = (N_1 - n_1) + .5(N_0 - n_0) + E[\text{\# of exported broker buys} \mid \theta_H)$$

$$B_L = .5(N_0 - n_0) + E[\text{\# of exported broker buys} \mid \theta_L)$$

$$B_H + B_L = (N_1 - n_1) + (N_0 - n_0) + E[\text{\# of exported broker buys} \mid \theta_H]$$
$$+ E[\text{\# of exported broker buys} \mid \theta_L]$$
$$= (N_1 - n_1) + (N_0 - n_0) + E[B - S \mid B - S > 0, \theta_H]$$
$$Pr(B - S > 0 \mid \theta_H) \, E[B - S \mid B - S > 0, \theta_H]$$
$$Pr(B - S > 0 \mid \theta_H) + E[B - S \mid B - S > 0, \theta_L]$$
$$Pr(B - S > 0 \mid \theta_L)$$
$$= (N_1 - n_1) + (N_0 - n_0) + 2E[B - S \mid B - S > 0]$$
$$Pr(B - S > 0)$$
$$= (N_1 - n_1) + (N_0 - n_0) + \phi(n_0, n_1)$$
$$B_H - B_L = (N_1 - n_1) + E[\text{\# of exported broker buys} \mid \theta_H]$$
$$- E[\text{\# of exported broker buys} \mid \theta_L]$$

Expanding the expression on the right-hand side and using the fact that

$$Pr\left(B_0 > \frac{n_0 + n_1}{2}\right) = Pr\left(B_0 < \frac{n_0 - n_1}{2}\right),$$

we get

$$B_H - B_L = N_1 + n_0\left(Pr\left(B_0 > \frac{n_0 + n_1}{2}\right) - Pr\left(B_0 \geq \frac{n_0 - n_1}{2}\right)\right)$$
$$+ 2E\left[B_0 \mid B_0 \geq \frac{n_0 - n_1}{2}\right]Pr\left(B_0 \geq \frac{n_0 - n_1}{2}\right)$$
$$- 2E\left[B_0 \mid B_0 > \frac{n_0 + n_1}{2}\right]Pr\left(B_0 > \frac{n_0 + n_1}{2}\right).$$

If $n_1 \geq n_0$, then $B_H - B_L = N_1$, since the $Pr(B_0 \geq (n_0 - n_1)/2) = 1$ and $Pr(B_0 > (n_0 + n_1)/2) = 0$. If $n_1 < n_0$, then when we expand the expression for $B_H - B_L$ we get

$$B_H - B_L = N_1 - \sum_{i=(n_0-n_1)/2}^{(n_0+n_1)/2} (n_0 - 2i) \binom{n_0}{i} .5^{n_0} = N_1.$$

The spread given in the text is found by substituting $B_H - B_L$ and $B_H + B_L$ into (3) and using the fact that $\phi(n_0, n_1) = n_1$ when $n_1 \geq n_0$.

PROOF OF COROLLARY 1. (1) The market bid-ask spread is increasing in n_0 if

$$n_0 - \phi(n_0, n_1) > n_0 - 1 - \phi(n_0 - 1, n_1),$$

which is equivalent to $\phi(n_0, n_1) < 1 + \phi(n_0 - 1, n_1)$. This follows from (A2).

(2) The market bid-ask spread is nondecreasing in n_1 if

$$n_1 - \phi(n_0, n_1) \geq n_1 - 1 - \phi(n_0, n_1 - 1),$$

which is equivalent to $\phi(n_0, n_1) \leq 1 + \phi(n_0, n_1 - 1)$. This follows from (A3).

PROOF OF PROPOSITION 3. Suppose that in equilibrium brokers selected two different customer mixes, n_0^1 and n_0^2. For this to be an equilibrium, it must be that $\lambda_i(n_0^1) = \lambda_i(n_0^2) = \lambda_i$. If profits are to be zero, the λ_i must satisfy

$$\phi(n_0^1) = n_0^1\lambda_0 + (W - n_0^1)\lambda_1,$$

and

$$\phi(n_0^2) = n_0^2\lambda_0 + (W - n_0^2)\lambda_1.$$

Now consider a broker who enters and selects quantity $\hat{n}_0$ such that $n_0^1 < \hat{n}_0 < n_0^2$. Let $\delta = (\hat{n}_0 - n_0^1)/(n_0^2 - n_0^1)$. By convexity,

$$\phi(\hat{n}_0) < \delta\phi(n_0^2) + (1 - \delta)\phi(n_0^1) = \hat{n}_0\lambda_0 + (W - \hat{n}_0)\lambda_1,$$

hence there are positive profits to entry.

PROOF OF LEMMA 3.1. Suppose it is optimal to deviate by j customers but not by one. Then we have

$$(m + j)\lambda_0(n_0) + (w - (m + j))\lambda_1(n_0) > \phi(n_0 + j),$$

and

$$(m + 1)\lambda_0(n_0) + (w - (m + 1))\lambda_1(n_0) < \phi(n_0 + 1).$$

These inequalities together imply

$$\phi(n_0 + j) + (j - 1)\phi(n_0) - j\phi(n_0 + 1) < 0,$$

which violates convexity.

PROOF OF LEMMA 3.2. Suppose that brokers lose money either by switching to mix $m + j$ or $m - i$.

$$(n_0 + j)\lambda_0(n_0) + (W - (n_0 + j))\lambda_1(n_0) < \phi(n_0 + j)$$
$$(n_0 - i)\lambda_0(n_0) + (W - (n_0 - i))\lambda_1(n_0) < \phi(n_0 - i)$$

Using the fact that in equilibrium

(A4) $$n_0\lambda_0(n_0) + (W - n_0)\lambda_1(n_0) = \phi(n_0),$$

we have

$$\phi(n_0) + j[\lambda_0(n_0) - \lambda_1(n_0)] < \phi(n_0 + j)$$

and

$$\phi(n_0) - i[\lambda_0(n_0) - \lambda_1(n_0)] < \phi(n_0 - i),$$

which implies

$$i\phi(n_0 + j) + j\phi(n_0 - i) > (i + j)\phi(n_0).$$

PROOF OF LEMMA 3.3. Straightforward computation verifies that this schedule satisfies (8), so that, given W, it is not optimal to select a different n_0. It is also necessary to verify that, given these prices, the broker will not accept fewer than W customers. Suppose the equilibrium is to accept W customers, n_0 of them uninformed. The broker fails to make money by accepting one less uninformed customer if

$$\lambda_0(n_0, W - n_0)(n_0 - 1) + \lambda_1(n_0, W - n_0)(W - n_0) \leq \phi(n_0 - 1, W - n_0).$$

Using (A2) and (A4), we can rewrite this as

(A5) $$0 \leq \lambda_0(n_0, W - n_0) - \tfrac{1}{2}\eta(n_0 - 1, W - n_0).$$

Similarly, it is unprofitable for the broker to accept one fewer informed customer if

$$\lambda_0(n_0, W - n_0)n_0 + \lambda_1(n_0, W - n_0)(W - n_0 - 1) \leq \phi(n_0, W - n_0 - 1).$$

Again using (A2), (A4), and (9), we can write this as

$$0 \leq \lambda_0(n_0, W - n_0) - \tfrac{1}{2}\eta(n_0 - 1, W - n_0).$$

We conclude that given the schedule (9), it is optimal to accept one less uninformed customer if and only if it is optimal to accept one less informed customer. We wish to verify that it is not optimal to accept one less customer. Using (A2) and (9), (A5) can be rewritten as

(A6) $$n_0\phi(n_0 - 1, W - n_0) + (W - n_0)\phi(n_0, W - n_0 - 1)$$
$$- (W - 1)\,\phi(n_0, W - n_0) \geq 0.$$

For simplicity, we will consider just the case of W even (when W is odd, the above expression can be shown to hold with equality). Using (A2), (A6) can be rewritten

$$(W - n_0)\phi(n_0, W - n_0 - 1) \geq (W - n_0 - 1)\phi(n_0, W - n_0),$$

which follows from lemma 1.

References

Admati, Anat, and Paul Pfleiderer. 1988. A Theory of Intraday Trading Patterns. *Review of Financial Studies* 1:3–40.
Angel, James. 1994. Who Gets Price Improvement on the New York Stock Exchange? Working paper, Georgetown University.
Black, Fischer. 1990. Bluffing. Working paper.

Chowdhry, B., and V. Nanda. 1991. Multi-Market Trading and Market Liquidity. *Review of Financial Studies* 4:483–511.

Easley, David, and Maureen O'Hara. 1987. Price, Trade Size, and Information in Securities Markets. *Journal of Financial Economics* 19:69–90.

Fishman, Michael, and Francis Longstaff. 1992. Dual Trading in Futures Markets. *Journal of Finance* 47:643–71.

Glosten, Lawrence, and Paul Milgrom. 1985. Bid, Ask and Transaction Prices in a Specialist Market with Heterogeneously Informed Agents. *Journal of Financial Economics* 14:71–100.

Grossman, Sanford. 1992. The Informational Role of Upstairs and Downstairs Trading. *Journal of Business* 65 (4):509–28.

Harris, L. 1992. Consolidation, Fragmentation, Segmentation and Regulation. Working paper, University of Southern California.

Kyle, Albert S. 1985. Continuous Auctions and Insider Trading. *Econometrica* 53: 1315–35.

Lee, Charles. 1993. Market Integration and Price Execution for NYSE-Listed Securities. *Journal of Finance* 48:1009–38.

Madhavan, Ananth. 1993. Trade Disclosure and the Integration of International Security Markets. Working paper, University of Pennsylvania.

Merton, Robert C. 1992. Operation and Regulation in Financial Intermediation: A Functional Perspective. Working paper, Harvard Business School.

National Association of Securities Dealers. 1991. Inducements for Order Flow: A Report to the Board of Governors, National Association of Securities Dealers, Inc. Washington, DC: National Association of Securities Dealers.

Pagano, Marco. 1989. Endogenous Market Thinness and Stock Price Variability. *Review of Economic Studies* 56:269–88.

Petersen, Mitchell A., and David Fialkowski. 1992. Price Improvement: Stocks on Sale. Working paper, Center for Research in Security Prices, University of Chicago.

Röell, Ailsa. 1990. Dual-Capacity Trading and the Quality of the Market. *Journal of Financial Intermediation* 1:105–24.

Comment   Lawrence E. Harris

This paper examines a formal model of brokerage crossing markets in which residual order flows are cleared in a central competitive dealer market. One purpose of the paper, to judge from its title, introduction, and conclusion, is to obtain some results about fragmented markets. Although the paper also addresses other issues, I will confine my remarks to this one.

The authors conclude that fragmentation may be a reflection of increased price competition. This conclusion is obtained in the following sense: brokerage crossing markets that are fragmented and competitive provide better prices for (uninformed) customers than do monopolistic brokerage crossing markets. The result follows from assumed inelasticities of customer demands to trade

Lawrence E. Harris is professor of finance and business economics at the University of Southern California.

and from zero-profit conditions applied to competitive brokers and to competitive dealers. These assumptions ensure that the pie of wealth that can be distributed among market participants is of fixed size. The monopolistic broker market structure provides inferior prices because the brokerage reduces the size of the pie by taking out monopoly profits.

Although I found the result interesting, it does not completely address the problem that I think about when I hear the adjective *fragmented* placed before the noun *markets:* I would like to know whether any broker should be allowed to cross orders internally. This question seems to be at the heart of many of the current controversies about fragmented markets.

This paper does not attempt to answer this question. To do so would require a welfare analysis that would have to consider how the interests of informed traders, uninformed traders, and securities industry intermediaries should be weighed relative to each other. Issues relating to the external benefits of price discovery and liquidity would also need to be considered. In addition, various agency problems and other issues too numerous to mention here would affect the analysis. These issues are all beyond the scope of this paper.

The paper does, however, provide a very important result about price discrimination among diverse traders. The authors formally prove that competitive brokers who can discriminate between informed and uninformed traders will, and must, charge different commissions to the two types of traders. Any crossing broker who tries to charge an intermediate price would get only informed traders. Pursuing this pricing strategy would be unprofitable.

This conclusion is very important because such discrimination can be effected only in a fragmented market. It cannot be provided in an anonymous central market to which all orders are routed.

The fragmentation that we see in the U.S. equity markets reflects this price discrimination. Many dealers pay brokers for order flows from retail traders who are widely believed to be uninformed. Competition among brokers will pass these payments through to the customer in the form of reduced commissions. The uninformed order flow will thereby pay lower transaction costs than they would pay in a completely anonymous market.

Having raised the issue of payment for order flow, I would like to finish by discussing a related public policy issue concerning best execution. Should brokers be required to search for best price for small orders when they can obtain the best wholesale price plus some payment for order flow? If the payments for order flow reflects the appropriate discount from the anonymous market price, the answer should be no.

Now, consider what happens if we require the broker to search anyway. Will the broker do it? Only if the benefits of an improved price can be measured by the customer. If the price improvement is not recognized by the customer, no competitive broker will search beyond the anonymous market price. To do so would incur search costs that would not produce recognizable benefits to the firm.

I believe that most retail clients cannot effectively audit their agent's search for best execution. They do not trade frequently enough, they do not trade with enough different brokers, and they cannot easily collect the information necessary to determine whether the trade prices are consistently good or bad. Retail clients know their commission costs, but they do not know how good their price is relative to what is appropriate for their order type.

The existing system thus helps solve the agency problem. By requiring brokers to search further for best price, we only exacerbate the agency problem because we force brokers to compete to provide immeasurable services. Agency problems are solved by improving measurement.

We might imagine that we could help small uninformed traders by requiring that their orders be consolidated to a single market that provides prices appropriate to them. The results in this paper suggest that market cannot exist without the brokers' active participation. They must discriminate among the orders. Otherwise, informed traders will try to use the uninformed traders' market. A broker must have an incentive to participate. Payment for order flow provides these incentives.

Comment   Geoffrey P. Miller

Kathleen Hagerty and Robert McDonald provide a theoretical exploration of one aspect of the phenomenon of market fragmentation and offer suggestions about the implications for public policy.

As a law professor with a strong interest in the regulation of financial markets and institutions, I found the paper to be stimulating and thoughtful, but ultimately not very informative about the proper direction of public policy. The conditions set up in the authors' model are so general and abstract that they don't allow for much purchase on real-world institutions. Beyond this, even under the constraints of the model, the authors are not able to draw unambiguous policy conclusions. This may not be a particularly telling critique of a piece of pure theory, but it is important to make the observation because those who are constructing social policy need all the help they can get from theory in an area as rapidly evolving and complex as this.

Perhaps I could summarize my basic critique by recommending that the authors revise the title of their paper—instead of "Brokerage, Market Frag-

Geoffrey P. Miller is the Kirkland and Ellis Professor, director of the Program in Law and Economics, and chairman of the Center for the Study of Central Banks at the University of Chicago Law School; a consultant for the Federal Reserve Bank of Chicago; and editor of the *Journal of Legal Studies*.

mentation, and Securities Market Regulation," they should strike all the words after "Market Fragmentation" and insert an "and" after "Brokerage"—the paper, in other words, might be more satisfying if it were simply about "Brokerage and Market Fragmentation," without venturing into the field of legal regulation.

The authors' general view of market fragmentation is that it might not be such a bad thing. Brokers receiving order flows from informed and uninformed customers can distinguish between them, and find that it is a profitable strategy to act as counterparties rather than as mere brokers when dealing with uninformed customers. Thus, trading gets diverted away from the centralized exchange. Because of competition among brokers, the benefits of this strategy are shared with customers. Both brokers and customers benefit from this kind of market fragmentation.

This model has some plausibility, but it leaves important questions unanswered.

The authors provide an account of market fragmentation that does not depend on the off-market transaction free riding on the price discovery function of a centralized market. But their account is not inconsistent with the free-riding theory, suggesting, at most, that there might be forces *other* than free riding that drive off-exchange trading.

The authors acknowledge the potential real-world importance of agency costs in this setting, but they abstract this factor out of their model. Yet the conflict of interest that arises when a broker has the opportunity to act as a counterparty is obvious. The model the authors propose places brokers in the role of protecting themselves against the costs of dealing with informed traders by directing a portion of the informed trades to the central exchange while keeping much of the uninformed trade for themselves. Yet it seems at least equally likely that it will be securities firms that are the informed traders relative to their customers, and that customers face the losses associated with dealing with their brokers as counterparties.

The authors recognize that market fragmentation in their model has potentially deleterious consequences for centralized markets. This includes a reduction in liquidity of the primary market and associated increases in bid-ask spreads. Presumably, under their model, you would also observe an increase in the proportion of informed to uninformed traders in the centralized market as a result of market fragmentation. Thus, uninformed traders dealing on the centralized market face a higher probability of trading with an informed counterparty. It might be worth exploring whether the Hagerty-McDonald model predicts a kind of snowball effect or variant of Gresham's law, as informed traders drive out uninformed traders on the centralized market. In any event, public policy analysis should look at the costs of market fragmentation on the centralized market and compare, if possible, these costs with the benefits realized in collateral markets.

The authors' model does not replicate the richness of observed markets.

They present a picture of trading that occurs either on a centralized market or with brokers, but they do not model the complex array of off-market trading that occurs in practice. Of course, this is a function of the constraints of formal modeling, which is difficult enough even in stylized settings, much less in settings that reflect the muddiness of real-world practice.

Perhaps more troubling, the model appears to have greatest application in settings where the prices and orders are determined in individual negotiations with a broker. This is more descriptive of over-the-counter markets for custom products such as derivatives than for organized equity trading. But such OTC markets have never been characterized by extensive trading on centralized exchanges, so with respect to these products we are not dealing with market fragmentation—these markets are fragmented to begin with. The authors are correct that their model has some application for equity trading, but they could usefully develop this point further.

This paper is premised on the assumption that brokers can distinguish the uninformed and informed traders in the order flow. This assumption might stand further support, given the possibility that informed traders might present themselves as uninformed traders in order to obtain the benefits of the favorable treatment that broker-dealers are capable of giving to uninformed traders. There may be ways that broker-dealers can make this distinction; for example, the broker's knowledge of the customer, or the size of the trade. But the authors might further elaborate this point.

In general, the paper asks an interesting question and makes an important contribution to the literature, but does not offer substantial insights into the identification of optimal social policy or the formulation of desirable legal regulation.

Authors' Reply

Both Lawrence Harris and Geoffrey Miller express the wish that we had engaged in a broader analysis of trade-crossing and market fragmentation. Before addressing their specific comments (many of which we are sympathetic with), we would like to place our paper in perspective. A crude but largely accurate characterization of the microstructure literature is that it assumes that all orders transact at one price in one location, although perhaps with competitive market makers (exceptions to this characterization were noted in our paper). Recent years have seen the rapid growth of off-exchange trading systems, including some that explicitly purchase order flow, cross offsetting orders, and then export to the central market (in effect hedging) any residual order flow.

We see our paper as a first attempt at understanding the economic effects of this kind of trade crossing. As we indicate in the paper, we think the stylized model is actually applicable to a wide variety of real market practices. Our model suggests that, even in a world where all traders trade one share, the bid-ask spread is at best a crude indicator of prices paid and received by investors. The model predicts that heterogeneous treatment of customers should be widespread. Somewhat surprisingly, competitive order-crossing brokers will seek to deal with both informed and uninformed traders.

Harris is concerned by the omission in our paper of a welfare analysis. In particular, how do we trade-off the interests of informed investors, uninformed investors, market intermediaries, and other market participants broadly defined? In some sense, the answer to this question represents the Holy Grail of security market policymaking. We did not attempt a welfare analysis in the paper, and our guess is that this kind of question is, in the end, unanswerable. Knowledgeable price discrimination by brokers will help uninformed traders and hurt those traders who pay the full market spread. We are pessimistic that there will ever be an unambiguous ranking of systems that hurt one group and help another. We think of efficiency questions as being more interesting, which leads to the next point.

Both Harris and Miller point out a closely related limitation in our analysis, one we agree is important. Markets in our model do not discover prices. There is no way for us to analyze the effect of brokers free riding off a central market price. If the siphoning of traders away from the central market reduces the informativeness of prices, financial markets will do a poorer job of providing signals useful in resource allocation. It is an interesting question whether complete reporting of trades makes prices sufficiently informative, even if the trades occur at disparate locations. There are reasons for thinking reporting alone is not sufficient, which is why this question is so important.

In our setting, the information content in orders is ultimately preserved via the export of net orders. It seems reasonable to speculate that trade crossing would reduce central market liquidity, however, since the market maker sees lower trade volume. This might be offset by the availability of greater liquidity from the crossing brokers, who know their customers and their trade motives well and hence will make deeper markets for them.

While we also agree with Miller that we have little to contribute in the way of active suggestions for market regulation, our paper does sound a cautionary note for regulators. The market in which all participants trade in one place at one price is not necessarily the market preferred by all traders, and there is no compelling reason for thinking it best in any sense. We view our contribution as describing a benefit associated with fragmentation which, while not a policy prescription, should have value for thinking about policy.

3   Competition, Fragmentation, and Market Quality

Thomas H. McInish and Robert A. Wood

3.1   Introduction

A key issue in the Market 2000 debate is whether the fragmentation of trading in individual stocks harms or enhances market quality. The New York Stock Exchange (NYSE) has steadily lost market share to the regional exchanges, to National Association of Securities Dealers (NASD) broker-dealers, and, more recently, to proprietary trading systems (PTSs) such as Instinet, Instinet Crossing, Posit, the Arizona Stock Exchange, and Lattice.[1] This increasingly effective competition naturally leads to the fragmentation of order flow. Although fragmentation disperses the orders, most competitors are informationally linked, so that all participants observe each others' trades and quotes within seconds of their execution.[2]

In the competition for order flow of listed securities, the NYSE is the dominant market center because of its natural advantages resulting from its historical position, from dominance in listings, and from a variety of rules that provide it with competitive advantages. In spite of these advantages, the erosion of NYSE market share appears to be increasing, particularly as the PTSs and third-market dealers—especially Madoff and Madoff clones—gain competitive strength. Perhaps the most important result of the Market 2000 debate will be the reaction of regulators and legislators to the fragmentation issue.

Branch and Freed (1977) investigate the relative impacts on spreads of increased competition and lost volume due to fragmentation of NYSE trading.

Thomas H. McInish is the Wunderlich Professor of Finance at the University of Memphis. Robert A. Wood is distinguished professor of finance at the University of Memphis.

The authors wish to thank the National Association of Securities Dealers for financial support and Ananth Madhavan for helpful suggestions.

1. See the report of the General Accounting Office (Bothwell 1993).
2. Some PTSs are not permitted to print their trades on the Consolidated Tape System at present.

These authors conclude that competition plays a much larger role in reducing spreads than loss of volume plays in increasing them. Hamilton (1979) notes that off-exchange trading of listed stocks can result in smaller and less volatile bid-ask spreads if effects due to increased competition predominate. If fragmentation of trading reduces economies of scale, spreads will be larger and more volatile. Hamilton concludes that at the time of his study the net effect of fragmentation is to reduce spreads and returns variance by at most a few percent. It should be stressed that the focus of these papers is on competition between the NYSE and other market centers.

Mendelson (1987) develops a model showing that fragmentation reduces the expected quantity traded, increases the price variance traders face, and reduces expected gains from trade. But the model also shows that fragmentation may improve the quality of market price signals. Although these theoretical arguments show that concentrating orders at one location can reduce spreads, a crucial assumption underlying this result is that the specialist, who is then given a monopoly position, will act altruistically for the public welfare rather than extract monopoly profits from traders.

Several studies have examined related topics. Cohen, Maier, Schwartz, and Whitcomb (1982) examine whether brokerage firms should be allowed to offer in-house execution services or all transactions should be forced instead to go through an exchange. These authors develop a model leading to the conclusion that the ancillary services exchanges offer, such as stabilization and surveillance, which have characteristics of public goods, will be undersupplied when fragmentation exists. Cohen and Conroy (1990) examine Securities and Exchange Commission (SEC) rule 19c-3, which allows off-exchange trading of NYSE stocks listed after April 26, 1979. They find that during 1983 increased fragmentation resulted in lower spreads but greater return variance.

This paper examines the impact of fragmentation on the quality of markets as measured by the bid-ask spread, premium (the difference between the midpoint of the outstanding spread and the price), and volatility (variance of return). The research design employed forms five stock portfolios that are equal in the attributes known to affect spreads and volatility. Firm attributes held equal include size, financial leverage, dividend payout, and market-to-book ratio. Trading characteristics held equal include stock price, market risk, dollar volume of trading, trading frequency, the availability of options for stocks, and membership in the S&P 500.

The key aspect of the research design is that the difference in the fragmentation of orders is maximized across the five portfolios. Hence the portfolios are nearly identical in attributes that affect their spreads, premiums, and volatility, and as different as possible in fragmentation of order share. Examination of the portfolio bid-ask spread, premium, and volatility supports the view that competition between market centers is beneficial for market participants.

The remainder of the paper is divided into seven sections. In section 3.2 the data are described. How fragmentation is measured, the variables used in the study, and how trading quality is measured follow. Next, the linear programming (LP) model is described. Section 3.7 presents the findings and the final section the conclusions.

3.2   The Data

Trading data for 1991 for NYSE-listed common stocks were obtained from the Institute for the Study of Security Markets (ISSM) tapes. Balance-sheet data for the three years ending in 1990 were obtained from Compustat files. The following criteria were used in selecting the sample. The data needed for each variable must be present on both the ISSM and Compustat tapes. To minimize thin trading problems, only common stocks with at least one thousand trades during the year are considered. To avoid the aberrant spread behavior of low-priced stocks, only stocks with an average price of at least $5 are included in the sample. A total of 980 firms met these criteria.

3.3   Measuring the Fragmentation of Trading

Fragmentation is measured using the Herfindahl index, which is commonly employed in the economics literature to assess the concentration of industries. For this study, the Herfindahl index calculation is based on the dollar volume of trading in NYSE-listed stocks during 1991 on the NYSE, each regional exchange, and Nasdaq. If trading occurs solely on the NYSE, the index value for that stock is 0.0. As trading becomes increasingly dispersed, the index value increases toward 1.0. Let P_i equal the dollar volume on an exchange for stock i divided by the total dollar volume for stock i on all exchanges. And let n_i equal the number of exchanges on which stock i trades. Define p_i as the summation of P_i^2 across n_i. Then the Herfindahl index for stock i is calculated as

$$\text{HERFINDAHL}_i = (1 - p_i)/((n_i - 1)p_i).$$

Examples of market shares based on dollar volume and Herfindahl indexes for the first ten securities in our sample are provided in table 3.1. The more dispersed the order flow, the greater the value of the Herfindahl index.

3.4   Equalizing Portfolio Trading Attributes

As noted above, the research design involves forming portfolios with similar attributes so that the spread, premium, and volatility are equalized, except for the influence of fragmentation. The average value for the period 1988–90 of the following firm attributes is held equal in the five portfolios.

LASSET	Log of assets
FINLEV	Financial leverage
PAYOUT	Dividend payout
MRKT/BK	Market-to-book ratio

Table 3.1   **Market Share on the NYSE, Nasdaq, and Regional Exchanges and**
                   Herfindahl Index Values for the Securities of Ten Firms, 1991

| | Market Share for Exchange (million $) | | | | | | Herfindahl |
Symbol	Boston	Cincinnati	Midwest	NYSE	Pacific	Nasdaq	Index
A	0	0	46	1,610	0	20	0.041
AA	521	465	1,342	40,882	1,304	530	0.042
AAF	0	0	47	487	0	43	0.191
AAL	46	0	336	3,64	72	22	0.063
ABF	28	0	385	4,50	139	66	0.068
ABK	0	0	60	2,04	0	53	0.039
ABM	12	0	11	293	19	143	0.285
ABP	0	0	25	357	0	18	0.123
ABS	553	0	903	20,997	760	648	0.062
ABT	499	718	3,856	62,888	3,882	2,182	0.075

Notes: The securities represent the first ten firms in the study sample. Market share is dollar trading volume for 1991. None of these ten securities had trades on the Philadelphia Stock Exchange.

FINLEV is defined as total debt/total assets $\times$ 100. Three years of data are used for each of these variables to reduce the impact of any unusual observations for an individual year. The attributes of the common stock that are held equal in the five portfolios are

AVGPRI	Average price
LN$VOLUME	Log of dollar volume of trading
BETA	Obtained from the 1990 Compustat tape
OPTION	Margin/option flag; 1 = optionable/marginable, 0 = not
S&P	S&P 500 flag; 0 = member, 1 = not member
NOTRADES	Number of trades per day

AVGPRI, LN$VOLUME, and NOTRADES are the averages for these variables over the year 1991. OPTION and S&P are 0/1 variables whose values are taken from the ISSM header record for 1991. LASSET and LN$VOLUME are in log form, since the distributions of these variables are highly skewed. Examination of the remaining variables does not indicate a need for log transformation prior to use.

The inclusion of each of these variables is based in part on the following articles: LASSET (Thomadakis 1977; Banz 1981; Reinganum 1981), FINLEV (Hamada 1972), PAYOUT (Ball 1978), MRKT/BK (Lustgarten and Thomadakis 1987), AVGPRI (Roll 1981; McInish and Wood 1992), LN$VOLUME (Jegadeesh and Subrahmanyam 1993), BETA (Sharpe 1964), OPTION (Fedenia and Grammatikos 1992), S&P (Harris and Gurel 1986; Jegadeesh and Subrahmanyam 1993), and NOTRADES (Stoll 1978; McInish and Wood 1992).

The LP holds both the first and second moments of the variables described above approximately equal across the five portfolios. Firm size is held constant by equalizing the log of assets. Holding the market-to-book ratio equal ensures that the growth expectations in all portfolios are the same. Note that this procedure results in holding market capitalizations approximately equal as well. Each of the trading attributes held equal is known to affect both the bid-ask spread and volatility. Equalizing the trading attributes as measured during the test year (with the exception of beta) rather than during a prior period better controls for the influence of these variables on fragmentation.

Table 3.2 presents the mean, standard deviation, minimum, and maximum values for each variable for the entire sample.

3.5 Trading Quality Measurement

Trading quality for the five portfolios is measured with three variables: bid-ask spread (SPREAD) in cents; PREMIUM, as measured by the absolute value of the difference between the midpoint of the outstanding NYSE bid and ask and the trade price; and VOLATILITY, calculated as the variance of the minute-by-minute returns for each portfolio over the year. SPREAD is formed by first obtaining the average for each stock in the sample over the year and then obtaining the weighted average within each portfolio where the weight is the LP solution level (discussed below). PREMIUM is calculated in the same manner. VOLATILITY is calculated by first forming a minute-by-minute return index for each portfolio (weighting the return for each stock by its LP solution level) and then calculating the standard deviation of the return series over the year.

3.6 Linear Programming Model

Before describing the LP model more formally, it may be helpful to provide an intuitive description. The LP forces the sample firms into five portfolios so that the attributes noted above are held equal in each portfolio. Both the mean

Table 3.2   **Sample Statistics for Each Variable for the Entire Sample (N = 980)**

Variable	Mean	Standard Deviation	Minimum	Maximum
LASSET	7.20	1.71	2.81	12.32
FINLEV	6.78	17.01	0.00	94.79
PAYOUT	49.97	57.65	0.00	445.94
MRKT/BK	2.06	1.43	0.02	9.31
AVGPRI	31.46	24.20	6.63	441.20
LN$VOLUME	12.18	2.81	−2.30	17.73
BETA	1.03	0.41	−0.10	2.70
OPTION	0.54	0.50	0.00	1.00
S&P	0.61	0.49	0.00	1.00
NOTRADES	122.91	196.83	4.29	37,132.57
HERFINDAHL	0.09	0.09	0.00	0.99

and the standard deviation of the attributes are held equal so that the LP will not, for example, have one extreme portfolio with very large and very small firms while the other extreme portfolio has all average-sized firms. Although the means of firm size would be equal across portfolios in this case, the size composition of firms in the portfolios would vary considerably. Holding equal the standard deviation of firm size in the portfolios alleviates this concern.

In considering the number of variables included, note that multicollinearity, which may be a significant problem when adding variables to any variant of the general linear model, is not of concern with the LP model. Although each added variable narrows the reach of the objective function somewhat, this is not a problem for most research designs. Thus, adding variables that might be considered overcontrolling, for example, using both the market-to-book ratio and the dividend payout ratio to control for growth, will not compromise the research. However, increasing the number of constraints may lead to spreading the sample firms across portfolios as discussed below.

The LP model used to form the five portfolios is

(1) $$\text{Maximize } \sum_j f_{5j} \text{ HERFINDAHL}_i$$

$$- \sum_j f_{1j} \text{ HERFINDAHL}_j, \qquad j = 1, \ldots, 980 \text{ firms},$$

subject to

(1a) $$\sum_j f_{i-kj} \text{ HERFINDAHL}_j - \sum_j f_{i-k-1} \text{ HERFINDAHL}_j =$$

$$\sum_j f_{i-k-1} \text{ HERFINDAHL}_j - \sum_j f_{i-k-2} \text{ HERFINDAHL}_j,$$

$$j = 1, \ldots, 980 \text{ firms}, \qquad i = 1, \ldots, 5 \text{ portfolios}, \qquad k = 3, 4, 5$$

(1b–1k) $$\sum_j f_{ij} X_j = \sum_j X_j/5 \pm \Delta, \qquad j = 1, \ldots, 980 \text{ firms},$$

$$i = 1, \ldots, 5 \text{ portfolios}$$

(1l–1u) $$\sum_j f_{ij} X_j^2 = \sum_j X_j^2/5 \pm \Delta, \qquad j = 1, \ldots, 980 \text{ firms},$$

$$i = 1, \ldots, 5 \text{ portfolios}$$

(1v) $$\sum_j f_{ij} = 980/5 \pm \Delta, \qquad j = 1, \ldots, 980 \text{ firms},$$

$$i = 1, \ldots, 5 \text{ portfolios}$$

(1w) $$\sum_j f_{ij} = 1 \pm \Delta, \qquad j = 1, \ldots, 980 \text{ firms},$$

$$i = 1, \ldots, 5 \text{ portfolios}$$

(1x) $$\Delta = 0.001$$

where f_{ij} is the LP solution variable that represents the amount of the ith portfolio's funds invested in firm j, X represents, in turn, each of the remaining variables described above, and X^2 represents the squared valued of these variables.

The objective function of the LP given in equation (1) maximizes the difference between the value of HERFINDAHL in portfolio 1 and the value of HERFINDAHL in portfolio 5. Hence, one extreme portfolio will have the least fragmentation of its trading, while the other extreme portfolio will have the most. Equation (1a) holds the distance between the HERFINDAHL values of the intervening portfolios equal. Equations (1b–1k) hold the first moments of the control variables equal, while equations (1l–1u) hold the second moments equal. Equation (1v) holds the number of stocks in each portfolio equal, while equation (1w) forces every stock into the solution.

As table 3.3 shows, the LP achieves the desired goal. The resulting portfolios are nearly identical in attributes that affect their trading quality, while the measure of trading fragmentation (HERFINDAHL) is spread evenly across the portfolios. The difference in the level of HERFINDAHL across the five portfolios is maximized. With these portfolios, we can isolate the effect of fragmentation on portfolio trading characteristics.

Table 3.3   **Statistics for Sample Portfolios: Mean and Standard Deviation (below)**

	Portfolio				
	1	2	3	4	5
HERFINDAHL	0.138	0.114	0.089	0.065	0.040
	0.089	0.064	0.032	0.017	0.012
LASSET	7.20	7.20	7.22	7.21	7.19
	1.70	1.73	1.62	1.71	1.76
FINLEV	26.77	26.72	26.78	26.83	26.78
	17.00	17.06	17.03	16.95	16.98
PAYOUT	49.90	49.98	50.06	50.08	49.88
	57.66	57.57	57.60	57.58	57.65
MRKT/BK	2.06	2.06	2.06	2.06	2.06
	1.43	1.43	1.43	1.43	1.43
AVGPRI	31.41	31.40	31.52	31.47	31.46
	24.24	24.23	24.14	24.20	24.16
LN$VOLUME	15.21	15.20	15.22	15.20	15.17
	1.60	1.64	1.61	1.72	1.88
BETA	1.03	1.03	1.03	1.03	1.03
	0.42	0.42	0.41	0.41	0.41
OPTION	0.54	0.54	0.54	0.54	0.54
	0.50	0.50	0.50	0.50	0.50
S&P	0.61	0.61	0.61	0.61	0.61
	0.49	0.49	0.49	0.49	0.49
NOTRADES	122.96	122.92	122.91	122.94	122.67
	196.62	196.59	196.86	196.85	196.74
N	208	211	210	215	205

Notes: The means and standard deviations of each variable for each of the five portfolios formed using the LP model are presented. The LP separates the Herfindahl index values as much as possible across the five portfolios. At the same time, it holds the values of each of the other variables approximately equal across the five portfolios.

The LP solution technique chosen results in continuous solution values rather than integer solution values. With an integer solution, firms would be totally in one of the five portfolios. Finance theory permits a continuous solution wherein a firm may be spread over more than one portfolio, since it is realistic to form portfolios in this manner. Since the LP formulation is basically an assignment problem, the solution values naturally gravitate to either 0.0 or 1.0 as long as the constraints are not too binding, so that relatively few firms are spread across portfolios. In the solution obtained, 88 percent of the nonzero solution values are 1.0. The results were replicated by rounding the solution values of 0.5 and above to 1.0 and those below 0.5 to 0.0 to ensure that significant bias did not result.

This low level of intermediate solution values is fortunate, since the size of the problem makes integer programming computationally intractable. The need to have a relatively low number of solution values between 0.0 and 1.0 arises because, as the number of intermediate solution values increases, the intent of the equality constraints is being defeated. To illustrate, if a $10 billion firm has a solution value of 0.5 for portfolio 1 and 0.5 for portfolio 2, the size equality constraints will indicate that a $5 billion firm is being included in each portfolio.

If strict equality were specified in the LP constraints, no feasible solution could be obtained. Hence, each equality constraint is held equal to 0.0 plus or minus 0.1 percent. Thus, rather than obtaining exactly 1.0 for most nonzero solution values, we obtain 0.999 or 1.001.

3.7   Why Use LP to Form Portfolios

The 980 sample stocks could be analyzed by applying a form of the general linear model to the individual trades and quotes. Three concerns arise from this procedure. First, the signal obtained in this manner is very noisy as a result of bid-ask bounce and the high level of idiosyncratic risk in each stock. Second, the functional form of the linear model must be specified. Third, multicollinearity among the dependent variables may confound the results. Each of these problems is minimized or avoided with the use of LP to form portfolios.

While portfolios are often used to avoid the noisy signal problem, the typical approach of ranking on a variable such as market capitalization does not avoid multicollinearity. To illustrate the problems that result from the traditional procedure, data for market capitalization (EQUITY), MRKT/BK, PAYOUT, AVG-PRI, and BETA are averaged for 3,995 firms on the Compustat Plus file for the three years ending in 1991. The Spearman correlations of EQUITY with the remaining variables are MRKT/BK 0.30195, PAYOUT 0.56676, AVGPRI 0.86729, and BETA 0.10597. All of these correlation coefficients are significant at the 0.0001 level. While data for spreads, trading frequency, and stock price were not available for this sample, we know from other research that these variables are highly correlated with market capitalization. Thus, ranking on market capitalization introduces considerable correlation in these variables across the portfolios. It is easy to see that many research designs will be confounded by these correlations. The LP approach controls this source of bias in portfolio formulation. While portfolios are often used to avoid the noisy signal problem, the typical approach of ranking on a variable such as market capitalization does not avoid multicollinearity. The determination of the number of portfolios to be formed involves a judgment between the advantage of reducing the noise of the signal in each portfolio by increasing it size versus the advantage of increasing the number of observations.

3.8   Findings

Table 3.4 repeats the values of HERFINDAHL for the five portfolios and reports the levels of SPREAD, PREMIUM, and VOLATILITY as well. The values of the liquidity and spread measures for each of the five portfolios are also presented graphically in figure 3.1. Note that both SPREAD and PREMIUM tend to decrease as fragmentation increases. The Pearson correlation coefficients presented in table 3.4 show that these relationships are significant at the 0.05 level. Volatility decreases from a level of 0.052 for portfolio 5, which has the least order flow fragmentation, to portfolio 3, but then increases for portfolios 1 and 2, reaching 0.073. The correlation between portfolio volatility and the Herfindahl index is not statistically significant.

Although the observed range of spread across the five portfolios is only 0.6 cent, this evidence nevertheless supports the hypothesis that competition between market centers, which, if effective, naturally results in fragmentation of the order flow, reduces both SPREAD and PREMIUM, thereby benefiting market participants. Further, VOLATILITY is not found to be affected significantly by fragmentation.

Table 3.4	Statistics for Analysis of the Effect of Trading Fragmentation			
Portfolio	HERFINDAHL	SPREAD	PREMIUM	VOLATILITY
1	0.138	0.241	0.059	0.073
2	0.114	0.239	0.058	0.062
3	0.089	0.244	0.060	0.035
4	0.065	0.244	0.061	0.038
5	0.040	0.247	0.064	0.052
Pearson correlation coefficient of		−0.9018	−0.8929	0.6366
HERFINDAHL (confidence level in parentheses)		(0.036)	(0.041)	(0.248)

Note: The means of Herfindahl index (HERFINDAHL), spread (SPREAD), premium (PREMIUM), and portfolio variance (VOLATILITY) are provided for each of the five sample portfolios.

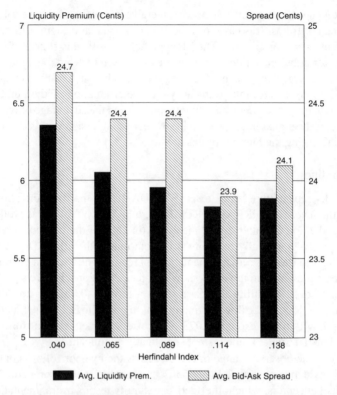

Fig. 3.1   Average spread and liquidity premium of five portfolios with varying levels of off-board market share

3.9   Conclusion

In the Securities Reform Act of 1975, Congress mandated an increase in competition between the regional exchanges, Nasdaq, and the NYSE for NYSE-listed securities. The NYSE has consistently argued that such competition fragments the order flow to the detriment of market quality. This study examines the NYSE concern by forming five portfolios of NYSE-listed common stocks. These five portfolios are nearly identical in attributes known to affect trading quality but have the maximum possible difference in the fragmentation of trading across competing market centers. These five portfolios isolate the effect of fragmentation on market quality.

The findings show that bid-ask spreads and premiums (the difference between the midpoint of the outstanding spread and the price) are significantly reduced by competition. This result is consistent with evidence reported by Branch and Freed (1977), Hamilton (1979), and McInish and Wood (1992) that competition reduces spreads. Volatility shows no significant change as fragmentation increases. Hence the traditional view that competition benefits society is found to apply to securities trading. This issue will be of continuing interest, since the General Accounting Office (Bothwell 1993) has urged the SEC to continue to monitor the issue of market fragmentation.

References

Ball, Ray. 1978. Anomalies in relationships between securities' yields and yield-surrogates. *Journal of Financial Economics* 6:103–26.

Banz, Rolf W. 1981. The relationship between return and market value of common stock. *Journal of Financial Economics* 9:3–18.

Bothwell, James L. 1993. Securities markets: SEC actions needed to address market fragmentation issues. In *Oversight Hearings on the Future of the Stock Market Focusing on the Results of a GAO Study on Market Fragmentation before the Subcommittee on Telecommunications and Finance of the House Committee on Energy and Commerce.* 103d Cong., 1st sess., 1993.

Branch, Ben, and Walter Freed. 1977. Bid-ask spreads on the Amex and the Big Board. *Journal of Finance* 32:159–63.

Cohen, Kalman, J., and Robert M. Conroy. 1990. An empirical study of the effect of rule 19c-3. *Journal of Law and Economics* 33:277–305.

Cohen, Kalman J., Steven F. Maier, Robert A. Schwartz, and David K. Whitcomb. 1982. An analysis of the economic justification for consolidation in a secondary securities market. *Journal of Banking and Finance* 6:117–36.

Fedenia, Mark, and Theoharry Grammatikos. 1992. Options trading and the bid-ask spread of the underlying stocks. *Journal of Business* 65:335–51.

Hamada, Robert S. 1972. The effect of the firm's capital structure on the systematic risk of common stock. *Journal of Finance* 27:435–52.

Hamilton, James L. 1979. Marketplace fragmentation, competition, and the efficiency of the stock exchange. *Journal of Finance* 34:171–87.

Harris, Lawrence, and Eitan Gurel. 1986. Price and volume effects associated with changes in the S&P 500: New evidence for the existence of price pressures. *Journal of Finance* 4:815–30.

Jegadeesh, Narasimhan, and Avanidhar Subrahmanyam. 1993. Liquidity effects of the introduction of the S&P 500 index futures contract on the underlying stocks. *Journal of Business* 66:171–87.

Lustgarten, Steven, and Stavros Thomadakis. 1987. Mobility barriers and Tobin's *q*. *Journal of Business* 60:519–37.

McInish, Thomas H., and Robert A. Wood. 1992. An analysis of intraday patterns in bid/ask spreads for NYSE stocks. *Journal of Finance* 47:753–64.

Mendelson, Haim. 1987. Consolidation, fragmentation, and market performance. *Journal of Financial and Quantitative Analysis* 22:189–207.

Reinganum, Marc R. 1981. Misspecification of capital asset pricing: Empirical anomalies based on earnings' yield and market values. *Journal of Financial Economics* 9:19–46.

Roll, Richard. 1981. A possible explanation of the small firm effect. *Journal of Finance* 36:879–88.

Sharpe, William F. 1964. Capital asset prices: A theory of market equilibrium under conditions of risk. *Journal of Finance* 5:309–27.

Stoll, Hans. 1978. The pricing of security dealer services: An empirical study of NASDAQ stocks. *Journal of Finance* 33:1153–72.

Thomadakis, Stavros. 1977. A value-based test of profitability and market structure. *Review of Economics and Statistics* 59:179–85.

Comment   Harold Mulherin

McInish and Wood present a timely piece on competition and fragmentation, a timeless topic that has induced heated debate among market participants for as long as organized exchanges have existed. The authors combine an innovative methodology with a clear and concise presentation to provide a significant contribution to the empirical literature on market microstructure. My primary reservation with the study is the particularly strong policy stance that the authors derive from their work. My comments include a review of the measurement ambiguities faced by any empirical study such as this but also advance a recommendation for a more novel approach to the competition/fragmentation debate that is rooted in the property-rights framework of Ronald Coase.

Overview of Their Approach

Let me first point to some of the notable features of the analysis. McInish and Wood position their research amid the ongoing debate of the trade-offs involved in the choice between consolidation and fragmentation of securities trading. The primary issue they seek to address is the effect that off-board trading has on the performance of the securities market in the United States. This question has repeatedly surfaced in the United States since the nineteenth-century battles between bucket shops and organized futures and securities exchanges. (See Mulherin, Netter, and Overdahl [1991a, 1991b].) The analysis of off-board trading is also highly pertinent to current-day matters tied to market automation as well as to much of the theme in the SEC's Market 2000 study.

The data used in the study include the bid-ask spreads, trading volume, and financial ratios of 980 NYSE-listed securities for the year 1991. The key innovation of the study is the use of a linear programming model that groups the 980 firms into five portfolios having remarkably similar trading and financial characteristics but having differing fractions of trading away from the NYSE. This detailed method of controlling for the characteristics of the firms under analysis is the significant contribution of the paper to the literature on competition and fragmentation.

Across the five portfolios, the analysis compares the amount of off-board trading, as captured by a Herfindahl measure of trading away from the NYSE, with measures of market quality including the bid-ask spread. The analysis distinguishes between a competition hypothesis, which predicts an inverse relation between off-board trading and spreads, and a fragmentation hypothesis,

Harold Mulherin is associate professor of finance at Pennsylvania State University.

which predicts that a larger Herfindahl measure will lead to wider spreads. The authors find that the portfolio with the greatest Herfindahl measure of off-board trading has a spread that is 0.6 cent narrower than the portfolio that has the least amount of off-board trading. They conclude that off-board trading advances competition and that the SEC and Congress should take efforts to facilitate more dispersion of trading across securities markets.

Measurement Issues

Although the analysis in the paper is quite sound, there are several measurement issues that temper the policy implications that can be drawn from the results. A query that immediately comes to mind regards the economic significance of the results. While the authors find statistical significance, the difference between the market quality of the two most extreme portfolios is still only 0.6 cent per share. Given the bid-ask spread of 24.1 cents per share for the most competitive portfolio, the savings to investors is around 2 percent. For the average security in the sample, which has 123 trades per day, this translates into a savings of 74 cents per day. Certainly one can quibble with the economic significance of these numbers, but an even more telling benchmark comes from Charles Lee's (1993, 1011) analysis of off-board trading in NYSE listings, which finds that "the price for non-NYSE trades is .7 to 1 cent per share less favorable than that for adjacent NYSE trades." Hence, even if McInish and Wood have successfully measured the effect of competition on NYSE market quality, it is not obvious that mandated increases in off-board trading will improve investor welfare. Indeed, welfare may decline if the trade execution of the regionals and Nasdaq is not as favorable as that of the NYSE.

A second concern that I have with the empirical design is the ambiguous interpretation of the Herfindahl measure used in the study. The authors present the measure as a clean proxy for both fragmentation and competition, being of the opinion that fragmentation and competition are pure synonyms. However, the Herfindahl formula suggests a less-than-perfect relation between fragmentation and competition. Consider table 3C.1, an example of three securities, all with 75 percent of their volume on the NYSE but with varying fractions of trading at competing venues. The example holds specialist competition at 25 percent but varies the dispersion of this competition across dif-

Table 3C.1   **Example of the Herfindahl Index**

Security	Fraction of Trading				Herfindahl
	NYSE	Midwest	Pacific	Nasdaq	
1	.75	.25	0	0	.60
2	.75	.125	.125	0	.34
3	.75	.0833	.0833	.0833	.24

fering numbers of alternative exchanges. In doing so, the Herfindahl index varies noticeably. Mechanically, therefore, fragmentation and competition are not perfect substitutes. More important, the given numbers raise thorny issues of a kind that have plagued the Justice Department as to whether specialist competition is greater when one or many competitors have 25 percent of the market.

An even more problematic aspect of interpreting the Herfindahl variable as a proxy for specialist competition stems from the lack of data on limit orders and floor trading activity in the sample of securities. Since the initial insights of Demsetz (1968), microstructure theory has recognized that one factor keeping specialists honest is the heated competition on the floor of the NYSE itself. I am concerned that such internal competition is likely to be correlated with the off-board trading measured by the Herfindahl index and that the reported association between the Herfindahl and spreads may be driven in whole or part by the incidence of limit orders and floor trading activity.

Similar missing-variable arguments can be made regarding the emphasis of bid-ask spreads as the measure of market quality. We know that market quality is multidimensional and includes, in addition to spreads, the depth of quotes and fraction of within-the-spread executions. Without the consideration of these aspects of market quality, the authors cannot unambiguously say that added off-board trading improves quality. It is possible that off-board trading lessens depth and thereby detracts from market quality.

Sample selection and endogeneity issues give further weight to the point that the reported results do not lead to the causal inference that added off-board trading will improve market quality. In spite of the careful work of the authors, their study still faces sample-selection biases because their data requirements lead them to analyze only the hi-cap segment of the NYSE. But what if the data were available to study all NYSE listings? I wager this would strengthen the results, as the second-tier NYSE firms likely have wider spreads and less off-board trading. But certainly we would not interpret the results from such extended analysis to say that more off-board trading will lead to narrower spreads, as we know that the selection of trading location is endogenously chosen in the market.

In the United States, there is a standard life cycle of a security from an OTC setting of many dealers, to the NYSE environment of a single specialist to a hybrid system of specialists and many dealers. Post–Big Bang London also is experiencing such a hybrid life cycle (Waters [1992]). For the purpose of the present study, this endogenous life cycle places further clouds over the interpretation of the Herfindahl measure. Does it really represent competition or are the off-board trading venues merely cream-skimming bucket shops? Blume and Goldstein (1991) as well as a companion piece by McInish and Wood (1992) find that the regionals and Nasdaq free ride at least 90 percent of the time on trading in NYSE-listed securities. This free riding may impede the depth and absolute level of quotes. Such effects on market quality cannot be captured in McInish's and Wood's cross-sectional analysis, thus tempering the authors' conclusion that increased off-board trading will improve overall market quality.

Opening the Black Box

Moving from specific measurement issues to a more general perspective, I think the authors must broaden the paradigm underlying their analysis. The authors are deeply rooted in the "NYSE-as-a-monopoly" viewpoint that strongly influenced economists at least up through May Day in 1975. This monopoly paradigm has gone the way of fixed commissions due to the practical fact of the many domestic and global alternatives for trading NYSE listings. From a more intellectual standpoint, the monopoly label for organized financial exchanges has been rendered obsolete by the property-rights model of Ronald Coase and others, which tells us not to attach the tag of monopoly to a complex organization simply because we do not fully understand it.

Coase (1988, 7–10) himself admits that many economists still assume that the rules of organized exchanges foment market power. But Coase chastises his colleagues for this presumption and notes that, for anything approaching perfect competition to exist, an intricate system of rules is required. For Coase, the term "rules" is synonymous with property rights and is quite distinct from SEC regulations.

In the Coasian spirit, I think that any perceived problems inherent in the competition/fragmentation debate can be mitigated via the allocation of property rights rather than by the extension of the arm of the SEC. What I have in mind is placing more solid property rights to listing in the hands of the listing corporations. Both initial listing decisions as well as additional trading locations would be at the discretion of corporations and would not be co-opted by the SEC's grant of unlisted trading privileges. As Coase has taught us, this clear definition of property rights in listing would internalize the cost-benefit trade-offs involved in the competition/fragmentation debate and would lead to the optimal number of trading locations for all publicly traded securities. The nice thing about the property-rights approach is that the amount of off-board trading for each security is determined by the invisible hand of the market rather than the visible, and clumsy, hand of the SEC.

References

Blume, Marshall E., and Michael A. Goldstein. 1991. Differences in Execution Prices among the NYSE, the Regionals, and the NASD. Working paper, Wharton School, University of Pennsylvania, September.

Coase, R. H. 1988. *The Firm, the Market, and the Law.* Chicago: University of Chicago Press.

Demsetz, Harold. 1968. The Cost of Transacting. *Quarterly Journal of Economics* 82 (February): 33–53.

Lee, Charles. 1993. Market Integration and Price Execution for NYSE-Listed Securities. *Journal of Finance* 48 (July): 1009–38.

McInish, Thomas H., and Robert A. Wood. 1992. Price Discovery, Volume and Re-
    gional/Third Market Trading. Working paper, Memphis State University, April.
Mulherin, J. Harold, Jeffry M. Netter, and James A. Overdahl. 1991a. Prices Are Prop-
    erty: The Organization of Financial Exchanges from a Transaction Cost Perspective.
    Journal of Law and Economics 34, part 2 (October): 591–644.
———. 1991b. Who Owns the Quotes? A Case Study into the Definition and Enforce-
    ment of Property Rights at the Chicago Board of Trade. *Review of Futures Markets*
    10 (1): 108–29.
Waters, Richard. 1992. SE Acts on Small Company Shares. *Financial Times,* October
    15, 21.

Comment   John C. Coffee, Jr.

Wood and McInish ask an important question: Does the fragmentation of trading in multiply listed stocks harm or enhance market quality? But this is not
the question they answer. Rather, they answer that in their study competition
among markets seems to be producing slightly tighter spreads and lower premiums without seriously affecting volatility. This is not fully responsive to
their own question, because more is involved in the assessment of market quality. A focus on the average spread can be misleading, particularly if any aggregate improvement in the average bid-ask spread comes at significant expense
to a discrete class of market participants (here, small shareholders). Because
there is evidence of such injury to at least one class of investors and because
the Wood and McInish study itself reveals only a very modest improvement in
price spreads, the result is an uncertain trade-off between aggregate efficiency
and distributive equity. In this light, it is far from self-evident that public policy
should permit the kind of nonprice competition by which emerging competitors in the third market and on regional exchanges seem to be diverting order
flow from the New York Stock Exchange (NYSE).

The first part of this brief comment examines this evidence that some investors systematically lose as the result of contemporary intermarket competition,
and the second part turns to the problematic character of competition based on
payments for order flow. Although payments for order flow are not addressed
in Wood's and McInish's paper, to omit this topic from a discussion of competition among market centers is frankly like casting *Hamlet* without the prince of
Denmark. Indeed, the prevalence of nonprice competition (such as rebates for
order flow), when coupled with the problem of informed trading, may explain
why intermarket competition has yielded only the scant improvement in bid-
ask spreads and Wood and McInish find.

John C. Coffee, Jr., is the Adolf A. Berle Professor of Law at Columbia University Law School.

Who Wins and Who Loses from Intermarket Competition

The magnitude of the price effect shown by the Wood and McInish data seems very modest. Comparing their portfolio 5 (which has the least order flow fragmentation) with their portfolio 1 (which has the most), one finds that the quoted spread falls by 0.6 cent and the liquidity premium declines by 0.5 cent. Although this change is certainly in the desired direction, such a slight improvement in market efficiency may be thought insufficient to justify the possibility that some classes of customers systematically lose when their transactions are diverted away from the primary market (NYSE or American Stock Exchange [AMEX]) to other markets. A number of recent studies reach essentially this conclusion, each stressing different evidence. Lee (1993) finds that in 1988 and 1989 "[t]he average price difference between the NYSE and matched off-Board trades is 0.7 to 1 cent per share." Examining liquidity premiums, he further reports "that off-Board trades generally involve higher execution costs in the order of 0.5 to 1.5 cents per share." The most illuminating data uncovered by Lee emerges when he breaks down the average liquidity premium by trade size. On trades of one hundred to four hundred shares (the typical trade of small retail customers), the average excess liquidity premium paid for off-board trades in matched samples in 1989 was 1.22 cents (and 1.58 and 2.65 cents per share when the trades were effected on the NASD or on the Cincinnati exchange, respectively). Yet, on larger trades above two thousand shares, some regional exchanges (most notably the Midwest and Pacific) offered significantly better executions than the NYSE. Thus, even if Wood and McInish are entirely correct in their conclusion that competition among market centers is reducing the average bid-ask spread, it appears that some rival market centers are besting the NYSE by offering superior execution services (chiefly for midsized blocks), but others are offering inferior executions while diverting order flow by means of nonprice competition.

Lee's study has received some methodological criticism (on the ground that it does not adequately distinguish market and limit orders) and is subject to the further objection that its 1988 and 1989 data are now out-of-date because some third-market dealers have subsequently introduced price-improvement programs under which they will in certain circumstances execute transactions between their own bid and asked quotations. Still, later studies have shown an even greater disparity between NYSE and off-board execution in the same stock. Blume and Goldstein (1993) employ 1990 data to examine the extent of price improvement on the NYSE versus other markets. Similarly to Lee, they find the NYSE to significantly outperform rival markets on trade sizes below five hundred shares, but to lag behind some other markets on transactions in the five-hundred- to three-thousand-share range. Mayer and Leigh (1991) report that daily extreme prices (highs and lows) are significantly more likely to be off-board trades than mere chance would dictate. If one accepts their assumption that the daily highs are disproportionately purchases by public customers and the daily lows are sales by them, this finding further corroborates the inferiority of off-board executions. Finally and most importantly, Fialkowski and Petersen (1992) use a data set consisting of the orders sent to all exchanges from a major retail brokerage firm through automated routing systems during two days in 1991. They report that the expected price improvement per trade was 3 cents per share higher on the NYSE than on off-board transactions. This result (which is three times above Lee's estimate of the disparity) may result both from the fact that they consider price improvement in one-eighth-point markets[1] and because a retail brokerage firm will chiefly be routing smaller orders.[2]

Another recent form of study has been to compare the bid-ask spreads on Nasdaq and exchange-listed common stocks, after controlling for differences in market capitalization. Grouping stocks into decile portfolios by market capitalization, Goldstein (1993) finds that all stock exchanges had significantly tighter price spreads (both in absolute terms and as a percentage of price) than Nasdaq in 1990. Indeed, he reports that 99 percent of the stocks traded on the exchanges had a lower average closing bid-ask spread than the median stock traded on Nasdaq's National Market System. Focusing just on stocks that would meet NYSE listing requirements, he finds that the spreads are 15–18 cents wider when the stocks trade only on Nasdaq. Similarly, Christie and Huang (1993) find that, when issuers move from Nasdaq to the NYSE or AMEX, the quoted spread narrows and the average liquidity premium declines. Such data are not inconsistent with the implication of the Wood and McInish study that intermarket competition reduces spreads, but they suggest that market structure is a critical variable.

Still, at least one study suggests that competition can produce undesirable market fragmentation and higher volatility. Porter and Thatcher (1992) compare daily spreads of NYSE-listed stocks that were also listed on at least one regional exchange from 1987 to 1989. For some stocks, as volume increased on the regional exchanges, they find that the NYSE quoted spread narrowed in apparent response to this competition. But for other stocks, as volume rose on the regional exchanges, the NYSE spread increased—apparently as the result of market fragmentation. The dividing line, they find, depended on whether the average bid-ask spread exceeded $0.3125. Above this level, increased volume on the regional exchange seemed to produce market fragmentation, not tighter spreads. Whether competition from regional exchanges will widen or

1. When the spread is an eighth of a point, price improvement typically occurs only in auction markets, because when public orders cross in them, one side by definition gets a superior price to the bid-ask spread in a dealer market. For example, if the spread is $10 to $10 1/8 and two public orders for one hundred shares cross, the transaction will be either at $10 (in which case the buyer does better than in a dealer market where it would normally be charged $10 1/8) or at $10 1/8 (in which case the seller does better than in a dealer market where it would normally receive $10 per share).
2. In this sample, 99 percent of the trades were under three thousand shares.

narrow the quoted spread on the NYSE depends, they surmise, on the volume of public limit orders in the stock. If they are correct, the direct challenge of a rival market (whether the third market or a regional exchange) may be less important in inducing narrower spreads than the influence of limit orders (which dealer markets may not process or may treat less favorably than do auction markets).

Price Competition versus Cream Skimming

When order flow is diverted from a primary exchange to a rival market center, proponents of intermarket competition assume that there is an efficiency gain: either (1) the customer is getting a better price (whether in the form of a tighter spread or a between-the-spread execution) or (2) the broker is receiving a rebate for its order flow, which it presumably passes on to the customer (either in whole or at least in part) in the form of a reduced brokerage commission. But this assumption of a net cost saving may be incorrect, for either of two distinct reasons.

First, the customer may experience a loss greater than the rebate paid to the broker. According to several commentators, the typical payment for order flow in the case of a NYSE-listed stock is 1 cent per share.[3] But, according to Fialkowski and Petersen (1992), the expected price improvement that is forgone when transactions are diverted away from the NYSE is 3 cents per share. Thus, there is an asymmetry between the broker's gain and the customer's loss. In effect, the customer loses the expected value of an execution between the bid and asked spread (worth 3 cents), and there is no way, even in a highly efficient market for brokerage services, that the broker can "pass on" the 1-cent rebate it receives so as to compensate the customer fully for its 3-cent loss.

Second, rival market centers appear to be following a general strategy of "cream skimming" rather than directly contesting the primary exchanges across the board. This is evident in three distinct respects. First, third-market dealers do not attempt to compete for order flow on most NYSE-listed stocks. The NYSE estimates that order flow payments are currently common with regard to some 428 NYSE-listed stocks,[4] and the practice of paying for order flow is far less pervasive with regard to AMEX stocks. Why? Seemingly, third-market makers find it profitable to pay for flow only in actively traded stocks. Second, rival market centers still engage in derivative pricing; that is, they simply match the NYSE specialist's quoted spread, rarely moving their own bid and asked quotations inside the specialist's. Although there is some evi-

3. Typically, a payment is made for order flow only if (1) the trading spread exceeds one-eighth of a point, (2) a minimum monthly order flow is promised (usually 100,000 shares), (3) the transaction does not exceed a maximum size (often 3,000 shares), and (4) certain source restrictions are observed (no professional traders). See Coffee (1991); National Association of Securities Dealers (1991).

4. I was provided this estimate by James E. Shapiro of the NYSE Research and Planning Division.

dence of change, the NYSE still largely monopolizes price discovery. Has-brouck (1993) examined quote data at one-second intervals for three high-volume NYSE-listed stocks that also trade heavily on other markets. He found that between 80 and 90 percent of price discovery occurred on the NYSE. McInish and Wood (1992) find that a better bid or offer is available off-board only 11 percent of the time for NYSE-listed stocks and 7 percent of the time for AMEX stocks (although they also identify some stocks in which a regional exchange has the "best bid or offer" as much as 40 percent of the time).

Third, the regional exchanges focus their efforts on competing for smaller trades in NYSE-listed stocks. In 1988, trades of nine hundred shares or less represented over 75 percent of all transactions in NYSE-listed securities on the Boston, Midwest, Pacific, and Philadelphia exchanges, as well as on the NASD (see Lee 1993, 1017). Why? The best explanation may be that rival market centers want to avoid the professional (or "informed") trader and obtain trans-actions from less sophisticated (or "uninformed") retail customers. Derivative pricing is a means to this end. By simply matching the bid-ask quotation of the NYSE or AMEX (and declining to pay for order flow on large or professional trades), the rival market center does not attract order flow from informed trad-ers. If instead the third-market maker or regional specialist were to quote the inside spread, it could not refuse to deal with the professional trader under the Intermarket Trading System's rules. The result is that the burden of adverse selection falls disproportionately on the primary exchange specialist, who loses the "safe" business of the retail customer but must accept the problematic trades of the professional.

If one accepts this premise that rival market centers do not want to expose themselves to informed traders and so will not quote a bid-ask spread inside that of the NYSE specialist, it may explain why the benefits of intermarket competition in the Wood and McInish study are so modest (i.e., no more than 0.6 cent). Moreover, the ability of the NYSE specialist to narrow its spreads further in response to competitive pressure would also appear to be limited. As uninformed trades are diverted to rival market centers, informed trades will represent an increasing percentage of the trades it handles, and the logical re-sponse to informed trading is to widen (not narrow) the bid-ask spread.

In this light, competition from rival market centers that is not based on price competition (i.e., payments for order flow and similar practices) may stalemate the public policy objective of narrower bid-ask spreads. Even reforms such as decimalization, which should induce a lower-cost market center to quote a tighter spread in order to obtain order flow, may be significantly frustrated if the more efficient market maker can hope instead to divert a nonrepresentative and "safer" order flow by offering rebates to the broker for desired transac-tions. To be sure, the extent of the "informed" trading problem has not been reliably estimated.[5] But beyond the traditionally cited reasons—unfairness to

---

5. New literature suggests that "informed trades are concentrated in the medium-sized cate-gory." See Barclay and Warner (1993). But, as noted earlier, midsized blocks appear to be the one

the customer and the asserted risk of market fragmentation—there may be a third reason for public policy to disfavor payments for order flow: it may chill price competition and reduce the efficiency gains that normally should accrue from intermarket competition.

References

Barclay, M., and J. Warner. 1993. Stealth Trading and Volatility: Which Trades Move Prices? *Journal of Financial Economics* 34:281–306.

Blume, M., and M. Goldstein. 1993. Dissimilar Market Structures and Market Liquidity: A Transaction Data Study of Exchange Listings. Working paper, Owen Graduate School of Management, Vanderbilt University.

Christie, W., and R. Huang. 1994. Market Structure and Liquidity: A Transactions Data Study of Exchange Listings. *Journal of Financial Intermediation* 3:320–26.

Coffee, J. 1991. Brokers and Bribery. *New York Law Journal,* September 27, 1991, 5.

Fialkowski, D., and M. Petersen. 1992. Posted versus Effective Spreads: Good Prices or Bad Quotes? Working paper, Center for Research in Security Prices, University of Chicago.

Goldstein, M. 1993. Competitive Specialist vs. Dealer Markets: Effective and Displayed Spreads on Nasdaq-NMS and the U.S. Stock Exchange System. Working paper, Graduate School of Business, University of Colorado, Boulder.

Hasbrouck, J. 1993. One Security, Many Markets: Determining the Contributions to Price Discovery. Working paper, Stern School of Business, New York University.

Lee, C. 1993. Market Integration and Price Execution for NYSE-Listed Securities. *Journal of Finance* 48:1009–38.

McInish, T., and R. Wood. 1992. Price Discovery, Volume, and Regional/Third Market Trading Volume. Working paper, Memphis State University.

Mayer, M., and B. Leigh. 1991. Does Off-Board Trading Compromise Execution Quality? The Evidence from High and Down Low. Working paper, American Stock Exchange Research Department.

National Association of Securities Dealers. 1991. Inducements for Order Flow: A Report of the Order Flow Committee to the Board of Governors. Washington, DC: National Association of Securities Dealers.

Porter, D., and J. Thatcher. 1992. Fragmentation, Competition, and Limit Orders: New Evidence from Interday Spreads. Working paper, Marquette University, Milwaukee.

Authors' Reply

The comments by Coffee and Mulherin have two focuses: (1) the economic perspective underlying our paper, and (2) technical questions about our procedures and findings. We will respond to each of these in turn.

The Economic Perspective

Philosophical differences exist between Mulherin's and Coffee's views and our views of the competition for order flow among the New York Stock Ex-

---

area where regional exchanges are attracting order flow away from the NYSE, based on traditional price competition. See Lee (1993); Blume and Goldstein (1993). Hence, the magnitude of informed trading as a barrier to price competition that tightens the bid-ask spread remains debatable.

change (NYSE), the regionals, and the third-market broker-dealers. We will outline their views and contrast them with ours.

Mulherin subscribes to a Coasian perspective in which, ideally, no regulatory intervention would interfere with the invisible hand's allocation of order flow so as to optimize global welfare. Corporations' property rights would allow them, within the framework of our legal system, to determine where their stock would be traded. With this view, corporations, acting in the interests of their shareholders, will determine an optimal allocation of order flow among the NYSE, regional exchanges, and third-market dealers. According to Coase, exchange rules such as those of the NYSE (perhaps complex and difficult to understand) may "exist in order to reduce transactions costs and therefore to increase the volume of trade" (1988, 9).

Coffee's philosophical perspective, which is primarily focused on price competition, leads to the view that the regionals and third-market broker-dealers are cream skimming, free riders that compete unfairly with practices such as the purchase of order flow and do not contribute significantly to the price discovery process. One might infer from Coffee's statements that investors would be better served if the regional exchanges were eliminated and third-market dealers were prohibited by fiat from trading listed securities. Then the order flow would be concentrated at the NYSE and the market depth maximized at one location. We are concerned that the NYSE specialists would not use their then supreme market power for the public benefit but rather for their own wealth enhancement.

Our philosophical view of the competition for listed order flow stems from (1) a pragmatic assessment of the present regulatory environment, and (2) Stigler's dominant-firm oligopoly model (1940, 1964), which, in our opinion, describes the competition for listed order flow. Garbade and Silber (1979) were the first to characterize the NYSE as the dominant competitor, with the regionals and third-market dealers offering satellite competition. In the dominant-firm oligopoly model, satellite competitors are unable to compete on price but rather must offer superior service through better technology and in other ways, attention to local clientele, and so forth (McInish and Wood 1995). The NYSE publicly invites price competition (bettering quotes) from the satellites, yet according to this model this is precisely the kind of competition that they are far less able to offer, particularly with trading in eighths. Thus, the principal arena for competition is technology, not price. In fact, before we seriously consider abolishing the satellite competitors we should remember that all of the extensive technological innovations in market mechanisms during the past thirty years have been initiated by the regional exchanges, the third-market dealers, and the proprietary trading systems (PTSs),[1] with the NYSE matching

1. PTSs include Instinet (continuous and crossing), Posit, and the Arizona Stock Exchange call auction system. Competition to NYSE specialists is also provided by Morgan Stanley's Market Match, Lattice, and Fidelity's Institutional Liquidity Network, all of which match buy and sell

innovations to avoid loss of market share. According to an early study by Garvey, "[t]he initiative of minor exchanges was of no less importance in inducing the Regular Board [NYSE] to modernize its trading technique" (1944, 142). Dominant competitors have little incentive to innovate.

Within the framework of the dominant-firm oligopoly model, Salop and Scheffman show that raising rivals' costs is a strategy used by dominant firms to gain market share: "It may be relatively inexpensive for a dominant firm to raise rivals' costs substantially" (Salop and Scheffman 1983, 267). "Possible cost-raising strategies include . . . lobbying legislatures or regulatory agencies to create regulations that disadvantage rivals." (Salop and Scheffman 1987, 19). We believe that evidence exists (discussed below) that supports the view that the dominant-firm oligopoly model and the strategy of raising rivals' costs accurately characterize the competition for order flow in listed stocks. Thus, Coffee appears to view the NYSE as a benevolent competitor without selfish motives while satellites possess less pure motives; our perspective is that NYSE behavior is better explained by the nonprice predation (i.e., cost predation) literature.

This philosophy leads to several positions that differ from the Mulherin and Coffee views.

Accusing satellite competitors of cream skimming and free riding reflects, in our opinion, a misunderstanding of the role of competition in a dominant-firm environment, which, as noted above, is not primarily focused on price.

As we and others have found, the satellites do contribute meaningfully to price discovery (McInish and Wood [1993a]; Harris, McInish, Shoesmith, and Wood [1995]; Hasbrouck [1993]; Garbade and Silber [1979]), providing price leadership 10–20 percent of the time. Assuming the dominant-firm oligopoly model is the appropriate paradigm to characterize the competition for listed order flow, it is not sensible to expect more of the satellites.

As Demsetz (1982) notes, a fine line exists between property rights and regulatory barriers to entry. Even Coase recognizes the possibility of exchange rules being administered so as to limit competition. Coase (1988, 9) quotes Adam Smith on this point: "To widen the market may frequently be agreeable enough to the interest of the public, but to narrow the competition must always be against it." We are concerned that property-rights arguments may lead to regulatory barriers to competition. To illustrate our concern, the Securities and Exchange Commission (SEC) has limited the trading hours of the Arizona Stock Exchange call auction system (AZX) to thirty minutes before the NYSE open and one hour after the NYSE close. This restriction imposes serious limitations on the use of the AZX: traders must stay late at the office to place

---

orders and print the resulting trades typically through third-market dealers. Additional order flow is matched internally and printed off-board by the large retail brokers such as Merrill Lynch and Shearson. The ability of brokers and large buy-side institutions to profitably cross orders internally is, in our opinion, further evidence of the existence of rents on the NYSE.

orders, indexers may not be able to capture market-on-close prices, and so forth. Many other NYSE and SEC rules and regulations hamper the use of the PTSs. We agree with Oesterle, Winslow, and Anderson (1992) that the NYSE quotes are not more proprietary than those of any other vendor. Can K-Mart prohibit their competitors from using their quoted prices? Since futures markets lead cash markets, does this mean that the NYSE is free riding on the futures markets?[2] We also think that the property rights of investors are being overlooked. Our discussions with institutional buy-side[3] traders reveals dismay that the property-rights argument is being used to limit their use of PTSs.[4] In their estimation, they own the quotes that stem from their limit orders, not the NYSE. Contrary to Mulherin, we submit that buy-side traders are far more qualified to make decisions about where orders should be executed than the boards of directors or executives of public corporations.

Purchase of order flow, instead of being a nefarious scheme to bilk investors, may merely reflect the fact that rents exist (i.e., that spreads are wider than are needed to generate a return required by the riskiness of market making) on the floor of the NYSE. Or it may simply be a way of separating informed from uninformed order flow. Further, these moneys flow into the competitive retail brokerage arena. At this point, we observe discount brokers offering trade executions for no commission. Further, we observe Madoff clones competing for his business.

Having established the differences among our views and those of our reviewers regarding the competition for order flow, we next consider evidence that can help discriminate among these views.

Evidence That Discriminates among the Three Perspectives

In this section, we offer evidence that supports our view that NYSE behavior can be explained with the paradigm of raising rivals' costs. We also offer evidence that discriminates between NYSE behavior that increases the *NYSE volume* at the expense of its competitors, versus behavior that increases the aggre-

2. We thank Robert Neal for this insight.
3. "Buy-side" refers to the money managers—mutual funds, pension funds, and so forth—and individual investors, while "sell-side" refers to the brokerage firms and the market centers. This terminology historically arose because stocks are considered to be sold.
4. The PTSs currently present the most serious threat to the NYSE, since they provide trading features that the more aggressive institutional buy-side traders desire: anonymity, which prevents front-running (they hate their agent's also being their competitor); transparency; the ability to enter and control orders directly without going through an intermediary; lower commissions, since they are not subsidizing immediacy; low trading costs; the ability to see depth for a montage of quotes—four price increments on either side (that is, they see the whole book); the ability to trade electronically; the opportunity to avoid subsidizing the liquidity needs of others; the ability to post quotes in decimals and to be able to gain priority by bettering quotes by 1 cent; and so forth. Liquidity naturally attracts order flow. This fact, combined with the NYSE's anticompetitive rules, provides the NYSE with a decided competitive advantage as the dominant market center. The recent rapid growth in trading on the PTSs that is occurring in the face of the natural NYSE advantage reflects the strong preference aggressive buy-side traders have for the PTSs. At this point, the PTSs threaten the existence of the weaker regional exchanges.

gate order flow from a Coasian perspective, the former behavior being anticompetitive. In addition to the evidence cited below, our views are also based on scores of discussions with investment professionals.

McInish and Wood (1995) show that the NYSE specialists fail to display about one-half of all limit orders that are inside existing quotes for a sample of 118 NYSE-listed stocks, in apparent contravention of SEC regulations. Why would the NYSE specialists engage in such conduct? As noted above, while satellite competitors are unable to beat the dominant firm on price, they must match its price. If the NYSE obfuscates true prices by systematically hiding limit orders, the satellite competitors, according to regional specialists with whom we have discussed this matter, must engage in costly procedures to discover true prices (Harris, McInish, and Wood 1993). Presently, the regionals do so by submitting their own limit and market orders in small quantities to the NYSE, while some third-market dealers engage in the costly practice of temporarily displaying limit orders if the spread is wider than one eighth.[5] To block this practice, the AMEX has submitted a proposed rule to impose restrictions on so-called competing dealers to the SEC, which, if implemented, would place regional specialists' orders at the end of the NYSE/AMEX queues (SEC 1994, III-11). If implemented, this proposal will seriously impact the ability of regional specialists to determine true prices. The SEC's Division of Market Regulation concludes that "the proposal's restrictions are imposed primarily for competitive reasons. Accordingly, the Division recommends that the AMEX amend or withdraw the proposal" (SEC 1994, III-11).

A NYSE rule that is anticompetitive in that it increases NYSE volume at the expense of their competitors is rule 390, which prohibits a broker from executing principal trades or agency trades, if the broker has both sides of the trade, off the exchanges (i.e., off the Intermarket Trading System) (McInish and Wood 1992b).

Rule 500 makes delisting from the NYSE extremely difficult, which, according to the SEC's Market 2000 report, is considered to be an anticompetitive rule by market participants.[6] The SEC's Division of Market Regulation

---

5. Other important aspects of hiding limit orders are that (1) the practice results in the illusion of price improvement, which the NYSE characterizes as market orders crossing within the spread but which in many cases results from executions against hidden limit orders; and (2) it creates a fiduciary responsibility on the part of money managers to execute trades on the NYSE, since illusion of price improvement exists. (We thank Junius Peake for this insight.) If the true spreads were revealed by the NYSE at all times, they would be matched by the satellites. Thus, the illusory price improvement would disappear. The practice of hiding limit orders is an example of the NYSE market power and its willingness to use such power to disadvantage the competition.

6. Rule 500 states, in part: "In the absence of special circumstances, a security considered by the Exchange to be eligible for continued listing will not be removed from the list upon request or application of the issuer, unless the proposed withdrawal from listing is approved by the security holders at a meeting at which a substantial percentage of the outstanding amount of the particular security is represented, without objection to the proposed withdrawal from a substantial number of individual holders." (CCH 1991, 2597) Thus, delisting cannot simply be approved by a company's board of directors, or even by a simple majority of the firms' stockholders.

"cannot identify any justification for the stringent approval requirements [for delisting] built into NYSE Rule 500" (SEC 1994, 31).

The NYSE policy that any new listing is prohibited from trading on regionals or in the third market for the first month does not foster increased aggregate trading volume. Rather, it is anticompetitive.

The NYSE resistance to decimal trading, which Peake (1995) perceives to be the last vestige of fixed commissions, can hardly be construed as a policy that will enhance aggregate volume. The NYSE policy of fixed commission, which ended by SEC fiat in 1975, clearly was not designed to increase order flow.

The Security Investment Automation Corporation (SIAC), which is two-thirds owned by the NYSE, rounds trades and quotes from PTSs to eighths, masking price advantages that might be offered by the PTSs. Thus competition is limited, and NYSE volume is enhanced, while aggregate order flow is not increased.

Response to Coffee and Mulherin Specific Concerns

Mulherin and Coffee note that we find only 0.6 cent difference in spread between the portfolios with the greatest and the least fragmentation, which averages $8.46 per trade, or $1,040 per day per stock. Yet this position ignores what spreads would be if the NYSE had no competitors. McInish and Wood (1992a) show that competition reduces spreads. As Neal (1987) finds for options markets, the mere presence of a competitor will reduce spreads. Our goal is to test the NYSE position that fragmentation harms markets. Our evidence does not support the NYSE position. Further, Branch and Freed state "that competition appears to play a much larger role in restraining NYSE spreads than increased volume might play if trading were more concentrated on the Big Board" (1977, 163).

Mulherin and Coffee point out that we do not address other market-quality issues such as depth and trades between quotes. To investigate this objection, we examine market depth. We find that market depth, as measured by the average bid depth plus ask depth for each quote, is essentially identical across the five portfolios for both the NYSE and for the other market centers. Thus, fragmentation does not alter depth. Given the finding in McInish and Wood (1995, in press) that NYSE specialists hide about half of all limit orders that are inside existing spreads, it may not be possible to measure trades between the quotes in a meaningful way.

Mulherin questions the use of the Herfindahl index as a measure of fragmentation. While other measures might be used, depending on one's conception of fragmentation, the Herfindahl index is widely employed as a measure of concentration (competition or lack thereof) in the industrial organization literature. To address Mulherin's concern, we create an alternate measure of competition motivated by Neal's findings cited above, by calculating the number of competitors for each stock with at least 1 percent of the dollar volume of trading.[7] The research design was replicated for this metric. The mean number of competitors for the five portfolios ranges from 3.1 to 5.2. The correlations of this metric with SPREAD, PREMIUM, and VOLATILITY are -0.94, -0.98, and -0.52, respectively, with corresponding confidence levels of 0.017, 0.004, and 0.38. These results, using the alternate measure of fragmentation, confirm even more strongly that fragmentation does not appear to harm markets.

Mulherin is concerned that the inferences drawn from the sample can be questioned because we use only hi-cap stocks, but, in fact, we have included stocks of all sizes in our sample. In fact, the market value of the smallest of our 980 firms is only $31 million. We exclude only NYSE stocks that do not have a minimal trading level of at least one thousand shares (to avoid thin-trading biases), that trade at less than $5 per share (to avoid aberrant spread behavior), or that do not have both Institute for the Study of Security Markets and Compustat data. Further, Mulherin conjectures that the second tier of firms in our sample "likely have wider spreads and less off-board trading." To test this conjecture, we divided the sample firms into two groups based on size and find that he is correct. The percentage of dollar volume traded on the NYSE for each group is large firms, 87.8 percent; small firms, 85.5 percent. While this difference is statistically significant, it does not seem to be practically significant.

Mulherin expresses concern that a positive correlation between the Herfindahl index and the limit orders and crowd activity may drive our results. Unfortunately, the NYSE does not release data that would permit us to evaluate this conjecture. (We are able to discriminate between block and nonblock trades—replicating our study with the elimination of block trades does not change our findings.) Yet in our opinion Mulherin's view seems unlikely since this would require stocks that have greater floor and limit order activity to also have *proportionally* greater regional trading activity.

Mulherin posits a life-cycle hypothesis wherein the age of the firm is positively correlated with the Herfindahl index and, in turn, with bid-ask spread, so that our research design may have been confounded. Yet this exactly is the kind of confounding that the linear program is designed to protect against. Note that the first and second moments of a number of variables related to the life cycle of firms are held equal in each of the five portfolios. Specifically, these are the dividend payout ratio, market-to-book ratio, asset value, financial leverage, dollar value of trading, and beta. Thus, we feel reasonably confident that the life-cycle concern has been accounted for to the best of our ability.

Coffee expresses concern that some investors are disadvantaged by trades on the satellites and cites a series of papers. In our opinion, he is drawing inferences concerning investor welfare that are not justified by our present knowledge of market microstructure. A great many issues about trading costs

---

7. For a discussion of additional studies that have used number of competitors as a proxy for competition, see McInish and Wood (1993a).

are not yet clearly understood.[8] He further cites evidence comparing Nasdaq quotes with NYSE quotes—our paper did not mention Nasdaq. However, for a perspective of NYSE versus Nasdaq spreads that differs from Coffee's, see McInish and Wood (1993b).

Mulherin also argues "that the selection of trading location is endogenously chosen in the market." This disregards the impact of anticompetitive NYSE rules such as rule 500 and rule 390.

Coffee points out that Porter and Thatcher (1992) find that increased competition from regional exchanges narrowed NYSE spreads for stocks with relatively low initial spreads, but increased spreads for stock with relatively high initial spreads. Coffee concludes from this finding that "increased volume on the regional exchange seemed to produce market fragmentation, not tighter spreads." We believe that the wider spreads in the face of increased regional competition are more likely to reflect an increased incidence of hiding limit orders as a competitive response by NYSE specialists.

Coffee argues that in the presence of asymmetric information the NYSE specialist must widen the spread even further if the probability of being picked off by an informed trader (in the midsize range especially) rises because uninformed order flow has been attracted by rebates offered by satellite competitors. But, if Coffee is otherwise correct, his thinking fails to incorporate (1) the fact that this process is, like all market phenomena, self-limiting and (2) the implication of the NYSE being the dominant competitor. To clarify, fragmentation, interacting with the asymmetric information to raise that component of the spread, drives both informed and uninformed order flow to the satellites. So it is not as though fragmentation has caused these higher spreads associated with the movement of order flow to the satellites; fragmentation is also the result of the dominant-firm price leader having the market power to raise spreads to cover the cost of being picked off. The satellites certainly do not have this option.[9]

To summarize, we continue to affirm that the data do not support the NYSE contention that fragmentation harms investors. We are sympathetic with the world Mulherin champions, where nothing stands in the way of the invisible hand's allocation of order flow among competitors. But our view that the dominant-firm oligopoly model is the appropriate paradigm to characterize the competition for listed order flow, combined with our pragmatic assessment of

8. For example, we are aware of two studies conducted by buy-side firms that extensively examine trading performance on the NYSE, regional exchanges, and Nasdaq, finding essentially no difference in execution costs. These studies have the advantage of knowing the characteristics of each order—data not yet made available to academics by the NYSE. Further insights are provided by Angel (1994) and Chan and Lakonishok (1991). Additional concerns are that trading-cost studies have not been extended to the PTSs and that they do not include all trading costs. For example, commission costs on the PTSs can be as low as 1–2 cents a share compared to 5–6 cents a share on the NYSE. Further, front-running costs, which may be largely avoided on the PTSs, are not yet measured.

9. We have benefited from discussions with Frederick Harris on this topic.

what can realistically be accomplished in the present regulatory environment, causes us to be less sanguine about moving from the present state of competition to our ideal trading world following the Mulherin path. It is not our goal, as Mulherin suggests, that the SEC extend its regulatory reach. We are encouraged that the Market 2000 report does not move in that direction. In our opinion, if the PTSs were able to compete without any regulatory obstacles, the costs of trading services presently being paid by the institutional buy-side to the sell-side would be reduced by 50–75 percent.

References

Angel, J. 1994. Who receives price improvement? Working paper, Georgetown University, Washington, DC.

Branch, Ben, and Walter Freed. 1977. Bid-ask spreads on the AMEX and the Big Board. *Journal of Finance* 32:159–63.

Chan, Louis K. C., and Josef Lakonishok. 1991. Institutional trades and intra-day stock price behavior. Working paper, University of Illinois, Champaign.

Coase, R. H. 1988. The firm, the market, and the law. Chicago: University of Chicago Press.

Commerce Clearing House (CCH). 1991. New York Stock Exchange, Inc.: Constitution and rules. Chicago: Commerce Clearing House.

Demsetz, Harold. 1982. Barriers to entry. *American Economic Review* 72:47–57.

Garbade, K., and W. Silber. 1979. Dominant and satellite markets: A study of dually traded securities. *Review of Economics and Statistics* 61:455–60.

Garvey, George. 1944. Rivals and interlopers in the history of the New York security market. *Journal of Political Economy* 52:128–43.

Harris, Frederick D., Thomas H. McInish, Gary L. Shoesmith, and Robert A. Wood. 1995. Cointegration, error correction and price discovery on informationally linked security markets. *Journal of Financial and Quantitative Analysis,* Spring.

Harris, Frederick D., Thomas H. McInish, and Robert A. Wood. 1993. Raising rivals' costs. Working paper, University of Memphis.

Hasbrouck, Joel. 1993. One security, many markets: Determining the contributions to price discovery. Working paper, New York University.

McInish, Thomas H., and Robert A. Wood. 1992a. An analysis of intraday patterns in bid-ask spreads for NYSE stocks. *Journal of Finance* 47: 753–64.

———. 1992b. The effect of NYSE rule 390 on spreads, premiums, and volatility. Working paper, University of Memphis.

———. 1993a, Price discovery, volume, and regional/third-market trading. Working paper, University of Memphis.

———. 1993b. Volatility of Nasdaq/NMS and listed stocks. Working paper, University of Memphis.

———. 1995. Hidden limit orders on the NYSE. *Journal of Portfolio Management.*

Neal, Robert. 1987. Potential competition and actual competition in equity options. *Journal of Finance* 42:511–31.

Oesterle, Dale Arthur, Donald Arthur Winslow, and Seth C. Anderson. 1992. The New York Stock Exchange and its outmoded specialist system: Can the exchange innovate to survive? *Journal of Corporation Law* 17:223–310.

Peake, Junius. 1995. Brother can you spare a dime? In Robert A. Schwartz, ed., *Global Equity Markets: Technological, Competitive, and Regulatory Challenges.* Burr Ridge, IL: Business One Irwin.

Porter, David, and John Thatcher. 1992. Fragmentation, competition, and limit orders: New evidence from interday spreads. Working paper, Marquette University, Milwaukee.

Salop, Steven C., and David T. Scheffman. 1983. Raising rivals' costs. *American Economic Review*, papers and proceedings issue, sect. "Recent Advances in the Theory of Industrial Structure," 73:267–71.

———. 1987. Cost-raising strategies. *Journal of Industrial Economics* 36:19–34.

Securities and Exchange Commission. Division of Market Regulation. 1994. Market 2000: An examination of current equity market developments. Washington, DC: Government Printing Office.

Stigler, George. 1940. Notes on the theory of duopoly. *Journal of Political Economy* 48:521–41.

———. 1964. A theory of oligopoly. *Journal of Political Economy* 72:44–61.

4 An Exchange Is a Many-Splendored Thing: The Classification and Regulation of Automated Trading Systems

Ian Domowitz

4.1 Introduction

In 1969, a company called Instinet established a computer-based trading facility as an alternative to the exchange markets. The Securities and Exchange Commission (SEC) responded by proposing rule 15c2-10, a filing requirement for automated trading and information systems.[1] The proposed rule was the first direct regulatory action aimed specifically at automated trading markets.

Since then, the growth in automated trade execution systems on a worldwide basis has been explosive. In the United States alone, there are roughly twenty such mechanisms, including completely automated exchanges, exchange facilities with automated trade execution components, and proprietary systems not currently regulated as exchanges.[2]

Growth in regulatory initiatives and analysis with respect to this new form of financial market structure quickly followed. These efforts can be classified in four general ways. There are the obvious hardware and software concerns that are generic in the oversight of any computerized system. Advances in this area include the Automation Review Policy put forward by the SEC.[3] Perhaps less obvious are the oversight issues posed by the nature of the computerized algorithms themselves, which govern the trade-matching mechanism and con-

Ian Domowitz is professor of economics at Northwestern University and a research associate of the Center for Urban Affairs and Policy Research.

Financial support from the Center for Urban Affairs and Policy Research, Northwestern University, is gratefully acknowledged. The author thanks Michael Simon of Milbank, Tweed, Hadley & McCloy for helpful comments with respect to some legal technicalities, without implicating him in any remaining errors in citation or interpretation.

1. See Securities Exchange Act Release no. 8661 (August 4, 1969), 34 *Federal Register* 12952.

2. See Domowitz (1993c) for a listing and classification of automated trading markets.

3. See Securities Exchange Act Releases no. 27445 (November 24, 1989), 54 *Federal Register* 48703, and no. 29185 (May 15, 1991), 56 *Federal Register* 22490, with respect to SEC policies. General Accounting Office (1989) contains some additional concerns.

tribute to the pricing and trade allocation properties of the price discovery process.[4] Computerized markets also lend themselves to cross-border trading, raising problems of jurisdiction and standardization.[5] Finally, there is the question of how to classify and regulate automated systems as a trading market. This includes such diverse issues as conformity with existing law, participant protection, and competition, among others.

The market regulation problem is the focus of this paper. The microcosm for the discussion is the issue of SEC regulation of proprietary automated trading systems. The primary emphasis is on the appropriate definition of an exchange for the purpose of regulation and whether the exchange/nonexchange distinction remains a viable regulatory construct.

Some history may help to motivate these issues. Rule 15c2-10 for the regulation of propriety systems was not adopted after its introduction in 1969. It was determined that Instinet did not share certain characteristics of a registered exchange, although it performed the function of an exchange with respect to trading activity. In particular, it was decided that Instinet did not fit into the statutory scheme contemplated for exchanges and, therefore, for exchange regulation.[6] This exhibited a decidedly institutional approach to trading market regulation on the part of the SEC. In fact, rule 15c2-10 was withdrawn in 1975, following the 1975 amendments to the Securities Exchange Act, on the basis of institutional considerations.[7] In response to increasing numbers of automated systems, the SEC adopted a policy of granting "no-action" positions with regard to the Securities Exchange Act's definition of the term "exchange" in 1984.

After some experience in overseeing proprietary trading systems and objections to the no-action approach from various exchanges, the SEC reintroduced rule 15c2-10 in 1989.[8] Some of this experience involved decisions with respect to the definition of an exchange, and how this definition should be applied to proprietary automated systems for purposes of regulation.[9] The rule is still pending approval, and its disposition, including possible amendments or even withdrawal, awaits the analysis to be put forth in the Market 2000 report on U.S. equity markets. If adopted, the new rule would provide regulatory requirements for such systems, which currently are subject to broker-dealer regulation

4. See, for example, Sundel and Blake (1991); Corcoran and Lawton (1993); Domowitz (1993a); and 55 *Federal Register* 17932 (April 30, 1990).
5. See, for example, International Organization of Securities Commissions (1991).
6. Securities Exchange Act Release no. 26708 (April 18, 1989), 54 *Federal Register* 15429.
7. See Securities Exchange Act Release no. 11673 (September 23, 1975), 40 *Federal Register* 4522. Automated trading systems were to be regulated as facilities of an exchange or "association," if the self-regulatory organization operated the system. Proprietary systems were to be regulated as broker-dealers or as securities information processors.
8. See Securities Exchange Act Release no. 26708 (April 18, 1989), 54 *Federal Register* 15429.
9. See, for example, Securities Exchange Act Releases no. 27611 (January 19, 1990), 55 *Federal Register* 1890, and no. 28899 (February 28, 1991), 56 *Federal Register* 8377.

and provisions set forth in individual no-action positions provided to system operators.

This paper is motivated by the following questions posed by the SEC for comment in the concept release of the U.S. Equity Market Structure Study and in the publication of the proposed rule 15c2-10. Might the SEC usefully revisit how it defines an exchange, and is the exchange/nonexchange distinction still viable for determining the regulatory treatment for a market system? Proposed amendments are sought as to how Congress might redefine an exchange in light of advances in automation. The SEC also is interested in whether the choice of designating a system as exchange or nonexchange is too limiting, in general. In fact, the SEC itself asks whether the classification could instead be based on functional attributes of a trading market, proprietary or otherwise. This leads naturally to the appropriateness of adopting a standards approach to the regulation of automated systems.[10]

Given the nature of these questions, this paper is in the spirit of the work in Domowitz (1990, 1993b) on the laws and regulatory definitions germane to the approval of automated trading systems in U.S. futures markets. The language of the law, precedents set in place by the regulatory authorities, and the nature of automated trade execution mechanisms are set out and compared. It will be argued that a functional approach to the regulation of trading markets is more appropriate in the face of automation, the case resting in part on the SEC's rulings. This conclusion is consistent with the analysis of Merton (1992) of financial products and intermediation and Lee (1992) on regulatory anomalies.

A brief discussion of trading systems appears in section 4.2. Regulatory background with respect to the institutional players, characteristics, and proce-dures relevant to the questions considered here is presented in section 4.3. Section 4.4 contains an analysis of the definition of an exchange, as distilled from legislative history and legal precedent. This definition currently is at the core of SEC regulatory policies with respect to trading systems. Examination of the issues that arise in maintaining this definition as a basis for trading sys-tem classification is contained in section 4.5. The emphasis is on exchange membership, liquidity requirements, and competition. The questions of re-definition and a functional approach to system classification occupy section 4.6. A classification scheme consistent with the idea of functional regulation is suggested, and its implications for current trading systems and registered exchanges are explored.

4.2 Automated Trading Systems

A trading system is defined by the SEC to be "any system providing for the dissemination outside the sponsor and its affiliates of indications of interest,

---

10. See Securities Exchange Act Release no. 26708 (April 18, 1989), 54 *Federal Register* 15429.

quotations, or orders to purchase or sell securities, and providing procedures for executing or settling transactions in such securities."[11]

An automated trading system typically includes computerization of order routing, information dissemination, and trade execution. The order-routing system brings buyers and sellers together so that they can trade. Computerized systems allow the transmission of real-time market information to a much larger group of potential participants than was previously possible. Automated trade execution systems are basically mathematical algorithms that enable trade matching without the person-to-person contact afforded by traditional trading floors or telephone networks. With one exception, discussion of regulation of trading systems has been focused on systems with some form of automated execution.[12]

An automated trade execution system can comprise the entirety of an exchange's trading operations, such as National Securities Trading System (NSTS) of the Cincinnati Stock Exchange or the single-price auction Arizona Stock Exchange. A system may simply be another facility of an exchange, operating in tandem with a traditional trading floor or telephone network, or after regular exchange hours. Examples include Retail Automated Execution System (RAES) of the Chicago Board Options Exchange, Scorex of the Pacific Stock Exchange, and the after-hours crossing networks of the New York Stock Exchange (NYSE). Finally, an automated market may be set up as a proprietary trading system, a for-profit entity, of which Instinet and Posit are examples.[13]

Automated trading markets have a varied microstructure. The following general divisions will be sufficient for the discussion of market definitions in sections 4.4 and 4.5.

4.2.1 Trading Systems with Passive Pricing

Automated trade matching can be based on time and order-type priorities, with the transaction price taken from a floor or telephone market. The trading system has no independent price discovery mechanism. The price may vary through the trading session, if the automated system operates at the same time as the floor/telephone market, or may be fixed at a closing price, say, for an after-hours trading session. Such systems are designed for the trading of individual issues (equities or options) or baskets of stocks.

---

11. This definition appears in the text of the proposed rule 15c2-10. The rule itself does not apply to facilities of a registered exchange, to systems in which all transactions are internally matched by a broker or dealer, or to "brokers' broker" trading systems. The rule does apply to clearing and settlement facilities, but the discussion in this paper is limited to trading systems with an execution component.

12. The exception is Delta Government Options, which is a trading system for options on federal government securities, comprising a broker, a clearing agency, and a bank. It is basically a blind brokerage system and does not involve computer-generated executions.

13. See Domowitz (1993c) for a listing of automated markets and their classification into various categories of operation.

It is possible to automate some form of price improvement on these systems. Generally speaking, the computer assesses market conditions and prices the trade accordingly for execution, possibly at a price better than the best quote available at the time of order entry. All such rules depend explicitly on pricing and sales in another market such as the NYSE, however. For this reason, systems with automated price improvement must still be considered passive pricing mechanisms.

4.2.2   Limit Order Book Systems in Automated Continuous Markets

In automated continuous markets, bids and offers are submitted continuously over time. Depending on the design of the system, transactions occur in one or both of two ways. First, transactions occur when the orders cross, that is, when the price of the best bid is equal to or greater than the best offer. Market orders are allowed on some systems, resulting in an immediate cross if a counterparty is available in the system. Second, a trader may participate in a trade advertised by an existing quotation on the electronic limit order book by touching a button.

There are many variations on this theme, but all such markets have a price discovery component. That is, price is determined endogenously within the system, based on order flow and the precise rules governing trade priority and execution. Some such systems have explicit provision for market-making operations in the form of a two-sided quotation facility.

4.2.3   Automated Periodic Single-Price Auction

In automated single-price auction systems, bids and offers are submitted over some period of time, and all trades are executed together at one price at a single point of time. The transaction price typically is calculated by maximizing the total volume traded over possible transaction prices, given the bids and offers resting in the system. Bids and offers eligible for a match at the system-calculated price are processed into trades, subject to a set of priority rules.

Once again, there are variations in this system structure, often depending on order types and order information display. Regardless, such systems are price discovery mechanisms, producing equilibrium prices at fixed points in time from order flow into the system. There typically is no provision for two-sided quotations. The only feature sometimes present that is in the spirit of market making is an order type designed to help equate supply and demand in the case of an order imbalance.

4.3   Some Regulatory Background

In the current regulatory environment, automated trading systems can fall within any of several statutory classifications. Three of these categories are relevant for the issues addressed here, namely broker-dealers, registered exchanges or facilities thereof, and exempt exchanges.[14]

Generally speaking, brokers make securities transactions for the accounts of their customers, while dealers transact for their own accounts in the process of handling customer orders.[15] They must register with the SEC and become a member of the self-regulatory organization (SRO), that is, with a registered exchange or securities association. Although they must comply with a variety of legal restrictions, their regulatory burden is light compared with registered exchanges, whether or not they operate a trading system. A trading system operating as a broker-dealer does not have the statutory burden of responsibility for real-time market surveillance, for example. Such trading systems may have no obligation to comply with the SEC's Automation Review Policy.[16] The broker-dealer regulatory framework does not apply to system access criteria, terms of trade execution, or the handling of quotations.[17]

The definition of an exchange is far from precise, and is the subject of section 4.4. For the moment, it suffices to think of an exchange in simple terms as a marketplace for securities transactions. Exchanges must register under section 6 of the Securities Exchange Act. Registration brings with it a host of regulatory requirements, duties, and responsibilities.[18] Copies of all rule changes must be filed for public comment and regulatory approval, for example, including development plans for automated systems. Automated systems operated by an exchange must comply with the principles of the Automation Review Policy and are subject to strict surveillance and reporting

14. A system may also be classified as a securities association, but such an association (e.g., the National Association of Securities Dealers [NASD]) is subject to very similar requirements as registered exchanges; see section 15A(b)(1)–(8) of the Securities Exchange Act. Other categories include clearing agency, transfer agent, and securities information processor. The first is not relevant, given the emphasis on the process of trading rather than on the clearing of transactions. The second involves issuance and registration of securities. The NASD has suggested that a trading system be categorized as a securities information processor. Registration as such is not required unless the trading system is first classified as an exchange or securities information processor that acts on an exclusive basis on behalf of a self-regulatory organization. See sections 3(a)(22)(B) and 11A(b)(1) of the Securities Exchange Act.

15. The law defines a broker to be "any person engaged in the business of effecting transactions in securities for the account of others, but does not include a bank." A dealer is "any person engaged in the business of buying and selling securities for his own account, through a broker or otherwise, but does not include a bank, or any person insofar as he buys or sells securities for his own account, either individually or in some fiduciary capacity, but not as a part of a regular business." See sections 3(a)(4) and 3(a)(5) of the Securities Exchange Act.

16. See Securities Exchange Act Releases no. 27445 (November 24, 1989), 54 *Federal Register* 48703, and no. 29185 (May 15, 1991), 56 *Federal Register* 22490. A system operating under a no-action letter may, however, be required to comply with the review policies. Some broker-dealer systems are not subject to this constraint, however.

17. See Domowitz (1993a) for discussion of the oversight problems involved in these areas for automated trading systems.

18. See, for example, Becker, Adkins, Fuller, and Angstadt (1991) and the discussion in Securities Exchange Act Release no. 28899 (February 28, 1991), 56 *Federal Register* 8377.

requirements. An exchange is not allowed to seek exemption from any regulatory burden on behalf of its automated trading system.[19]

An exchange may seek an exemption from registration, however, under section 5 of the Securities Exchange Act. Thus, an automated trading system can be classified as an exchange and can ask for exemption from the regulatory requirements associated with registration. The scope for this action is quite narrow, however. Exemptions are granted based on a "limited volume" provision; that is, in the case of a "limited volume" of transactions, it may not be considered practical or necessary in the public interest to regulate the exchange or system as an SRO. The statute provides no firm standard as to what level of volume would justify a continuing exemption. The guideline recently used is the volume of the smallest of the fully regulated national exchanges.[20]

The decision that proprietary trading systems did not fit into the statutory classification of an exchange led to the regulation of proprietary systems as broker-dealers, with any additional stipulations contained in no-action letters.[21] These conditions generally include the provision of quarterly operational data, notice of any material change to the system, and individually tailored requirements that the SEC sees fit to impose. There is no public notice and comment period in the no-action process, unlike the approval process for trading systems operated as facilities of existing exchanges.

The conditions imposed in the no-action approach imply only sporadic reporting of trading, product, and system innovations. Proprietary systems began to grow in volume terms and in the number and types of securities to be traded. System innovation increased as technology improved, and systems became more complex. Faced with these developments, some experience in monitoring, and complaints with respect to unfair competition under the no-action approach, the SEC reconsidered the problem.

The result is the reintroduction of rule 15c2-10 for the regulation of trading systems, over and above the statutory requirements for broker-dealers. The proposed rule contains a variety of requirements, but it is effectively a vehicle to create a statutory classification (i.e., a market participant) somewhere between a broker-dealer and an exchange. In the proposed rule, the SEC reemphasizes

19. This follows from the classification of an automated trading system associated with an exchange as a "facility" of the exchange; see section 3(a)(2) of the Securities Exchange Act. The statute further does not allow exchanges to be exempt from parts of the act; it is an all-or-nothing provision. In contrast, section 17(b)(1) provides such exemptive authority regarding the registration of clearing agencies.

20. The SEC exempted seven exchanges from 1935 to 1936 on the basis of low volume. The only other such action in history is the exemption of the Arizona Stock Exchange, an automated trading system, in 1991; see Securities Exchange Act Release no. 28899 (February 28, 1991), 56 *Federal Register* 8377. The volume standard used was that of the Cincinnati Stock Exchange, which averaged 717 trades per day with daily share volume of 1,238,241 in 1990.

21. A no-action letter states that the SEC staff agrees not to recommend enforcement action to the SEC with respect to the nonregistration of the trading system as an exchange. The letters are not subject to judicial review; that is, they are not "orders" of the SEC.

its position that proprietary trading systems do not fit into the statutory classification of an exchange. The commission further believes that subjecting trading systems to exchange registration would deter innovation in trading system structure.[22]

Renewed concern with the issue of the allocation of regulatory costs between exchanges and competing systems, even under a scheme of "heightened broker-dealer regulation," has surfaced, however (see SEC 1991). This has led to reconsideration of the definition of an exchange and the viability of maintaining the exchange/nonexchange distinction.

4.4   The "Generally Understood" Meaning of Exchange

The Securities Exchange Act defines an exchange to be "any organization, association, or group of persons, whether incorporated or unincorporated, which constitutes, maintains, or provides a market place or facilities for bringing together purchasers and sellers of securities or for otherwise performing with respect to securities the functions commonly performed by a stock exchange *as that term is generally understood,* and includes the market place and the market facilities maintained by such exchange" (section 3[a][1], emphasis added). The legislative history of the Securities Exchange Act gives the SEC considerable leeway in interpreting what trading systems should be classified as exchanges.[23] Even very recent decisions have deferred to SEC interpretations of what the phrase "generally understood" is supposed to mean, and invite reinterpretation of the phrase over time.[24]

There is concern that an overexpansive interpretation would make certain types of operations "exchanges" automatically, so it is important to clarify the obvious exceptions. The definition specifically does not apply to broker-dealers operating systems that limit use to their own retail customers. Such systems are considered to be simple automation of the internal trade execution functions traditionally managed by a broker-dealer. The definition also does not apply to certain systems operated by brokers' brokers for nonequity, generally government or municipal, securities. Such a system permits dealers to advertise their trading interests anonymously and provides a means of executing transactions based on those indications of interest. This type of system is excluded from the discussion by existing law. The apparent reason for this exclu-

---

22. Such language in the proposed rule was considerably reinforced in later decisions, in which membership requirements were cited as a large barrier to entry, and the "straitjacket" of exchange regulation with respect to evolving systems is mentioned.

23. This dates back to 1934. Congress decreed that stock exchanges could not be regulated under a rigid statutory definition. See "Stock Exchange Practices," 73d Congress, 2d session, 1934, Senate Report 792, 5.

24. See, for example, *Board of Trade of the City of Chicago v. Securities and Exchange Commission,* no. 90-1246 (7th Circuit, February 4, 1991). The court noted specifically that the wording was not "crystal clear," and affirmed the SEC's interpretation at the time.

sion is the classification of a brokers' broker as performing "traditional" broker-dealer functions.[25]

Given these exceptions, it is possible to clarify the issues surrounding what is "generally understood" to be an exchange. These issues can be aggregated into the categories of pricing, trading conventions, access, and liquidity. The discussion is limited to the general definition of an exchange, whether it be required to register or it obtains exemption from registration.[26]

4.4.1   Price Discovery and Information in the Definition of an Exchange

A system that does not provide trade execution facilities cannot be considered an exchange. Procedures for executing transactions include any rules, guidelines, or facilities for order entry and execution. Automated execution facilities qualify under this definition. Execution facilities, automated or otherwise, even combined with price information dissemination, are not sufficient to qualify a trading system as an exchange, given congressional and SEC rulings.[27]

Execution of trades does not imply price discovery, as illustrated in section 4.2. Price discovery is held to be an essential element of an exchange. Lack of price discovery is a major factor in the SEC's decision to consider proprietary systems as fundamentally different from exchanges.[28] The Instinet system engaged in price discovery at the time of this ruling, however, and is not classified as an exchange. On the other hand, the SEC determined that the Wunsch Auction System should be defined as an exchange, in part because its automated procedures set an equilibrium price for securities.[29] Thus, proprietary systems engaged in passive pricing cannot be considered exchanges, but price discovery, even combined with price information dissemination, is not sufficient to qualify.

Price information dissemination is, however, a component of the exchange definition. The requirement does not include a transparency restriction, that is,

---

25. When Congress enacted the Government Securities Act, it added the definitions of government securities broker and dealer to the Securities Exchange Act. Congress did not feel the need to create a category of "government securities exchange," given the fact that, traditionally, blind brokers in nongovernment securities had been regarded as broker-dealers. See 55 *Federal Register* 1899 (January 19, 1990).

26. Typically, a determination first is made as to whether or not a system is an exchange. Once the determination is made, a system that is classified as an exchange may then seek exemption status. See, for example, Securities Exchange Act Release no. 28899 (February 28, 1991), 56 *Federal Register* 8377, particularly footnote 36.

27. See 93d Congress, 2d session, 1974, Senate Report 865, 4–7, in which Congress recommended that "communications and execution" systems such as Instinet should be registered as securities information processors, rather than as exchanges. The SEC finally chose to regulate Instinet as a broker-dealer under a no-action provision; see Richard G. Ketchum to Daniel T. Brooks, Cadwalader, Wickersham and Taft, August 8, 1986, SEC files.

28. See Securities Exchange Act Release no. 26708 (April 18, 1989), 54 *Federal Register* 15429.

29. See Securities Exchange Act Release no. 28899 (February 28, 1991), 56 *Federal Register* 8377.

a statement as to the degree to which prices and volumes are made publicly available on a real-time basis. It does mandate that the exchange's design makes buy and sell quotations available on a regular or continuous basis. In fact, the SEC has gone so far as to use the publication of two-sided (simultaneous buy and sell) quotations as part of its exchange definition.[30]

4.4.2   Trading Rules and Conventions in the Definition of an Exchange

The legislative history surrounding trading systems clearly shows that having an arbitrary set of rules and conventions that centralize trading does not qualify a system as an exchange. The SEC requires that the system have either a formal market-maker structure or a consolidated limit order book, or be a single-price auction to be considered an exchange.

An automated system clearly can fulfill any or all of these requirements. In practice, automated markets that have been classified as exchanges embody both a market-maker system and a limit order book or employ a periodic auction for trade execution and pricing.[31] If the system lacks market makers, there are apparent restrictions on the operation of the limit order facility. Limit order protection for customer orders is expected. This is a trivial detail for automated continuous auctions, for example, which usually embody such protection as part of their design. The SEC has also objected to a limited duration for orders resting on the book in a system. Removal of unfilled orders at the end of a day is considered to be at odds with expected exchange operations.[32]

Although the courts have occasionally ruled otherwise,[33] the SEC has decided that lack of a traditional trading floor does not eliminate the classification of a system as an exchange. This is evident simply from the existence of the Cincinnati Stock Exchange and the Arizona Stock Exchange. The requirement is centralization of trading for the purpose of trade execution. The means can range from the traditional trading floor to a computer system allowing access across geographical boundaries.

Negotiation facilities also are not required for classification as an exchange. Once again, although the courts have found that an exchange is in part defined as a place to negotiate transactions, the SEC has decided otherwise.[34] This is

---

30. See Securities Exchange Act Release no. 27611 (January 19, 1990), 55 *Federal Register* 1890.

31. The Cincinnati Stock Exchange essentially operates as a consolidated limit order book, but "designated dealers" are assigned to each security. These dealers commit to an obligation to fill agency orders of limited size under certain conditions. The Arizona Stock Exchange is a single-price automated auction.

32. See Securities Exchange Act Release no. 27611 (January 19, 1990), 55 *Federal Register* 1890.

33. In *Board of Trade of the City of Chicago v. Securities and Exchange Commission,* the court held up the lack of a trading floor as a way in which a trading system did not fulfill the functions commonly expected of an exchange.

34. See *LTV v. UMIC Government Securities, Inc.,* 523 *Federal Supplement* 819 (1981), where the court stated that an exchange was a place or means through which persons meet to negotiate securities transactions.

also evident from the existence of automated systems classified as exchanges, which do not have negotiation capabilities.

4.4.3   Access and the Definition of an Exchange

Traditionally, an exchange is composed of members, who have a proprietary interest in the exchange. In fact, the Securities Exchange Act mandates that a registered (nonexempt) exchange provide for fair representation of its members under section 6(b)(3).

The term "member" is defined in some detail under section 3(a)(3)B. Generally speaking, a member is a registered broker-dealer or any person associated with a broker-dealer under section 6(c)(1). Institutions that must comply with the rules of an exchange are also included in the definition of member for the purpose of regulation under the act.

A member need not have a proprietary interest in the exchange under the law. Thus, an individual or institution participating in a trading system owned by others could still be considered a member if the system were classified as an exchange.

More important, the act does not specifically prohibit an exchange from giving direct trading access to individuals who are not broker-dealers.[35] Most automated trading systems permit access to individuals or institutions that are not registered as broker-dealers. This does not mean that they could not be considered exchanges, registered or exempt.

4.4.4   Liquidity and the Definition of an Exchange

Liquidity is a difficult concept, and many definitions have been proposed. The discussion here is limited specifically to the way the SEC defines liquidity in the context of the "generally understood" terminology defining an exchange.

It may help first to clarify what is not liquidity in the classification of a system as an exchange. Liquidity is not immediacy, in the usual sense of being able to transact quickly and in a continuous fashion. Liquidity also is not based on volume considerations.[36]

The SEC holds that having two-sided quotations on a "regular or continuous basis" is a guiding principle for liquidity, and has judged a system to be illiquid on the basis of a low percentage of two-sided quotes, relative to overall buy and sell quotations.[37] In this context, the SEC has virtually identified liquidity

35. Compare section 6(b)(8) with section 6(f). See also section 6(o)(1) regarding denial of membership.

36. Both of these conclusions are based on the SEC's recent decisions regarding the Wunsch Auction System, now known as the Arizona Stock Exchange. The commission determined that the system is indeed an exchange, based in part on its belief that the market fosters liquidity, but the auction mechanism is periodic, not continuous. Liquidity is not immediacy. Once the commission reached this conclusion, it then granted a low-volume exemption from registration. Liquidity for the purpose of exchange definition is therefore not based on volume. See Securities Exchange Act Release no. 28899 (February 28, 1991), 56 *Federal Register* 8377.

37. See Securities Exchange Act Releases no. 26708 (April 18, 1989), 54 *Federal Register* 15429, and no. 27611 (January 19, 1990), 55 *Federal Register* 1890, with respect to liquidity and a low percentage of two-sided quotations.

with the specialist/market-maker/dealer function, by stating that liquidity by the definition above is provided only through a formal market-making mechanism.[38] This would make a formal market-making mechanism part of the definition of an exchange, in contradiction to commission statements that the market-making function could, at least in principle, be replaced by a consolidated limit order book.

The commission has relaxed the provision of requiring two-sided quotes in the definition of liquidity provision in at least one case. The SEC still requires the entry of buy and sell quotations on a regular basis such that purchasers and sellers have a reasonable expectation that they can "regularly" execute their orders at those quotes. The same standard is applied to "elements" of a trading system, most notably the mechanism for setting transaction prices. The trading system itself must be designed to create liquidity in the sense that buyers and sellers have a reasonable expectation that they can regularly execute orders.[39]

For a trading system to be classified as an exchange, it must make an attempt to assure liquidity provision by these definitions. In the case of an automated system, this means that the design of the system itself must be expected to create a liquid market through its rules and trading procedures. The key word here is "expected." In particular, only the likelihood that the trading mechanism would create liquidity by the commission's definitions is required for a trading system to be classified as an exchange.[40]

4.4.5   What Is an Exchange?

It is now possible to define what is "generally understood," at least by the SEC, to be an exchange. To be classified as an exchange, a trading system must

provide trade execution facilities;

provide price information in the form of buy and sell quotations on a regular or continuous basis;

engage in price discovery through its trading procedures, rules, or mechanism;

have either a formal market-maker structure or a consolidated limit order book, or be a single-price auction;

centralize trading for the purpose of trade execution;

have members; and

---

38. See, for example, Securities Exchange Act Release no. 27611 (January 19, 1990), 55 *Federal Register* 1890. Even the discussion of an automated exchange in that reference emphasizes liquidity provision through the market-making function.

39. See ibid., on the first point, and Securities Exchange Act Release no. 28899 (February 28, 1991), 56 *Federal Register* 8377, with respect to trading mechanisms.

40. See, for example, Securities Exchange Act Release no. 27611 (January 19, 1990), 55 *Federal Register* 1890, particularly footnote 100, but this idea also appears elsewhere.

exhibit the likelihood, through system rules and/or design, of creating liquidity in the sense that there be entry of buy and sell quotations on a regular basis, such that both buyers and sellers have a reasonable expectation that they can regularly execute their orders at those quotes.

This definition, distilled from legislative, legal, and commission decisions, remains flexible with respect to regulatory action. A trading system cannot avoid classification as an exchange simply by omitting "particular characteristics" of exchange markets (as generally understood).[41] A trading system that appears likely to result in a regular centralized securities market, in the commission's opinion, would be classified as an exchange.

4.5   The Exchange/Nonexchange Distinction

The SEC has requested comments as to whether the exchange/nonexchange distinction is still viable, given the introduction of automated trading systems. The purpose of this section is to examine some of the issues that arise by maintaining the existing definition as a basis for regulatory action.

4.5.1   Members versus Participants

Direct access to the trading facilities provided by an exchange has traditionally been limited to members, who are registered as, or associated with, broker-dealers and have a proprietary interest in the exchange. The technology behind automated systems eliminates the need for a physical presence, and rules limiting access to a narrow class of traders typically are lessened in proprietary trading systems.[42] In particular, institutional traders may deal directly with each other, without the need for the financial intermediation provided by broker-dealers.

It was argued in section 4.4 that members need not have a proprietary interest in the system, and that direct access to a system classified as an exchange can be allowed to participants who are not broker-dealers. These points were based on a rather literal interpretation of the law and on a single precedent, the classification of the Wunsch Auction System as an exchange.

Both points are more easily challenged than upheld by the SEC in maintaining the exchange/nonexchange distinction. Institutions are members only for the enforcement of certain narrow provisions of the Securities Exchange Act, for example. There is the question of whether interpreting section 6(f)(1) as allowing institutional participation is consistent with the intent of Congress as expressed in section 3(a)(3)A of the act with respect to limitations on exchange membership. It might also be argued that the Wunsch system is a spe-

---

41. Examples given in ibid. include omission of affirmative market-making obligations or a limit order book.
42. Complete elimination is impossible, of course, for a variety of reasons. A participant must, at the minimum, demonstrate the financial means to settle transactions.

cial case, given the periodic nature of the price discovery process, and that continuous trading systems require membership in order to be classified as an exchange. Finally, the SEC has noted that the legal question of whether the act prohibits an exchange from granting direct trading access to participants who are not broker-dealers has not been settled (see SEC 1991).

There are competitive questions that would arise from this prohibition, and from a strictly traditional definition of membership. Exchanges would be legally limited with respect to access, while proprietary trading systems would not. Trading systems without members would further not be subject to the potential barrier to entry of the act's provision regarding fair representation of members, should they otherwise be forced to register as an exchange. Exchange classification and possible registration are avoided simply by a lack of membership, which has nothing at all to do with the actual function of trading market operations.

Maintenance of the membership requirement in the definition of an exchange may further serve to create a two-tier market, splitting institutional order flow from retail customer order flow.[43] It is not clear that such an outcome is desirable.

4.5.2   Liquidity and Two-Sided Quotations

By its definition of liquidity in terms of two-sided quotations, the SEC virtually forces a formal market-making system to be an essential element of an exchange. Although it was noted in section 4.4 that the requirement had seemingly been relaxed to that of regular buy and sell quotations, this observation was based on the single precedent provided by decisions concerning a single-price auction. Market making is associated with continuous auction and dealer markets, and the SEC could make this case in its classification of continuous trading systems as exchanges.

One of the functions of an exchange is to provide a basis for liquidity, defined more broadly than in the SEC's use in classifying trading systems. Part of the SEC's definition will serve as a basis for discussion: the creation of liquidity in the sense that both buyers and sellers have a reasonable expectation that they can regularly execute their orders at those quotes.

Liquidity might then be distinguished in two fashions. The first is "inside liquidity," which is the liquidity provided by market makers. The second is "outside liquidity," which is provided by investors, institutional or otherwise.[44] Outside liquidity is provided when one investor's position in a security is sold to another investor, regardless of whether the financial intermediation of a market maker is involved. Inside liquidity can be important with respect to the

---

43. Some might well argue that this has happened already, in part because of the differences in execution costs between proprietary systems allowing direct participation by institutions and exchanges that enforce the financial intermediation of broker-dealers.

44. See Miller and Upton (1989) with respect to immediacy and Domowitz (1995) for discussion in the context of automation.

definition proposed above, but need not be required. The market must produce outside liquidity for the market to fulfill its basic function.

The SEC definition is tantamount to stating that the basic function of providing outside liquidity cannot be accomplished without inside liquidity for a trading system to be classified as an exchange. Regulating immediacy by means of rules with respect to the affirmative obligations of specialists, for example, is indeed part of regulating trading operations. This is regulation of the market-making function, not of the function of producing outside liquidity. In fact, regulation of the market-making function does not necessarily mean that inside liquidity aids outside liquidity.[45]

It may be the case that a market-making system does encourage relatively more outside liquidity than a limit order book system. Relative liquidity is not the issue, however. A trading system operating with a limit order book and without a formal market-making structure is capable of generating the likelihood of liquidity in the sense of buyers and sellers expecting regular execution of orders. There are many examples of such systems operating overseas.[46]

4.5.3   Passive Pricing, Competition, and the Low-Volume Exemption

Although passive pricing trading systems might satisfy most of the requirements for exchange classification, the lack of price production rules out such a determination.[47] Such systems use automation to directly appropriate quotes from another price-producing trading system. The passive system then may operate at a lower cost relative to an exchange, because it does not bear the burden of the production of prices and the associated higher cost of regulation. Existing exchanges are unhappy about the situation, claiming unfair competitive advantage in favor of such proprietary systems.[48]

It is interesting that one of the reasons given for not regulating such systems as exchanges is possible adverse effects on innovation and competition.[49] It is not clear what kind of competition is being cited, and one must look to history for some guidance. Following the 1975 amendments to the Securities Exchange Act, the SEC promoted the development of the National Market Sys-

45. Franks and Schaefer (1990) report, for example, that a large proportion of trades on Nasdaq are matched; that is, dealers sometimes do not complete a transaction until a counterparty has been found.

46. Some such systems do embody a design detail allowing the input of two-sided quotations, encouraging informal market making for profit. Some others, particularly the larger ones, such as the Paris Cotation Assistée en Continu (CAC) and the German Deutsche Terminbörse (DTB), have some sort of market making or dual-capacity dealing formalized as part of market operations. Market makers on the DTB, however, must exhibit quotes on either side of the market only upon request, and need not do so on a regular or continuous basis. The DTB is considered very liquid, with over 3.7 million futures contracts and 9 million options contracts traded in 1991.

47. Two-sided-quotation dissemination is included here. Some systems simply generate automatic quotations based directly on the prices on the NYSE.

48. See Securities Exchange Act Release no. 26708 (April 18, 1989), 54 *Federal Register* 15429, footnote 6, for a list of such complaints from every major exchange.

49. See, for example, Securities Exchange Act Release no. 27611 (January 19, 1990), 55 *Federal Register* 1890, and SEC (1991).

tem. This concept was based on the idea that trading systems would compete on the basis of superior quotations. It follows that competition is meant to foster better price discovery. On the other hand, the diversion of order flow to the lower-cost producer of the execution service, the passive pricing system, can result in the inability of orders in all markets to interact with one another. This diversion of outside liquidity away from the price-producing market may then cause an erosion in the quality of price information, hence a deterioration of the price discovery process. Protection of passive pricing systems on the basis of competition, using the definition of exchange as the excuse, may be misplaced.

Fostering the development of innovative price-producing systems to promote competition is a useful goal, however. The SEC believes that the costs of exchange regulation do not decrease linearly with volume, and that there are large fixed costs of compliance, especially for new systems that handle institutional order flow.[50] Classification as an exchange does not necessarily mean registration and regulation as an exchange. New systems can be expected to have low volume, and the low-volume exemption can be used as a tool to foster price competition. Exempt exchanges can be usefully regulated under the types of restrictions envisioned under proposed rule 15c2-10. Such a course of action is sensible, given that large volume is an important pressure for tighter regulation in the interest of protecting the overall market.[51]

4.6 A Functional Approach to Trading Markets

The SEC has asked for proposed amendments as to how Congress might redefine an exchange in light of advances in automation. A suitable reinterpretation might involve dropping requirements for, or restrictions on, membership, as well as eliminating the market-making requirement in the form of two-sided quotations. The commission would still be left with the problem of passive pricing systems, forcing another look at the price discovery element in the definition. All in all, such a substantial redefinition could occasion a major revision of regulatory law in order to accommodate its application and enforcement. Perhaps realizing this, the commission also queried whether classification and regulation might instead be based on functional attributes of a trading market. The regulatory rewrite could then be oriented toward functions that are more stable than their associated institutions in the light of continued innovations in trading market infrastructure.

The intent of this section is not to discuss the economic-philosophical foundations of functional versus institutional regulation, nor the regulatory dialec-

---

50. See Securities Exchange Act Release no. 28899 (February 28, 1991), 56 *Federal Register* 8377.

51. This point also is made by Lee (1992). He goes a bit farther, however, in proposing that volume alone might be used as the appropriate definition of an exchange.

tic and process of change associated with regulatory avoidance. This has been done elsewhere.[52] The purpose here is to delineate some of the lines of inquiry with respect to a shift from institutional to functional regulation of trading systems in the face of the technical advances in trading market structure. A bit of general background is necessary, however.

The SEC talks of regulating "functional attributes," which is in line with Lee (1992), who defines functional regulation as the determination of the functions that require regulation and the rationale for such regulation. Merton (1992) uses the term to mean regulation of different products that are nearly perfect substitutes from the perspective of their users.[53] The discussion here uses both definitions, taking the users to be participants in the trading process.[54] Either way, regulation along functional lines would not require constant changes over time in the regulations surrounding trading systems as they further develop.

4.6.1   Price Discovery

Economists would generally agree that the price discovery process, with the associated dissemination of price information, is a primary market function. Trading systems that produce prices are substitutes. Regulatory initiatives that promote quality price production and competitive pressures would qualify such systems as nearly perfect substitutes. The mechanism of price production can vary, from automated limit order books to formal market-making systems. Combinations of both currently exist in both automated and nonautomated execution settings. Obviously, the quality of price production may still vary, and differential costs to the participants necessitate the usual trade-offs.

A functional approach to the classification and regulation of trading systems then implies that price discovery systems be regulated on equal terms. The legal focus of inquiry will naturally shift to the definition of price discovery.[55] This should not be too difficult a task, however. Any reasonable definition would imply that the floor of the NYSE, Instinet, Delta Government Options, and the periodic-auction mechanism of the Arizona Stock Exchange would be classified and regulated as price discovery markets. Such a determination also calls the exclusion of brokers' broker systems, mentioned in section 4.4, into serious question.

52. See, for example, Kane (1986), Lee (1992), and Merton (1992), and the references therein.
53. Some of Merton's (1992) discussion is a bit broader philosophically, giving functional regulation the perspective of taking as given the economic functions of markets and intermediaries, and questioning what is the best institutional structure to perform those functions.
54. The discussion here narrows with respect to services provided by trading markets. In particular, companies desiring listing services are classifiable as "users," but this is considered a different "function," and may possibly destroy perfect substitutability between trading systems with and without listing facilities from the viewpoint of the companies whose shares are traded. In any case, listing services can be regulated separately. Lee (1992) even makes a case for separating the listing function from the sponsor of a trading system on economic and incentive grounds.
55. For example, computer-generated quotations at or at most an eighth away from "primary market quotes" might not be reasonably classified as a price discovery mechanism.

Classification and concomitant regulation along price discovery lines helps to clearly answer some hypothetical questions posed by the SEC with respect to proprietary trading systems.[56] For example, if five broker-dealers or five institutions developed a trading system among themselves, would this be an exchange? The question is irrelevant in the context of functional regulation. If this system engages in price discovery, it is regulated accordingly.

Would a price discovery system merit different regulatory treatment from one operating as a passive pricing mechanism? The answer is yes, in the sense of an additional layer of regulatory oversight relative to that required for mere trade execution. Given the importance of price discovery to the public-interest mandates of regulatory legislation, surveillance of the process and rules with respect to price reporting are natural additional requirements.[57]

This does not necessarily mean that price discovery systems need operate at a significant handicap relative to passive pricing mechanisms. Price discovery systems can obtain incremental profits from the sale of price information. Passive pricing systems cannot operate without such information, and should expect to pay for it. The lesser regulatory burden of passive pricing systems also does not imply that price discovery markets will lose enough market share to make operating not worthwhile and quality price discovery impossible.[58] In fact, the NYSE claims an increase in the percentage of large trades executed on the NYSE over the past few years and best pricing, despite the proliferation of proprietary trading systems (see Shapiro 1995). The price production mechanism and its associated liquidity bring participants to price discovery markets.

4.6.2   Trade Execution

Centralization for the purpose of trade execution also is a basic function of trading systems. Such execution at low cost is a major motivation for institutions moving to trading systems that do not necessarily offer price improvement through the price discovery process. The minimum quality of trade execution in terms of price is already legally defined in terms of best quotations in consolidated markets. From the functional perspective, centralization for trade execution can be considered a means of regulatory classification independent of pricing, conditional on such a minimum pricing standard.

Execution relates to the basic economic function of resource allocation at given prices, and therefore deserves a level of regulatory oversight. Passive pricing systems as well as price discovery markets execute trades. Volume reporting requirements are important, for example, as well as the design and integrity of the system. The latter implies that the SEC's Automation Review

---

56. See Becker, Adkins, Fuller, and Angstadt (1991) for this, and other, examples.

57. See, for example, Corcoran and Lawton (1993) and Domowitz (1993a) for additional discussion with respect to different oversight for varying levels and functions of automated systems.

58. Obviously, a fully specified equilibrium model of both price and nonprice competition in the exchange services industry would be helpful in qualifying the balance between system types as a function of services and costs. This model has yet to be formulated in the literature.

Policy and some form of proposed rule 15c2–10 be applied in the case of functional regulation of automated trade execution.

This is not currently the case for all execution systems. In fact, rule 15c2-10, which is largely oriented toward execution, is not applicable to a potentially large number of broker-dealer systems as it now stands. The functional perspective would discard prohibitions on the regulation of execution that are purely historical and apply to the institutional definition of broker-dealers. If the trading system executes trades, it is regulated as a trade execution system. This would also prevent proprietary trading systems from hiding as broker-dealers simply to avoid regulation under something like the proposed rule 15c2-10 and the related review policies.

Classification along the functional line of execution also means that execution systems that do not engage in price discovery, but are currently facilities of registered exchanges, would be regulated simply as execution mechanisms. Thus, the NYSE after-hours crossing network would have equal standing with Instinet's or Posit's crossing systems. The all-or-nothing provision with respect to exchange regulation would no longer necessarily be applicable. From the competitive point of view, currently registered exchanges could compete on an equal footing with proprietary trading systems in the market for passive pricing execution services.[59]

4.6.3   Liquidity

There may be a legitimate argument as to whether liquidity creation is a basic function of a market or a measure of the quality of the market's product. The position taken here views liquidity as something to be fostered through regulation, but not necessarily as a line of classification that promotes different regulation for liquid versus illiquid markets.

Liquidity, in the regulatory context of system classification, is embodied in the notion that both buyers and sellers have a reasonable expectation that they can regularly execute their orders at quotes resting on the system. Liquidity by this definition could be considered likely in both price discovery and passive pricing trading systems. Although good-quality price discovery and execution require some level of liquidity, it is unnecessary to legislate liquidity or the means of its provision. The process of trading will drive markets with too little liquidity out of business and motivate additional innovation with respect to mechanisms friendly to liquidity provision.

In particular, a functional perspective need not draw regulatory classification lines between systems differentiated by direct outside liquidity and inside liquidity that is used to promote outside liquidity.[60] Merton (1992) characterizes

---

59. This could introduce issues of vertical integration into the discussion of trading system regulation, since a passive pricing system could be using prices produced by the same entity on a different level.

60. This does not mean that a formal market-making mechanism does not need oversight, but that the liquidity-provision mechanism requires oversight. The general nature and degree of that

innovation in part by the cyclic pattern of the replacement of financial intermediaries by market mechanisms, followed by the entry of intermediaries using
the new mechanism. Limit order book systems have replaced, or are used instead of, formal market-making mechanisms in some international jurisdictions. Market makers have not necessarily disappeared, but have adapted to the
new technology and offer services accordingly.

4.6.4   The Question of Standards

The SEC has requested comment on the appropriateness of a "standards"
approach for the regulation of proprietary systems. This includes standards
under which systems and system amendments would be approved and standards for exemption from certain regulatory burdens.[61] These questions are
equally appropriate in the context of functional classification and regulation of
trading systems.

A standards-based approach to the approval process clearly could be beneficial, if not too broadly applied. Ambiguities with respect to the frequency
and nature of risk assessments, surveillance requirements, record keeping for
system development and operations, and the like, can easily be avoided.[62] Consistent application across all trading systems of the current Automation Review
Policy is one step in this direction. A system either conforms to the standards
or not, the determination of which should then speed up the regulatory approval process.

A standards approach with respect to system configuration is not appropriate. One of the avowed aims of the SEC is to encourage innovation in trading
market infrastructure. A reinterpretation of the theoretical work of Shy (1991)
on international standardization suggests that the frequency of innovation is
potentially much lower under a uniform standards approach to trading system
configuration. The reason is that a market structure adopted widely is less
likely to be abandoned by traders, causing an incentive problem with respect
to the introduction of new market systems.[63] This problem has also been noted
by Amihud and Mendelson (1989) in the context of SEC approval of an options
market integration system. They characterize adoption of a certain standard in
terms of "technological lockup," noting barriers to future innovation. An ex-

---

oversight will depend on the classification of the system with respect to execution and price discovery.

61. As opposed to the delineation of general categories of information that must be contained
in those plans, for example. The exemption issue is posed in the context of exemption from exchange registration.

62. The model here is Securities Exchange Act Release no. 16900 (June 17, 1980), 45 *Federal
Register* 41920, concerning clearing agency operations.

63. This incentive problem also explains why automated systems have not made much headway
in replacing traditional market-maker and/or open outcry auction systems in the United States,
while automated auctions are commonplace in countries without such traditions. See Domowitz
(1993c).

ample to which their argument applies directly would be configuration standards that effectively mandate a formal market-making mechanism.[64]

It was argued earlier that fostering competition in the area of superior price discovery is appropriate, while such nurturing in the case of passive pricing systems is not in accordance with the SEC's definition of competition. A low-volume exemption for price discovery systems is justifiable on the same grounds as applied in the case of exemption from exchange registration. Large volume remains an important pressure for tighter regulation, all the more so since price discovery at low volumes is arguably less important to the overall price discovery function of the national market. Such a standard could, in principle, be unambiguously defined. In practice, however, this could be difficult. Lines of demarcation based on dollar volume would certainly depend on the particular securities traded on the system, for example. The same might be said for a standard including the number of market participants as a factor.

4.7   Concluding Remarks

If the SEC's decision classifying the Wunsch Auction System as an exchange is viewed as setting legal precedent, failure to reclassify some existing trading systems might bring about further legal action from established exchange markets. Such action could transpire in the event of a new continuous trading system that satisfied the guidelines laid down in the latest decision, but that applied for registration as a broker-dealer. Given the difficulties with redefining what is meant by an exchange, the SEC might be expected to justify its latest ruling by appealing to the single-price auction nature of the trading mechanism.[65] Legal precedent suggests that the SEC would win.

The strict definition of an exchange in terms of membership and two-sided quotations has been argued to be unsatisfactory, given the advances in technology and the current design of automated trading systems as exhibited worldwide. It is arguably the case that such systems fulfill all the trading functions of an exchange, including the likelihood of liquidity provision without two-sided quotations on a continuous basis.

This observation leads to the suggestion that the exchange/nonexchange distinction be dropped in favor of a more functional approach to the classification and regulation of trading systems. The nature of regulation is based on the functional lines of centralization for trade execution and price discovery. The dividing line distinguishes systems that engage in price production from those executing transactions based on passive pricing.

Classifying and regulating price discovery systems uniformly, subject to

---

64. See also Domowitz (1993a) on the potential harm to liquidity from tight regulation of system configuration.

65. This potential problem is consistent with the interpretation of Lee (1992), who regards the Wunsch decision as a regulatory anomaly, and provides a variety of reasons for the decision, none of which concern exchange redefinition.

possible volume exemptions, puts systems such as Instinet, the Wunsch Auction System, and Delta Government Options on the same footing as the floor of the NYSE. The exclusion from such regulation of brokers' broker systems, currently exempted from exchange classification and the proposed rule 15c2–10 based solely on the traditional classification of such operations as broker-dealers, would be considered inappropriate.

This view would also promote the uniform regulation of execution services. The required oversight would still be considered less than for systems engaged in price discovery over and above execution. Such a uniform standard questions the exclusion of a number of broker-dealer systems from regulation under some form of proposed rule 15c2–10. It further suggests that some facilities of established exchanges, operating as passive pricing mechanisms, be regulated on an equal basis with proprietary trading systems that do not engage in active price discovery. Thus, the NYSE after-hours crossing network would compete on a level playing field with such crossing systems operated on a proprietary basis.

These observations have been made within the fairly narrow scope of stock trading systems, relative to overall financial market operations. This was considered necessary in order to be very specific with respect to the legislative details leading to the issues and the factors involved in the determination. Similar questions are arising in the derivatives markets, however, both in the context of established exchange operations and over-the-counter derivative market activity.[66] The Chicago Board of Trade is requesting an exemption from regulation as a "professional trading market," for all instruments that would otherwise be regulated under the Commodity Exchange Act. The Chicago Mercantile Exchange seeks regulatory exemption for its rolling spot currency contract, because it has close affinity to cash market instruments currently traded over the counter. The argument is that considerable benefits would accrue by allowing trading in this contract to operate on regulatory parity with the cash market. The implication of the analysis in this paper is that the establishment of additional statutory classifications, in the form of "new" market participants, is not necessarily an appropriate response to technological advances in market infrastructure or new product development. On the other hand, regulation along functional lines invites consideration of easing some restrictions on established exchanges.

66. See Bronfman (1995), for example, for discussion of Chicago Board of Trade and Chicago Mercantile Exchange initiatives aimed at exemptions from exchange regulations for certain types of trading participants and products.

References

Amihud, Yakov, and Haim Mendelson. 1989. Option Markets Integration: An Evaluation. Manuscript, New York University.

Becker, Brandon, Alden Adkins, Gordon Fuller, and Janet Angstadt. 1991. The SEC's Oversight of Proprietary Trading Systems. Paper presented at the Conference on Securities Markets Transaction Costs, Owen Graduate School of Management, Vanderbilt University.

Bronfman, Corinne M. 1995. In the Public Interest? Reassessing the Regulatory Role in the Financial Markets. In Robert A. Schwartz, ed., *Global Equity Markets: Technological, Competitive, and Regulatory Challenges*. Burr Ridge, IL: Business One Irwin.

Corcoran, Andrea, and John Lawton. 1993. The Effect of Variations among Automated Trading Systems on Regulatory Oversight. *Journal of Futures Markets* 13:213–22.

Domowitz, Ian. 1990. When Is a Marketplace a Market: Automated Trade Execution in the Futures Market. In Daniel R. Siegel, ed., *Innovation and Technology in the Markets: A Reordering of the World's Capital Market Systems*, 183–96. Chicago: Probus.

———. 1993a. Automating the Price Discovery Process: Some International Comparisons and Regulatory Implications. *Journal of Financial Services Research* 6:305–26.

———. 1993b. Equally Open and Competitive: Regulatory Approval of Automated Trade Execution in the Futures Market. *Journal of Futures Markets* 13:93–113.

———. 1993c. A Taxonomony of Automated Trade Execution Systems. *Journal of International Money and Finance* 12:607–31.

———. 1995. Financial Market Automation and the Investment Services Directive. In Robert A. Schwartz, ed., *Global Equity Markets: Technological, Competitive, and Regulatory Challenges*. Burr Ridge, IL: Business One Irwin.

Franks, Julian R., and Stephen M. Schaefer. 1990. Large Trade Publication on the International Stock Exchange. Manuscript, London Business School.

General Accounting Office. 1989. Automation Can Enhance Detection of Trade Abuses, but Introduces New Risks. GAO/IMTEC-89-68. Washington, DC: General Accounting Office.

International Organization of Securities Commissions. 1991. Screen-Based Trading Systems for Derivative Products. Report of the Technical Committee.

Kane, Edward J. 1986. Technology and the Regulation of Financial Markets. In Anthony Saunders and Lawrence J. White, eds., *Technology and the Regulation of Financial Markets*, 187–93. Lexington, MA: Heath.

Lee, Ruben. 1992. What Is an Exchange? Discussion paper, Capital Markets Forum, International Bar Association.

Merton, Robert C. 1992. Operation and Regulation in Financial Intermediation: A Functional Perspective. Working Paper no. 93–020. Division of Research, Harvard Business School.

Miller, Merton H., and Charles W. Upton. 1989. Strategies for Capital Market Structure and Regulation. Manuscript, University of Chicago.

Securities and Exchange Commission. 1991. Automated Securities Trading: A Discussion of Selected Critical Issues. Paper prepared for the International Organization of Securities Commissions 1991 Annual Meeting, Panel on Automated Trading, Burgenstock, Switzerland, June.

Shapiro, James E. 1995. U.S. Equity Markets: A View of Recent Competitive Developments. In Robert A. Schwartz, ed., *Global Equity Markets: Technological, Competitive, and Regulatory Challenges*. Burr Ridge, IL: Business One Irwin.

Shy, Oz. 1991. International Standardization and Protection. Seminar Paper no. 505. Institute for International Economic Studies, Stockholm University.

Sundel, Michael B., and Lystra G. Blake. 1991. Good Concept, Bad Executions: The Regulation and Self-Regulation of Automated Trading Systems in United States Futures Markets. *Northwestern University Law Review* 85:748–89.

Comment   Ananth Madhavan

Ian Domowitz's paper concerns a timely and interesting topic. In a narrow sense, the key question posed by the paper is, what determines whether a trading system is an exchange or a broker-dealer? The proliferation of new trading systems complicates the task of regulators, who previously relied on definitions that corresponded relatively closely to economic realities (see, e.g., Madhavan [1992] for an analysis of various trading systems). Modern technology has blurred the traditional definitions and boundaries. For example, some crossing systems are classified as brokers, but these systems can be extended easily to incorporate computer algorithms that make possible some limited price discovery within the prevailing quotes (see, e.g., Leach and Madhavan [1992, 1993] for a discussion of price discovery). Exchanges argue that regulation places an unfair burden on them and limits their ability to innovate. The question is a crucial one for policymakers as well as market participants.

The answer to the narrow question proposed in this paper is that the function of the trading system should determine the appropriate classification, and hence the amount of regulation required of the trading system. Just as advances in genetic research raise new ethical questions (e.g., can a corporation patent a genetically engineered mouse?), the new technologies of trading create new challenges for regulators and policymakers. Taking a functional approach over the current statutory approach makes sense, given the rapidly changing technology. Domowitz makes a forceful argument that the functional approach should be based on price discovery, and that this would promote more efficient regulation as well as fairness.

However, there is a broader issue, that is, whether we need such classifications in the first place, and if we do, how to operationalize the functional definition proposed here. To answer the broader question, we need to step back and ask ourselves about the purpose of regulation. Public regulation of the securities markets is generally designed to build trust in the financial system, by protecting investors (especially "small" retail investors who may underestimate the potential risks associated with trading securities) from defaults, fraud, insider trading, and market manipulation of various types. In addition, regulation also serves as a method to monitor and control financial markets, a function that is important because these markets play a crucial role in financing new investment and allocating resources. From this perspective, the trading

Ananth Madhavan is associate professor of finance at the University of Southern California.

systems most important for regulation are those that have the highest volume, where trading by professional market participants (e.g., market makers and brokers) can affect the integrity of prices. These are the systems that should be subject to the most stringent regulation, that is, regulated as exchanges are today.

But the need for regulation must be balanced against the costs imposed by such rules. What are these costs? There are both explicit and implicit costs to regulation. Explicit costs imposed on exchanges include the costs of compliance, market surveillance, reporting requirements, and disseminating quotes and maintaining system access. The implicit costs imposed on exchanges by regulation are in terms of the limits placed on the ability to innovate because of the difficulty in changing trading arrangements.

Both explicit and implicit costs are significant, but there are reasons to err on the side of excess. First, some of the explicit costs are for functions required of exchanges that might be performed anyway. For example, of the fifteen hundred or so New York Stock Exchange (NYSE) employees, roughly a third are involved in market surveillance required by law. However, even if there were no such regulations, the NYSE would probably still continue to devote resources to maintaining a "fair and orderly" market, simply because it is in the interest of the NYSE to develop a reputation for trust. Second, the explicit costs of collecting real-time market information and the ability to analyze these data (e.g., to detect episodes of insider trading) will continue to decline as the technology improves. Implicit costs, however, induced by the limits placed on innovation by cumbersome and slow regulatory approval for new changes, may be significant and may be growing. These costs are largely discretionary, however, and can be reduced by shortening the approval process. These arguments would suggest that we exercise some caution in terms of changing the regulatory environment too rapidly in the direction of less regulation.

Given this, how should the functional approach be implemented? Again, although I agree with the basic thrust of Domowitz's argument, I would argue for caution in implementing his proposal. Extending the regulatory burden to small trading systems trying to develop new methods for price discovery may ultimately reduce the incentives for innovation. To some extent, this is the approach practiced now. For example, the Arizona Stock Exchange, an electronic batch auction system providing price discovery, is exempted from the traditional requirements imposed on an exchange because its volume is low. This makes sense; it allows newer systems the freedom to experiment and alter their trading arrangements to capture more volume without costly and lengthy regulatory oversight. Similarly, less regulation of high-volume trading systems without price discovery may expose investors to potential risks that may damage trust in the financial system.

In summary, the paper provides a very careful and insightful analysis, and raises a number of highly important issues for further research. Domowitz's proposal deserves to be taken extremely seriously, and his paper should be required reading for all those affected by this issue.

References

Leach, C., and A. Madhavan. 1992. Intertemporal Price Discovery by Market Makers: Active Experimentation versus Passive Learning. *Journal of Financial Intermediation* 2:207–35.
———. 1993. Price Experimentation and Market Structure. *Review of Financial Studies* 6:375–404.
Madhavan, A. 1992. Trading Mechanisms in Securities Markets. *Journal of Finance* 47:607–41.

Comment   Chris A. Hynes

Ian Domowitz's paper focuses on the problem of market regulation of computer-based trading facilities. After categorizing the various systems according to functional criteria, he traces the history of regulatory thought and action concerning them.

While discussing this history, he raises the issue of the confusion generated by the definition of an exchange contained in the Securities Exchange Act. This definition is critical to the level of regulatory burden placed upon the system, or exchange, as the interpretation may determine, and forms a battleground between the traditional exchanges and their newer competitors, the proprietary trading systems.

He then goes on to define the requirements for categorization as an exchange, and discusses the issues involved. Two important items discussed are "inside liquidity" and "outside liquidity." Inside liquidity is supplied to an exchange or system by its market makers, while outside liquidity is provided by investors. The consistency of liquidity, and the immediacy that results from this consistency, are important to the SEC. However, since market makers rarely provide enough liquidity to provide immediacy for large institutional investors, and retail investors can generally satisfy their demands for immediacy through the bids and offers of market makers, is it any wonder that retail investors are happy with exchanges and third-market-maker executions, while an increasing share of institutional business is moving to trading systems offering outside liquidity? Perhaps Domowitz should examine the significance of this difference between traditional exchanges and the new electronic marketplaces, even if they are classified as exchanges.

When discussing the system/exchange attributes of passive pricing versus price discovery, Domowitz has the insight that, while price discovery systems need another layer of regulation relative to passive pricing systems, this burden needn't be excessive. He also points out that the differential regulatory burden

Chris A. Hynes is a managing director of State Street Global Advisors and president of State Street Brokerage Services, Inc., a subsidiary of State Street Bank and Trust Company.

alone shouldn't cause a market share drain from one system/exchange to another. This point should be emphasized, since cross-border proprietary trading systems are having a difficult time gathering business, even though they have a dramatically lower regulatory burden than the international bourses. The problem is simple: investors are reluctant to trade passively unless they have a price discovery system providing accurate information to the passive pricing system.

Continuing the quest for the level, rational playing field, Domowitz suggests that separate facilities of exchanges devoted to passive pricing structures be separated from the regulation of the parent and carry a regulatory burden equal to that of stand-alone systems with similar structure. Is it sensible, though, that regulatory burdens for systems/exchanges with electronic audit trails, even with different pricing structures, should be substantially different in cost? While he has previously stated that the difference needn't be excessive, he is implying here that it is important enough to be a concern. He has also pointed out the desirability of the low-volume exemption for new systems. Since so much of the regulatory burden is designed to stop fraud occurring when agency and principal functions are mixed, and to ensure that trading rules are followed, why should there be a great regulatory cost when participants are on an equal footing and algorithms enforce trading rules?

This question is indirectly addressed as the article moves on to standards, where Domowitz points out that standards can be valuable in the approval process, but pose a danger to innovation in the control of system configuration. According to the SEC's definition of competition, says the author, fostering competition for superior price discovery is appropriate, while doing so for passive pricing systems is not. The SEC should realize that both are quite valuable to the investment ecosystem. To fight competition from a passive pricing system, a price discovery system has to tighten its markets to decrease the price paid for immediacy relative to the passive market. It would help if the size of markets increased to provide real immediacy to the institutional investor population. In this way, the existence of passive pricing systems fores the improvement of price discovery systems, and should certainly be worthy of some nurturing.

I am concerned about the article's conclusion that regulation move to a more functional approach. Without major legislative overhaul, this would place proprietary trading systems with no principal-agency conflicts directly into a regulatory scheme fixed years ago that contemplates these conflicts as being at the heart of the regulatory mission. We cannot adopt a functional approach without functional legislation.

Author's Reply

You must not say, what is this? Why is that? All things have been created for their proper functions.

—Sirach 39:21

The regulation of trading markets is a sensitive, even emotional, subject for many people. Mention of the topic itself strikes at the heart of what individuals and organizations believe "should be done" to organize market activity in non-market fashions to protect the public interest. One response is to turn immediately to a discussion of the purpose and function of market regulation. This reaction was particularly pronounced in open discussion at the NBER Conference. Opinions varied, ranging from "regulation is unnecessary" to the use of trading system classification as an antitrust device.

Ananth Madhavan outlines the functions of regulation as the building of trust, participant protection, and the monitoring and control of market activity. Government regulation is thought to be necessary in support of these functions. Chris Hynes does not appear to disagree with the desirability of such goals, but believes that the market user base can be relied on as the sole regulator. I concur with the functional description, and have some sympathy with both of these positions. Both can muster theoretical support, depending on the assumptions made on the underlying nature of the market and the potential for market failure with respect to one or more of these functions.

My paper, however, is not about the purpose and functions of regulation, nor does it address the issue of "what should be" in the context of trading market regulation. There is already a large literature on the former, and many opinions exist with respect to the latter. I take as given the functions outlined by Madhavan, broadly interpreted. I would add only the consenting opinion that the functions of trading systems and the functions of regulation are not independent. I implicitly adopt the pragmatic view that government regulation of trading markets exists and will continue. The paper concerns the nature of that regulation. Legislative history and legal precedent are used to develop a taxonomy of system classification that is shown to be at the core of regulatory policy. This taxonomy is compared to the new developments in the technology of trading market structure. It is argued to be weak in some respects and inconsistent in others with respect to its use in establishing policy, in the face of these technical advances. Functional regulation is suggested, in part because it is more closely related to the taxonomy than is the current institutional structure. The purpose of the remainder of the paper is simply to delineate some lines of

The author has benefited greatly from conversations with James E. Shapiro and George Sofianos.

inquiry with respect to a shift from institutional to functional regulation of trading systems.

Once the hurdle of the purpose and function of regulation is passed, the discussants' broad concerns are quite similar. The issues are regulatory costs, competition for exchange services, and practical implementation of the functional approach along the lines suggested in the paper.

Madhavan correctly notes the need for balance between the need for system regulation and costs imposed by the rules. He would discount regulatory cost in the equation on the basis that much of it would be incurred anyway as a natural by-product of providing quality exchange services. I am inclined to agree, but industry participants, if not the facts, are seemingly against us. System operators uniformly have made a concerted effort to avoid costs associated with regulation as a registered exchange. The comment letters from existing exchanges cited in the paper forcefully argue that the lower cost associated with avoiding exchange registration is a strong competitive advantage in the exchange services business. The SEC has made the same point, but used it as a rationale to promote new system development, allowing the avoidance of such costs through nonregistration.

Hynes addresses costs in the context of an implication of the functional view, that regulatory burdens carried by electronic crossing facilities of exchanges should be on the same level as that born by stand-alone systems with the same structure. He queries the sense in assuming that regulatory cost differences exist. Under the Securities Exchange Act, a crossing facility operated by a registered exchange is necessarily subject to regulatory costs associated with registered exchanges. A stand-alone system is not bound by the same requirements if registered as a broker-dealer or under the proposed rule 15c2-10. Hynes also points out that there should not be a large regulatory cost for automated systems, when participants are on an equal footing. I agree, but the point is that automated systems are not currently competing on a completely level regulatory playing field. Further, the details of system design may mandate different levels of regulatory oversight; this point is discussed in Domowitz (1993).

Both discussants mention some details with respect to the competition for exchange services. This is an area that deserves much more attention on theoretical, empirical, and policy levels. Madhavan believes in more stringent regulation for higher-volume systems, and cites a low-volume exemption as a tool for promoting competition through innovation in exchange design and implementation. I agree, and these points are discussed in more detail in the paper.

Hynes indirectly gets to the heart of the issue of competition in the presence of both price discovery and execution-only markets. On the one hand, he notes that passive pricing trading systems require price discovery systems that produce accurate prices. On the other, he argues that passive pricing systems are important to the investment ecology, and that a price discovery market must decrease the price paid for immediacy relative to the passive market in order to compete. The desirable balance between these markets and the equilibrating forces promoting a healthy trade-off between accurate price discovery and lower price for immediacy are not well understood. A fully specified equilibrium model of both price and nonprice competition in the exchange services industry would be most helpful in qualifying the balance between system types as a function of services and costs. This model has yet to be formulated. Regulation cannot mandate the growth of market size suggested by Hynes as a solution to the problem; it can only encourage it.

The discussants also touch upon the implementation of the functional approach to market regulation, with seemingly different perspectives that are not too far apart as a practical matter. Madhavan reiterates the point concerning low-volume exemptions as a policy tool, noting that the regulatory apparatus is already in place for its use. The discussion of this issue in the paper further supports his argument. He also mentions the difficulty of deciding upon the demarcation between price discovery and passive pricing systems. This is a very practical concern, requiring consideration of pricing activity within quotes put out by a market that is obviously of a price discovery type. The issue might be resolved, for example, by maintaining the current regulatory standard for price discovery in terms of quotation activity. Computer-generated quotations at or at most an eighth away from "primary market" quotes also might not be reasonably classified as a price discovery mechanism.

The link to Hynes's concern about implementation is that the legal focus of inquiry will naturally shift to the definition of price discovery. Hynes cites the necessity of major legislative overhaul to accommodate a functional approach, noting that the current system was put in place years ago. Both points are correct and important. In fact, legal scholars at the conference termed the Securities Exchange Act obsolete in the presence of the technological advances in market structure. Discussion in the paper notes that even a redefinition of an exchange to accommodate the current system would occasion a major revision of regulatory law in order to allow its application and enforcement. In other words, a rewriting of the law may be necessary in any case. The paper simply asks whether such a regulatory rewrite might be oriented toward functions that are more stable than their associated institutions in the light of continued innovations in trading market infrastructure.

Finally, the discussants both raise the issue of the level of regulation. This is a return to the "what should be" question noted at the beginning of this reply. The paper has nothing to say about the absolute level of regulation. The emphasis is on the relative levels of regulation across market environments. As Hynes says, this is a quest for the level, rational playing field. The point is not that more or less regulation is needed to fulfill the goals and perform the functions of regulation. Rather, a need for a shift in focus of the ways in which these ends are achieved in the current technological environment is the logical conclusion of the analysis in the paper.

Reference

Domowitz, Ian. 1993. Automating the Price Discovery Process: Some International Comparisons and Regulatory Implications. *Journal of Financial Services Research* 6:305–26.

5 Transaction Costs in Dealer Markets: Evidence from the London Stock Exchange

Peter C. Reiss and Ingrid M. Werner

5.1 Introduction

New electronic trading technologies have drastically reduced the costs of financial transactions and put tremendous pressure on financial exchanges to lower their costs. In 1986, the London Stock Exchange (LSE) responded to these pressures by switching from a closed, floor-based, broker-dealer market to an open electronic quotation system dubbed SEAQ. The LSE's SEAQ system operates much like the National Association of Securities Dealers' Nasdaq dealer system. On SEAQ, competing market makers post bid and ask prices and guaranteed trade sizes. Although SEAQ also displays trade information, brokers and dealers still negotiate trades by phone. Besides changing its quotation systems, the LSE enacted new rules designed to encourage competition and narrow quoted spreads. These rules included the elimination of fixed commissions and member entry barriers, and the adoption of best execution rules. The exchange also imposed minimum quote sizes. The minimum quote size for a security is the number of shares market makers must stand ready to trade at their posted prices. On SEAQ, these minimums are large, equaling 2, and

Peter C. Reiss is professor of economics at Stanford Business School and a research associate of the National Bureau of Economic Research. Ingrid M. Werner is associate professor of finance at Stanford Business School, a research fellow of the National Bureau of Economic Research, and a research fellow of the Stockholm Institute for International Economic Studies.

The authors thank Stephen Wells and Graham Hart of the London Stock Exchange's Quality of Markets Group for providing data and answering questions. Goldman Sachs, Preferred Technology, Salomon Brothers, and Union Bank of Switzerland graciously granted access to their trading operations. The authors had the good fortune to observe Xavier Rolet, Richard O'Hare, Dan Pizza, and George Gray make markets. Kathleen Tyson of the U.K. Securities Investment Board explained the intricacies of U.K. security regulations. The Stanford Graduate School of Business funded part of this research through its Financial Services Research Initiative and a Robert M. and Ann T. Bass Faculty Fellowship to Werner. Werner also acknowledges her stay at the London School of Economics. The authors are responsible for the paper's analysis and conclusions.

sometimes more, percent of a security's average daily trading volume. To reduce the capital risks associated with large trades, the exchange granted market makers the right to delay their disclosure. During 1991, SEAQ delayed releasing information on large trades for up to ninety minutes. Currently, they delay disclosing information on extremely large trades for up to one week!

The LSE's emphasis on liquidity over transparency has renewed debate about whether such rules affect the costs of financial transactions. A recent International Organization of Securities Commissions report (1993) observed that few studies have examined the determinants of transaction costs in dealership markets. Several empirical studies report substantial intersecurity and interday variation in Nasdaq and SEAQ dealer spreads. Few examine the relationship between spreads and transaction prices, or consider how exchange rules might affect spreads. This paper uses newly available SEAQ intraday quotation and transaction data to analyze the relationship between investor transaction costs and best bid-ask spreads. Using unique information in SEAQ data, we show that LSE rules lead dealers to offer systematic discounts from posted prices. These discounts vary across traders, securities, and trade characteristics.

We also argue that conventional transaction cost measures do not recognize important institutional features of dealership markets. On SEAQ, these include minimum quote sizes and best execution rules. These rules affect dealers' quoted prices and their willingness to offer traders discounts. Contrary to the assumptions of many theoretical models, SEAQ market makers do not compete by narrowing (symmetric) quotes. Indeed, they almost *never* narrow the quoted spread between their bid and ask prices. They instead compete by positioning their bid or ask on or at the market bid or offer. Curiously, they may maintain these positions for hours or days, offering traders discounts instead of changing what they advertise on SEAQ screens. We find, as some theoretical models do, that dealer discounts usually increase with the size of a trade. We also find puzzles. Surprisingly, discounts for customers, brokers, and market makers all decrease with market-maker concentration and increase with market depth. These heterogeneities raise new theoretical and empirical questions about how dealer competition affects the relation between quoted prices and transaction prices.

Section 5.2 begins with a review of prior research on transaction costs, particularly transaction costs in dealer markets. We then show that several standard transaction cost measures may over- or underrepresent dealer discounts from quoted spreads. We illustrate our arguments using SEAQ and Nasdaq intraday trade and quotation data for Cadbury Schweppes, a heavily traded FTSE-100 (Financial Times–Stock Exchange) equity. We find that SEAQ Cadbury quoted bid-ask spreads are slightly higher than Nasdaq spreads. More notable are differences in the price discounts offered by Nasdaq and SEAQ market makers. Though some research suggests that dealers offer only other dealers discounts from quoted prices, this is not true on SEAQ. SEAQ market makers grant discounts to medium and large retail orders more often than they do to each other. The median retail discount increases uniformly with order size, and applies to many orders larger than the Cadbury minimum quote size. We conclude the Cadbury example by developing a new measure of transaction costs, what we term the *adjusted apparent spread*. This measure reveals how dealers vary spreads and discounts with trade characteristics. We estimate these adjusted apparent spreads using quantile regression techniques. These regressions flexibly describe the distribution of Cadbury discounts conditional on trade size and trader identities.

Section 5.3 analyzes 1991 quotation data for 1,887 U.K. and Irish equities to isolate inter- and intrasecurity variations in quoted prices. We find striking variation. Best bid-ask spreads range from less than 1 percent of share value to over 50 percent! Much of this variation is systematic. As on Nasdaq, quoted and best bid-ask spreads decline as the number of posting market makers increases. It also appears that greater capital risks associated with higher minimum quote sizes may cause market makers to widen their spreads. Dealer participation in actively "making the market" also falls as turnover increases. At any instant, nearly one-third of the market makers in a heavily traded equity post noncompetitive prices. While our empirical methods do not disentangle the interplay among dealer concentration, spreads, and volume, we examine whether trade-size economies or order-processing costs could explain these correlations. We find limited evidence that they do.

Section 5.4 analyzes a smaller sample of sixty SEAQ securities divided equally among three market capitalization classes. Conventional transaction cost statistics imply that each capitalization class has best bid-ask spreads comparable to Nasdaq spreads. Our conditional apparent spread measures show that transaction costs for individual securities differ substantially because of differences in the extent of discounting. Some of these differences occur because trade characteristics differ across market capitalization classes. For instance, FTSE-100 equities appear to have lower transaction costs because they have relatively more discounted interdealer trades. Other differences occur because market makers and brokers charge different customers different prices. The median customer trade is never discounted by market makers, but nonregistered dealers give their median customers substantial discounts. We also show that market makers appear unwilling to give each other price breaks over the phone, but do when trading anonymously through interdealer brokers. Finally, we find some evidence that large orders receive greater discounts in less concentrated markets.

5.2   Measuring Transaction Costs in Dealer Markets

Investors incur several types of transaction costs each time they trade. These include commissions, differences between purchase and sale prices, and costs related to the price impact of trades. This paper exclusively analyzes differences between purchase and sales prices. We analyze spreads largely because we do not have detailed data on commissions. In 1991, the exchange estimated that commissions on trades between £50,001 and £100,000 averaged 0.23 percent of price. Smaller round lots paid as much as 6.11 percent, and orders greater than £1,000,000 an average of 0.15 percent.[1] These commissions only accentuate the spread-related size discounts we report below.

Prior theoretical and empirical market microstructure research has devoted considerable effort to modeling how market makers set spreads. Most conceptual models focus on a single market maker or specialist. These models show how factors such as limit order competition and a trade's size affect specialists' spreads. Many models, for instance, conclude that larger trades will be charged larger spreads. In inventory models, this occurs because of inventory risk; in adverse selection models, it occurs because large trades move prices.[2]

Empirical research on the determinants of spreads has struggled with the question of how to estimate transaction costs when transaction prices differ from dealers' posted quotes. Much of this research relies on New York Stock Exchange (NYSE) intraday transaction and quotation data. This research reveals that specialists vary their spreads in systematic ways (e.g., Brock and Kleidon [1992]; McInish and Wood [1992]; and Foster and Viswanathan [1993]). These findings have inspired new theoretical models of trade between different types of investors and market intermediaries.

Fewer papers have modeled the behavior of market makers in dealer quotation markets. Models by Ho and Stoll (1983), Grossman and Miller (1988), Glosten (1992), Madhavan (1992), Biais (1993), Dennert (1993), and others show that strategic interactions among market makers can considerably complicate relationships between spreads and trade characteristics. Consider, for example, the conclusion cited above that specialists will charge large orders larger spreads. In dealership markets, such a policy would give large traders an incentive to split trades among dealers. Absent centralized information on the identities of traders, dealers will have a harder time identifying and pricing informed trades. Recently, Glosten (1994) has shown that minimum tick sizes may similarly constrain dealers' abilities to charge large orders high spreads. His model also provides some intuition for how SEAQ minimum quote sizes may affect spreads. By forcing dealers to accept large and small trades at the same price, SEAQ rules on minimum quote size give market makers incentives to widen spreads. By widening spreads, SEAQ market makers can protect themselves against inventory imbalances and informed trades while simultaneously retaining an option to offer execution within their guaranteed quotes. What is unclear is whether competition will force market makers to offer discounts. Studies of NYSE specialists suggest that they offer only small orders

---

1. *Quality of Markets Review, Summer 1991* (London: London Stock Exchange, 1991), 17–24.
2. Some of these predictions carry over to models of dealer markets. For papers that model inventory risks, see, e.g., Garman (1976); Amihud and Mendelson (1980); and Ho and Stoll (1981, 1983). Admati (1991) surveys papers that model adverse selection risks.

discounts. Large floor trades receive less favorable execution at or outside the bid and ask.[3]

Few studies have examined the relation between quoted prices and transaction prices in dealer markets. Some descriptions of Nasdaq claim that only interdealer or Instinet transactions trade within the quoted spread. A recent study by the LSE's Quality of Markets Group estimated that nearly 35 percent of SEAQ trades occur within the best bid-ask spread.[4] Some researchers speculate that these are interdealer trades. Others interpret this statistic as evidence that SEAQ quoted prices do not contain much information. The LSE's *Quality of Markets Review* and Neuberger and Schwartz (1989) report that not all trades within the spread are dealer trades. These comparisons do not show, however, whether other characteristics also affect discounts. The analysis below shows that while many trades within the best bid-ask spread on SEAQ are interdealer trades, large customer trades also receive favorable execution. Small and very large trades usually do not.[5] We now illustrate how trader identities and other factors affect SEAQ transaction costs.

5.2.1   Cadbury Schweppes: An Introductory Example

We begin our analysis of SEAQ transaction costs by analyzing what conventional transaction cost measures reveal about the cost of trading Cadbury Schweppes, a heavily traded FTSE-100 stock. We analyze Cadbury for several reasons. First, by focusing on a single security we can more clearly describe SEAQ trading rules that might affect transaction costs. Second, during the period we studied Cadbury Schweppes, market makers had to accept trades as large as £100,000—quite large by Nasdaq and SEAQ standards. Third, Cadbury Schweppes shares also trade on Nasdaq as American Depository Receipts (ADRs). This dual trading of Cadbury shares allows us to compare transaction costs in two very similar dealer markets.

The Cadbury SEAQ data come from separate settlement and quotation records maintained by the LSE. The Nasdaq data come from the Institute for the Study of Security Markets. Subsequent sections and an appendix describe these data in greater detail. Table 5.1 provides conventional descriptive statistics on Cadbury transactions during 1991. The top section of the table contains transaction costs statistics developed in prior studies. Following convention, we express each as a percentage of Cadbury's average share price. For comparison, we also convert each to a pound sterling estimate of the spread cost on a median-size SEAQ trade (roughly 1,500 shares). These measures convey very

---

3. Lee (1993) finds liquidity premiums, defined as an absolute difference between trade prices and the bid-ask midpoints, that increase with trade size.
4. See *Stock Exchange Quarterly and Quality of Markets Review: Spring Edition* (London: London Stock Exchange, 1992), 27.
5. SEAQ does not require market makers to offer best execution to very large trades. For additional evidence on SEAQ size discounts, see Breedon (1993); De Jong, Nijman, and Röell (1993); and Hansch and Neuberger (1993).

Table 5.1   SEAQ and Nasdaq Descriptive Statistics for Cadbury Schweppes

Average Transaction Cost Measure	SEAQ		Nasdaq	
	Percent of Price	Cost for Median SEAQ Trade (pounds)	Percent of Price	Cost for Median SEAQ Trade (pounds)
Touch spread[a]	0.85	49.90	0.71	41.68
Roll's spread[b]	0.73	42.86	0.53	31.12
Effective spread[c]	0.72	42.27	0.60	35.23
Effective spread excluding trades outside touch	0.70	41.10	0.58	34.05
Weighted effective spread[d]	0.63	36.99	0.50	29.36
Weighted effective spread excluding trades outside touch	0.54	31.70	0.47	27.59

Percent Distribution of Trades by	SEAQ		Nasdaq	
	Value	Number	Value	Number
Trades outside touch	7.6	2.3	2.3	1.6
Trades at touch	40.8	70.8	65.9	78.3
Trades inside touch	51.6	26.9	31.8	20.1

Bid-Ask Discounts	SEAQ		Nasdaq	
	Average as Percent of Price	Estimated Discount for Median SEAQ Trade (pounds)	Average as Percent of Price	Estimated Discount for Median SEAQ Trade (pounds)
All trades[e]	0.075	4.40	0.052	3.05
Excluding trades outside touch	0.085	4.99	0.063	3.70

Percent Distribution of the Touch by	SEAQ			Nasdaq		
	Minutes Market Is Open	Times When Trades Occur	Value of Trades Occurring	Minutes Market Is Open	Times When Trades Occur	Value of Trades Occurring
Touch < −0.01 pence	0.0	0.0	0.0	0.0	0.2	0.1

	(1)	(2)	(3)	(4)	(5)	(6)
−0.01 ≤ Touch < 0.50 pence	0.0	0.0	0.1	0.1	0.0	0.1
0.50 ≤ Touch < 1.50 pence	0.5	0.7	1.0	8.4	6.3	8.3
1.50 ≤ Touch < 2.50 pence	16.0	17.6	19.6	27.2	36.2	41.5
2.50 ≤ Touch < 3.50 pence	46.5	46.6	45.6	22.9	25.1	24.0
3.50 ≤ Touch < 4.50 pence	26.3	25.2	24.3	39.0	28.5	23.7
4.50 ≤ Touch < 5.50 pence	10.7	9.8	9.3	2.4	3.0	1.7
5.50 ≤ Touch < 6.50 pence	0.0	0.0	0.0	0.0	0.7	0.4
6.50 ≤ Touch < 7.50 pence	0.0	0.0	0.0	0.0	0.1	0.1
Average touch by time (pence)	3.257			2.860		
Intraday standard deviation (pence)	0.547			0.649		
Interday standard deviation (pence)	0.484			0.595		

General Characteristics

	(2)	(5)
Average transaction price (pounds)	3.84	3.96
Number of market makers	16	>25
Capital risk at minimum quote size (pounds)[f]	95,906	15,823
Number of trades	24,967	5,837
Average trade size (pounds)	58,115	42,044
Median trade size (pounds)	5,871	15,840
Total trading volume (1,000 pounds)	1,450,957	241,991

Sources: SEAQ data were drawn from the LSE computer records for the periods January 14–March 18, April 2–June 24, July 1–September 24, and October 14–December 27, 1991. The missing periods are due to retrieval problems. Nasdaq data were drawn from the Institute for the Study of Security Markets tapes for January 1–December 31, 1991. All statistics exclude trades before 8:30 (9:00) A.M. and after 4:30 (4:00) P.M. for SEAQ (Nasdaq).

[a]The touch spread is the average across transactions of 100 (Ask−Bid)/Trade Price.

[b]Roll's spread measure is two times the square root of minus the serial covariance of price changes.

[c]The effective spread is the average across transactions of $2 \times 100 \times |$Trade Price − (Best Ask + Best Bid)/2$|$/Trade Price.

[d]The volume-weighted average of the equation in note c. See Lee and Ready (1991).

[e]The average discount is the average across transactions of $100 \times |$Trade Price − Best Quote$|$/Trade Price, where the Best Quote is the bid (ask) for a customer sell (buy).

[f]Capital risk is calculated based on the average stock price. The minimum quote size for Cadbury Schweppes is twenty-five thousand shares on SEAQ. Exceptions are given for two market-making firms who may post smaller quote sizes. The maximum quote size for Nasdaq trading of Cadbury Schweppes was one thousand ADRs.

different impressions of transaction costs, both on the same exchange (reading down columns) or between exchanges (reading across pairs of columns). SEAQ spread-related cost estimates range from 0.54 to 0.85 percent, a difference of £18 on the average trade. Nasdaq cost estimates range from 0.47 to 0.71, a difference of £13.5. On both exchanges, the difference between the best bid and ask is clearly a weak upper bound on costs. The average discount from the best bid or ask on SEAQ is 0.07 percent, or roughly £4.4 on a median-size trade.

Comparing spreads across exchanges, we find that Nasdaq has lower spread-related transaction costs. The best bid-ask statistics show that on a median-size SEAQ trade, Nasdaq traders save £8.2! The value-weighted Nasdaq measures also show that large Nasdaq trades receive substantial discounts from quoted prices. When one excludes trades outside the best bid-ask and weights spreads by value, however, it appears that there is no substantial difference between SEAQ and Nasdaq. The distribution of trade values about the best bid-ask prices provides one possible explanation for the difference narrowing. Although SEAQ has wider best bid-ask spreads, a larger percentage of large SEAQ trades go through inside the best bid-ask prices. The difference between the SEAQ value-weighted and the unweighted effective spreads suggests that SEAQ transaction costs fall substantially with the size of a trade. The difference between the effective spreads of £5.3 roughly equals the commission on a £2,300 trade.

Although the statistics in table 5.1 suggest that Cadbury traders receive better prices on Nasdaq, these average comparisons mask systematic differences in Nasdaq and SEAQ dealer discount policies. The middle section of table 5.1 shows how the timing of trades affects the cost comparisons in the top section. It reports the percentage distribution of the best bid-ask spread by minutes the markets are open, number of trades, and trade value. On SEAQ, for example, 26.3 percent of the time (two hours and six minutes of a trading day) a trader can expect to pay a four-pence spread. Roughly one-fourth of SEAQ trades and shares transact at this spread. On Nasdaq, however, the best bid-ask spread is around four pence 39 percent of the time, yet few trades or shares transact at this spread. There are several possible explanations for this phenomenon. Nasdaq traders might be in a better position to trade when spread costs are low, or Nasdaq market makers might compete more for trades during high-volume periods. Our general point is that traditional comparisons of average transaction costs do not distinguish between these explanations. In what follows, we propose measures that isolate these differences better.

Before developing our measures, we first describe features of Nasdaq and SEAQ that influence how we construct and interpret our measures. Figures 5.1 and 5.2 display quotation and trading histories for Cadbury on two arbitrarily chosen days, October 16 and 17, 1991. These figures illustrate where trades occurs relative to the best bid and ask on SEAQ and Nasdaq. The solid lines are the best bid and offer. London traders call this the "touch." The dashed vertical lines mark the official open and close on Nasdaq and the unofficial open and close on SEAQ. (The appendix describes the SEAQ data and trading procedures in greater detail.) Figures 5.1A and 5.1B show the unique information we have on SEAQ trades. They display customer orders, interdealer trades, and crossing trades. Figures 5.1C and 5.1D display the Nasdaq data. Like most publicly available data, the Nasdaq data do not identify trade counterparties. Figures 5.1A and 5.1B show that the SEAQ touch does not vary much during the course of the trading day. Most customer trades (dots and triangles) go through at the touch. By contrast, many dealer trades (circles and stars) execute within the touch. The figures also show that SEAQ market makers do not use a fixed tick-size rule when offering discounts. The black stars represent interdealer broker (IDB) trades executed on one of four anonymous electronic bulletin boards. The four IDB systems provide services similar to those offered to Nasdaq dealers by Instinet. Generally, it appears that SEAQ trades are distributed randomly throughout the day, and there are no obvious anomalies when Nasdaq opens. On both days, at least one customer sell order executes outside the touch. These trades seemingly violate SEAQ's best execution rule (see the appendix).

During this period, sixteen SEAQ market makers and over twenty-five Nasdaq market makers posted quotes and took trades. Though not pictured, each SEAQ market maker had a quoted spread of five pence. That is, the difference between their quoted bid and ask prices was five pence. Cadbury market makers maintained this spread virtually the entire year![6] Since the market touch was four pence or less on these two days, no SEAQ market maker ever simultaneously posted at the best bid and best ask. Unfortunately, we do not have similar information for Nasdaq. Other studies, however, suggest that Nasdaq market makers rarely post both the best bid and ask (see Chan, Christie, and Schultz [1995]).

Comparing contemporaneous touch spreads, we see that SEAQ has a slightly larger spread on October 16 and a smaller one on the 17th. These differences are not large enough to cause arbitrage. Figure 5.2 provides information about the size of trades. In each panel, we have scaled the area of the circles to represent the number of shares traded. This figure suggests that, in contrast to the NYSE, some but not nearly all large trades execute inside the touch. The IDB trades and broker trades are also larger than the average customer trade. Finally, the figure suggests that large interdealer trades usually, though not always, execute within the spread.

5.2.2   Estimating Transaction Costs: Adjusted Apparent Spreads

Table 5.1 and figures 5.1 and 5.2 together reveal substantial differences in transaction spreads. The obvious challenge is to devise measures that isolate

---

6. There are a few instances when market makers posted wider spreads (seven, eight, and ten pence) but these are extremely rare.

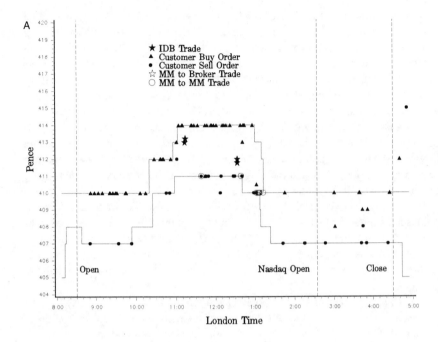

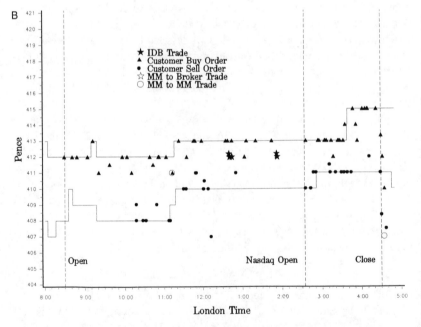

Fig. 5.1   Trade types and best bid-ask, Cadbury Schweppes, 1991. London: *A*, October 16; *B*, October 17. Nasdaq: *C*, October 16; *D*, October 17.

Notes: IDB = interdealer broker; *MM* = market maker.

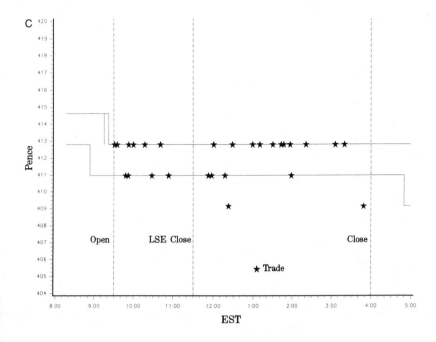

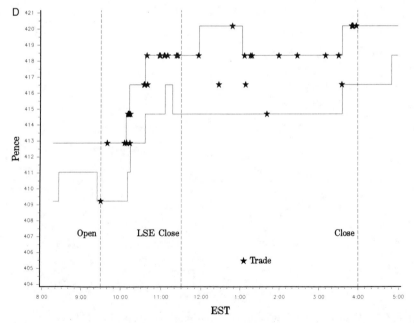

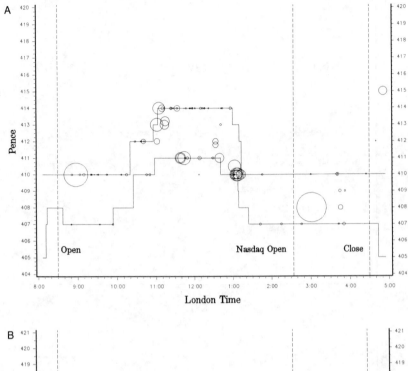

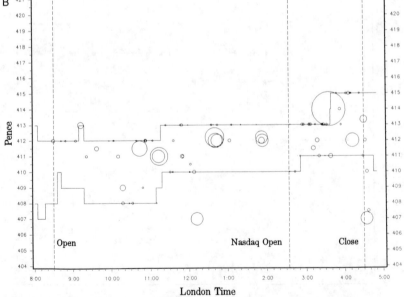

Fig. 5.2   Trade sizes and best bid-ask, Cadbury Schweppes, 1991. London: *A,*
October 16; *B,* **October 17. Nasdaq:** *C,* **October 16;** *D,* **October 17.**
Note: Circle area is proportional to trade size.

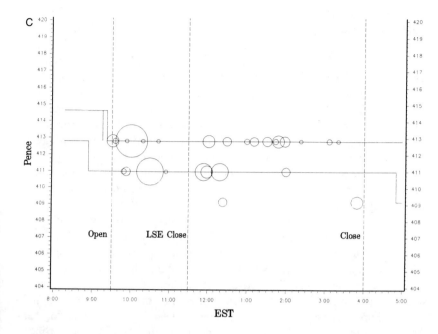

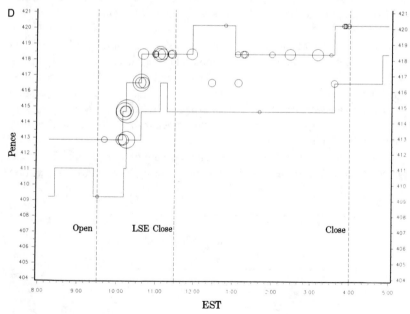

these differences. Demsetz's (1968) original work suggested one should interpret the quoted spread as a security dealer's price for immediacy. In theory, the price of immediacy is the difference between an investor's purchase or sales price and the asset's "true" or "immediate" value. As Demsetz and others note, researchers and dealers rarely know an asset's true value. There is little agreement among researchers, however, on how to define or measure immediate value. The definition we adopt is the instantaneous cost of a round-trip transaction—what we call the apparent cost or *apparent spread* incurred by *simultaneously purchasing and selling shares.* We adopt this definition because it follows Demsetz's concept of immediacy and because it pairs the costs of comparable trades. The obvious practical problem with our definition is that one rarely observes comparable simultaneous buy and sell orders. To explain how we overcome this problem, we briefly summarize other approaches.

Prior researchers have measured transaction costs by averaging best bid-ask spreads or by inferring implicit spreads from neighboring transaction prices. Figure 5.3 illustrates several problems with these approaches. For simplicity, it presumes that the touch is constant. As in figure 5.2, the areas of the circles represent each trade's size. The effective spread at time $t - 1$, $2 \times E_{t-1}$, measures transaction costs as the deviation of price from the touch midpoint. This measure implicitly assumes that the midpoint is the asset's "true value," or that the discount on a reverse transaction would receive the same discount. Since on SEAQ the same dealer rarely posts both the best bid and ask, it is unclear why the touch midpoint is the best way to measure a SEAQ security's true value. Indeed, the Cadbury data reveal that the average of dealers' quotes can differ substantially from the touch midpoint. For instance, occasionally fifteen market makers will be at the ask and only one at the bid. Do these positions signal that the touch midpoint is not the "average" or true price? This question is difficult to answer. We would like in principle to have a measure of transaction costs that incorporates this information, since the positions of dealers may affect their willingness to offer discounts.

Figure 5.3 also displays another popular measure of spread-related transaction costs, those based on differences in neighboring buy and sell transaction

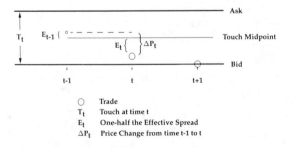

Fig. 5.3   Conventional spread measures

prices. At time t, ΔP_t measures the difference between a small buy and a large sell order. This implicit spread measure has the advantage that it does not require quotation information. The figure, however, reveals a potential drawback. Since it compares the discounts of different-size trades, it can mask size discounts. The same caveat applies to spread measures proposed by Roll (1984) and others. These measures estimate spreads from serial covariances of transaction price changes. Although subsequent research has refined Roll's measure to allow for drifting spreads and dealer inventories, few studies condition these serial covariances on other observable trade characteristics, such as order size. Some studies also have used regression analysis to condition price changes on past price changes and trade characteristics.[7] These regressions, however, usually do not relate price changes to information about the touch or dealers' quotes.

Figure 5.4 illustrates how we propose to use trade characteristics and price information to develop a measure of transaction costs. The figure displays a sell order receiving a discount D_t from the best quoted bid. We define the apparent spread on this transaction, AS_t, as the difference between the transaction price P_t and the quoted *ask*. The apparent spread provides an upper bound on transaction costs because SEAQ's best execution would guarantee a reverse purchase execution at or within the ask. An obvious question is, why is the quoted ask the appropriate benchmark for the reverse (round-trip) transaction? Aside from SEAQ best execution rules, there is no guarantee that a market maker will execute the reverse buy order at the touch.

Since we do not observe the reverse discount, we propose to estimate it. One possible estimate of what a market maker might offer is the discount D on the customer's original sale. If this discount is applied to the ask, we obtain the effective spread. If this discount is applied to a dealer's ask price above the market ask, then we can obtain a price that is outside the touch. This assignment rule therefore can violate the exchange's best execution rule. Since there is little reason to believe that the same dealer will execute the reverse transaction at the same discount, we propose an econometric model of discounts that uses past information to predict what dealers would offer under current conditions. Using this model, we construct an estimate of the reverse transaction discount $\hat{D}$ and then define the round-trip transaction cost as the *adjusted apparent spread*, that is, the difference between the apparent spread and the estimated discount, or $\widehat{AAS} = AS - \hat{D}$.

The key element of our approach is the econometric model that predicts discounts using trade information. Ideally, we should develop this model from a rich theory that predicts how dealers use information to set spreads and discounts. Formally, we would like to know the structure of $D = D(\Omega_t)$, where Ω_t

---

7. Compare Ho and Macris (1984); Glosten (1987); Glosten and Harris (1988); Stoll (1989); Harris (1990); Madhavan and Smidt (1991); Hasbrouck (1991); Lee and Ready (1991); and Lee, Mucklow, and Ready (1993).

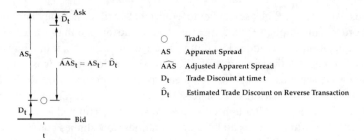

Fig. 5.4   Adjusted apparent spread

represents the market maker's information at the time of trade. Because we are unlikely to observe everything in Ω_t, we must adopt an alternative model. We formulate a conditional prediction model by assuming discounts are random draws from a density

$$(1) \qquad\qquad f(D_t \mid \omega_t).$$

Here f represents the observed density function of discounts, and ω_t represents our information. By examining how the observed conditioning variables ω_t affect f, we hope to identify what factors determine dealer discounts, and thus transaction costs.

In principle, we would use a variety of statistical techniques to estimate how the conditioning variables ω_t affect f. We chose to use quantile regressions. These regressions describe how the quantiles (or percentiles) of D vary with ω_t (see Koenker and Basset [1978]). We chose conditional quantiles over means primarily to minimize the influence of misclassified trades, a problem present in most intraday transaction data sets. To underscore the point that these quantile regressions do not produce "structural" estimates of parameters underlying $D(\Omega_t)$, we suppress the coefficients from the underlying regressions and instead report point predictions and approximate standard errors. To the extent that we have statistical hypotheses, they are that particular variables do not explain observed discounts. In work not reported here, we have explored the robustness of our predictions using split-sample techniques. These checks convince us that the quantile estimates are reasonably accurate for all but very large trades.

5.2.3   Apparent Spreads for Cadbury Schweppes

To date, we have estimated very simple models of discounts and spreads. In future work, we plan to experiment with other conditioning variables, such as the direction of trades. The specifications we report here examine whether and how discounts vary with the trade counterparties (for SEAQ only), the size of trades, and the touch. While previous studies have examined the separate impact of the touch and the size of trades, our specifications allow for interactions between the two. To our knowledge, we are the first to estimate counterparty effects.

Since we do not use conditioning variables that would generate asymmetric discounts, we treat discounts symmetrically by modeling apparent spreads. We assume SEAQ apparent spreads (AS = Touch − Discount) equal

(2) $AS_i = $ Touch $-$ Discount$_i = \sum_{j=0}^{3} [\beta_{0,i} + \beta_{1,i}$ Touch$]$

$\times$ (Trade Size$_i$)$^j + \varepsilon_i$,

where i indexes types of trades (IDB, customer, market-maker, and broker trades), the β's are unknown coefficients, and ε is an unobserved error. In words, the apparent spreads are a polynomial in trade size and interactions with the touch at the time of the trade. We include touch interactions on the right-hand side to allow for the possibility that apparent spreads may depend on the (guaranteed) touch spread. The Nasdaq regressions have a similar structure. They use quartic polynomials in trade size and do not have coefficients that depend on trade types.

Figures 5.5A–5.5C plot the estimated apparent spread quartiles by size of trade, the touch, and trader identities. To simplify comparisons between SEAQ and Nasdaq, we have expressed the apparent spreads as a fraction of the prevailing touch. The vertical differences between the top horizontal curves and the horizontal axis equal the estimated apparent spread divided by the touch. The vertical differences between pairs of similarly shaped curves are the estimated adjusted apparent spreads, our measure of the cost of an instantaneous round-trip transaction. Figure 5.5A displays how the median cost for a SEAQ customer trade depends on the touch and the trade's size. The vertical dashed lines mark the median Cadbury trade size (approximately £4,500) and the largest trade Cadbury market makers must accept at their posted bid or ask prices (approximately £100,000). The median-size customer trade executes at the touch, no matter what the touch. As Cadbury's touch widens from two to three to four pence, the median large customer trade receives deeper and deeper discounts. At four pence, a trade larger than £1,000,000 receives roughly a 25 percent discount (one pence per share, or £2,600 total). These estimates confirm that only very large (usually institutional) trades are likely to receive discounts. Even these large trades, however, are not assured discounts. The graphs also show that trade discounts do not widen at the same rate as the touch. That is, when the touch widens by one pence, the total discount from the bid and the ask does not increase by one pence. This shows that market makers do not use discounts to maintain a constant pence spread.

Figure 5.5B summarizes the variation in customer transaction costs holding the touch constant at three pence (the sample median). The three curves represent the first, second (median), and third apparent spread quartiles. Vertical differences between similar curves again equal estimated adjusted apparent

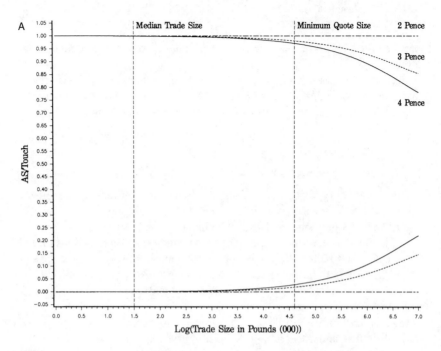

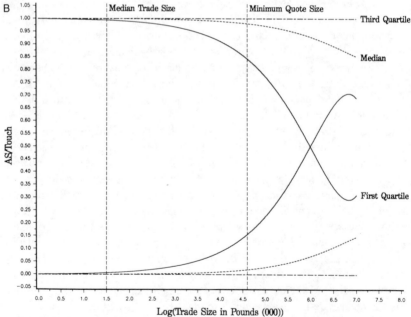

Fig. 5.5   Apparent spread by log(trade size), Cadbury Schweppes, 1991. Customer trades: *A,* London, median apparent spread/touch. *B,* London, apparent spread/touch quartiles. *C,* Nasdaq, apparent spread/touch quartiles. Dealer trades: *D,* London, median apparent spread/touch.

Notes: IDB = interdealer broker; *MM* = market maker.

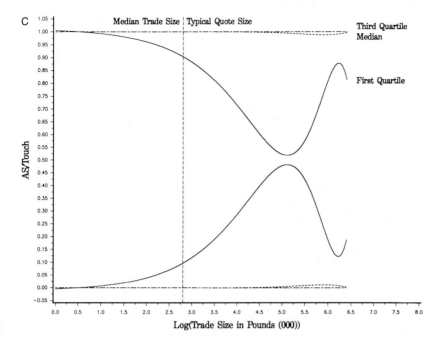

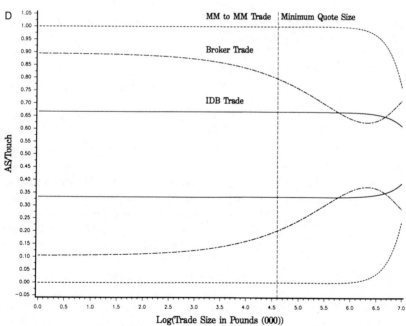

spreads. Note that there is no interquartile difference in apparent spreads at or below the median trade size. In other words, nearly all small retail orders pay the quoted spread. This finding appears at odds with asymmetric information models that predict small uninformed trades will receive more favorable execution. Upper-quartile customer trades appear to receive no discount up to the minimum quote size of £100,000. Surprisingly, beyond the minimum quote size the dispersion in discounts increases. Nearly 25 percent of customer trades larger than £400,000 receive at least 50 percent discount, implying the adjusted apparent spread is zero or negative. The infrequency of large trades, however, reduces the precision of our estimates.

The frequency with which we observe trades of a given type and size is a key determinant of the statistical precision of our estimates. Generally, we observe many more small trades than we do large, and many more trades at three pence than we do at two or four pence. A plot of apparent spreads by trade size also reveals that market makers tend to clump discounts on whole pence, though the exchange does not have tick-size rules. To provide an indication of the precision of our point estimates across ranges of trade values, we calculated standard errors using Chamberlain's (1993) suggested approximations. These estimated standards confirm that the (point) precision of our estimates in figure 5.5B deteriorates as the size of the trade increases. At the median trade size, the standard deviation of the median apparent spread to touch ratio is 0.02. Thus, at a touch of three pence, a 95 percent confidence interval for the median apparent spread is 2.79 to 2.91 pence. For transactions near £150,000, the standard deviation rises to 0.04, by £300,000 it is 0.10, and by £400,000 it is 0.19. Thus, we do not estimate apparent spreads precisely beyond two to three times the minimum quote size (£100,000).

Figure 5.5C shows the estimated distribution of spreads for Nasdaq, holding the touch constant at three pence. We estimate that more than 50 percent of Nasdaq trades execute at the touch and thus receive no discount. Lower-quartile trades receive discounts at most sizes. The Nasdaq quartiles are more curved than SEAQ quartiles, with discounts of 50 percent effectively eliminating the spread for trades over £150,000. At larger sizes, the discount diminishes and then appears to increase. Since we observe few trades in this range, we do not attach much significance to this increase. For now, we tentatively conclude that Nasdaq and SEAQ market makers have roughly comparable discount policies.

Finally, figure 5.5D displays how the median spreads of IDB, market maker–to–market maker, and dealer-to-dealer (or market maker) trades vary with a trade's size. Our calculations assume the touch is three pence. Because the SEAQ data do not identify which of the two SEAQ dealers initiates a trade, we classify dealer trades as buy (sell) orders based on whether the observed price is above (below) the touch midpoint. The vertical dashed line indicates the minimum quote size. Each type of interdeal trade has a median size roughly equal to the minimum quote size. The median market maker–to–

market maker trade below £400,000 pays the full spread. This is perhaps not too surprising, since dealers negotiate these trades over the phone and market makers cannot tell whether the order is for the market maker or a customer. When market makers deal anonymously with each other using IDBs, however, they discount the spread by about one-third, or one pence. This also is not surprising, since IDB users purchase for (sell from) their own account so that they can subsequently sell to (buy from) a customer. SEAQ brokers seem to grant market makers and other brokers deep discounts. This results from an exchange rule requiring that dealers, when acting as a principal in a trade, have to deal at better prices than the touch. The median broker discount reaches a maximum of more than one-third the touch, or one pence, for trades around £540,000. Curiously, we observe few broker trades compared to the number of market maker–to–market maker trades.

5.3   Intersecurity Variations in Quoted and Touch Spreads

The Cadbury example suggests that transaction costs vary systematically with trader identities and order sizes. This leads us to question whether the Cadbury example is representative of SEAQ transaction costs. Ideally we would like to answer this question by using quantile regressions to estimate which factors affect each SEAQ security's adjusted apparent spread. These calculations would allow us to distinguish between security, security class, and exchange-specific variations in transaction costs. Unfortunately, our data and econometric methods currently do not allow us to analyze a large sample of SEAQ securities. The main obstacle we face is the time required to match separate transaction and quotation records. The exchange transaction records, for example, require extensive checking to identify IDB trades and to match "shape" trades (see the appendix).

Although we continue to work toward a longer-term goal of matching all SEAQ quotation and transaction data, this paper examines two narrower SEAQ samples. This section analyzes the fourth quarter 1991 quotation records of 1,887 U.K. and Irish equities. The main advantage of this sample is its broad coverage. These securities accounted for over 95 percent of 1991 SEAQ trading volume. Its main drawback is it contains only quotation information. Consequently, we can make statements only about how quoted prices and volumes vary across securities. Section 5.4 uses matched quotation and transaction data on sixty of these securities to find whether customers pay quoted spreads.

The Cadbury results suggest that we should find differences in spreads across securities, if only because the size of trades and characteristics of traders will vary across securities. The main issue we address here is, are there other factors that may cause residual differences? We can think of several, including the inherent riskiness of securities, the amount of total trading volume, and the number and identities of market makers.

Previous studies of Nasdaq spreads have found significant cross-section variation in best bid-ask spreads. Much of this variation appears related to trading volume, with spreads declining rapidly as share volume increases and dealer concentration decreases. Some researchers interpret these relations as evidence of the benefits of market-maker competition. That is, market makers compete harder when there are more market makers. Other researchers attribute the decline to the high cost of marketing low-volume equities. What is unclear is why dealers of low-volume stocks have high costs. Given the similarities in the SEAQ and Nasdaq quotation systems, we also might expect to see spreads on SEAQ securities fall as trading volume increases. Indeed, we do. This raises the issue, how should one interpret the rate at which spreads decline? Our answer is that the decline reveals the economies of scale in market making.

Several rules introduced by the LSE in the mideighties encourage market-maker competition on SEAQ. First, the exchange allows free entry into market making, provided market makers have adequate capital. Second, the exchange allows market makers to quit or add securities on short notice. Third, the major costs of making markets, the market makers' time and capital, are largely fixed and not sunk costs. Together these conditions suggest that even market makers for small-volume stocks face substantial (potential) competition. Provided there is some slope to the demand for any individual market maker's services, this competition will result in a familiar monopolistic competition equilibrium: competitive entry will make each market maker's demand curve tangent to their average dealing-cost curve. If trading volume in a stock increases, competing market makers will enter, and reestablish the tangency condition. Afterward, each market maker will operate at a higher volume and charge a lower spread (since average dealing costs decline with volume). Thus, in a monopolistically competitive dealer market, the fall in spreads with trading volume reveals the shape of market makers' average dealing cost function and the extent of scale economies (see Bresnahan and Reiss [1991]). Also, this theory predicts that it is the number of actual and not potential competitors that best predicts the decline in spreads. For example, if the number of market makers that could potentially make a market increases from two to ten, we would see no change in spreads. Whereas, if the ten entered, we would see a decrease in spreads.

Table 5.2 and figure 5.6 report how the distribution of quoted spreads and best bid-ask spreads vary across the 1,887 SEAQ equities. We condition spreads on the number of market makers posting quotes, as opposed to the number of market makers eligible to post quotes. We note again that this conditioning does not have a causal interpretation. Instead, we base this conditioning on the monopolistic competition prediction that securities with little trading volume will have few dealers, and that each of these dealers will have higher costs. The spreads underlying the table and figure are quarterly medians of average daily spreads. We calculated a security's average daily spread by aver-

Table 5.2 SEAQ Quote Statistics by Number of Market Makers

Number of Market Makers	Number of Securities	Quoted Spread (% of price) Quartiles			Touch Spread (% of price) Quartiles			Median Cost for 1,000-Share Trade at Touch[a] (pounds)	Median Number of Market Makers at			Median Number of Quote Postings[b] per Day and Market Maker	Median-Minimum Quote Size (pounds)
		1	2	3	1	2	3		Best Ask	Best Bid	Neither		
1	22	6.19	14.84	28.57	6.19	14.83	28.57	57.28	1.00	1.00	0.00	1.00	386
2	551	5.18	9.01	15.38	4.65	8.02	13.95	29.97	2.00	2.00	0.00	1.00	374
3	454	3.76	6.47	11.11	3.12	5.25	9.17	23.82	2.00	2.00	0.00	1.00	454
4	355	3.11	5.51	10.75	2.43	4.31	8.45	19.40	2.74	2.69	0.00	1.00	1,800
5	211	1.68	4.05	7.48	2.32	2.79	5.15	15.55	2.96	2.89	0.00	1.20	3,345
6	158	2.01	2.76	4.50	1.38	2.02	3.70	16.27	3.06	3.00	0.06	1.50	8,052
7	89	1.95	2.68	4.60	1.37	1.91	3.39	19.95	3.13	3.21	0.87	1.71	20,888
8	43	1.68	2.52	3.54	1.22	1.77	2.53	21.04	4.01	3.92	0.77	2.12	23,775
9	34	1.68	2.04	3.32	1.04	1.57	2.31	20.42	4.49	4.03	1.08	3.56	39,026
10	25	1.40	1.82	3.29	0.97	1.44	2.48	14.77	5.39	5.14	1.02	4.20	51,300
11	22	1.53	2.51	3.74	1.10	1.65	2.40	20.17	4.98	4.69	1.44	3.64	61,120
12	30	1.28	1.75	3.31	0.91	1.16	2.13	20.02	4.14	4.30	3.56	5.79	86,310
13	59	1.31	1.57	2.29	0.88	1.29	1.61	19.83	6.57	5.69	2.00	5.46	76,860
14	66	1.28	1.60	2.33	0.79	1.13	1.67	15.54	6.20	5.27	2.87	5.25	137,480
15	53	1.35	1.59	2.31	0.74	1.12	1.65	14.93	5.04	4.71	5.17	6.07	133,310
16	20	1.26	1.43	1.99	0.69	0.90	1.23	13.69	4.85	4.92	6.81	6.03	152,070
17	7	0.95	1.30	1.53	0.69	0.79	0.91	15.01	7.44	6.14	4.37	7.35	142,541

Notes: Based on 1,887 U.K. and Irish equities with more than twenty days of trading activity during the period October 14–December 27, 1991. The number of sample observations exceeds 1,887 because some securities experienced changes in the number of market makers during the sample period. The underlying data are daily averages (8:30 A.M. to 4:30 P.M.) of minute-to-minute quotation histories. Quantiles are computed by calculating medians across days by security and across market-maker concentrations.

[a]The median cost for trade at the touch is estimated as the difference between the touch and the touch midpoint times the value of a thousand-share trade.

[b]Number of quote postings = 1.0 means that one quote was posted at the start of trading and was not changed during the day.

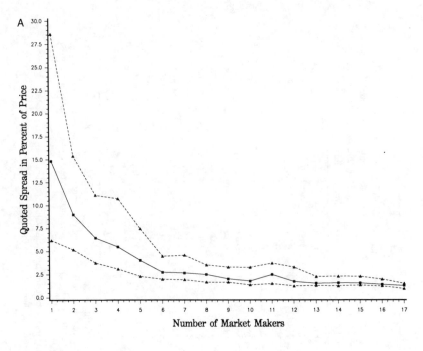

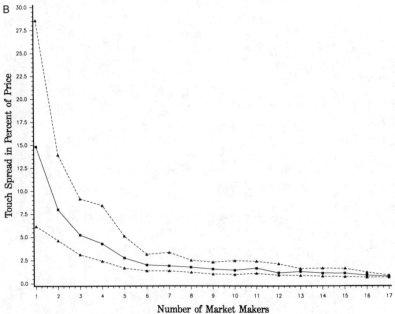

Fig. 5.6   Spread quartiles by number of market makers for 1,887 SEAQ ordinary equities, fourth quarter 1991. *A*, quoted spread. *B*, touch spread.

aging minute-to-minute spreads during the quotation period: 8:30 A.M. to 4:30 P.M. To summarize the variation in these median spreads given a particular number of quoting market makers (i.e., market structure), we report the *quartiles of these medians*. Thus, the median of the median touch spreads of monopoly dealers is 14.83 percent of price. The median touch spread in the highest six monopoly markets is greater than 28.57 percent of price, and so on. Table 5.2 shows that the difference in the median touch spreads for markets with one versus five market makers is 12 percent of price. The interquartile range for five market makers is only 2 percent of price. This large drop suggests there are scale economies at small volumes, and that low-volume dealers have excess capacity. The median minimum quote sizes in the far right column, which are based on the past twelve months' trading volume, confirm that customer transaction costs, as measured by touch spreads, fall with trading volume.

Figure 5.6A graphically displays how quickly the interquartile range and medians of quoted spreads fall as market concentration decreases and share volume increases. Figure 5.6B does the same for touch spreads. The figures and table suggest that dealers achieve most scale economies in markets with minimum quote sizes of £15,000 to £25,000, which roughly corresponds to a market with five to eight dealers. Table 5.2 provides additional evidence. It shows that the median cost of a thousand-share trade executed at the touch falls from £57.28 when trading with a monopolist to around £16–£20 when trading with a dealer with four to seven competitors. The quoted spreads of the largest stocks in our sample, the FTSE-100 equities, exhibit little interquartile dispersion, conditional or unconditional on the number of market makers. A monopolistic competition model would predict that these dealers are near the bottom of their average dealing-cost curves, which roughly corresponds to minimum quote sizes of £50,000 to £75,000. Based on the exchange's rule for calculating minimum quote sizes, this corresponds to an annual trading volume of between £500 and £700 million.

The figure and table 5.2 reveal other interesting regularities. Touch spreads fall at roughly the same rate as quoted spreads. In percentage terms, the gap between the two widens as the number of market makers increases. This perhaps suggests that market makers allow themselves more leeway in moving quotes when they face greater competition. The relation is still somewhat odd, since there is no obvious reason why quoted (as opposed to equilibrium spreads) should change with the number of competitors. Table 5.2 also reveals how dealers' posting behavior may affect the difference between quoted and touch spreads. Columns ten through twelve of table 5.2 show that market makers are usually either at the best bid, best ask, or setting quotes outside the market. For instance, the median security with nine market makers will have four market makers at the best bid and four at the best ask. The gap between the touch and quoted spread suggests the four dealers setting the best ask are not the same four setting the best bid. The remaining market maker straddles both the best bid and ask. By doing so, this market maker avoids most of the inventory and information risks associated with unsolicited trades.

The second to last column of table 5.2 reports the median number of times per day a market maker changes its price quotes. Although we know of no obvious benchmark for this number, we were struck by how infrequently market makers adjust their stated willingness to take trades. One might attribute constant quoted prices to infrequent turnover, yet even FTSE-100 market makers change their quotes less than once per hour! One explanation for these persistent prices is that the large minimum quote sizes substantially increase market makers' capital risk. This risk causes them to widen spreads. By fixing wide spreads, they retain the option to vary transaction prices without changing quotes. We now consider how frequently they offer discounts from the touch spread.

5.4   Further Evidence on Apparent Spreads

The analyses in sections 5.2 and 5.3 reveal substantial variation in spreads by security, trader, time, and trade size. This section estimates an econometric model that isolates the contribution of these factors to apparent spreads. Our data sample consists of fourth-quarter 1991 quotation and transaction histories for sixty SEAQ securities. We randomly chose the sixty securities so that they would equally represent large (i.e., FTSE-100), medium, and small capitalization SEAQ securities. We limited the sample to sixty securities because of the time required to match and check quotation and trade data. The fourth quarter is the most recent we have (see the appendix).

The three market capitalization classes roughly divide the sixty securities into three volume, market-structure, and price-size classes. Tables 5.3 and 5A.1 provide information on these classes and the sample securities. Comparing tables 5.2 and 5.3, it appears that the sample represents the range of SEAQ dealer concentration and trading volumes. During the mandatory quotation period, the FTSE-100 securities averaged 106 trades per day, totaling £7,156,000, compared to 13 trades totaling £646,000 for medium equities and 5 trades totaling £83,000 for smaller equities. The average number of market makers ranges from 12.6 for FTSE-100 equities, to 6.2 and 4.7 for medium and small equities. The quoted and touch spread statistics in table 5.3 also span those in table 5.2.

Table 5.3 provides median quoted, touch, effective, and adjusted apparent spreads for each security. Although these medians mask intrasecurity variation in transaction costs, they reveal considerable variation in spreads within and across size classes. Most of this intersecurity variation occurs because these securities have different security prices, and not because they have different pence spreads. For instance, Cadbury Schweppes (CBRY) has median touch, apparent, and effective spreads of three pence. So does Abbey National (ANL). The percentage differences in table 5.3 occur because Abbey's price is two-

Table 5.3 SEAQ Median Spreads as a Percentage of Average Trade Price

FTSE-100 Size Class					Medium-Size Class					Smaller-Size Class				
Security Code	Adjusted Apparent Spread	Touch Spread	Effective Spread	Quoted Spread	Security Code	Adjusted Apparent Spread	Touch Spread	Effective Spread	Quoted Spread	Security Code	Adjusted Apparent spread	Touch Spread	Effective Spread	Quoted Spread
BT.A	0.56	0.56	0.56	0.83	SVC	1.05	1.26	0.84	1.69	ANU	4.45	4.45	4.45	5.93
GUIN	0.67	0.67	0.67	1.17	BOS	1.24	1.24	1.24	1.55	SEP	3.63	3.63	3.63	6.05
MKS	0.70	0.70	0.70	1.05	THK	1.07	1.29	1.07	2.15	LILY	2.74	4.12	2.74	5.49
RTZ	0.77	0.77	0.77	1.35	BNZL	2.87	3.44	2.29	4.59	BDN	2.65	2.65	2.65	3.53
LLOY	0.78	1.05	0.78	1.31	COST	4.59	4.59	4.59	7.64	BYNS	3.31	3.31	3.31	4.96
ANL	1.08	1.08	1.08	1.43	WOLV	1.21	1.38	1.21	1.73	OWN	1.31	1.75	1.31	1.75
SUN	0.96	0.96	0.96	1.28	SCPA	1.19	1.79	1.19	2.39	SNGT	0.99	1.49	0.99	1.49
CBRY	0.73	0.73	0.73	1.22	HETH	1.01	1.42	1.01	1.42	GDG	1.62	3.24	1.62	3.24
WHIT	0.68	0.68	0.68	1.13	PFG	1.12	1.12	1.12	1.56	ROG	12.15	18.23	12.15	18.23
LGEN	0.94	1.08	0.81	1.34	PFA	0.76	1.02	0.81	1.27	WHWY	6.61	6.61	6.61	13.22
ABF	0.67	0.67	0.67	1.12	LEIH	1.13	1.51	1.13	1.89	EXG	4.31	6.47	4.31	8.62
UBIS	0.78	0.78	0.78	1.30	BRFD	8.95	8.95	8.95	13.43	SMN	6.27	6.27	6.27	9.41
RR.	1.53	1.53	1.53	2.29	SPX	1.21	1.62	1.21	2.02	MSY	2.46	2.95	2.46	3.93
RBOS	1.48	1.77	1.18	2.37	BODD	1.87	2.49	1.87	3.11	SMP	11.07	11.07	11.07	16.60
RMC	0.93	1.31	0.93	1.87	SREL	2.29	2.29	2.29	3.06	RHT	3.10	3.10	3.10	5.17
WILC	1.13	1.50	1.13	1.88	BLGH	2.40	2.40	2.40	3.20	HAMP	5.26	5.26	5.26	7.89
TATE	0.80	0.80	0.80	1.33	FRG	1.61	2.14	1.61	2.68	PDG	2.80	2.80	2.80	2.80
AW	0.85	1.14	0.85	1.42	LVLL	11.99	11.99	8.99	14.99	ELWK	8.59	8.59	8.59	11.45
NFDS	0.55	0.55	0.55	0.92	THT	1.60	1.60	1.60	2.13	COI	14.52	18.16	10.89	18.16
NFC	1.36	1.36	1.36	2.27	ATV	2.48	3.47	2.48	4.96	BFG	4.85	7.28	4.85	9.70
Overall	0.71	0.86	0.57	1.14	Overall	1.31	1.75	1.31	2.19		2.28	2.28	2.28	3.43

Source: Data were drawn from the LSE's computer records for the period October 14–December 27, 1991.

thirds Cadbury's price. Although on other exchanges the fixed spread might occur because of tick-size rules, the LSE does not regulate tick sizes. Thus, it is puzzling that absolute SEAQ spreads do not vary more with price. We also observe that the variation here is similar, though perhaps more substantial, than that reported for Nasdaq firms by Stoll (1989). He reports spreads for Nasdaq/ National Market System stock size deciles. They range from 1.2 to 6.9 percent of price. A recent study by Chan, Christie, and Schultz (1995) using a more recent time period reports higher average percentage spreads for large Nasdaq stocks.[8]

The within-class variation in spreads and discounts in table 5.3 does not appear related to dealer concentration or volume. Compare, for example, the two oil companies, Richmond Oil and Gas (ROG) and Crossroads Oil (COI). They have the same touch and the same number of market makers. Richmond, however, has a much greater median discount. The greater discount granted the median Richmond trade may reflect Richmond's larger average trade size. Yet, if trade size explains this difference, then why do we not observe greater differences between Richmond and other securities?

As suggested by the analyses in sections 5.2 and 5.3, the interclass differences in spreads might reflect differences in trade counterparties and the volume of trade. Table 5.4 reports information on the distribution of trade counterparties and trade sizes for each of the three size classes. Most trades in each class are "customer bargains," that is, trades where a retail customer is a counterparty. Market makers execute between 60 and 75 percent of these trades. This is somewhat surprising, since the exchange has more than three hundred brokers and just twenty-seven market makers. When brokers do trade with customers, they typically execute large transactions. Relative to other trades, we rarely observe agency crosses, or customer-to-customer trades. Curiously, these trades occur more frequently among smaller (less liquid) issues. The average FTSE-100 equity has 106 customer trades per day, which vastly exceeds the number of customer trades for medium (13) and small (5) equities. Although the number of trades per day differs substantially, the average and median trade sizes do not.[9] Thus, this table suggests that average trade sizes alone do not explain differences in median spreads.

The next section of table 5.4 examines whether interdealer trade discounts differ. If particular types of interdealer trades receive large discounts, then we might expect this to affect average spreads. As a group, the FTSE-100 sample equities have considerably more interdealer trades than either the medium or small equities. Table 5.3, however, shows that the smaller equities receive greater percentage discounts. Thus, the total volume of interdealer trades does

8. Several studies report lower spreads for NYSE stocks. For instance, Kleidon and Werner (1993) report an average quoted spread of 0.6 percent for S&P 100 stocks in 1991.
9. Median trade sizes (not reported in table 5.4) are FTSE-100 £3,744, medium-size £4,550, and small equities £2,625.

Table 5.4   SEAQ Trading Volume by Type of Trade

Type of Trade	FTSE-100 Size Class			Medium-Size Class			Small-Size Class		
	Number of Trades	Pound-Volume (% of total)	Average Trade Size (1,000 pounds)	Number of Trades	Pound-Volume (% of total)	Average Trade Size (1,000 pounds)	Number of Trades	Pound-Volume (% of total)	Average Trade Size (1,000 pounds)
Customer trades									
MM sells to customer	39,333	28.9	54	6,922	35.7	42	1,990	37.0	26
Customer sells to MM	67,471	33.1	36	6,791	40.2	49	3,185	36.5	16
Dealer sells to customer	487	1.2	183	230	3.1	111	32	3.0	133
Customer sells to dealer	557	1.5	201	121	2.4	161	32	4.4	193
Customer sells to customer	222	0.7	229	113	1.8	130	88	12.8	203
Total volume	108,070	65.4	44	14,177	83.2	48	5,327	93.7	25
Interdealer trade									
MM sells to MM	3,400	10.0	216	431	3.4	64	107	1.4	19
IDB trades	8,168	19.6	176	783	9.9	94	125	3.5	39
MM sells to dealer	1,401	2.5	132	241	2.5	87	52	1.0	26
Dealer sells to MM	1,500	2.5	123	105	0.9	73	32	0.4	16
Dealer sells to dealer	3	0.0	109	2	0.1	229	0	0.0	0
Total volume	14,472	34.6	176	1,562	16.8	83	316	6.3	28
All trades	122,542	£7,348,199	60	15,739	£821,199	52	5,643	£140,049	25

Source: Data were drawn from the LSE's computer records for the period October 14–December 27, 1991.

Notes: The number of trades is cumulative for the entire sample period and includes all firms in each group. *IDB* = interdealer broker; *MM* = market maker.

not obviously appear related to discounts. Table 5.4, however, also shows that the four IDB systems account for an appreciable fraction of total interdealer trades. This suggests that market makers can take advantage of discounts offered on electronic systems that are not offered over the phone. Together, these results suggest that, while differences in the mix of customer and interdealer trades can explain some variation in spreads and discounts, they are not the only sources of variation.

Table 5.5 describes how median apparent spreads and discounts differ with trade counterparties. To facilitate comparison, it contains apparent spreads and discounts expressed as fractions of the prevailing touch. No adjustment is made for differences in the size of trades or trading volume. As in the Cadbury example, the median trade between a customer and a market maker receives no discount. The median customer trade through a broker does receive a discount. These discounts are small for FTSE-100 securities and large (one-quarter to one-third of the touch) for medium- and small-size class securities. Customer crosses receive large discounts. This is not too surprising, since these trades usually involve large institutions swapping equity "baskets." Median interdealer trades receive modest discounts, more so in the medium and smaller equity size classes. Most IDB trades and trades between dealers occur at or close to touch midpoints.[10] Infrequent dealer crosses usually occur at one-half the touch. The table also shows that asymmetries exist. For example, the median discount on a medium-class customer buy from a dealer is 25 percent of the touch. The corresponding discount for a customer sell is 8 percent. This asymmetry reinforces our earlier point that dealer discounts may have little to do with the touch midpoint.

Following the Cadbury Schweppes analysis, we can use quantile regressions to decompose apparent spreads for these sixty securities into volume, trader, and security-specific components. In principle, we could proceed by estimating separate regressions for each security. In practice, this approach is computationally and descriptively unwieldy. We instead estimated separate models for each size class. These specifications include security fixed effects. Additionally, because spreads differ across securities in relation to the security's price, we scaled the apparent and touch spreads by security prices. Experimentation with functional forms led us to the following specification describing customer trades for security j:

$$(3) \qquad \frac{AS_j}{P_j} = \beta_0 + \frac{\text{Touch}_j}{P_j} \times \left[\theta_j + \beta_{00} \frac{\text{Touch}_j}{P_j} \right.$$
$$\left. + \sum_{i=1}^{4} \left[\beta_i + \beta_{0i} \frac{\text{Touch}_j}{P_j} \right] (\text{Trade Size})^i \right] + \varepsilon.$$

---

10. The negative adjusted apparent spreads occur because we separately estimate median spreads and discounts.

Table 5.5   SEAQ Median Apparent Spreads and Discounts by Type of Trade (percentage of touch)

Type of Trade	FTSE-100 Size Class			Medium-Size Class			Smaller-Size Class		
	Apparent Spread	Discount	Adjusted Apparent Spread	Apparent Spread	Discount	Adjusted Apparent Spread	Apparent Spread	Discount	Adjusted Apparent Spread
Customer trades									
MM sells to customer	1.00	0.00	1.00	1.00	0.00	1.00	1.00	0.00	1.00
Customer sells to MM	1.00	0.00	1.00	1.00	0.00	1.00	1.00	0.00	1.00
Dealer sells to customer	1.00	0.02	0.98	0.75	0.08	0.67	0.75	0.00	0.75
Customer sells to dealer	0.98	0.00	0.98	0.92	0.25	0.67	1.00	0.25	0.75
Customer sells to customer	0.75	0.25	0.50	0.60	0.40	0.20	0.75	0.25	0.50
Interdealer trades									
MM sells to MM	1.00	0.00	1.00	1.00	0.00	1.00	1.00	0.00	1.00
IDB trades	0.50	0.50	0.00	0.42	0.58	−0.16	0.50	0.50	0.00
MM sells to dealer	0.50	0.50	0.00	0.58	0.67	−0.09	0.64	0.50	0.14
Dealer sells to MM	0.50	0.50	0.00	0.33	0.42	−0.09	0.50	0.36	0.14
Dealer sells to dealer	0.75	0.25	0.50	0.73	0.27	0.46	NA	NA	NA
Median touch spread	3 pence			4 pence			2 pence		

Source: Data were drawn from the LSE's computer records for the period October 14–December 27, 1991.

Notes: Reported numbers are medians across trades for all securities in each group. *IDB* = interdealer broker; *MM* = market maker.

In words, we represent the conditional quantiles of apparent spreads as a quartic in the trade's pound value interacted with the touch and the square of the touch. The coefficient β_0 is the apparent spread when the touch is zero. The coefficient θ_j is a security-specific fixed effect that captures differences in discounts from the touch across securities. The polynomial in size and the squared touch give added flexibility to the shape of the conditional median discount function. To capture differences in customer and noncustomer trades, we included additional zero-one dummy variables interacted with the touch and the touch squared when the trade involved an IDB, a dealer, or two market makers.

Table 5.6 summarizes the results of the conditional median regressions for each size class. The first panel describes the fit. While there is no natural measure of fit, the average absolute error is small, and the conditional medians explain about 60 percent of the variation in apparent spreads (over price). Figure 5.7 plots actual versus fitted values for the medium-size class. It shows that the model does reasonably well explaining the substantial variation in apparent spreads. The security-specific fixed effects explain little of the variation in apparent spreads. In future work, we plan to investigate whether there are more complicated security-specific size and trader effects. The other three panels in table 5.6 suggest that the model explains a large fraction of the variation across securities, but also that there are exceptions. The interquartile range statistics (columns 3 and 6) show that trade size, touch, and trade type explain variation in apparent spreads. The large absolute errors and standard deviations show, however, that there are outlying spreads the model does not explain. We do not have an explanation for these unusual spreads, although most occur because of trades outside the quoted spread. These observations may represent match or coding errors.

Figures 5.8A–5.8C display estimated conditional median apparent spreads for customer trades by size class. The vertical distance between the upper curves and the horizontal axis is the estimated apparent spread. As in the Cadbury example, the vertical distance between similar curves equals the adjusted apparent spread. Each median is evaluated at the average of the firm effects. Figure 5.8A plots median adjusted apparent spreads for FTSE-100 equities as the touch ranges from 0.5 to 1.5 percent of price. These estimates are similar to those for Cadbury. Medium and large trades (£75,000–£500,000) receive only slight discounts when the touch is 0.5 percent of price. As the touch widens, the median FTSE-100 trade obtains a greater discount.

Figures 5.8B and 5.8C repeat the format of figure 5.8A for medium- and small-size equities. The sample average touches are 1.3 percent of price for the medium-size class and 2.3 percent of price for the small class. For the medium-size class, median spreads fall monotonically as the size of the trade increases. The same is true for the small-size class, but the decline is less pronounced. For instance, when the touch is 1 percent of price, trades greater than £4,500 receive virtually no discount. Table 5.3 shows that a 1 percent touch-to-price

Table 5.6   **Summary of Apparent Spread Quantile Regressions**

		FTSE-100 Size Class	Medium-Size Class	Smaller-Size Class
Sample size		122,542	15,722	5,546
Parameters		42	42	42
Apparent spread/transaction price mean (%)		0.83	3.09	3.73
Apparent spread/transaction price median (%)		0.82	3.30	4.00
Apparent spread/transaction price standard deviation (%)		0.44	3.86	3.45
Quantile standard error		0.25	1.38	1.34
Average error		−0.05	−0.20	−0.30
Average absolute error		0.10	0.47	0.50

					Regression Error		
Security Code	Median AS/P (1)	Standard Deviation of AS/P (2)	Interquartile Range of AS/P (3)	Quantile Regression Average Absolute Error (4)	Standard Deviation (5)	Interquartile Range (6)	$(1 - x^2)$ $x = (5)/(2)$ (7)
			FTSE-100 Size Class				
BT.A	0.51	0.26	0.28	0.05	0.21	0.00	0.35
GUIN	0.61	0.30	0.41	0.10	0.19	0.14	0.60
MKS	0.69	0.25	0.19	0.07	0.19	0.00	0.42
RTZ	0.75	0.29	0.75	0.09	0.21	0.00	0.48
LLOY	0.79	0.31	0.43	0.11	0.21	0.12	0.54
ANL	1.05	0.91	0.36	0.04	0.20	0.00	0.95
SUN	0.90	0.44	0.40	0.18	0.38	0.26	0.25
CBRY	0.73	0.28	0.29	0.09	0.21	0.04	0.44
WHIT	0.66	0.27	0.38	0.09	0.19	0.18	0.50
LGEN	1.00	0.42	0.36	0.14	0.35	0.19	0.31
ABF	0.65	0.31	0.42	0.14	0.26	0.21	0.30
UBIS	0.78	0.30	0.29	0.11	0.22	0.13	0.46
(continued)							

Table 5.6   (continued)

Security Code	Median AS/P (1)	Standard Deviation of AS/P (2)	Interquartile Range of AS/P (3)	Quantile Regression Average Absolute Error (4)	Regression Error Standard Deviation (5)	Regression Error Interquartile Range (6)	$(1 - x^2)$ $x=(5)/(2)$ (7)
RR.	1.47	0.55	0.76	0.12	0.35	0.00	0.60
RBOS	0.64	0.59	0.64	0.27	0.50	0.35	0.28
RMC	0.98	0.48	0.53	0.19	0.40	0.19	0.31
WILC	1.08	0.49	0.61	0.21	0.36	0.29	0.46
TATE	0.77	0.31	0.32	0.10	0.23	0.06	0.45
AW.	0.92	0.94	0.39	0.12	0.27	0.03	0.92
NFDS	0.57	0.21	0.31	0.06	0.13	0.00	0.62
NFC	1.35	0.50	0.79	0.15	0.31	0.00	0.62
Medium-Size Class							
SVC	1.05	0.35	0.45	0.11	0.23	0.01	0.57
BOS	1.20	0.37	0.44	0.14	0.28	0.16	0.43
THK	1.13	0.59	0.75	0.22	0.44	0.23	0.44
BNZL	2.56	1.29	1.50	0.47	0.82	0.59	0.60
COST	4.37	1.66	2.57	0.78	1.33	1.16	0.36
WOLV	1.20	0.40	0.47	0.20	0.35	0.19	0.23
SCPA	1.30	0.67	0.64	0.30	0.52	0.34	0.40
HETH	1.02	0.34	0.42	0.18	0.31	0.21	0.17
PFG	1.06	0.39	0.39	0.21	0.34	0.25	0.24
PFA	0.76	0.48	0.63	0.27	0.43	0.30	0.20
LEIH	1.09	0.47	0.66	0.23	0.36	0.36	0.41
BRFD	7.41	2.85	3.82	1.14	1.95	1.48	0.53
SPX	1.36	0.56	0.75	0.22	0.36	0.38	0.59
BODD	1.82	0.81	1.22	0.32	0.52	0.50	0.59
SREL	2.23	0.84	1.34	0.38	0.67	0.69	0.36
BLGH	2.36	0.85	0.27	0.51	0.81	0.76	0.09

FRG	1.57	0.69	0.97	0.40	0.60	0.53	0.24
LVLL	13.95	7.11	9.39	2.22	5.31	2.78	0.44
THT	1.45	0.46	0.60	0.13	0.27	0.01	0.66
ATV	2.67	1.21	1.44	0.45	0.85	0.47	0.51
Smaller-Size Class							
ANU	3.69	1.63	1.67	0.76	1.31	0.85	0.35
SEP	3.59	1.41	0.89	0.83	1.19	1.25	0.29
LILY	1.80	0.94	1.49	0.36	0.60	0.46	0.59
BDN	8.22	2.90	4.61	1.15	1.93	2.07	0.56
BYNS	3.17	2.23	2.79	0.73	1.41	0.56	0.60
OWN	1.71	2.05	1.28	0.25	0.61	0.00	0.91
SNGT	1.02	0.37	0.49	0.16	0.34	0.00	0.16
GDG	4.23	2.15	4.16	1.04	1.83	1.17	0.28
ROG	6.45	2.39	1.61	0.94	1.60	1.23	0.55
WHWY	6.45	2.59	1.83	1.00	1.89	0.91	0.47
EXG	2.37	0.80	0.06	0.03	0.68	0.01	0.28
SMN	6.25	1.99	0.86	1.17	1.94	2.45	0.05
MSY	1.29	0.44	0.86	0.18	0.37	0.31	0.29
SMP	12.50	5.30	5.69	3.00	4.43	3.74	0.30
RHT	1.73	2.65	4.44	0.71	1.47	0.52	0.69
HAMP	3.47	5.28	3.52	1.11	1.82	1.62	0.88
PDG	2.96	3.57	1.86	0.61	1.41	0.51	0.84
ELWK	4.17	2.48	2.86	0.89	1.59	0.75	0.59
COI	1.82	1.45	0.91	0.17	0.31	0.22	0.95
BFG	2.39	1.64	1.37	0.64	0.68	0.02	0.83

Note: The median apparent spreads in table 6.5 differ because they are median spreads divided by average price.

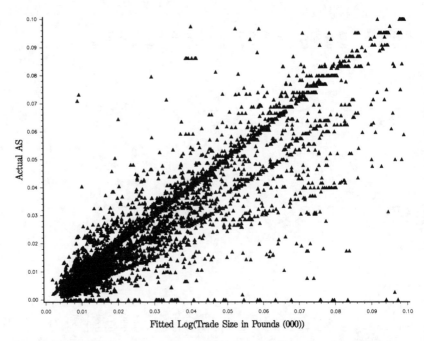

Fig. 5.7   Apparent spread by log(trade size) for a medium size class sample, fourth quarter 1991. Actual apparent spread versus median predicted apparent spread.
Note: AS = apparent spread.

ratio is at the low end of medium- and small-size class spreads. The median FTSE-100 trade receives a larger discount the wider the touch, although for the very largest trades (not pictured) there is evidence that such discounts disappear. These differences in discounts across size classes suggest that large orders have either very different competitive consequences or cost consequences for market makers.

Figure 5.8D shows the estimated apparent spreads granted by dealers of FTSE-100 securities, holding the touch constant at 1 percent of price. Again, these results parallel those in the Cadbury example. Dealer trades have a profile similar to customer discounts, though the discount levels differ. Market makers do not discount the median trade. Brokers discount the spread by one-third when dealing with each other, and IDB trades execute at roughly the touch midpoint. Translated into adjusted apparent spreads and not adjusting for the direction of trades, this corresponds to a one-third broker-to-broker spread and no IDB spread.

5.5   Conclusions

This study used unique SEAQ transaction and quotation data to document SEAQ spreads and market-maker discounts. To the best of our knowledge, this is the first study to account simultaneously for differences by type of trade, trade volume, and security. We began by first developing a new measure of transaction costs, the adjusted apparent spread. This measure calculates the hypothetical cost of an (immediate) round-trip transaction using information on dealers' quotes and investors' transactions. Specifically, we used quantile regressions to model how these spreads varied with trade, trader, and security characteristics. Our estimates reveal that medium to large trades on average receive discounts from the touch spread. These discounts increase, the wider the touch. Small and very large trades pay the touch (and sometimes more). Dealers and market makers price customer trades differently. Market makers discount only very large trades; dealers regularly discount medium and large trades. Market makers rarely discount trades with other market makers over the phone, but do so when trading anonymously using IDBs.

The practice of discounting the touch raises many fascinating questions that need further study. We would like to develop theoretical models that explain why dealers grant discounts and how discounts affect spreads. We also would like to understand why dealers link these discounts to size. The pattern we observe suggests that neither simple asymmetric information nor inventory risk models can easily explain why dealers widen spreads and then selectively discount. The anonymous role of IDBs in interdealer trades also deserves further study. Finally, it would be useful to develop a monopolistic competition model of market making that recognizes how market makers spread their dealing costs across securities.

Our empirical analysis is preliminary and leaves many issues untouched or partially addressed. We clearly should estimate adjusted apparent spreads using information about who originates trades. We also need to extend the data samples to explore whether dealers individually have different discount policies. Other market-maker information also should enter our regressions. For instance, although we condition on the touch at the time of trade, we do not control for market depth at the bid and the ask, or past information. Additional variables might include market indexes, and capital or price risk measures.

Finally, our findings suggest that researchers should not use average spreads to measure the efficiency of a market. Instead, one should compare measures that hold constant characteristics that market makers "price." While our research does not provide an analytical understanding of how dealers decide on quoted and transaction prices, it provides a place to begin.

Appendix

Quotation and Transaction Data

The Cadbury Schweppes Nasdaq transaction data come from the Institute for the Study of Security Markets. On Nasdaq, Cadbury Schweppes shares

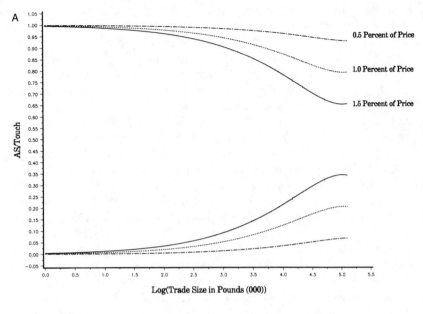

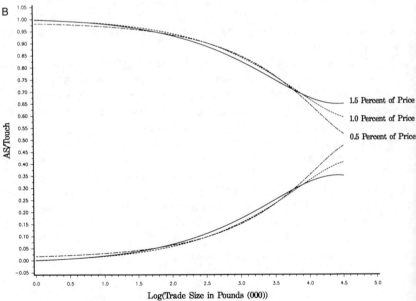

Fig. 5.8   Apparent spread by log(trade size) and touch, fourth quarter 1991. Customer trades, median apparent spread/touch: *A,* FTSE-100 size class sample; *B,* medium-size class sample; *C,* small-size class sample. Dealer trade median AS/ touch: *D,* FTSE-100 size class sample.

Notes: AS = apparent spread; *IDB* = interdealer broker; *MM* = market maker.

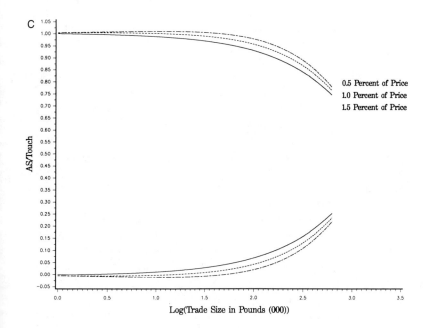

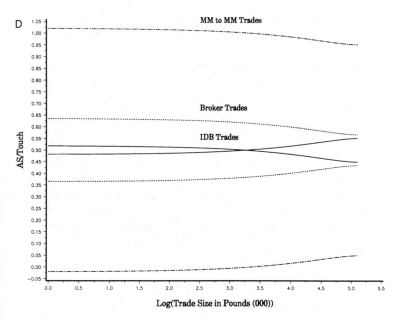

trade as ADRs. We converted the Nasdaq shares to pound-equivalent shares using daily FT-Actuaries foreign exchange rates quoted in London.

The SEAQ data come from the Quality of Markets Group at the LSE. Both the SEAQ transactions and quotations data required extensive editing to match samples and dealer codes. For the Cadbury analysis, we use all overlapping trade and quotation data. These data cover January 14 to March 18, April 2 to June 24, July 1 to September 24, and October 14 to December 31. In sections 5.3 and 5.4 we use October 14 to December 31. The quotation data cover two thousand U.K. and Irish ordinary shares. Some securities are missing data because of retrieval problems, new listings, delistings, or trading halts. SEAQ rules require market makers to quote guaranteed prices and volumes between 8:30 A.M. and 4:30 P.M. London time. Dealers sometimes post prices for up to one-half hour before the mandatory open and close. These quotes are not binding. During the mandatory quote period, market makers must accept trades as large as 2.5 percent of the security's previous twelve months' average daily trading volume. Dealers must also offer "best execution." During 1991, this meant SEAQ market makers had to execute trades at less than the minimum quote size or inside the prevailing touch. Market makers away from the touch had to execute orders at the touch price (or better) or transfer the order to another market maker.

We obtained transaction data for 907 larger U.K. and Irish securities. Approximately 840 of these equities appear in the quotation sample. The transaction data come from end-of-day settlement reports filed with the Central Checking Section of the LSE. These reports do not necessarily reproduce the original ticker tape. Each trade has two time stamps, one reported by the seller and one by the buyer. We use the seller's time stamp unless it indicates a trade outside the prevailing touch. If the seller's time stamp would classify the trade as outside the touch, we check the buyer's time stamp. If the buyer's time stamp puts the trade at or within the touch, we use the buyer's time. If neither time stamp appears valid, we use the seller's time. This reduces the number of trades that execute outside the touch, but does not eliminate them. Trades outside the touch are sometimes "average price" basket trades. Dealers execute baskets using prearranged pricing formulas. The data also contain coding anomalies. The most significant are "shapes." Shapes occur when a dealer matches several customer orders with one (sometimes two) other customer order(s). These appear in the data as a series of unbalanced customer transactions.

Pilot Sample with Quotes and Transactions

We constructed the sample of sixty securities by randomly sampling names from a list of all SEAQ equities. We first assigned securities on this list to market capitalization classes based on their March 31, 1991, market capitalization.[11] We then randomly sampled within classes, rejecting any security lacking

---

11. *Quality of Markets Companies Book 1991* (London: London Stock Exchange, 1991), table 1, "1000 largest listed UK companies by market valuation," 19–38.

complete data. We also required that it have a minimum quote size of at least two thousand shares and more than seven hundred trades between March 31, 1990, and March 31, 1991. We chose the twenty FTSE-100 firms so that they would overlap with previous LSE studies.

Table 5A.1 provides additional information on the sixty firms.

References

Admati, A. 1991. The Information Role of Prices: A Review Essay. *Journal of Monetary Economics* 48, no. 3:347–61.

Amihud, Y., and H. Mendelson. 1980. Dealership Markets: Market-Making with Inventory. *Journal of Financial Economics* 8:31–53.

Biais, B. 1993. Price Formation and Equilibrium Liquidity in Fragmented and Centralized Markets. *Journal of Finance* 48:157–85.

Breedon, F. J. 1993. Intraday Price Formation on the London Stock Exchange. Financial Markets Group Discussion Paper no. 158, London School of Economics.

Bresnahan, T. F., and P. C. Reiss. 1991. Entry and Competition in Concentrated Markets. *Journal of Political Economy* 99:977–1009.

Brock, W. A., and A. W. Kleidon. 1992. Periodic Market Closure and Trading Volume: A Model of Intraday Bids and Asks. *Journal of Economic Dynamics and Control* 16:451–89.

Chamberlain, G. 1993. Quantile Regression, Censoring, and the Structure of Wages. Working paper, Economics Department, Harvard University.

Chan, K. C., W. G. Christie, and P. H. Schultz. 1995. Market Structure and the Intraday Pattern of Bid-Ask Spreads for NASDAQ Securities. *Journal of Business* 68:35–60.

De Jong, F., T. Nijman, and A. Röell. 1993. A Comparison of the Cost of Trading French Shares on the Paris Bourse and on SEAQ International. Financial Markets Group Discussion Paper no. 169, London School of Economics.

Demsetz, H. 1968. The Cost of Transacting. *Quarterly Journal of Economics* 82:33–53.

Dennert, J. 1993. Price Competition between Market Makers. *Review of Economic Studies* 60:735–51.

Foster, F. D., and S. Viswanathan. 1993. Variations in Trading Volume, Return Volatility, and Trading Costs: Evidence on Recent Price Formation Models. *Journal of Finance* 48:187–211.

Garman, M. 1976. Market Microstructure. *Journal of Financial Economics* 3:257–75.

Glosten, L. R. 1987. Components of the Bid-Ask Spread and the Statistical Properties of Transactions Prices. *Journal of Finance* 42:1293–1307.

———. 1993. Intra- and Inter-Market Competition. Working paper, Graduate School of Business, Columbia University.

———. 1994. Is the Electronic Open Limit Order Book Inevitable? *Journal of Business* 49:1127–61.

Glosten, L. R., and L. Harris. 1988. Estimating the Components of the Bid-Ask Spread. *Journal of Financial Economics* 21:123–42.

Grossman, S. J., and M. H. Miller. 1988. Liquidity and Market Structure. *Journal of Finance* 43:617–37.

Hansch, O., and A. Neuberger. 1993. Block Trading on the London Stock Exchange. Working paper, London Business School. Prepared for the Conference on Global Equity Markets, New York University.

Harris, L. E. 1990. Liquidity, Trading Rules, and Electronic Trading Systems. Mono-

Table 5A.1   Descriptive Statistics for Transaction Sample

Code	Firm	Market Capitalization (million pounds)	Average Price (pounds)	Median Trade Size (pounds)	Normal Market Size (pounds)	Transactions in Mandatory Quote Period	Number of Market Makers
		FTSE-100 Firms					
BT.A	British Telecommunications	20,882	3.60	2,494	360,000	13,571	15
GUIN	Guinness	8,062	5.99	6,902	299,500	8,724	14
MKS	Marks & Spencer	6,432	2.85	3,267	213,750	12,937	14
RTZ	RTZ	5,530	5.20	5,820	260,000	7,296	13
LLOY	Lloyds Bank	4,171	3.83	5,908	191,338	5,845	14
ANL	Abbey National	3,564	2.79	576	139,495	19,122	14
SUN	Sun Alliance Group	3,002	3.13	13,600	78,138	2,486	12
CBRY	Cadbury Schweppes	2,681	4.11	6,015	102,666	5,309	16
WHIT	Whitbread	2,298	4.41	6,071	110,227	3,285	14
LGEN	Legal & General	2,242	3.72	7,782	92,939	2,771	12
ABF	Associated British Foods	2,121	4.48	21,950	44,801	900	10
UBIS	United Biscuits Holdings	1,752	3.84	7,860	96,000	3,207	16
RR.	Rolls-Royce	1,557	1.31	774	65,371	8,798	15
RBOS	Royal Bank of Scotland	1,440	1.69	7,867	84,563	4,572	14
RMC	RMC Group	1,348	5.35	14,910	53,466	1,397	12
WILC	Willis Corroon	1,084	2.66	24,808	66,411	1,406	7
TATE	Tate & Lyle	1,147	3.76	7,720	93,985	3,083	14
AW	Anglian Water	1,061	3.52	3,480	88,000	1,958	13
NFDS	Northern Foods	965	5.44	4,891	54,400	2,639	8
NFC	NFC	884	2.20	4,158	32,932	2,559	5
Average		**3,611**	**3.69**	**7,843**	**126,399**	**5,593**	**12.6**

Medium-Size Firms

SVC	Salvesen (Christian)	583	2.37	4,720	23,700	813	9
BOS	Body Shop	501	3.23	3,480	32,269	1,907	5
THK	Tiphook	446	4.65	12,925	23,250	1,978	6
BNZL	Bunzl	400	0.87	5,832	43,500	614	7
COST	Costain Group	362	0.65	2,220	16,319	2,839	11
WOLV	Wolverhampton & Dudley	324	5.78	5,880	11,560	203	6
SCPA	Scapa Group	284	1.67	16,191	8,370	454	7
HETH	Heath (C.E.)	263	4.93	9,905	14,790	305	7
PFG	Provident Financial	251	4.47	9,821	8,940	300	6
PFA	Proudfoot (Alexander)	225	3.93	62,730	19,650	250	5
LEIH	Leigh Interests	208	2.65	11,400	13,234	454	6
BRFD	Berisford International	181	0.22	2,050	5,459	618	7
SPX	Spirax-Sarco Engineering	169	2.47	7,816	4,936	148	5
BODD	Boddington Group	157	1.61	7,335	4,816	454	6
SREL	Suter	145	1.31	2,810	13,087	306	4
BLGH	Bullough	139	1.25	6,500	6,228	114	4
FRG	FR Group	127	1.87	17,226	9,342	359	6
LVLL	Lovell (Y.J.) Holdings	118	0.33	950	1,650	895	4
THT	Thorntons	110	1.88	1,386	5,633	532	5
ATV	Anglia Television Group	100	2.02	4,812	4,039	525	7
Average		**255**	**2.41**	**9,799**	**13,539**	**703**	**6.2**

(continued)

Table 5A.1   (continued)

Small-Size Firms

ANU	Anglo United	92	0.34	2,950	8,500	171	4
SEP	Southend Property Holdings	88	0.83	4,654	2,490	118	3
LILY	Liley	86	0.36	1,720	3,600	296	7
BDN	Bridon	77	1.13	1,545	11,346	186	6
BYNS	Bayens (Charles)	69	0.60	5,392	3,022	281	5
OWN	Owners Abroad	63	1.14	4,680	11,406	1,409	4
SNGT	Silentnight Holdings	56	2.01	4,900	4,030	290	5
GDG	Gardiner Group	54	0.62	16,062	6,200	87	5
ROG	Richmond Oil and Gas	48	0.16	2,000	802	163	2
WHWY	Wheway	45	0.30	1,950	1,501	262	7
EXG	Excalibur	40	0.46	3,060	926	89	4
SMN	Starmin	37	0.16	1,625	479	155	5
MSY	Misys	33	2.04	10,400	6,120	137	5
SMP	St. Modwen Properties	30	0.18	454	900	109	4
RHT	Resort Hotels	30	0.97	2,805	9,665	526	6
HAMP	Hampson Industries	29	0.38	1,436	1,902	81	4
PDG	Pendragon	25	1.78	232	5,349	311	5
ELWK	Elswick	23	0.09	793	1,309	321	5
COI	Crossroads Oil	22	0.28	702	560	31	2
BFG	Bennet & Fountain Group	21	0.21	1,024	1,030	128	6
Average		**48**	**0.70**	**3,419**	**4,057**	**258**	**4.7**

Sources: Market capitalization on March 31, 1991, as reported in *Quality of Markets Companies Book 1991* (London: London Stock Exchange, 1991), table 3. Transactions data were drawn from the LSE computer records for the period October 14–December 27, 1991. The average price is calculated based on all trades during the sample that took place during the mandatory quote period. The median trade size is based on the pound value of all trades during the mandatory quote period for the sample. Normal market sizes in number of shares are from the computer records of the LSE. The pound value of the normal market sizes are the number of shares times the average price of transactions.

graph Series in Finance and Economics 1990–4. New York University, Salomon Brothers Center.

Hasbrouck, J. 1991. Measuring the Information Content of Stock Trades. *Journal of Finance* 46:179–207.

Ho, T., and R. Macris. 1984. Dealer Bid-Ask Quotes and Transaction Prices: An Empirical Study of Some AMEX Options. *Journal of Finance* 39:23–45.

Ho, T., and H. Stoll. 1981. Optimal Dealer Pricing under Transactions and Return Uncertainty. *Journal of Financial Economics* 9:47–73.

———. 1983. The Dynamics of Dealer Markets under Competition. *Journal of Finance* 38:1053–74.

International Organization of Securities Commissions. 1993. Transparency on Secondary Markets: A Synthesis of the IOSCO Debate, Ore Societa Editorale Media Economici. Milan: Seme S.p.A., Divisione Libri.

Kleidon, A. W., and I. M. Werner. 1993. Round-the-Clock Trading: Evidence for U.K. Cross-Listed Securities. NBER Working Paper no. 4410. Cambridge, MA: National Bureau of Economic Research.

Koenker, R., and G. Basset. 1978. Regression Quantiles. *Econometrica* 46:33–50.

Lee, C. M. C. 1993. Market Integration and Price Execution for NYSE-Listed Securities. *Journal of Finance* 48:1009–38.

Lee, C. M. C., B. Mucklow, and M. J. Ready. 1993. Spreads, Depths, and the Impact of Earnings Information: An Intraday Analysis. *Review of Financial Studies* 6:345–74.

Lee, C. M. C., and M. J. Ready. 1991. Inferring Trade Direction from Intraday Data. *Journal of Finance* 46:733–46.

McInish, T., and R. Wood. 1992. An Analysis of Intraday Patterns in Bid/Ask Spreads for NYSE Stocks. *Journal of Finance* 47:753–64.

Madhavan, A. 1992. Trading Mechanisms in Securities Markets. *Journal of Finance* 47:607–41.

Madhavan, A., and S. Smidt. 1991. A Bayesian Model of Intraday Specialist Pricing. *Journal of Financial Economics* 30:99–134.

Neuberger, A. J., and R. A. Schwartz. 1989. Current Developments in the London Equity Market. Working paper, London Business School.

Roll, R. 1984. A Simple Measure of the Effective Bid/Ask Spread in an Efficient Market. *Journal of Finance* 39:1127–39.

Stoll, H. R. 1989. Inferring the Components of the Bid-Ask Spread: Theory and Empirical Results. *Journal of Finance* 44:115–34.

Comment   F. Douglas Foster

The paper by Reiss and Werner provides an interesting introduction to price formation and trading costs on the London Stock Exchange (LSE). The authors appear to be less interested in testing a specific set of hypotheses. Rather, their paper provides a thorough overview of the LSE, with a particular interest in how trading costs in this market can be measured, and how these costs compare with other exchanges (in particular with the Nasdaq market in the United

F. Douglas Foster is associate professor of finance at the College of Business Administration at the University of Iowa.

States). The authors demonstrate that (1) bid-ask quotes on the LSE are relatively large and rarely change. Competition in this market is related, in part, to discounts from the quoted bid-ask spread; and (2) different classes of investors (customers, market makers, brokers, and interdealer broker [IDB] trades) appear to be offered different discounts from the best bid and ask (the touch). Because of these effects, simply using the quoted bid-ask spread to measure trading costs can be very misleading. Reiss and Werner provides us with a very carefully constructed analysis of trading data that describes this problem, with particular attention to the role of the trade size and customer identity in determining trading costs.

In my view, the most important innovation in the paper is the estimation technique used to isolate trading costs. Because the bid-ask quotes seldom change, and because transaction reporting can be delayed, an important part of measuring transaction costs is the estimation of the discount offered from the touch. Reiss and Werner suggest a cost measure that is based on an immediate purchase and sale of the stock (or the converse). Using the current trade, they compute the apparent spread, which is the current quote less the discount on the first transaction. To get the round-trip trading costs, the authors then estimate the *expected* discount on the offsetting trade and subtract this amount from the adjusted spread. This value, defined to be the adjusted apparent spread, becomes the trading cost of interest (although in their figures the authors only report the apparent spread value). This cost measure is an important innovation. It reflects the discount offered in the current trade, as well as the discount likely to be offered on the return trade. Importantly, it appears that the extent of the discount is related to the characteristics of the order in very interesting ways.

Because of the emphasis on an empirical overview, Reiss and Werner spend less time discussing why the trading environment on the LSE evolved the way it has. They leave the details of a specific model for other research. This raises a natural question. If a specific model were to be tested, are Reiss and Werner's techniques likely to be useful for a direct test of that model? For example, Hansch, Naik, and Viswanathan (1993) in a related paper suggest that LSE market makers quote larger spreads and then execute trades inside the spread for three reasons: (1) following an informational change, it gives the market makers some elbow room before they alter their quotes; (2) it enables them to service customer orders without frequently adjusting their quotes, and thus signaling their inventory; and (3) the process of negotiation reveals something about the identity of the customer as well as the motive of the trade. Does the current work of Reiss and Werner allow us any additional insights to these arguments? If not, what more needs to be done?

Reiss and Werner condition on the information in the order flow and estimate trading costs using quantile regressions. For Cadbury Schweppes, this functional form is given in expression (2). Specifically, the authors use the trade size and the interaction between the touch and the trade size, as well as the traders' identity, to estimate the (adjusted) apparent spread. This bring us to the most controversial part of the paper. Why are these variables the correct ones to condition on? Why condition on them in this form (trade size and the interaction between trade size and touch)? Can this conditioning set be related to a theoretical model, or to the intuition given by Hansch, Naik, and Viswanathan?

This complication in choosing a conditioning set becomes more complex when the authors estimate trading costs across a sample of stocks. Expression (3) gives the functional form used for such tests. At first it appears that they use expression (2) and scale it by dividing both sides by the transaction price. However, now the authors condition on touch and trade size in a different way—the form of the interactions is significantly different. Little explanation is offered for the change, and it is not clear which specification is appropriate. This serves to highlight the need for a theoretical basis for quote formation on an interdealer market like the LSE.

In summary, the paper provides a fascinating array of evidence on the market structure of the LSE. In presenting this information, the authors raise more questions than any one paper can hope to address. The estimation procedure that is used is innovative in that it provides an economically relevant, forward-looking measure of costs. Its drawback, however, is that without a firm theoretical footing it is difficult to interpret, and will be controversial to many readers. Linked to a rigorous model of quote formation, this procedure promises to be an effective method of estimating costs. In my mind, the most interesting insight of the paper is "[b]y widening spreads, SEAQ market makers can protect themselves against inventory imbalances and informed trades while simultaneously retaining an option to offer execution within their guaranteed quotes." This insight echoes that of Hansch, Naik, and Viswanathan (1993) and suggests an interesting path for theoretical researchers who wish to understand better interdealer competition. Interested theorists should read Hagerty's and McDonald's chapter in this volume for a related theoretical paper.

Reference

Hansch, O., N. Naik, and S. Viswanathan. 1993. Market Making on the London Stock Exchange: An Empirical Observation. Working paper, London Business School.

Comment   Bernard S. Black

This paper has a lot of interesting data in it as well as the most careful measure of effective buy-sell spread that I've seen. It is no criticism of the authors to say that their data raises as many questions as it solves.

Bernard S. Black is professor of law at Columbia University Law School.

One weakness is the theoretical model of competition among market makers as oligopolistic competition, of the kind that once characterized the steel or auto industry, where the oligopolists earn positive economic profits, or perhaps dissipate potential oligopoly profits through various inefficiencies. I think this is implausible. Entry costs into the business of making a market in common stock are likely to be low by the standards of nonfinancial industries. For firms that are already making markets in other stocks, entry costs into making a market in the stock of a particular company are surely small.

So even if there are only a small number of market makers in the stock of ABC Corporation, there is lots of *potential* competition from broker-dealers who *could* become market makers in ABC Corporation if the market price of liquidity services—the effective buy-sell spread—is significantly above the cost of producing this product. That potential competition ought to keep effective buy-sell spreads close to competitive levels.

How then does one explain the strong picture that the authors present in figure 5.6 of declining spreads with increasing number of market makers? The alternate story that I'd like to offer posits several features of market making.

1. *Some* costs associated with making a market in ABC Corporation stock are largely independent of trade volume, including keeping up with information about ABC's business and about trading in ABC stock. These costs must be borne even if trading volume is zero. At low trading volumes, the need to recover these costs may significantly increase effective spreads. As trading volume increases, these costs become smaller per trade.

2. These information-collection costs of market making decline with the number of *other* market makers. Market maker 17 can, in large part, skimp on its own research and instead rely on market transactions, and on quoted spreads from other market makers, to find out what's happening in the market for ABC stock. Conversely, market maker 1, with a larger market share, can't learn much from the behavior of piggybacking market makers like 17. So there can be an equilibrium where one or a few market makers enjoy high volume, which they use to cover their relatively high information-gathering costs, while market makers like 17, with low volume, can offer competitive spreads because they incur low information-gathering costs. In this respect, market making is quite unlike conventional product markets, where competitor 17 can't piggyback on the capital investments made by number 1.

3. Some trades are more information intensive than others. On average, larger trades will come from more knowledgeable traders. Market maker 17 won't dare handle these trades. These trades will primarily flow to market makers like number 1 that invest heavily in gathering information.

If we had the data to look behind the simple correlation that the authors present between effective spreads and the *number* of market makers, and could disaggregate the data, I would want to examine the market share of different market makers, broken down in various ways, including trade size. That might tell us whether the model of the industrial organization of market making that I've described captures some of the truth—perhaps more than the authors' model of oligopolistic competition.

This model, where small market makers piggyback on the information-gathering efforts of large market makers, could also provide a window into one of the puzzles in the data—why doesn't any one market maker offer a quoted spread equal to the touch? The combination of quoted spreads greater than the best published bid-ask spread, and relatively frequent discounts, may hide from other market makers some of the information that a particular market maker has collected. That's a speculation in search of a model, I recognize.

I would like also to comment on two surprising features of the data. First, we apparently have large-company percentage spreads of about 0.6 percent for S&P 100 stocks, on the NYSE, 0.9 percent on SEAQ for FTSE-100 stocks, and, depending on the study, between 1.2 percent and 2 percent on Nasdaq for large-company stocks. These are large differences, for markets that increasingly compete with each other, both for listings and order flow.

I'd like to know whether these are really comparable numbers. If they are, then I would like to know why these price differences survive. One reason might be *nonprice* differences in the quality of execution. Let me offer two examples. A thousand-share trade on the NYSE is exposed on the floor and sometimes is executed between the best quoted bid and the best quoted asking price. That narrows the effective spread. But it takes time—a minute or two. Maybe speed of execution, which reduces transaction costs, explains why third markets can take transactions away from the NYSE even though their apparent price is higher. But this is not necessarily a happy outcome. The advantages of speed might accrue to the broker, not to the customers.

There is a way to find out who benefits from sending trades to third markets, suggested by Jack Coffee. The SEC could require brokers to offer clients an explicit choice: faster execution or the possibility of a better price. My bet: the vast majority of small investors would opt for a better price.

Second example: informed traders like to hide their trades. Maybe London competes with the NYSE by offering secrecy, in return for a higher effective spread. We might prefer that delayed transaction reporting not be allowed. I'm one of the people who think that price disclosure has important external benefits. But for present purposes, we could *explain* a difference in effective spreads based on these kinds of nonprice factors.

Second data feature: the authors report that "IDB trades"—broker-to-broker-dealer trades intermediated by interdealer brokers—occur at better prices than direct broker-to-broker trades. At first impression, this makes no sense. Shouldn't it be, if anything, the other way around?

Let me offer a possible explanation. The better pricing accorded to IDB trades could reflect a gentlemen's understanding that only informationless trades go through IDB. Such an understanding, even if it would break down in the United States, could survive in the much more close-knit British investment community. IDB brokers could kick cheaters out of the club by refusing to take their orders. Information trades would then go direct broker to broker, and properly get worse pricing.

Here the authors ought to *ask* British dealers about the reasons that might underlie this difference. They might get a simple, plausible explanation rooted in price discrimination between high-information and low-information trades.

Authors' Reply

Increased competition between exchanges for order flow has renewed debates about which trading systems offer "better execution." As the discussion at this conference testifies, the quality of execution is a difficult concept to measure. Many studies regard the quality of execution as synonymous with the spread cost of an average trade. Our paper illustrates why in dealer markets average comparisons may mask or, worse, obscure systematic differences in transaction costs. In particular, on SEAQ, the practice of discounting the posted quotes raises new questions about how one should assess the quality of execution in dealer markets. We are grateful to our discussants and conference participants for their observations about our overall approach and our methods. We now briefly revisit several of these points and relate them to our overall objective.

We began studying SEAQ dealer markets thinking that we could use existing models and measures to explain SEAQ dealer pricing policies. Interviews with SEAQ officials and market makers quickly convinced us that SEAQ rules led to behavior not captured by standard models or measures. We thus began with a narrower objective, how to summarize these differences. Our adjusted apparent spread measure recognizes that both minimum quote sizes and best execution rules affect quoted spreads and the ultimate relation of transaction prices to quoted prices.

Our paper emphasizes that one must condition comparisons of transaction costs on factors that dealers use when pricing trades. The estimations in this paper use simple quantile regression equations to make this point. As Douglas Foster observes, these specifications should ideally come from a model of dealer behavior. They should probably also contain other variables. We agree. Unfortunately, we were unable to find a structural model in the literature that captures dealer interaction in markets like SEAQ. We also note that it will be difficult to obtain an empirically tractable model of dealer behavior. Nevertheless, Foster's point is well taken and is one we plan to pursue. Our regression results are thus best viewed as a first attempt at describing the facts that require explanation.

Besides the findings highlighted in Douglas Foster's comment, we again emphasize the important interactions between trade size and the touch at the time of trade. Medium to large trades receive favorable execution, whereas small and very large trades at best get "best execution." Favorable execution increases, the wider the spread. These findings contrast with the predictions of some theoretical models and the results of previous empirical studies. As Foster notes, our finding that quotes change infrequently is also noteworthy. Hansch, Naik, and Viswanathan (1993) also make this observation. While their story suggests reasons for why spreads might move infrequently, it does not explain why we see systematic patterns by the size of the touch, trade size, and trader identity. Finally, contrary to the predictions of some second-price auction models, we find order flow does not always go to a SEAQ dealer advertising the best price. There are at least two reasons for this. First, dealers have the option to take trades at the best bid and offer. Second, traders know that dealers discount.

Bernard Black raises an interesting observation about market-maker trading and IDB discounts. We disagree, however, that what we observe is the result of a "gentlemen's agreement" among SEAQ dealers. An alternative story, suggested to us by several market makers, is that market makers use direct negotiation only as a last resort. That is, they use the phone to resolve inventory imbalances only after they have exhausted all other means. (These include all four IDBs and customers.) This explanation suggests that the difference in transaction costs we observe between phone trading and IDB trading reflects a dealer "impatience" cost.

Black also rightly observes that we omit important nonprice differences in the quality of execution, such as the speed of execution (immediacy) and information disclosure. We agree. We did not mean to suggest that our apparent spreads capture all that is important. While we would like to measure these dimensions, it is very difficult to measure the speed of execution without time-stamped order information. Similarly, it is difficult to quantify the costs of reduced transparency without knowing where and when information arrives.

Reference

Hansch, O., N. Naik, and S. Viswanathan. 1993. Market Making on the London Stock Exchange: An Empirical Observation. Working paper, London Business School.

6 The Effect of Integration between Broker-Dealers and Specialists

Robert Neal and David Reiffen

6.1 Introduction

In recent years, the New York Stock Exchange (NYSE) and the American Stock Exchange (AMEX) have relaxed their rules concerning the relationship between "upstairs" brokerage firms and "downstairs" specialists. Since 1986, large broker-dealers have acquired specialist units on the floor of the NYSE, and some smaller broker-dealers have acquired specialists on the floor of the AMEX. This paper exploits this structural change to evaluate whether the previous restrictions against integration of brokerage and specialist functions served investors' best interests.

The traditional objections to this integration suggest two mechanisms by which integration can lead to higher trading costs.[1] First, integration between broker-dealers and specialist units might lead to agency problems. For example, suppose that a customer can readily observe the quoted spread, but has difficulty determining if she received best execution. An integrated broker might provide a worse execution because of its incentive to route its trades through its affiliated dealer, rather than searching for the best price. Second, integration could lead to higher trading costs for unintegrated brokers, what Salinger (1988) has referred to as "foreclosure." As applied to this industry, integration may allow the specialist to increase trading costs for trades from other broker-dealers. In general, the degree of vertical integration within a firm is endogenous, and changes in the degree of vertical integration are rare and

Robert Neal is an economist at the Federal Reserve Bank of Kansas City. David Reiffen is a senior economist at the Federal Trade Commission. The views expressed in this chapter are those of the authors and do not represent those of the Federal Trade Commission or any individual commissioner.

1. We use the term trading cost to refer to the costs of making a trade, taking into account effective bid-ask spreads, commissions, and so forth. While this term is often used interchangeably with "transactions" cost by financial economists, "transactions" cost may mean something completely different to industrial organization economists.

result from (typically) unobserved events. For this reason, it is difficult to test theories of vertical integration. In this industry, however, the recent integration resulted from a policy change, mitigating the usual identification problem.

Using data on combinations of broker-dealers and specialist units between 1987 and 1993, we test for evidence supporting these two hypotheses. The tests consist of comparisons of bid-ask spreads, execution quality, depth, volume, and order flow patterns for a one-month period before the integration to the corresponding post-acquisition period. In each case, we test the null hypothesis that integration does not increase trading costs against the one-sided alternative that integration is associated with higher trading costs.

The two hypotheses suggest different sources of higher trading costs. The pure agency hypothesis predicts that there will be no change in spreads (which are relatively easy to monitor), but execution quality (which is difficult to monitor) will decrease for the integrated exchange, as the integrated firm shifts its order flow pattern. Execution quality on the nonintegrated exchanges would be unaffected. The pure foreclosure hypothesis predicts that, across all exchanges, spreads will widen, execution quality will diminish, and aggregate volume will be reduced.

Our results provide little support for these hypotheses. We do not find evidence that execution quality has suffered. There is no virtually no change in NYSE execution quality for the NYSE integrated stocks, and a slight increase in execution quality for the integrated stocks on the regional exchanges. We do, however, find a diversion of order flow and a reduction in average trade size on the regional exchanges. These findings are consistent with the rerouting of retail orders and suggest some alternative motivation for these acquisitions.

We offer two conjectures. First, vertical integration may facilitate profitable trading against uninformed retail orders. Second, it is possible that the specialist units that were acquired had been managed in a way that did not maximize their value. While we present some evidence consistent with these alternatives, such analysis is not the focus of this paper. However, since on average investors have not been hurt by integrations, we believe a policy of restricting these acquisitions is ill-advised.

6.2 Overview of Industry Structure

6.2.1 Overview of the Markets

Two distinct market transactions are involved in turning a retail customer's wish to trade into an executed trade. First, the customer places the order with a retail broker, who charges a price (commission) for this service. The broker then arranges for the order to be executed, usually on an organized market.[2] If the trade is executed on an organized market, there is typically a bid-ask

---

2. Some trades are executed internally (or "crossed") at the firm.

spread, which provides revenue to the firm executing the transaction, be it a specialist or a market maker. The two transactions—order taking and execution—are complementary in the usual economic sense that a decrease in the cost of execution will increase the demand for retail brokerage services. Alternatively, one can view executions as an input into the "retail trades" product sold by broker dealers. From this perspective, one can view the two markets as vertically related to one another.[3]

The right to trade any individual security on the NYSE is a proprietary right assigned to a single specialist. While the NYSE specialist is the only agent on the floor of that exchange making a market in any particular stock, that specialist faces competition from other sources, such as the specialists on the regional exchanges, private crossing networks, and the National Association of Securities Dealers (NASD) for stocks listed after 1979. The right to trade a stock on each regional exchange is similarly proprietorially assigned to one firm. Hence, one specialist on each regional exchange competes, or potentially competes (since not all NYSE stocks are actively traded on every regional exchange), with the NYSE specialist in that stock.

The competition between specialists is restricted by Securities and Exchange Commission (SEC) regulations. Specifically, barring unusual circumstances, no trade can be executed outside the best intermarket bid or ask. For example, suppose the specialist on the Chicago exchange offers a bid of $59\frac{1}{2}$, and the best bid among other exchanges if $59\frac{5}{8}$. The Chicago regional specialist must pay at least $59\frac{5}{8}$ if he is to execute that trade. It is important to recognize that this does not mean that all exchanges offer the same price. This holds for two reasons. First, the Chicago specialist is not obligated to trade at $59\frac{5}{8}$, while the specialist offering $59\frac{5}{8}$ is obligated to purchase some shares at that price. Second, and more interesting from our perspective, specialists may offer better prices than the best intermarket bid or ask. This phenomenon, known as price improvement, is fairly common. In their study of realized retail trading prices, Petersen and Fialkowski (1994) find that price improvement occurred for 35 percent of trades, while Blume and Goldstein (1992) estimate the figure to be between 12 and 31 percent. Evidence also suggests that the extent of price improvement varies across exchanges. Lee (1993) finds significant differences in realized spreads across exchanges, with the NYSE generally offering better prices than the regional exchanges, NASD, or Instinet.[4]

The relevance of specialist competition to the retail customer is that a broker can obtain different prices from different specialists. Hence, ignoring the broker's cost of searching, retail customers will be best served by brokers shopping across different exchanges. In this sense, specialists compete by offering more price improvement to the broker (and ultimately to the customer).

---

3. As Tirole notes (1988), the same analysis applies whether one thinks of the two markets as vertically related or complements.
4. For Lee's sample stocks in 1988 and 1989, only the Cincinnati Stock Exchange offered lower effective spreads in most size categories.

Offering price improvement is not the only means by which specialists compete. At least two other means of competing have been observed. First, exchanges may choose different rules governing transactions, which in turn affect the broker's choice of exchange. For example, during the time period we examined, the NYSE rules mandated that a "crossed" trade (where a broker-dealer represents private parties on both sides of the trade) must "clear" the order book.[5] The regional exchanges are not limited by such restrictions, so that certain types of trades are attracted to the regional exchanges.

Second, exchanges might offer other inducements to attract trades. In particular, some specialists (and third-market firms) offer direct payments to brokers in exchange for the opportunity to trade against retail transactions. This practice, known as payment for order flow, has been criticized by both academics and practitioners. For example, Lee (1993) questions the "propriety of order flow inducements which may impair broker's independence in pursuing best execution" (1009). Similarly, Blume and Goldstein (1992) raise the concern that payment for order flow results in worse prices for retail consumers. This same issue has been raised by NYSE chairman William Donaldson, who has argued for regulatory action to ban such payments.[6]

Clearly, a similar incentive might be created by the broker owning a specialist. In fact, it seems reasonable that the potential for consumers to receive inferior execution would be amplified by integration. As compared to contractual arrangements such as payment for order flow, vertical integration harmonizes the incentives of the broker and the market maker. For example, suppose that it is more profitable to trade against retail transactions than professional traders, so that specialists are only willing to pay for retail order flow. An integrated broker will have more incentive to screen out professional trades than a broker receiving payment for order flow.[7] Given the obvious similarity between integration and payment for order flow, however, our analysis of the effect of integration on trading cost offers insight on the effect of both practices.

6.2.2 Exchange Rules Governing Broker-Specialist Relations

Prior to 1986, both the NYSE and AMEX had rules governing broker-specialist relations, which had the effect of preventing such ownership.[8] Individuals affiliated with member firms of the exchange ("approved persons") could not simultaneously own a specialist unit and carry out normal brokerage

---

5. Clearing the order book means that all limit orders at prices more favorable than the crossing price must be executed before the crossed trade is executed. For example, suppose the specialist's bid is 59, his ask is 60, and there is a limit order to buy at 59¾. If two other agents agree to trade at 59½, NYSE rules require that the specialist or the broker take the opposite side of the limit order.

6. See David A. Vise, "NYSE Chief Urges Ban on Cash Payments," *Washington Post,* April 15, 1993, D11.

7. This is discussed more fully in section 6.5.

8. NYSE rules 104, 104–13, 105, 113–20; AMEX rules 190, 193.

operations.[9] Changes in the rules were proposed in 1985 and enacted in 1986. These rules allowed brokers affiliated with specialists to continue their brokerage operations in all securities as long as appropriate steps were taken to prevent certain abuses. In particular, a "Chinese Wall" was to be established to prevent the exchange of certain information between the specialist and brokerage units. For example, individuals associated with the brokerage unit are not allowed access to the specialist's "order book." Similarly, individuals at the brokerage entity who are privy to nonpublic information about the specialist's securities cannot relate that information to the affiliated specialist.

When the rule changes were proposed, the SEC issued a release describing the proposed changes and soliciting comments on the issues raised.[10] The commission received thirteen comment letters, including seven by firms or organizations opposed to the rule change.[11]

These seven commentators pointed to two general concerns regarding broker-specialist integration. First, several expressed concern that the integrated brokers would route orders toward their affiliated specialists, to the detriment of other specialists and retail customers. In the following sections, we describe several reasons that changes in order flow can both be profitable and reduce welfare. The second general concern was that the Chinese Wall procedure would be inadequate to prevent information from passing between specialists and brokers.

Those commentators supporting the change, as well as the SEC staff, noted the potential for increased capitalization of specialists that would result from integration. These comments suggested that this would result in increased liquidity and deeper markets. While these claims may describe the effect of integration, they do not explain the broker's incentive to integrate. That is, why is it profitable to increase the capitalization of a specialist? Moreover, if increased capitalization increases profits, why are brokers particularly well positioned to supply that capital?

Since 1988, several large brokers have taken advantage of the rule changes and acquired specialist units. Table 6.1 lists the acquisitions. From the standpoint of our analysis, the most relevant aspect of these acquisitions is that the broker acquires the right to act as a specialist in the NYSE stocks previously served by the independent specialist. This is the relevant aspect because, to

---

9. An approved person affiliated with a specialist could not (1) trade in securities in which the specialist made the market, (2) trade options on those securities, (3) accept orders in those securities, (4) undertake research in those securities, or (5) "popularize" those securities.

10. Securities Exchange Act Release no. 22396 (September 11, 1985), 50 *Federal Register* 37925.

11. These comments include those of the Boston exchange and Chicago Board of Exchange; Morgan Stanley; AT&T; Wertheim and Co. (NYSE brokers); Faganson, Frankel, and Steicher (NYSE specialists); and Wedbush, Noble, and Cook (brokers and specialists on other exchanges). Favorable comments were filed by most major NYSE brokers and several small NYSE brokers and specialists. These letters are public, and copies can be obtained from us.

Table 6.1   **Sample of Integrated Stocks and Control Stocks**

Acquiring Firm	Specialist Unit	Acquisition Date	Stocks
Boston Exchange			
BHR Securities	Corey MacTavish	7/22/91	BCC, CCK, ENS, EP, ETN, GCI, GPC, GRA, GRN, GSX, KMB, KR, KRI, MEA, MU, NLB, PPG, SNT, TMC, TRB, VFC
Canatella Specialist Corp.	Burlington Securities	10/16/91	AMW, BIC, BZR, CET, EXC, FGF, FGI, GHM, GOT, GRM, HPX, JHI, KVN, NAB, NNY, NPK, NWN, OBS, OXM, PNY, PWN, RBC, SCX, SIE, SNO, STW, SYM, TDS, TPL, TR, TXI
Natl. Financial Services Corp. (Fidelity)	Agoston	11/1/90	AA, ABX, AFL, AIR, ALD, ALX, AMR, APA, AR, BGE, BRC, CC, CCB, CLE, CPB, CS, DBD, DDS, DRM, EGG, EY, FOE, FRP, FTX, GTY, HSY, ICE, IF, KAB, MAS, MCK, MMC, MST, MXM, MXS, NCC, NSI, NWL, PHI, PLL, RYC, SB, SC, SPW, TNV, UCC, WIT
Natl. Financial Services Corp. (Fidelity)	Ocean Hill Securities	11/1/91	AFP, BRO, CMB, CQB, CW, CYR, DWW, ELJ, ESY, FMR, FSS, HI, ICL, KBH, LTD, LUV, LZB, MGF, SCT, SCZ, TDM, TEK, TJX, TYC, UCO, UCU, UJB, URS, USH, USR, UTR, UVX, WBN, WFC
Natl. Financial Services Corp. (Fidelity)	Chicago Corp.	1/4/93	AGL. AIZ, AME, APH, BAC, BBT, BDG, BDK, BGT, BKT, BNE, BTV, CAG, CCL, CHH, CMO, CMZ, CNG, CSC, CTS, ED, FQA, FWC, GII, GIM, GMT, GNC, GPS, GWW, I, IMC, ISS, JF, KEM, KUT, KIM, KMM, KTF, KTM, MDA, MHP, NBL, NEF, NMG, NPI, NT, OII, PCH, PCP, PGT, PIR, PMM, PNC, PPT, RBD, REL, ROK, RYL, SME, TMX, TRH, VFM, VIT, VKM, VLT, VMT, VNM, VOD, VSH, WGO, WIN, WNC, WR, XRX, ZE
Gowell Securities	Meldon	11/9/92	ACK, AMI, AMP, BNL, CCN, CMY, DH, DOV, FDO, FSI, LM, LOW, OHM, SEE, SK, V, WHT, WMT
Jefferies & Co.	Kemper Securities	5/6/91	ACY, ADI, ALG, AMD, APC, APD, AVE, BCP, BEV, BFI, BS, BYS, CH, CIR, CKE, CSM, DJ, FAX, FTU, GT, HE, HMS, HPC, HPH, KKS, LDS, LIT, LLX, MAH, MCN, NCM, NIC, NMI, PGR, PIF, PKD, PKN, PWJ, PZL, RCP, REC, RGS, RPC, SI, SVT, TMD, TRW, TSO, UAL, UK, UNM, UNP, WWW

Table 6.1 (continued)

Acquiring Firm	Specialist Unit	Acquisition Date	Stocks
NYSE			
Bear Stearns	Asiel & Co.	1/1/88	AA, AET, BK, DNB, HF, HMC, JC, MUO, PRE, PST, TX
Drexel Specialist Co.	Pforzheimer & Co.	3/1/88	AFL, AN, ANC, BCF, DEX, GAB, GMI, HNH, HYP, IAD, JCI, KU, KUH, NUV, OPC, PNS, TII, USR, WDG
Merrill Lynch	A. B. Tompane	10/26/87	ALN, CHL, CRN, DLT, ENE, FQA, FTK, GFC, HB, HFF, MST, RD, STY, TEP, WMB, X
Paine Webber	deCordova Cooper	9/1/89	ABY, ACP, BP, BTU, CBT, CHG, DRV, E, EXP, FW, GEC, GPO, GWW, HTN, HUG, IBM, LAW, MEI, SDP, SWX, TAC, TAN, WAG, WIC, Z, ZE
Philadelphia Exchange			
Shearson Lehman	Bloom Stalof	6/26/91	AA, AIG, AMB, AMR, AN, AR, ARC, ASA, AU, BAC, BCC, BCS, BEL, BZF, CBS, CCI, CDE, CHV, CLD, CLX, CWE, F, GP, GPU, GRN, HL, ITT, LNC, MDR, MMM, MOT, MRO, MTC, NVO, ORX, P, PBI, PD, PDG, PG, PH, RTZ, S, SBO, SO, SUN, SYN, TX, USR, WBB, WMT, WY, X, XON, ZE
Control stocks			ACB, AEG, AIP, AL, AP, ASO, ATN, AVY, BAX, BEN, BK, BKR, BN, BRK, C, CAS, CBR, CFI, CHX, CLT, CMA, CNL, CPH, CRS, CTC, CTK, CVT, DEC, DJI, DNB, DSP, EDE, EEI, EMR, ETZ, FCA, FLM, FPC, GAL, GER, GM, GOU, GRO, HCA, HEI, HMC, HRE, HWL, IEI, IR, JBM, JH, KEY, KML, KNO, KZ, LGN, LPI, LPX, MA, MAM, MD, MGC, MM, MRT, MXF, NER, NL, NSP, OIL, OSL, PAT, PEG, PIN, POR, PSC, RAY, RJF, ROG, RUS, SCE, SDY, SGI, SJT, SNA, SRR, SVM, TAC, TBP, TEF, TIN, TOY, TXF, UFF, UPT, VAT, VRC, WID, WOL, WRE, Y

the extent that the acquisitions adversely affect trading costs, those adverse consequences can be observed on the stocks in the integration.

In section 6.5, we describe how trading costs have been affected by integration. We find that trading costs do not appear to have changed much following the NYSE integrations. The evidence on the regional integrations is more ambiguous, although it is difficult to ascribe the observed effects to any one cause.

To generalize from past experience to future acquisition, however, would require that future acquisitions resemble past acquisitions. Based on our conversations with practitioners, we think that the specialists acquired on the NYSE since 1988 have generally been less well capitalized and had received lower rankings from the exchange than the average NYSE specialist.[12] Hence, in generalizing these results to future acquisitions, one must consider how these selectivity issues influence the effects of integration. For example, it may be that, while the effect of an acquisition on undercapitalized specialists is to reduce trading costs, the effect of integration between a broker and a well-capitalized specialist might increase trading costs.

6.3   Formalizing the Objections to Vertical Integration

As we discussed in the introduction, many of the comment letters expressed concern that trading costs would increase following integration. In this section, we develop descriptive and highly stylized models to provide economic content to these concerns. In constructing these models, our goal is to include enough relevant features of the market to generate testable predictions.

6.3.1   Agency Problems with Integration

SEC rules require stock brokers to provide "best execution" for retail customers. This does not mean that brokers are at all times required to maximize the price a retail seller receives (or minimize the price a retail buyer pays), since other factors, such as timeliness of the execution, are also relevant. Nevertheless, brokers do have a fiduciary responsibility to obtain the best price, other things equal.

It is possible that integration between brokers and specialists would undermine the broker's best execution responsibilities.[13] As noted above, brokers can frequently obtain "price improvement" on customer's trades: obtaining offers from competing specialists that are better than the best intermarket bid or ask. On the other hand, if an integrated broker routed its orders through its affiliated specialist, rather than comparing offers of competing specialists, it is possible that the integrated broker's customers would receive an execution inferior to that received by an unintegrated broker's customers. This possibility has also been raised by Hasbrouck, Sofianos, and Sosebee (1993).

To formalize this potential agency problem, we present a simple model in which integration can affect realized trading costs. First, we assume that there

---

12. The NYSE ranks specialists according to several criteria of efficacy. These rankings are not made public, but our understanding is that most of the acquired specialists were in the lower half of all specialists by this measure.
13. See Comments of Chicago Board of Exchange, 2.

exists a class of customers for whom specialists are willing to give discounts (price improvement).[14] We assume all of these customers can observe the commissions charged by brokers, but only α percent of them can determined whether they received best execution. Further, we assume that a dissatisfied customer can cancel the transaction, resulting in lost commission.[15] Finally, we assume that the broker has zero cost of obtaining quotes from specialists. Then a broker's gain from searching is αC (where C is the profit margin on commissions), and its cost is zero. Hence, absent integration, brokers will search for the best price.[16]

Consider the incentive of an integrated broker-specialist, under the assumption that the vertically integrated specialists can distinguish the orders of these customers from the rest of their orders.[17] Such an integrated firm gains αC from trying to obtain best execution for its customers, but loses the opportunity to trade its internal order flow at the posted bid or ask. The gains to trading these orders at the posted bid or ask is $(1 - m)(1 - \alpha)T + m(1 - \alpha)(T - t)$, where $T = |(\text{posted price}) - (\text{the cost of making the trade})|$ (i.e., the integrated specialist's trading profit); t is the trading profit on the trades the specialist would have made (i.e., absent "misrouting" due to agency problems); and m is the integrated specialist's market share, absent misrouting.[18] It will pay to route these orders internally as long as $\alpha C < (1 - \alpha)(T - mt)$. That is, for α, m, and t sufficiently small, and T high, it will pay to direct order flow internally. When this inequality holds, $(1 - \alpha)$ of this firm's customers are worse off.

If these conditions hold, testable predictions arise for changes in spread, execution quality, and order flow following integration. First, since the integrated broker-specialist wants to target retail customers, it will adjust the trading price for those customers only. This is most easily accomplished by the

14. Specifically, we are thinking of retail customers (who typically place small orders) as a class likely to obtain price improvement. Several sources provide evidence consistent with this assumption. First, Lee (1993) notes that orders sold for payment must be of small size and nonprofessional. Second, Petersen and Fialkowski (1994), whose data consist of retail orders only, report a greater degree of price improvement than Blume and Goldstein (1992), whose data include all trades. Finally, the assumption is consistent with Easley and O'Hara (1987) and Keim and Madhavan (1992), who argue that small orders are less likely to be information based.

15. This assumption simplifies the model by allowing us to incorporate "punishment" into a static game. Seppi (1990) employs a similar assumption to explain why informed investors do not behave opportunistically in a static model. More realistically, we could obtain similar results if α percent of customers choose their brokers on the basis of past price improvement, or if the SEC would (with some probability) impose a sanction on brokers who did not provide best execution.

16. More generally, brokers will search as long as their search cost is less than αC.

17. This assumption seems realistic. For example, among the information available to NYSE specialists on SuperDOT orders are the type of order (market, limit, or tick sensitive), buys, and the member firm originating the order. Hasbrouck and Sosebee (1992) also state that the identity of the member firm originating the order is a valuable signal of the underlying strategy of the trade. Virtually all NYSE retail orders go through SuperDOT.

18. One way of thinking about T and t is to suppose there are implicitly two spreads—one for retail customers and a larger one for professional customers—and both spreads are equal to the cost of trading with those customers. Then $t = 0$, and $T > 0$ is the difference in trading cost across the two classes.

integrated firm's reducing execution quality on orders for their own retail customers, without changing bid-ask spreads. Second, the incentive to provide
execution quality on orders from other brokers is unaffected by integration, so
that the integrated specialist continues to compete with other specialists to
obtain these orders.[19] This means that execution quality on other exchanges
will be unaffected by integration. Third, since the integrated broker shifts some
orders to its integrated specialist, the market share of the integrated exchange
will rise following integration. Finally, since m is smaller on the regional exchanges, the agency problem is most severe there.[20] The first column of table
6.2 summarizes these predictions, which are then tested against our data.

In addition to the predictions that are testable with our data, this model suggests other changes that are potentially measurable. For example, this model
suggests that the market share of the integrated broker declines (since α percent of its would-be customers go elsewhere). Also, the model suggests that
the retail customers of the integrated firm get less price improvement on the
integrated exchange than other retail customers *on that exchange.* Similarly,
these customers get worse execution on vertically integrated stocks than they
do on other stocks, ceteris paribus. With a more refined data set, it may be
possible to test these predictions.

6.3.2   Foreclosure Effects of Integration

Judicial interpretation of antitrust law has long viewed vertical mergers as
having a potential for "foreclosing" rivals. The fear expressed has been that
the acquisition of a customer or supplier would lead the integrated firm to
reduce or eliminate its trade with nonintegrated suppliers or customers. As
Chief Justice Warren put it in *Brown Shoe,* "the diminution of the vigor of
competition which may stem from a vertical arrangement results primarily
from a foreclosure of a share of the market otherwise open to competitors."[21]
A more rigorous conceptualization of foreclosure was developed by Salinger
(1988). According to Salinger, a vertical merger leads to foreclosure if it increases the input cost faced by unintegrated firms.[22]

Whether a vertical merger can result in foreclosure has long been debated
in the economics literature.[23] Recent work by Ordover, Saloner, and Salop

19. We assume away the possibility that other brokers, because of payment for order flow or
reciprocal agreements, are not acting in consumer interest. The benefit of integration relative to
other means of competing for order flow is discussed below.
20. This discussion abstracts from the constraints imposed on the specialist by competition from
floor traders who wish to trade against the incoming orders. This suggests a second reason that
agency problems may be more severe on regional exchanges, since the NYSE is a thicker market,
and hence the NYSE specialist is more likely to face competition from floor traders on that exchange. This also suggests that the agency problem will be most severe for thinly traded stocks on
any exchange.
21. *Brown Shoe Co. v. United States,* 370 U.S. 294 (1962), 328.
22. As discussed below, foreclosure in this sense is a necessary, but not sufficient, condition for
welfare to fall with integration.
23. See, for example, Comanor (1967).

Table 6.2   **Summary of Agency and Foreclosure Model Predictions for Integrated and Nonintegrated Exchanges**

Variable	Agency Model	Foreclosure Model
Volume	Decrease in total	Decrease in total
Effective spread	Increase for integrated	Increase for both types
	No change for nonintegrated	
Median spread	No change for either type	Increase for both types
Price improvement	Decrease for integrated	Ambiguous for integrated
	No change for nonintegrated	Increase for nonintegrated
Percentage of volume	Increase for integrated	Ambiguous for both types
	Decrease for nonintegrated	
Trade size	Decrease for integrated	Ambiguous for both types
	Increase for nonintegrated	
Depth	No change for either type	Decrease for both types

(1990, 1992) provides a formal model under which vertical integration can result in foreclosure. In their model, firms that produce differentiated products compete in each of the two related markets.[24] The markets are related in that firms in one market sell a product that is an input used by firms in the second market. Because firms are differentiated, the Bertrand equilibrium prices for all firms exceed marginal cost.

In applying this model to financial markets, we view exchanges as supplying "execution services" to brokers. Brokers combine this input with retail brokerage services, and sell the combined package as a "retail execution" to customer. Exchanges are differentiated in that they offer different execution speed, depth, and the ability to execute prearranged crosses. The Ordover-Saloner-Salop model assumes that prior to integration, at the equilibrium prices (effective spreads), each broker routes some orders to each exchange. Following the integration, the foreclosure model predicts that the increased market power created by the integration allows the integrated firm to increase the effective price its specialist unit charges nonaffiliated brokers. This can be accomplished by increasing realized spreads, reducing depth, or similar means of making the integrated exchange less attractive to other brokers. The direct effect of this change shifts out the demand facing specialists on other exchanges, whose optimal response is to increase their effective prices.[25] Ultimately, by increasing its rival brokers' costs and prices, the integrated firm

24. In their 1990 paper, input producers manufacture undifferentiated products, which implies that foreclosure can occur only when there are *exactly* two input producers. As this assumption does not fit the market of interest here, the model we present incorporates the suggestion made in their 1992 reply, that differentiated firms exist in both markets. We assume the differentiation in the two markets to be "orthogonal"; that is, consumers' preferences across brokers are independent of their preferences across exchanges.

25. Recall that exchanges are viewed as differentiated, so that an exchange would not capture 100 percent of the market by keeping its effective price constant when the integrated exchange raised its price.

is able to increase its market share and/or increase the price it charges for retail executions.

Note that, while both the agency and the foreclosure theories imply higher trading costs, the means by which trading costs rise is likely to be different in the two cases. In the foreclosure model, the integrated firm wants to increase its rivals' costs of executing all trades in the integrated stock. Since most trades occur at the bid or the ask, this requires increasing spreads, or reducing depth. Hence, the foreclosure model implies higher spreads after integration, while the degree of price improvement received by other brokers on the integrated exchange need not change. Further, the model predicts that the other exchanges would increase their prices, but by less than the integrated exchange. This implies that the extent of price improvement (measured from the inside bid or the ask) would rise, although the realized trading cost (the absolute percentage difference between the trade price and the quote midpoint) would increase. These predictions are summarized in the second column of table 6.2.

6.4   Data and Summary Statistics

Our analysis is based on all integrations that occurred on the New York, Boston, or Philadelphia stock exchanges since 1987. There are four integrations at New York, seven at Boston, and one at Philadelphia. The corresponding numbers of stocks in these integrations are 72 in New York, 279 in Boston, and 55 in Philadelphia. For each integration, the date, brokerage firm, and ticker symbol of the associated stocks are presented in table 6.1. This table also contains the sample of 101 control stocks. Randomly selected from NYSE, these stocks were continuously listed from 1987 to 1993 and were not involved in any of the above integrations.

The data for our analysis are intraday bid, ask, and execution price data from the Securities Industry Automation Corporation (SIAC). To the extent possible, we examine four weeks of trade data from a period three months before the integration, and another four weeks from a period three months after the integration. Because the SEC only periodically saved the SIAC data, in some cases we can analyze only two weeks of data, in other cases the before/after window is reduced to two months.

It is an unfortunate fact of life that there are gremlins in the SIAC data. We have attempted to filter out obviously inconsistent values and used estimation procedures that minimize the impact of outliers. Nevertheless, the raw data set contains eighteen million observations, and undoubtedly some gremlins remain.

Summary statistics for the integrated and control stocks are presented in table 6.3. Each panel contains four groups of statistics, and each group contains before-integration and after-integration statistics. In panels B and C, the first group contains observations for the integrated stocks on the integrated exchange. The second group contains observations for the control stocks on the

Table 6.3 **Summary Statistics**

A. Integrations on the New York Stock Exchange[a]

	Integrated Stocks, NYSE		Control Stocks, NYSE		Integrated Stocks, non-NYSE		Control Stocks, non-NYSE	
	Before	After	Before	After	Before	After	Before	After
Median spread	1.469	1.359	1.568	1.788	2.812	2.073	2.322	2.648
	1.197	1.242	1.208	1.197	1.666	1.593	1.795	2.061
	0.143	0.138	0.07	0.098	0.118	0.085	0.055	0.062
Effective	0.730	0.612	0.898	0.794	0.740	0.608	0.830	0.806
spread	0.715	0.574	0.738	0.596	0.631	0.458	0.658	0.618
	0.048	0.043	0.032	0.031	0.030	0.028	0.018	0.017
Improvement	0.158	0.195	0.162	0.237	0.047	0.086	0.072	0.158
≤ 3,000	0.110	0.159	0.132	0.166	0.018	0.039	0.016	0.061
shares	0.022	0.017	0.011	0.011	0.011	0.010	0.008	0.008
Improvement >	0.089	0.164	0.072	0.232	0.077	0.075	0.073	0.065
3,000 shares	0.076	0.083	0.044	0.146	0.000	0.000	0.000	0.000
	0.030	0.031	0.014	0.020	0.022	0.021	0.014	0.011
Price	35.71	34.68	30.56	26.56	40.88	39.69	35.66	30.00
	21.13	23.70	24.84	22.24	37.12	31.22	28.49	24.30
	3.663	3.888	1.439	1.234	1.905	1.952	0.846	0.670
% of volume	85.04	87.47	88.84	87.27	3.948	4.774	6.291	7.363
	87.06	89.43	86.22	90.13	1.748	1.823	1.464	1.869
	1.625	1.418	0.836	0.859	0.462	0.820	0.521	0.561
% of trades	78.97	81.08	83.44	80.45	5.672	6.322	7.789	9.127
	80.51	80.40	84.72	82.03	3.454	3.342	3.158	3.571
	1.658	1.352	0.918	0.896	0.464	0.707	0.501	0.534
Average trade	1634	1608	1694	1622	2261	1736	2085	2333
size	1449	1363	1212	1417	570.0	400.0	531.9	535.2
	129.4	105.8	209.7	65.85	372.5	338.6	310.0	498.0
Traded	1.674	1.518	1.474	1.280	0.276	0.246	0.222	0.252
volume	0.673	0.409	0.395	0.334	0.118	0.081	0.048	0.046
(millions)	0.425	0.463	0.150	0.140	0.067	0.026	0.026	0.051
Depth	31.00	44.22	28.76	34.78	5.027	4.651	4.560	5.417
	15.00	20.00	14.50	17.50	1.000	1.000	1.000	1.000
	6.499	10.33	2.522	3.534	0.743	0.763	0.346	0.860
Observations	71	67	302	291	65	61	279	283

B. Integrations on the Boston Stock Exchange[b]

	Integrated Stocks, Boston		Control Stocks, Boston		Integrated Stocks, NYSE		Control Stocks, NYSE	
	Before	After	Before	After	Before	After	Before	After
Median spread	2.628	2.629	2.694	2.547	1.421	1.127	1.424	1.263
	2.088	2.144	2.006	1.826	1.007	0.917	0.909	0.790
	0.126	0.119	0.098	0.096	0.095	0.074	0.073	0.064

continued)

Table 6.3 (continued)

B. Integrations on the Boston Stock Exchange[b]

	Integrated Stocks, Boston		Control Stocks, Boston		Integrated Stocks, NYSE		Control Stocks, NYSE	
	Before	After	Before	After	Before	After	Before	After
Effective	0.759	0.739	0.805	0.721	0.770	0.702	0.797	0.715
spread	0.582	0.583	0.598	0.516	0.670	0.586	0.631	0.555
	0.036	0.034	0.032	0.029	0.033	0.030	0.028	0.024
Improvement	0.144	0.165	0.179	0.191	0.147	0.141	0.166	0.157
≤ 3,000	0.078	0.104	0.088	0.090	0.122	0.115	0.118	0.119
shares	0.015	0.017	0.017	0.016	0.009	0.007	0.008	0.006
Improvement	0.090	0.092	0.080	0.076	0.098	0.084	0.093	0.106
> 3,000	0.000	0.000	0.000	0.000	0.070	0.071	0.075	0.080
shares	0.021	0.022	0.021	0.019	0.012	0.012	0.012	0.010
Price	32.28	32.39	26.74	29.24	30.80	32.46	27.15	30.21
	25.67	25.88	25.18	28.09	23.31	25.72	24.15	27.95
	2.655	2.411	0.766	0.839	2.522	2.503	0.846	0.955
% of volume	1.571	2.188	5.099	4.435	85.16	84.09	83.57	83.84
	0.745	0.980	1.323	1.284	87.80	87.52	85.91	85.90
	0.262	0.492	0.754	0.653	0.726	0.760	0.582	0.521
% of trades	2.300	3.817	6.573	5.742	73.76	72.12	70.91	70.42
	1.333	2.384	3.019	2.952	75.21	73.74	69.96	69.43
	0.231	0.524	0.704	0.548	0.976	0.918	0.727	0.728
Average trade	1470	697.9	860.3	905.8	2078	1960	1733	1780
size	614.2	530.1	551.1	553.1	1678	1185	1469	1478
	41.53	41.19	82.26	93.83	225.5	89.47	56.3	59.63
Traded	0.034	0.038	0.062	0.074	2.606	2.750	2.940	3.401
volume	0.013	0.015	0.019	0.019	1.405	1.359	1.052	1.183
(millions)	0.004	0.005	0.009	0.012	0.255	0.297	0.261	0.334
Depth	1.000	1.214	1.011	1.000	63.19	68.98	43.37	42.39
	1.000	1.000	1.000	1.000	25.00	30.00	25.00	27.50
	—	0.214	0.011	—	8.543	9.169	3.134	2.602
Observations	209	228	359	375	222	219	403	409

C. Integrations on the Philadelphia Stock Exchange[c]

	Integrated Stocks, Philadelphia		Control Stocks, Philadelphia		Integrated Stocks, NYSE		Control Stocks, NYSE	
	Before	After	Before	After	Before	After	Before	After
Median spread	1.831	2.383	2.684	2.802	0.709	0.709	1.516	1.355
	1.263	1.536	1.951	2.150	0.488	0.459	0.904	0.793
	0.220	0.327	0.259	0.276	0.082	0.085	0.197	0.179
Effective	0.657	0.583	0.795	0.830	0.495	0.478	0.743	0.733
spread	0.459	0.435	0.630	0.686	0.336	0.319	0.522	0.531
	0.080	0.060	0.071	0.073	0.059	0.055	0.065	0.067

Table 6.3 (continued)

C. Integrations on the Philadelphia Stock Exchange[c]

	Integrated Stocks, Philadelphia		Control Stocks, Philadelphia		Integrated Stocks, NYSE		Control Stocks, NYSE	
	Before	After	Before	After	Before	After	Before	After
Improvement	0.045	0.053	0.119	0.131	0.101	0.095	0.192	0.155
≤ 3,000	0.010	0.009	0.026	0.034	0.073	0.068	0.126	0.110
shares	0.012	0.018	0.037	0.034	0.012	0.0341	0.020	0.016
Improvement	0.026	0.020	0.140	0.010	0.066	0.067	0.144	0.095
> 3,000	0.000	0.000	0.000	0.000	0.057	0.053	0.102	0.075
shares	0.016	0.029	0.085	0.058	0.020	0.010	0.023	0.025
Price	46.06	44.47	28.75	29.52	31.37	28.80	26.80	29.24
	39.40	39.89	27.39	30.63	39.63	39.89	25.16	30.63
	4.235	3.815	2.279	2.180	4.309	3.884	2.017	2.306
% of volume	1.159	1.932	3.000	4.803	85.23	86.08	82.88	82.62
	0.813	1.539	0.865	1.109	85.87	87.16	83.71	86.04
	0.139	0.226	1.166	1.537	0.822	0.792	1.261	1.622
% of trades	2.615	5.537	3.826	5.865	68.60	66.35	70.14	71.65
	1.997	5.523	2.222	2.431	67.85	67.50	68.62	72.30
	0.334	0.504	0.683	1.461	1.627	1.600	1.803	1.977
Average trade	789.7	581.9	1497	1182	2008	2196	1687	1636
size	576.1	451.6	412.0	425.0	1973	2020	1534	1532
	94.24	57.29	932.6	481.2	111.0	132.1	102.1	111.2
Traded	0.082	0.120	0.037	0.053	5.887	4.728	2.509	2.009
volume	0.041	0.056	0.015	0.013	4.725	3.055	0.968	0.874
(millions)	0.015	0.021	0.018	0.018	0.748	0.636	0.489	0.390
Depth	1.842	1.455	1.000	1.065	52.81	66.94	36.78	39.85
	1.000	1.000	1.000	1.000	35.00	46.00	23.50	23.00
	0.612	0.389	—	0.065	6.841	10.20	5.362	6.959
Observations	54	56	54	61	53	55	67	69

Notes: For each group of statistics, the reported numbers are the mean, median, and standard error. These numbers refer to averages across firms.

These statistics are based on four vertical integrations on the New York Stock Exchange (NYSE).

These statistics are based on seven vertical integrations on the Boston Stock Exchange.

These statistics are based on one vertical integration on the Philadelphia Stock Exchange.

integrated exchange. The third group contains NYSE observations for the integrated stocks. The fourth group contains NYSE observations for the control stocks. Panel A, which presents the NYSE integrations, differs in that the third and fourth groups contain observations from the other exchanges for the integrated and control stocks.

To analyze the effects of integration, we examine several measures of trading costs and trading volume. The median spread is computed from all bid and ask quotes. We focus on the medians to mitigate the effect of outliers. The effective spread is defined as twice the absolute value of difference between the trade price and the midpoint of the spread. This value is then scaled by the price level. The midpoint is obtained from the highest bid price and lowest ask price, across all markets. The price improvement variables are defined as the minimum of the ask price minus the trade price, or the trade price minus the bid. This variable is scaled by the price level and computed for trades less than or equal to three thousand shares, and trades more than three thousand shares. The percentage of trades and percentage of volume correspond to the fraction executed on the specified exchange (Boston, Philadelphia, or New York). Trading volume represents the volume on the designated exchange. The depth is defined as the average of the quoted bid size and the quoted ask size. For each variable, the values reported in table 6.3 represent averages across firms. The numbers presented in the table are the mean, median, and standard error.

It is useful to compare these summary statistics on spreads and price improvement to those in other recent work. The data on NYSE price improvement is consistent with Angel's (1993) findings. He finds that on NYSE SuperDOT markets orders, average price improvement is 0.19 percent on buy orders, and 0.23 percent on sell orders. In our data, price improvement on small trades ranges from 0.16 percent to 0.24 percent. Lee (1993) finds that effective spreads are about 14 cents on the NYSE and about 15 cents on the Boston and Philadelphia exchanges, or about two-thirds the level suggested by our data.

The summary statistics suggest the impact of NYSE integrations on trading costs is minor. Relative to the control group, the NYSE integrated stocks show a similar decline in effective spreads. The spreads for the control stocks rise following the integration, but this is offset by greater price improvement among the control stocks. Following integration, the integrated stocks capture a larger fraction of trades and trading volume than the control stocks.

Panels B and C show a roughly similar pattern for the Boston and Philadelphia integrations. The effective spreads for the integrated stocks appear to decrease by slightly more than the control stocks. Relative to the control stocks, however, the median spreads rise slightly following integration. As with the NYSE integrations, the integrated stocks exhibit an increase in the fraction of trades and the fraction of trading volume following integration. Unlike the NYSE integrations, however, the average trade size shows a clear decrease following the regional integrations. Overall, these statistics are consistent with the interpretation that vertical integrations do not adversely affect trading costs.

6.5   Regression Tests of Agency and Foreclosure Models

In this section, we examine evidence from past acquisitions, with three purposes in mind. First, we look at measures of trading cost and volume to determine whether the net effect of integration has been to increase or to decrease the quality of executions. Second, we use information about trading costs and market shares to test the models described in section 6.3. Finally, to the extent that the two proposed models do not explain the existing pattern, we present hypotheses that are consistent with the data, and offer some additional suggestive evidence.

6.5.1   Overall Cost of Trading

As noted in section 6.2, there are two components to retail trading cost: the bid-ask spread (the specialist's price) and the broker's commission. Since we have no data on the latter component, we use two approaches in order to draw some inferences from the changes resulting from broker-specialist integration. First, we assume that commissions are unaffected by integration and examine the effect of integration on measures of effective bid-ask spread. Second, we assume that, like other products, the demand for trading any stock is a decreasing function of the cost of doing so. This implies that changes in volume move inversely with changes in trading costs.

The regression results in table 6.4 offer additional evidence that broker-specialist integration on the NYSE has had little impact on trading costs. We measure this impact by regressing the difference between the median percentage spreads after the integration and the median prior to integration against the percentage change in price, percentage change in trade size, change in the standard deviation of quote midpoint returns, and the change in total volume across all exchanges. Parallel regressions are presented for the change in effective spreads and for two measures of the change in price improvement. The first price improvement measure is based on all trades, while the second is computed only for small trades of less than three thousand shares.

Panel A examines how the trading costs of NYSE integrated stocks change relative to nonintegrated NYSE stocks. Panel B examines how NYSE integrations affect the trading costs on the regional exchanges. The underlying stocks are the same in both panels, but panel A uses trades and quotes only from the NYSE, while panel B uses observations from the regional exchanges. In both panels, the dummy coefficients for the NYSE integrated firms are uniformly small, and the t-statistics are less than 1.25 in absolute value. The economic magnitude was similarly small. For example, in panel A, the median spreads increased by 0.027 percent following integration. This value is about 2 percent of the average percentage spread.

The effects of integration on trading costs at the regional exchanges is presented in table 6.5. Panel A examines how the trading costs of integrated stocks on the Boston (or Philadelphia) exchange change relative to other stocks on Boston (or Philadelphia). Panel B examines whether the regional integrations affect the trading costs on the NYSE. Panel A uses trades and quotes only from the regional exchanges, while panel B uses observations from the NYSE.

Overall, the results are largely consistent with table 6.4. There is no significant change in the median or effective spreads following integration. While the spreads tend to rise following integration, the only statistical difference is in

Table 6.4   **The Effect of NYSE Integrations on Trading Costs**

			Dependent Variable	
	Change in % Median Spread	Change in % Effective Spread	Change in Price — All Trades	Improvement — Small Trades
A. Effect on NYSE trading costs[a]				
Intercept	.03331	−.00071	.00057	.00050
	(1.71)	(−4.85)	(4.18)	(3.64)
% change in price	−.68705	−.00480	−.00320	−.00315
	(−7.64)	(−7.04)	(−5.05)	(−4.96)
% change in trade	−.04640	−.00119	.00044	−.00040
size	(−1.53)	(−0.82)	(2.06)	(−1.88)
Change in standard	−.00710	−.00061	.00028	.00021
deviation of returns	(−0.11)	(−0.26)	(0.63)	(0.47)
Change in volume	.00099	−.00003	.00007	.00007
(millions)	(1.11)	(−0.52)	(1.16)	(1.15)
Integrated stock	−.02765	.00018	−.00037	−.00030
dummy	(−.065)	(0.55)	(−1.25)	(−1.00)
R^2	.181	.163	.127	.116
Observations	278	278	278	278
B. Effect on regional exchange trading costs[b]				
Intercept	.12932	−.00074	.00090	.00151
	(5.17)	(−.99)	(1.22)	(1.31)
% change in price	−.84628	−.00541	−.00135	−.00085
	(−7.22)	(−1.53)	(−0.39)	(−0.19)
% change in trade	−.00711	.00011	−.00012	−.00025
size	(−0.64)	(0.82)	(−0.37)	(−0.51)
Change in standard	−.05373	−.00063	.00035	.00056
deviation of returns	(−0.63)	(−0.24)	(0.14)	(0.14)
Change in volume	.00209	−.00003	.00000	.00004
(millions)	(2.15)	(−0.10)	(0)	(0.09)
Integrated stock	−.01334	.00035	−.00062	−.00010
dummy	(−0.25)	(0.22)	(−0.4)	(−0.44)
R^2	.232	.014	.003	.00:
Observations	180	180	180	18

Notes: These cross-sectional regressions are based on four vertical integrations on the NYSE. Each observation for the dependent variable is the before/after change for the same firm. The dummy variable is on for the integrated stocks and zero otherwise.
[a]All variables, both integrated and control, are measured on the NYSE.
[b]All variables, both integrated and control, are the average for the two regional exchanges.

the price improvement regressions. Integration on the regional exchanges is associated with somewhat more price improvement for small trades ($t = 1.39$) and with less price improvement for small trades on the NYSE ($t = -2.36$).

Table 6.6 presents additional evidence on trading costs by examining the change in trading characteristics following integration. The change in share of trades executed, the percentage change in the trade size, the change in the

Table 6.5   **The Effect of Regional Integrations on Trading Costs**

	Dependent Variable			
	Change in % Median Spread	Change in % Effective Spread	Change in Price — All Trades	Improvement — Small Trades
A. Effect on regional trading costs[a]				
Intercept	.01741	.00008	.00003	−.00002
	(1.42)	(0.52)	(0.14)	(−0.08)
% change in price	−.76576	−.00411	.00173	.00274
	(−15.70)	(−6.26)	(1.97)	(0.39)
% change in trade size	−.00506	−.00002	.00004	.00007
	(−1.14)	(−0.34)	(0.6)	(0.68)
Change in standard	.03875	.00086	−.00037	−.00021
deviation of returns	(0.56)	(0.94)	(−0.3)	(−0.13)
Change in volume	.00024	.00002	−.00000	−.00000
(millions)	(1.77)	(0.99)	(−0.09)	(−0.21)
Integrated stock	.01694	.00031	−.00033	−.00059
dummy	(0.92)	(1.26)	(−1.1)	(−1.39)
R^2	.513	.151	.025	.037
Observations	257	257	257	257
B. Effect on NYSE trading costs[b]				
Intercept	.04311	−.00010	.00032	.00030
	(3.79)	(−0.65)	(0.23)	(2.37)
% change in price	−.55254	−.00557	.00016	.00006
	(−12.74)	(−8.91)	(0.31)	(0.12)
% change in trade size	−.01336	−.00011	.00013	.00014
	(−0.59)	(−0.34)	(0.47)	(0.58)
Change in standard	.09306	.00286	−.00206	−.00206
deviation of returns	(1.54)	(0.33)	(−2.64)	(−3.03)
Change in volume	.00318	.00002	.00001	−.00001
(millions)	(1.16)	(0.51)	(0.43)	(−0.59)
Integrated stock	−.00479	.00034	−.00054	−.00048
dummy	(−0.26)	(1.32)	(−2.31)	(−2.36)
R^2	.178	.103	.016	.020
Observations	763	763	763	763

Notes: These cross-sectional regressions are based on eight vertical integrations on the two regional exchanges. Each observation for the dependent variable is the before/after change for the same firm. The dummy variable is one for the integrated stocks and zero otherwise.
[a]All variables, both integrated and control, are measured on the relevant regional exchange.
[b]All variables, both integrated and control, are the average for the two regional exchanges.

percentage of volume executed, and the change in total volume are all regressed against a dummy variable for the integrated stocks. Panel A presents these regressions for the NYSE integrations and is based on NYSE observations. Panel B contains the corresponding regressions for the regional integrations and is based on observations from the regional exchanges.

An alternative way to measure the change in trading costs following integra-

Table 6.6   The Effect of Integrations on the Characteristics of Trading

	Dependent Variable			
	Change in Trade Share	% Change in Trade Size	Change in Volume Share	Change in Total Volume (millions)
A. Integrations on the NYSE[a]				
Intercept	−2.7974	.16907	−1.8981	−.1779
	(−5.83)	(4.60)	(−2.44)	(−1.42)
Integrated stock	2.8431	−.10485	2.7938	−.0476
dummy	(2.53)	(−1.22)	(1.53)	(−0.16)
R^2	.022	.005	.008	0
Observations	278	278	278	278
B. Integrations of the regional exchanges[b]				
Intercept	.1339	.4440	.1286	1.2191
	(0.45)	(2.80)	(0.66)	(2.34)
Integrated stock	1.7844	−.5493	.0660	−.18862
dummy	(3.8)	(−2.18)	(0.21)	(−2.27)
R^2	.053	.018	0	.02
Observations	257	227	257	257

[a]These cross-sectional regressions are based on four vertical integrations on the NYSE. For all equations, the dependent variable is the before/afer change in that variable for the NYSE. The dummy variable is one for the integrated stocks and zero otherwise. All variables, both integrated and control, are measured on the NYSE.
[b]These cross-sectional regressions are based on eight vertical integrations on the two regional exchanges. For all equations, the dependent variable is the before/after change in that variable for that regional exchange. For the final equation, the dependent variable is the before/after total volume traded in the stock on all three exchanges. The dummy variable is one for the integrated stocks and zero otherwise. All variables, both integrated and control, are measured on the affected regional exchange.

tion is to examine the change in trading volume. For the NYSE integrations, trading volume fell by 0.047 million shares relative to the control stocks, but the t-statistic is only −0.16. A much stronger volume effect is observed for the regional exchanges. Relative to the control stocks, trading volume fell by 1.88 million shares, and the t-statistic changes to −2.27. This corresponds to a substantial decrease in total trading volume. Overall, these results are consistent with no change in trading costs for the NYSE integrations but provide some support for increased trading costs following the regional integrations.

The results in table 6.6 also suggest changes in the characteristics of the trading process for the regional exchanges. Relative to the control stocks, stocks involved in the regional integrations captured an additional 1.78 percent of the total number of trades executed and average trade size on the regional exchange decreased by 54 percent. The corresponding t-statistics are 3.80 and −2.18. The fraction of trading volume rose by 0.06 percent ($t = 0.21$), which reflects a trade-off between an increasing number of trades and a smaller trade size. The NYSE integrations show a somewhat different pattern. The integrated stocks increased their fraction of trades by 2.83 percent ($t = 2.53$) and their fraction of volume by 2.79 percent ($t = 1.53$). Similar to the regional integrations, however, there is some evidence of a decrease in trade size.

6.5.2   Testing Implications of the Agency and Foreclosure Models

Our analysis of the effect of integration on trading costs suggests that the NYSE integrations had little effect on trading costs, while the regional integrations may have increased trading costs. While both the agency and the foreclosure explanations predict higher trading costs, their predictions for the effect of integration on effective spreads, trade size, and depth differ. The predictions of the two models are detailed in table 6.2.

Our results, detailed in tables 6.4–6.6, suggest that neither model explains the mechanism by which integration can lead to higher trading costs. For the NYSE integrations, the only significant changes are an increase in depth on the NYSE, and increased market share on the NYSE (particularly of trades). Neither of the changes are in the direction predicted by the foreclosure model, and only the increased market share is as predicted by the agency model. As predicted by the agency model, there is a small, although not statistically significant, reduction in price improvement on the integration stocks, but two other effects undermine this interpretation. First, the size of the reduction in price improvement is smaller on the NYSE than on the regionals for the NYSE-integrated stocks. Second, the decrease in NYSE price improvement is larger (and more significant) for all trades than for small trades. This is contrary to the notion that small, naive traders would be disadvantaged. Also note that while none of the changes in trading costs that occurred on the regional exchanges are consistent with the foreclosure model, none of the changes are significant.

There are some significant changes associated with the regional integration (most importantly the effect of total volume), but again, most of the changes are not along the lines predicted by either model. For example, these integrations seem to have reduced price improvement significantly on the NYSE, but neither model predicts such a change. We also note that effective spreads actually fell on the NYSE, albeit not significantly. Similarly, median posted and effective spreads rose (not significantly) on the regional exchange experiencing the integration, while price improvement actually increased. This is not the pattern associated with either model. Hence, even if trading costs did rise, as the volume data suggest, some other explanation needs to be found.

6.5.3   Other Potential Motivations for Integration

The evidence presented thus far supports the notion that the NYSE integrations have not resulted in higher trading costs, while the effect of the regional integrations is ambiguous. If the motivation for integration was not of the type described in section 6.3, an alternative motivation must exist.

One potential motive for an acquisition is to better distinguish among classes of traders. For example, as discussed in section 6.2, suppose it is more costly for the specialist to trade against orders from those who have better information than he has (informed traders), than to trade against those with the same or worse information as the specialist (uninformed traders). If the specialist can limit his transactions to trading against uninformed traders he can, ceteris paribus, earn higher profits.

This view provides an explanation for the practice of payment for order flow, and is consistent with specialists willing to pay for small, retail (i.e., nonprofessional) order flow only. It is reasonable to assume that brokers possess knowledge regarding which traders are professional, and that professional orders are more likely to be information based.[26] If one assumes that the broker has useful information regarding whether the trader is informed, this explanation implies that the payment the specialist makes to the broker is one way that specialists compete for the opportunity to trade against uninformed retail orders. In turn, competition among brokers may then result in lower commissions being charged to retail customers. That is, payment for order flow results in a kind of market segmentation; retail orders implicitly face lower trading cost reflecting the lower cost of dealing with such customers.

Broker-specialist integration may be an alternative, and more complete, means of accomplishing the same objective. Integration may dominate payment for order flow because an integrated broker has more incentive to separate informed from uninformed traders.[27] Integration would allow the specialist to outbid other floor traders for the orders from the integrated broker because only the specialist knows that the orders are retail (uninformed) orders. This is similar to the model in Seppi (1990). In his model, because the broker can identify the individual institutional trader, a separating equilibrium emerges where uninformed institutions trade with the broker, and informed institutions trade with an unaffiliated market maker. In both models, the information about the identity of the customer allows the broker to trade with uninformed (and hence less costly) customers.

This "separation" hypothesis implies that, following integration, the integrated specialist's trades will be characterized by a reduction in average trade size or, equivalently, by an increase in market share of trades and, to a lesser extent, market share of volume. One would also anticipate improved execution for small trades on the integrated exchange, and worse execution for trades on

26. Keim and Madhavan (1992) and Easley and O'Hara (1987) show that small orders are less likely to be information based as well. Since specialists know the size of an order, however, the valuable component of the broker's knowledge concerns the identity of the individual placing the order.

27. In a static (i.e., no repeat interaction) environment, the unintegrated broker has no incentive to screen out informed traders, since it realizes none of the costs of the specialist trading against informed traders. As the perceived length of its relationship with the specialist increases, the broker's incentive to screen increases, but can never exceed the incentive of the integrated broker.

the other exchanges. Finally, one would expect to observe larger effective spreads on small trades for those stocks when they are traded on other exchanges.

The results in tables 6.4–6.6 are broadly consistent with this conjecture. The integrations on the regional exchanges resulted in an increased market share of trades and a decreased trade size. Additionally, price improvement on small trades increased on the regional exchanges, but declined on the NYSE following the regional integrations. The NYSE integrations led to a similar effect on market share, although the statistical significance is lower. However, price improvement declined on all exchanges following the NYSE integration, not just on the regionals, contrary to the conjecture. Another implication of this explanation is that the integrated broker's ability to attract retail customers should increase as a result of integration. This implication is potentially testable if data on individual broker's market shares of order flow at the retail level were available.

A second potential motivation for a broker to acquire a specialist is one that is not unique to the broker-specialist relationship, but rather common to many acquisitions. If any firm is managed in a way that does not maximize the value of that firm, alternative management teams may attempt to acquire control of the firm. Thus, specialist firms may be acquired simply because they are not well managed. One reason brokers may be the acquirers is that, by virtue of their relationship with many specialists, brokers know which specialist units are poorly managed.

Data on profitability of specialists is not readily available. However, one measure of how well a specialist is managed is the ranking it gets from the NYSE. The NYSE ranking is based on characteristics such as average spread and depth in the traded stocks. As noted above, although the rankings are nonpublic, industry sources indicate that the acquired specialists had relatively low rankings. This is consistent with our data. On all three exchanges, the stocks of the acquired specialists had significantly lower market shares (of both volume and trades) than the average stock on that exchange. Moreover, for all three exchanges, the share of the affected stocks being traded on the integrated exchange rose. For the Boston and New York exchanges, this increase occurred despite a general reduction in the market share of that exchange over the period. While the Philadelphia exchange's share of trading in all stocks increased over the sample period, the increase in the affected stocks far exceeded the general increase in the exchange's market share. A second factor supporting the idea that ratings rose is that the depth increased in Boston and New York following integration. Average depth on the Boston exchange rose by nearly three standard errors, and the New York change was about two standard errors. The effect of the Philadelphia acquisition, however, was to reduce depth by about two-thirds of a standard error.

6.6   Conclusion

This paper examined the effect of brokers acquiring specialists on the NYSE and two regional exchanges. These acquisitions, particularly those on the NYSE, provide us an opportunity to examine the effect of an increase in the degree of vertical integration within a firm.

Two theories have been proposed that suggest that such an increase may work to the disadvantage of investors: an agency theory and a foreclosure model. We derived testable implications of these theories and, using transaction data, tested some of the implications. We find that, even for acquisitions where investors may have been harmed, neither theory accounts for the mechanism. Hence, neither provides much insight into the motivation for these acquisitions.

The changes we do observe are reductions in average trade size on the integrated exchanges, and a divergence of order flow. These findings are consistent with the rerouting of retail orders and suggest some alternative motivation for these acquisitions. We offer two conjectures in this regard. First, vertical integration may facilitate profitable trading against uninformed retail orders. Second, it is possible that the specialist units that were acquired had been managed in a way that did not maximize their value. We offer some suggestive evidence consistent with these alternatives. Further work, or alternative models, would expand our understanding of financial markets and, more generally, the determinants of the degree of vertical integration.

References

Angel, J. 1993. Who Gets Price Improvement on the NYSE? Working paper, Georgetown University.

Blume, M., and M. Goldstein. 1992. Differences in Execution Prices among the NYSE, the Regionals, and the NASD. Working paper, Wharton School, University of Pennsylvania.

Comanor, W. 1967. Vertical Mergers, Market Power, and the Anti-Trust Laws. *American Economic Review* 57:254–65.

Easley, D., and M. O'Hara. 1987. Price, Trade Size, and Information in Securities Markets. *Journal of Financial Economics* 19:69–90.

Hasbrouck, J., and D. Sosebee. 1992. Orders, Trades, Reports, and Quotes at the New York Stock Exchange. NYSE Working Paper 92-01.

Hasbrouck, J., G. Sofianos, and D. Sosebee. 1993. New York Stock Exchange Systems and Trading Procedures. NYSE Working Paper 93-01.

Keim, D., and A. Madhavan. 1992. The Upstairs Market for Large Transactions: Analysis and Measurement of Price Effects. Working paper, Wharton School, University of Pennsylvania.

Lee, C. 1993. Market Integration and Price Execution for NYSE-Listed Securities. *Journal of Finance* 48:1009–38.

Ordover, J., G. Saloner, and S. Salop. 1990. Equilibrium Vertical Foreclosure. *American Economic Review* 80:127–42.
———. 1992. Equilibrium Vertical Foreclosure: Reply. *American Economic Review* 82:698–703.
Petersen, M., and D. Fialkowski. 1994. Posted versus Effective Spreads: Good Prices or Bad Quotes. *Journal of Financial Economics* 35:269–92.
Salinger, M. 1988. Vertical Mergers and Market Foreclosure. *Quarterly Journal of Economics* 53:345–56.
Seppi, D. 1990. Equilibrium Block Trading and Asymmetric Information. *Journal of Finance* 45:73–94.
Tirole, J. 1988. *The Theory of Industrial Organization.* Cambridge: MIT Press.

Comment   Philip H. Dybvig

The effect of vertical integration by broker-dealers and specialists is a very good example of the theme of this conference. This question of whether such vertical integration is good or bad is not firmly within the domain of either industrial organization or finance, and benefits from simultaneous illumination from both disciplines. From industrial organization, we have traditional views of vertical integration producing possible synergy gains or reducing competition. From finance, we have views that such mergers may increase the conflict of interest between broker-dealers and their clients (which conflict is already significant absent the integration, especially given that broker-dealers can trade on their own account), and we have the notion that the more highly capitalized broker-dealers will tend to increase liquidity and stabilize the market. Constraining all of these effects is the impact of regulation, both by the SEC and by the exchanges. Neal and Reiffen have started the process of sorting out the relative importance of some of these effects.

The most interesting part of the paper is the empirical analysis, and the interesting result is that there is no smoking gun that suggests that performance of the specialists degrades significantly after acquisition by a broker-dealer. This result must be qualified by a number of limitations of the analysis (most of which are due to data problems). For example, we have no data on commissions, whose contribution is ironically the part of performance that is easiest for the customer to observe.

Price improvement is one of the important variables in the paper. Unfortunately, the measure of price improvement in the paper is not very satisfactory, due to data limitations. The measure in the paper takes the distance to the closest side of the spread, normalized to the spread midpoint. When the spread is one-eighth, according to this definition there is no price improvement (since

Philip H. Dybvig is the Boatmen's Bancshares Professor of Banking and Finance at Washington University in Saint Louis.

the stocks are quoted in eighths), but that is not necessarily the case. As I understand the data, we do not even know which trades were made by the specialist (or which side the specialist took), and which trades were undertaken by floor traders or were negotiated upstairs and merely cleared on the floor of the exchange.

The nature of price improvement can make vertical integration profitable for subtle reasons, given that the specialists have the discretion to give special treatment to orders from their own firms. One form of price improvement is the stopping of a trade by the specialist, who later has the option of letting the trade stand with a counterparty from the limit order book or improving the price on own account. This is a free option that allows the specialist to profit with the submitter of the market order at the expense of the limit order book. For example, if the spread is 50–50¼, a market order to buy may be stopped by the specialist at 50¼, and tentatively matched with a limit order to sell at 50¼. If the stock price subsequently falls (say to 49¾–50), the specialist can improve the market order's price to 50⅛ and take the other side of the trade. Selling at 50⅛ is now profitable to the specialist, and the submitter of the market order also profits, both at the expense of the limit order. If the price rises, however, the submitter of the limit order is stuck with a losing sell.

How can specialists use this price improvement mechanism to favor trades from their own firm and its customers? When given a choice of what orders to stop for possible price improvement, specialists can stop orders stamped with their firm's name, which favors the firm's customers and the firm's own trade. Similarly, when tentatively matching a limit order to a stopped trade, the specialists can avoid doing so with orders from their own firms. This is a subtle way that vertical integration can profit a specialist, and this could not be detected without much finer information.

I liked the argument in the paper that a vertical integration of a specialist and a broker-dealer is a way for capturing the same rents one would obtain by selling order flow without such an obvious conflict of interest between the broker-dealer and its clients. Of course, this conflict of interest is no less strong, even if it is less obvious. A broker-dealer that profits either from selling order flow or from sending the order flow to its own subsidiary specialist would have less incentive than it should to seek out the best execution for its clients. This is a clear conflict of interest and is probably not in the public interest. Unfortunately, the paper has very little to say about this argument empirically. On a related note, it would be useful if we could measure the increased robustness of the specialists, given a larger capital base.

It is worth mentioning a few minor statistical issues. In general, I like the paper's attempt to find controls for some of the effects, but this could be carried further. For example, normalizing spread by price controls somewhat for the size of the stock price, but we do know that the proportional spread is related systematically to the size of the stock price. Similarly, there may be some selection bias in the population of specialists who are for sale. We know that some merged because they were insolvent after the crash, and it came out in the discussion that the specialists who merged were generally on the exchanges' problem lists. It might be useful to compare these mergers to a sample of acquisitions by firms that are not broker-dealers. It might also be useful to categorize the results by large and small stocks. On a final statistical note, use of median statistics leaves out the outliers that may be the most interesting cases: median statistics suggest that there is no problem in the typical case, but in rare cases the mergers might be a real disaster. Of course, such analysis would require particular care to make sure that the outliers are not simply due to data problems.

To summarize, the integration of broker-dealers and specialists is a very interesting policy arena in with both finance and industrial organization are important. It is interesting that the paper does not find any strong evidence of big changes in the performance of specialists following these mergers. However, tests of many of the potential effects are beyond our reach, given the current data availability, and much work remains.

Comment   Michael D. Robbins

I believe the paper would have added value if it addressed the question, Who is advantaged when a broker directs order flow to his own captive specialist and who is disadvantaged? A distinction between regional specialists and NYSE specialists should be sharpened. The issue of "price improvement" when orders are exposed to the primary market should also be addressed. Are price improvement and fiduciary obligation quaint ideas?

A clear study of the history, both recent and not-so-recent, of broker-dealer specialist integration would be useful. How did Merrill Lynch back into the specialist business during the tumult of the 1987 crisis? How does it view the business today (1994)? Would it expand today? What caused the exit of Paine Webber from the specialist business? How much are regional specialists dependent upon the liquidity exit they have on the NYSE? What about the stealth specializing done by retail firms under rule 19c-3? Why do institutional (informed) investors get treated differently by integrated broker-dealer specialists than retail (uninformed) investors? My viewpoint, of course, is more pragmatic than theoretic because of my background—I am a businessman rather than an academic, and I earn my living as an agent in the marketplace day after day.

Experience has shown me that the major attribute of a specialist organization has to be an understanding of the nature of risk. This is not always avail-

Michael D. Robbins is a member of the New York Stock Exchange and serves on the board of directors of the exchange.

able abundantly in large, broad-based, integrated broker-dealers, but may be present in good measure in a small, tightly knit group of risk takers.

Authors' Reply

We would like to thank Philip Dybvig, Michael Robbins, and conference participants for their thoughtful commentary on our work. We would also like to thank Andrew Lo for organizing this conference.

Our goal in studying the effect of integration between specialists and broker-dealers was twofold: to see if we could understand the motivation for the integrations, and to draw policy implications concerning the desirability of future integration and payment for order flow. The comments of Dybvig and Robbins illustrate the significance of the issue discussed, as well as the potential pitfalls in our study.

A central issue addressed by both commentators is selectivity bias; that is, how does one explain which integrations took place, and how does the nonrandomness of integrations affect the inference one can draw from our study?

Dealing with the first issue, since these four NYSE specialists were presumably viewed by broker-dealers as the most desirable candidates for acquisition, it seems reasonable that the four differ from the fifty or so NYSE specialists that were not. We agree with the commentators that it would be valuable to gain some understanding of why these particular transactions occurred. To some extent, each event may be idiosyncratic, and hence it may be difficult to systematically explain the transactions. For example, it was suggested by both commentators that the first integration (Merrill Lynch acquiring Tompane) was motivated by the specialist's impending insolvency following the 1987 market decline.

While newspaper accounts of that transaction confirm the specialist's predicament, they also suggest that something else was going on. For example, while the timing of the acquisition was influenced by the market decline, the acquisition apparently was not; negotiations between Merrill Lynch and Tompane had been ongoing for eighteen months prior to the acquisition (i.e., since the rule change). Similarly, the notion that Merrill Lynch bailed out a failing company does not appear consistent with the fact that there were other bidders for Tompane after the market decline, and that Merrill Lynch paid $10 million for a company with $5 million in debts. Finally, the Brady commission report noted that thirteen specialists had run out of liquidity on October 19, 1987, and most of those did not sell out to a broker-dealer, so clearly there were other sources of capital available to these specialists.

In order to learn about whether there is a systematic relationship between the characteristics of the specialist and the likelihood of integration, however, would require extensive information about the specialists. Unfortunately, it is difficult for someone outside the industry to learn much about the operating characteristics of the four specialists, as information such as profitability is not publicly available. Similarly, the NYSE ranks specialists in terms of the quality of their market making, but these ratings are not publicly available.[1]

One type of information that is available is the stocks in which each specialist makes a market, and some measure of the specialists' performance. These data are displayed in table 6.3 in our paper. Those data suggest that the stocks in acquired specialists' portfolios tended to be slightly larger volume stocks, selling at higher prices. In regard to performances of the specialists, the information is somewhat mixed; while the four NYSE specialists were worse than the control group in capturing trading volume (as measured in their market share), they did tend to have lower effective spreads than the control group. One final observation is that the four firms had on average a portfolio of eighteen stocks, which is about half the average for all NYSE specialists. This difference may reflect the lower NYSE ranking, as new listings are generally given to more highly rated specialists. Alternatively, it could be that smaller portfolios are not viable and must be combined with other business activities or other portfolios to achieve minimum viable scale.

To the extent that the four specialists were atypical of NYSE specialists, inference about future integrations from our work would be limited. If the agency motivation were a valid explanation of the reason for integration, then these four integrations would represent those with the greatest potential for harm. To the extent that no such harm was found, future integrations may be even less likely to produce these adverse consequences.

Dybvig notes that, while our theoretical analysis is based on specialists' taking the opposite side of all incoming orders, in reality the NYSE specialists' participation rate is considerably lower.[2] Many retail orders execute against NYSE floor traders and against existing limit orders, or are matched with other retail orders. This fact by itself mitigates, but does not eliminate, the kinds of problems we describe. For example, one can think of agency problems existing even if the probability is less than one that the integrated specialist has the opportunity to trade against the uninformed order flow.

One way of evaluating the consequences of our assumption is to examine how our results change as the percentage of trades that involved the specialist changes. Of course, we cannot observe the percentage. One proxy for participation rate of the specialist is the trading volume in a stock. Logic, as well as casual empiricism, suggests that floor traders tend to congregate around the posts of heavily traded stocks. Additionally, it seems likely that crosses occur less frequently and limit orders are less effective in thinly traded stocks. For

---

1. As Dybvig notes, the general impression among professionals is that these four specialists tended to be among the lower-rated specialists.

2. In the discussion during the conference, it was suggested that roughly 10 percent of NYSE trading involves the specialist's taking one side of the transaction.

both of these reasons, we would conjecture that, for any effective spread, the percentage of trades involving the specialist would be higher for thinly traded stocks.

Based on this, we examined whether the effect of integration was different for thinly traded stocks. If in fact we see diminution of execution quality on these integrated stocks, but not on integrated stocks in general, it would suggest that the agency theory may be relevant when the specialist faces reduced competition from floor traders (as generally occurs on the regional exchanges). To test this, we reran the regressions in panel A in tables 6.4 and 6.6, using only those test and control stocks in the lower 50th percentile of all stocks in the relevant group. We found no significant differences between these results and those reported in the paper; the coefficients changed little, although the standard errors rose due to smaller sample size. While it may be true that price improvement occurs less frequently for low-volume stocks, whatever advantages broker-dealers get from owning specialists do not appear to depend on the stock's trading volume.

Dybvig is correct when he notes that our measure of price improvement (and hence effective spread) is imperfect. Since we cannot observe whether an order is a buy or a sell, we cannot know the actual price improvement (or effective spread). In addition, our algorithm does not allow for price improvement when the bid-ask spread is one-eighth. These problems may contribute to the relatively low significance levels in our study.

In sum, we agree that the study does not fully explain the motives for integration, nor completely measure the effect. Nevertheless, we find it interesting that the data do not suggest that trading costs rose following integration. Our results therefore have significant implications for future integrations and for payment for order flow.

7 International Regulation of Securities Markets: Competition or Harmonization?

Lawrence J. White

7.1 Introduction

Since World War II, the rapid improvements in the technologies—data processing and telecommunications—underlying financial services have increasingly allowed firms in these markets to offer more financial services over wider geographic areas. One important consequence has been the potential or actual internationalization of many financial services.[1] Firms in the financial services industries are increasingly operating and offering their services in multiple countries; savers and investors are increasingly willing to channel their capital flows across national boundaries; and borrowers and securities issuers are increasingly seeking sources of funds across those same national boundaries.

In this environment, the national regulatory regimes that were designed for an earlier era, when financial markets were largely local or national in scope, are under strain. National regulators are clearly concerned about their ability to exercise their regulatory authority in this era of international flows and functions.[2] It is no accident that a number of international coordinating organizations—for example, the Cooke (Basel) Committee for commercial banks and the International Organization of Securities Commissions (IOSCO)—have been formed during these recent decades.

A recurring plea by national and international regulatory officials is that important aspects of financial regulation should be harmonized internationally—in essence, made uniform across the major countries involved in these

Lawrence J. White is the Arthur E. Imperatore Professor of Economics at the Stern School of Business, New York University.

The author is indebted to John Campbell, Mary Ann Gadziala, Dana Jaffe, Roberta Karmel, Michael Klausner, Millard Long, and Eugene Sherman for valuable comments on earlier drafts.

1. For general discussions, see Stoll (1990); Kosters and Meltzer (1990); Siegel (1990); Fingleton (1992); Edwards and Patrick (1992); and Stansell (1993).

2. See, for example, Walker (1992); Breeden (1992); Guy (1992); and Quinn (1992).

financial services.[3] This, it is claimed, will create a "level playing field" for market participants and prevent a "race to the bottom" among competing countries' regulatory regimes, which would harm financial market participants. There are others, however, who believe that much national financial regulation has the effect (whether by design or by inadvertence) of *preventing* the efficient allocation of resources by financial markets.[4] In this view, the harmonization of these regulations would reinforce and perpetuate these inefficiencies, and *competition* among regulatory regimes would likely enhance the efficiency of capital flows.

This paper provides an analytical framework for evaluating these conflicting approaches to the international regulation of financial services. In this paper, I focus primarily on securities markets,[5] but the lessons are valid for other financial services as well. The framework that I employ is that of analyzing both "market failure" (the structural conditions under which a market may fail to deliver the efficiency results promised by the textbook model of competition) and "government failure" (the reasons that government regulation may fail to correct and may even exacerbate the market imperfections that an omniscient and benevolent government might otherwise be expected to eradicate).[6] I argue that this framework applies to competition between exchanges and between national regulatory regimes as well as to competition between firms.

Using this framework, I find that there may be some regulatory areas where effective harmonization could improve the efficiency of securities markets. But in many other areas, competition among regulatory regimes is likely to be the best way to achieve efficiency in capital markets. One of the major goals of this paper is to provide the basis for distinguishing between the two approaches.

This paper proceeds as follows: In section 7.2, a vocabulary and taxonomy of different types of regulation—useful for the analysis that follows—is established. Section 7.3 discusses the main categories of market failure and relates these categories to the types of regulation that might be used to remedy them; it also outlines the major sources of government failure. In section 7.4, I pull these strands together to analyze the harmonization-versus-competition questions. Section 7.5 offers a brief conclusion.

7.2   Types of Regulation

For the purposes of this paper, I define regulation to mean any nonfiscal governmental intervention (i.e., excluding specific taxes or subsidies) in the

3. See the references cited in footnote 2. See also Grundfest (1990); Steil (1992, 1993); Worth (1992); and Karmel (1993).
4. See Kane (1991, 1992); Benston (1992a); and Steil (1992, 1993).
5. By securities markets, I mean the markets (which need not be organized around an exchange) for financial instruments of all kinds, including foreign exchange; in essence, I am excluding primarily the financial intermediation that occurs directly through banks, insurance companies, and pension funds (though these institutions are often involved in transactions that encompass the instruments that are the focus of this paper).
6. This approach is somewhat similar to that followed by Wolf (1989).

operation of private-sector markets. This regulation can be in the form of laws passed by legislatures, formal edicts issued by regulatory bodies, or informal guidance or interpretations offered by a government agency. This definition of regulation clearly encompasses a broad range of governmental intervention in markets. But regulation is not simply an undifferentiated mass of governmental intervention. It is possible to find commonalities among major types of regulation, which will prove useful for the discussion in the later sections in this paper. I offer three major categories.

Economic regulation usually involves limitations on prices, profits, and/or entry into or exit from an activity.[7] Familiar examples outside the financial services area would include the pre-1980s regulation of airline prices and routes by the U.S. Civil Aeronautics Board (CAB); the regulation of local electricity, natural gas, and telephone company prices and profits by individual state regulatory commissions; and limitations on local taxicab fees and entry by many cities.

Within the financial securities area, the pre-1970s blessing by the U.S. Securities and Exchange Commission (SEC) of the New York Stock Exchange's (NYSE) system of minimum fixed commissions would be one example; the American Glass-Steagall Act's limitations, which largely prevent commercial banks from entering the securities business and prevent securities firms from operating commercial banks, are a second;[8] limitations by various national governments as to what kinds of firms (including a determination of the nationality of their owners or their country of incorporation) can engage in various kinds of securities activities are a third.[9]

Health-safety-environment (H-S-E) regulation typically involves mandated changes in production processes and/or product qualities or types.[10] Nonfinance examples include the U.S. Federal Aviation Administration's safety requirements for airlines (including minimum requirements for their aircraft, pilots, and procedures); the U.S. Food and Drug Administration's (FDA) safety requirements with respect to pharmaceuticals and food additives; the U.S. Environmental Protection Agency's maximum limits on the emissions of air pollutants from electric utilities (and other stationary sources) and from motor vehicles; and the U.S. Occupational Safety and Health Administration's requirements for workplace safety.

In the securities area, examples would include the SEC's minimum capital requirements for broker-dealers; its requirement that securities firms' "registered representatives" should be licensed, should "know their customers," and should recommend only investments that are suitable for the specific circum-

---

7. For overviews, see Breutigam (1989); and Joskow and Rose (1989).

8. Loopholes, discovered by sharp-eyed lawyers in the 1980s, have allowed a few commercial banks to engage in securities underwriting and have allowed some securities firms to operate "nonbank banks."

9. These limitations extend beyond considerations of safety and soundness.

10. Together with information regulation, this form of regulation is sometimes described as "social regulation." For an overview, see Gruenspecht and Lave (1989).

stances of their customers; its requirement that only accredited investors (e.g., institutions) be allowed to purchase private-placement securities; and its requirement that money market mutual funds limit their holdings of low-quality commercial paper.

Information regulation typically involves the requirement that sellers attach specified types of information to the goods and services that they sell. Nonfinance examples include the U.S. Department of Transportation's requirement that an airline's ads for special fares should include (in fine print) the major details of the special fares' limitations; a state utility commission's requirements that electric or telephone utility bills include specified types of information; the FDA's requirements for labeling to accompany pharmaceuticals and processed foods; and a local taxicab commission's requirement that a cab driver's name and license number be prominently displayed.

In the securities area, examples of information regulation abound: for example, the SEC's requirements that issuers of publicly traded securities should disclose extensive information at the time of issuance and then disclose extensive information at periodic intervals and on a uniform (generally accepted accounting principles, or GAAP) basis; its requirement that mutual funds should report yield information on a specific and standardized basis; and its requirements that a publicly traded company's insiders disclose their holdings and trading activities.

These three regulatory categories are not airtight and may blur at the edges. Some forms of economic regulation may have some real or alleged H-S-E justifications or effects (e.g., the CAB's airline regulation or the Glass-Steagall restrictions). Also, the CAB's entry restrictions on airlines clearly impeded the development of an important production technology ("hub and spokes" scheduling), which emerged only after deregulation; and profit limitations in the form of rate-of-return restrictions are likely to influence input choices in production.[11] Further, virtually all forms of H-S-E and information regulation have some cost consequences, with implications for prices, profits, and possibly even entry. Nevertheless, the intent, form, and direct consequences of these three types of regulation are generally distinct enough that this typology is useful for furthering our understanding of regulatory goals, processes, and effects.

7.3   Market Failure and Government Failure

7.3.1   Market Failure

What might justify the forms of regulation just described? In principle, perfectly competitive markets ought to achieve efficient outcomes without the

---

11. This is frequently described as the Averch-Johnson effect; for a summary, see Baumol and Klevorick (1970).

need for any governmental intervention. But real-world markets may exhibit one or more types of "market failure" that would preclude their achieving those efficient outcomes. These market failures can be categorized as follows.

Market power. If one or a few sellers are present in a market and entry is not easy, the quantity sold is likely to be smaller and the equilibrium price is likely to be higher than would be true for an otherwise similar competitive industry. This is frequently described as the problem of monopoly or oligopoly.

Market power can arise (when entry is not easy) through explicit or implicit collusion among sellers (e.g., price-fixing conspiracies); through mergers that significantly reduce the numbers of firms and increase their market shares, thereby making explicit or implicit collusion easier; through technological conditions (e.g., economies of scale) that limit the number of efficient-size firms that can serve a market (e.g., the monopolies of local exchange telephone service or of local electricity generation); or through government restrictions that prevent entry and thereby protect market incumbents (e.g., the CAB's restrictions on entry into the airline industry). In the securities area, the pre-1970s agreement among NYSE member firms as to minimum brokerage commissions collectively gave those firms market power. The protected position of specialist market makers in most stocks listed on the NYSE similarly gave them market power. Specialists today in stocks where trading volumes are insufficient to permit competitive market makers may still enjoy some residual market power.

Economies of scale. The presence of economies of scale may serve as a source of pricing inefficiency even if the seller is not exploiting market power. If the technology of production in a relevant market is such that larger volumes (per unit of time) always imply lower unit costs,[12] then the efficient outcome of setting price equal to marginal costs may not be feasible, since it would not allow the firm to recover its full costs. Systems of local telephone service or electricity distribution may be of this nature. In the finance area, securities markets appear to exhibit economies of scale, since greater volumes of transactions (greater liquidity) are usually accompanied by smaller transaction costs (narrower spreads).

Externality (spillover) effects. If, as a consequence of a firm's production or an individual's consumption, there are direct and uncompensated effects on others—negative or positive—outside of a market framework, then the market outcome (even with a competitive structure) will not be efficient. With negative externalities (e.g., air or water pollution or traffic congestion), too much of the

---

12. This is a separate phenomenon from that of a "learning curve," which involves reductions in unit costs as a consequence of the accumulated production volume over any extended period of time. This latter phenomenon more closely resembles a process of gradual technological change.

good or service will be produced or consumed, and the price will be too low; also, too little effort and resources will be devoted to correcting or reducing the externality. With positive externalities (e.g., when one firm learns about improved production processes because of the efforts of other firms), too little of the good or service will be produced, and its price will be too high; also, too little effort will be devoted to enhancing the externality.

The usual source of externalities is the absence or poor specification of property rights and/or difficulties in enforcing them. For example, problems of air or water pollution can arise from the absence of clearly defined property rights in clean air or water and/or the free-rider problems that would accompany any single party's efforts to enforce its property rights. In the securities area, an example of negative externalities would be the negative consequences for other securities firms if the fraudulent actions of one firm were to cause the public to believe that other firms could or would act fraudulently; an example of positive externalities would be one firm's learning about another firm's development of a new securities product and thereby being able to develop and offer a similar product.

Public Goods. A "public good" is one in which the marginal costs of an extra party's enjoying the benefits of the good are relatively low or zero and exclusion from those benefits is difficult or impossible. In essence, a public good is one in which the positive externalities are substantial and pervasive.[13] Again, competitive markets will produce too little (or none) of the good or service, and its price will be too high. The provision of national defense, a police force's accomplishments in reducing the level of criminal activity in a community, a community's effort to control or eradicate mosquitos, and an individual's creation of an idea (information) that is useful to others would all be examples of public goods.

In the securities area, the previous example of one firm's developing a product that other firms can copy would qualify as an example of a public good; similarly, the price established in one market for a security may be useful to participants in other markets and would constitute a public good, as would the information developed by a securities analyst for distribution to his or her clients.

Uncertainty and the absence of complete knowledge. If individuals do not have complete knowledge about the present and future choices that are before them, they face uncertainty and risk as to the consequences of their choices and actions. Since most individuals are likely to be risk averse, they are likely to take ameliorating or offsetting actions—for example, acquiring information, forming portfolios, hedging—to reduce their risk exposure. These offsetting

13. Many of the phenomena that are identified as negative externalities, such as air and water pollution, are thus really "negative public goods."

actions often mean that additional resources must be expended. Also, with the presence of any uncertainty, individuals' ex ante choices may yield ex post mistakes.

In the securities area, uncertainty and incomplete information are pervasive, but a major fraction of securities services offered are designed to ameliorate or offset the effects of uncertainty: for example, the services of research firms and of rating firms; the diversified portfolios offered by mutual funds; and the options, futures, and swaps instruments that are now an active part of the securities world.

Asymmetric information. Problems of "asymmetric information" arise when a party on one side of a transaction has relevant information that the other side does not have.[14] For example, a seller of a good or service is likely to know more about its qualities and properties than does the buyer; an agent (e.g., a lawyer) is likely to know more about its actions than is the principal (e.g., a litigant) on behalf of whom the agent is expected to perform services; a borrower is likely to know more about its own prospects of repaying a loan than is a lender; a buyer of insurance is more likely to know about its own risk characteristics and the risk consequences of its prospective behavior than is a seller of insurance.[15] In the absence of any amelioration of these conditions, market participants may initially be "burned" by the outcome of these transactions but then learn to adjust their behavior—perhaps by participating less in these transactions. Output of the relevant good or service is likely to be lower than if the asymmetric information phenomenon did not exist. Over time, markets may develop institutions and practices—for example, information-generating entities, certifying agencies, reliance on reputation, reliance on "signals"—that can ameliorate the problems of asymmetric information. But these institutions and practices, in turn, involve costs and imperfections that would not be present if the asymmetric information problem were somehow absent.

Securities markets are an area where the problems of potential or actual asymmetric information are pervasive. Securities issuers know more about themselves than do prospective purchasers of the securities. Corporate managers know more about their activities than do shareholders or bondholders. A stock broker knows more about the quality of his or her services and recommendations than do the customers. Various information-based institutions—

14. For an overview, see Stiglitz (1989).

15. These asymmetric information phenomena can usefully be grouped as "hidden information" problems (the "lemons" problem of the buyer's knowing less about the qualities of the seller's product than does the seller, or the "adverse selection" problem of the insurance company's knowing less about the risk attributes of its insureds than do the latter) or as "hidden action" problems (the "agent-principal" problem of the buyer of services knowing less about the agent's actions than does the latter, or the "moral hazard" problem of the buyer of insurance engaging in more risky behavior because it is covered by insurance than it would if it did not have coverage). See Arrow (1985).

accounting firms, securities analysts, research firms, rating agencies, investment advisers—have developed and flourished in efforts to ameliorate these problems of asymmetric information, although these institutions in turn are likely to embody their own potential problems of asymmetric information.

Individuals who are unable to know their own best interests. If individuals do not know their own best interests, then even complete information will not prevent mistaken choices. This form of market failure is generally different from the problem of asymmetric information. If individuals are overwhelmed by the complexity of choices—for example, judging the safety of an airline or the quality of a hospital's services—they may rely on agents to help them (but with concomitant agent-principal problems). But if individuals do not know their own best interests, they may not even realize that they should be relying on agents, and they are unlikely to learn from their mistakes.

This "widows and orphans" approach to individuals' behavior is clearly a popular one for legislators, as is evidenced by numerous regulatory laws—including laws in the securities area—that require that "unsafe" products and services be banned from markets (rather than allowing individuals, or their agents, to make their own choices and trade-offs). Even if it is an accurate characterization of a portion of a society (beyond the categories of "children" and "mentally incompetent" to which it clearly would apply), the presence of others who are capable of making sensible choices then poses a difficult problem of how best to deal with safety issues in a society with diverse decision-making capabilities.

Problems of "second best." If an uncorrected market imperfection or failure exists in one market, then it will generally be true that unhindered competition in that market or in a related market (i.e., one in which there are demand or supply consequences from the initial imperfection) will not yield socially optimal results (see Lipsey and Lancaster 1956–57).

7.3.2 A Caveat and a Linkage

This listing of the major forms of market failure may initially encourage the impression that virtually all markets are ripe for governmental intervention. After all, few (if any) real-world markets would fit the textbook ideal of a perfectly competitive market. As will be argued below, however, governments also are far from perfect. The notion of the omniscient and benevolent governmental agency that can perfectly correct the failures of the private sector is also a textbook construct that few (if any) real-world government agencies could replicate. In sum, since both real-world markets and real-world governments exhibit varying degrees of imperfection, the actual policy debate concerning regulation (e.g., whether to regulate, how to regulate, the breadth of regulation, etc.) must always involve choices among imperfect markets and imperfect governments.

Subject to this caveat, this listing of the sources of market failure can be linked to the types of regulation discussed in section 7.2. The problems of market power and of economies of scale may be best treated through economic regulation;[16] externalities, public goods, and individuals' being unaware of their own best interests may be best approached through H-S-E regulation;[17] the problems of incomplete information and asymmetric information may be best approached through some combination of H-S-E and information regulation; and problems of "second best" are, in principle, the domain of any form of regulation.

7.3.3   Government Failure

Though government regulation can in principle improve the efficiency of imperfect markets, governments too can fail to deliver their promised outcomes, and their efforts at intervention can cause the efficiency of markets to deteriorate rather than increase. This government failure can occur for a number of reasons.

Difficulty in formulating clear and implementable goals. Without the specific profit goal that motivates most private enterprises, a government agency may well be buffeted by diffuse goals (e.g., improve the economy's efficiency, improve the economy's income or wealth distribution, avoid economic disruptions, treat individuals fairly) that are likely to be conflicting and difficult to translate for specific implementation. Overarching goals (e.g., "serve the people") may be even more subjective and open to conflicting interpretations and haphazard implementation.

Weak (or absent) incentives. Again, without profit incentives or the threat of bankruptcy, the diffuse goals of a government agency may make difficult the development of incentives to motivate government employees to work toward those goals. Also, societal values concerning income distribution and greater equality of incomes are more likely to hold sway in the public sector, making a link between a government employee's performance and his or her wages (with the likely consequences of wage differentials) more difficult to implement. Further, agency personnel may act in ways that enhance the importance and security of their own jobs rather than pursuing the larger public interest that is supposed to be the mission of their agency.

Difficulties of management. To be effective, organizations have to be well managed. With diffuse goals, government agencies are likely to be more difficult

---

16. Government ownership and taxes and subsidies are other possible tools of intervention.

17. Again, taxes (effluent fees) and subsidies are other possible tools for dealing with externalities and public goods. The creation and enforcement of property rights in "intellectual property" (i.e., patents, copyrights, and trademarks) is yet another way of dealing with the public goods problems that arise in the context of the creation of ideas and information.

to manage than are organizations with more specific goals. And in any event, good management is a relatively scarce skill that usually commands premium wages in an economy. The egalitarian ethos that makes performance-linked pay difficult to implement in government agencies also tends to cause compression in the overall government wage scale, so that low-skill jobs are usually overpaid (as compared to their private-market counterparts) and high-skill jobs are underpaid. As a consequence, governments frequently have difficulty in attracting and retaining highly skilled individuals, including managers, and government effectiveness suffers.[18]

Inadequate information. Government agencies may be no better at acquiring and using information than private-sector entities.[19] Indeed, the previously described problems of incentives and management would argue that government agencies may well have substantial difficulties in this respect. But with inadequate information, government agencies are likely to be plagued by the same types of problems and inefficiencies that were raised as potential market failures for private-sector entities. Regulatory controls based on poor information could well be costly; government regulators are likely to face asymmetric information problems vis-à-vis their regulated entities.[20]

Rent-seeking behavior. In an economy of gain-seeking individuals, those who are significantly affected by government action are unlikely to remain passive.[21] Instead, they are likely to try to influence governmental processes to achieve outcomes that are favorable to themselves ("rent seeking") and will find worthwhile the expenditure of considerable resources (ranging from outright bribery and corruption to more subtle lobbying and promises of electoral support) in efforts to twist government policy and actions in their favor. Even if these rent-seeking individuals and groups do not succeed in affecting policies (i.e., in "capturing" an agency or a legislature, as is discussed below), their efforts may well use up substantial real resources.

Rent-creating capture. Comparatively small groups of individuals who are potentially affected a great deal by government actions will have the most to gain

18. Government agencies may be able to attract some highly skilled individuals who hope to acquire the specific skills related to government operation and then leave to use those skills in the private sector. For example, the U.S. government has been able to attract young lawyers, even though its entry-level pay scale has been below the levels of the private-sector alternatives. But the flow of skilled human resources at senior levels is usually one-way—from government to the private sector—with the exception of short-term political appointments. The exceptions to this overall pattern are individuals who strongly believe that government service has an important intrinsic value and are willing to enter and remain in government service despite unfavorable pay differentials vis-à-vis the private sector.
19. For overviews and further discussion, see Stiglitz (1988, 1990).
20. For an overview, see Baron (1989).
21. See Krueger (1974); and, for an overview, Noll (1989).

from organizing themselves to influence government policy in their favor. Their success in achieving rent-creating policies—for example, regulatory protection—is likely to be at the expense of the general public. The latter, with each individual suffering only a small loss as a consequence of the altered policies, find the organizational costs of trying to oppose the changes to be too high. Consequently, rent-creating "special interest" regulatory measures and outcomes are likely to prevail, at the expense of the general population and of efficiency in the economy.[22]

Pursuit of income redistribution. A society may well decide that it is dissatisfied with the income distribution among individuals that would arise as the consequence of the workings of markets, whether those markets are operating perfectly or imperfectly. Government action is the vehicle for redistribution, and regulation can be an important means of implicitly affecting the distribution of income (see Posner 1971) (though taxes and subsidies are more common and more direct). But these actions surely create inefficiencies, even if they are successful at redistributing income (see Okun 1975). Further, the greater is the perceived legitimacy of government as a redistributive force, the greater is the potential for the rent-seeking behavior and rent-creating capture discussed above.

Regulatory efforts to achieve "fair" outcomes—as is true of much regulation in the securities area—would fall into this same general category. Though the regulation may apparently be aimed at correcting specific imperfections (for example, informational deficiencies or asymmetries or market power problems), the inclusion of "fairness" as a goal will usually imply some explicit or implicit notions of income redistribution (as compared with what an unregulated market would yield).

7.3.4   A Stronger Caveat

The combination of rent-seeking and rent-creating behavior and societal concerns encompassing income distribution and "fairness" can create potent regulatory forces that impede the efficient functioning of markets. The American regulatory landscape is littered with instances in which government agencies have practiced extensive economic regulation with the proffered justification of restricting the exercise of market power but with the reality of protecting and enhancing it. Examples at the federal level include airlines, rail transportation, trucking, banking, stock brokerage commissions, long-distance telephone service, and broadcasting; examples at the state and local levels include trucking, banking, long-distance and local telephone service, and taxicabs.[23]

---

22. See Stigler (1971); Posner (1974); Peltzman (1976); and, for an overview, Noll (1989).
23. Discussion and examples can be found in Phillips (1975); Weiss and Klass (1981, 1986); and Joskow and Rose (1989).

Further, the regulatory goal of cross-subsidy—achieving income redistribution by keeping prices paid by some users above long-run marginal costs so as to be able to use the surplus to keep the prices paid by other users below long-run marginal costs—has been an additional force for the employment of the tools of economic regulation in ways that protect and enhance market power. If prices are to be kept above long-run marginal costs, entrants must be prevented from "cream-skimming" or "cherry-picking" these supraprofitable markets, and market incumbents must also be protected from "excessive" competition among themselves in these markets; hence, these regulatory regimes must prevent entry and restrict competition among incumbents. Many of the perverse examples of economic regulation that were just cited have involved, at least in part, efforts to achieve cross-subsidy.

At first glance, H-S-E regulation would seem less susceptible to the forms of abuse and perverse application just described. But there are "winners" and "losers" arising from virtually every H-S-E regulatory action; and the combination of less-than-omniscient regulatory bodies, rent-seeking and rent-creating behavior, and the importance of "fairness" as a societal goal can lead to regulatory efforts and outcomes that involve substantial market distortions and inefficiencies.[24] The mantle of H-S-E goals can also serve to cloak protectionist and exclusionary measures, such as the Glass-Steagall Act's barrier between commercial banking and investment banking.[25]

Further, the costs of regulation can have disproportionate effects on some types of firms as compared with others; for example, there are frequently substantial fixed costs to complying with H-S-E regulation, which thereby favors larger firms (which can spread these costs over larger volumes of output) over smaller firms.[26] If the form and extent of the regulation is otherwise appropriate, then these are just the legitimate social costs of doing business, which may have the same kind of uneven effects as the purchase of a necessary but expensive piece of equipment.[27] But if the type or extent of regulation is inappropriate and it has an uneven impact (e.g., disadvantaging smaller or newer firms), protectionism in outcome—and possibly in intent—is an added feature of such regulation.[28]

Information regulation almost always has costs as well as benefits and thus is susceptible to the same problem of potential inappropriateness of types and levels as was just described for H-S-E regulation. And, though information

24. For examples and further discussion, see White (1981); Gruenspecht and Lave (1989); and Viscusi (1994).
25. Similarly, safety claims are sometimes used to justify the Bank Holding Company Act's general separation of commercial banking and insurance.
26. This disproportionate impact on small firms is exacerbated when H-S-E regulation takes the form of "design standards" (i.e., a specific process or type of equipment is mandated) rather than "performance standards" (i.e., a specific result on performance is required). The latter type of standard would give smaller firms greater flexibility in meeting a given requirement.
27. Again, the inflexibility of design standards would exacerbate the impact.
28. For a discussion, see White (1993) and the references cited there.

regulation is less likely to be explicitly exclusionary, the combination of inappropriate levels and large fixed costs is likely to have implicit exclusionary effects on smaller firms.

In sum, the real-world imperfections of government have yielded numerous instances of the regulatory process's being used for abusive purposes and reaching inefficient outcomes. Indeed, the deregulation movement of the late 1970s and the 1980s was a reaction to these abusive purposes and inefficient outcomes, especially in the economic regulation areas.[29] These abuses need not lead to the conclusion that all governmental regulation should be forsaken. But they do point toward constant caution in embracing new regulation (national or international) and toward the value of frequent reassessments of the motives, methods, and outcomes of existing regulatory regimes.

7.4   Harmonization versus Competition

7.4.1   The Widening Scope of Competition

The process of competition among firms can be analyzed as occurring within the confines of a market; indeed, one useful definition of a market is the collection of sellers that are in effective competition with each other.[30] This market may be embodied in a formal structure, with a physical representation and legal ownership framework, as is true for securities exchanges; or the market may simply be a group of firms that are effectively competing with each other.

As the costs of transacting over longer distances fall (e.g., because of improvements in the technologies of transportation, telecommunications, and/or data processing), markets widen: buyers and sellers that are located farther apart can now more easily transact with each other. Also, if changes in production or product technologies allow incumbent firms more easily to produce and sell a wider array of products and/or allow new opportunities for entrants, markets are again widened: buyers face more sellers that are competing for the former's purchases.

In the absence of formal market structures, the process of market widening is fully described by the larger numbers of sellers and/or buyers that are encompassed. To the extent that groups of sellers initially believe that they constitute a local market and then find themselves enmeshed in a larger market, the description below of wider competition among formal market structures, such as exchanges, may apply as well; a local trade association may be the vehicle through which the concerns of the local group are expressed.

---

29. See, for example, Weiss and Klass (1986); Joskow and Rose (1989); White (1993, n.d.); Winston (1993); and Joskow and Noll (1994).

30. This is approximately the market definition approach underlying the "Merger Guidelines" that guides U.S. merger antitrust policy. See U.S. Department of Justice (1992); and, for discussion, Kwoka and White (1994).

But where formal market structures are present, there is an additional element: the wider markets mean that the formal market structures (e.g., securities exchanges) themselves are in competition with each other—for sellers as well as buyers (see Bradley 1992). In essence, with improved technology both buyers and sellers can "evade" (or arbitrage) any higher costs of transacting in a "local" market by conducting their transactions in a more "distant" market—where "distance" may represent either geographic mileage or the extent of product dissimilarity. Securities exchanges in the United States have historically experienced such market widening as well as the concomitant intensified competition: geographically separated stock exchanges have increasingly competed among themselves (and with the less formally organized Nasdaq market system) for members, for listings, and for order flow. The stock exchanges have increasingly competed with the exchanges that trade other (but somewhat similar) kinds of instruments (e.g., options and futures). All exchanges are increasingly competing with over-the-counter (OTC) transactions in stocks and in customized swaps, options, and futures. And in the 1990s, the U.S. markets and exchanges are facing increased international competition, as are the markets and exchanges located in other countries.[31]

Similarly, if regulatory regimes have responsibility for local markets or exchanges, the widening of the markets represents a potential erosion of their authority: buyers or sellers can more easily evade these regimes' regulatory strictures (if they are burdensome) by transacting in an out-of-jurisdiction market or exchange. Previously separate and autonomous regulatory regimes are increasingly conscious of each other's jurisdiction and potential for snaring transaction volumes by reducing their regulatory burden. To the extent that regulatory agencies are concerned about avoiding the loss of transactions from their jurisdictions—because of concern as to the possible consequences for buyers or sellers within their jurisdictions of such out-of-jurisdiction transactions,[32] or because of worries by agency personnel that reduced within-jurisdiction volumes might bring into question the size of their agency and perhaps even the justification for their agency—they are thereby implicitly or explicitly in competition with each other.[33]

Again, the American experience is instructive. So long as the widening of securities markets remained within the United States and was largely confined to equity instruments, the SEC did not feel seriously threatened, although it

31. It is worth noting that the globalization of markets has displayed a pattern that is quite consistent with the predictions of the asymmetric information paradigm. An overview (Bodner 1990) describes the process of globalization as most advanced for foreign exchange, next for government obligations, third for corporations' debt (bonds), and least for corporate equity markets. This ranking is consistent with the transparency and simplicity of the various types of instruments and the information disadvantage that nonnational transactors would experience relative to national entities.

32. For example, the regulators may be concerned that within-jurisdiction sellers are unduly losing sales or that within-jurisdiction buyers are not being adequately protected.

33. See, for example, Scott (1977); Bloch (1985); Isaac (1994); and Coffee (1995).

clearly felt more comfortable dealing with the NYSE and its member firms and was somewhat worried about its weakened control over OTC and off-floor transactions. With the rise of the financial options and futures markets in the early 1970s—largely in Chicago, away from the SEC's traditional eastern seaboard focus—and the establishment of the Commodity Futures Trading Commission (CFTC) in 1975 to regulate some of these markets,[34] however, the SEC faced more serious challenges to its authority and jurisdiction. Its two decades of coexistence with the CFTC have been marked by alternating periods of open political battles for jurisdiction, uneasy political truces, and sporadic efforts at harmonization (see, e.g., Kane 1986 and Johnson 1992). And both agencies now face international competition in the 1990s—as do the national regulatory agencies of other countries.

A current regulatory issue typifies the SEC's concerns about transnational regulatory competition:[35] Should the SEC maintain its requirements that all companies whose equity shares are listed for trading in the United States (on an exchange or in other markets) must report their financial information according to U.S. GAAP? Or will unyielding insistence on this requirement cause non-U.S. companies (for whom a restatement of their financial information to conform with U.S. GAAP is an extra cost) to decline to list their shares for trading in the United States, thereby disadvantaging U.S. exchanges and market makers? But would relaxation of the GAAP reporting requirements for all firms mean that U.S. investors would be less well informed and protected? Or if the SEC relaxed the GAAP reporting requirements only for non-U.S. firms, would U.S. firms be somehow disadvantaged? And would U.S. investors in these non-U.S. companies' shares thereby be at an information disadvantage because of the less-complete information that they would receive? But, if the SEC maintains its strict GAAP requirements, will U.S. investors simply evade the SEC's efforts to protect them by purchasing these non-U.S. companies' shares through markets or exchanges abroad, albeit with larger transaction costs?

7.4.2 Some Generic Answers

We can now restate the questions that have motivated this paper. In an environment of near-global securities competition, when (if ever) is international harmonization of national securities regulation likely to improve the efficiency of securities markets? Conversely, when (if ever) is an absence of international harmonization, and thus a process of implicit or explicit competition among national regulatory regimes, likely to improve the efficiency of securities markets?

---

34. The CFTC also acquired regulatory authority over the agricultural and mineral (metals) commodities futures markets. The former set of markets had previously been regulated by the U.S. Department of Agriculture; the latter set had been largely unregulated.

35. For further discussion, see Edwards (1992); Freund (1993, 1995); Shapiro (1993); and Torres (1993).

The framework of section 7.3 provides a basis for generic answers to these questions:[36] for international harmonization to be potentially worthwhile, there must be some form of market failure (e.g., market power or externality) that transcends national boundaries and for which individual national regulatory efforts are somehow inadequate. But even in such instances the dangers of internationally harmonized *government failure* should lead to caution in endorsing a harmonization approach.

The application of these principles to securities markets leads to the following general approach to the international harmonization questions.

Proharmonization. The conditions under which international harmonization of a specific regulatory provision could improve the efficiency of securities markets would be one or more of the following: (1) The specific national regulatory provision is efficiently addressing a genuine market-failure condition and "evasive" transactions abroad would somehow undermine that effort. (2) The process of harmonization itself may be a vehicle for relaxing the stringency of protectionist national regulations that have created pockets of market power. (3) The process of harmonization itself may be a means of simplifying and making more uniform a diverse set of different national rules and procedures, with the consequence of lowering the transaction costs for those who try to transact on a multinational basis. (There is a separate question—whether harmonization, even if desirable, can succeed in an environment of international competition—to which we will return below.)

Procompetition. The conditions under which international competition among specific regulatory requirements could improve the efficiency of securities markets would be one or both of the following: (1) The regulatory provision is not efficiently addressing a genuine market failure but instead is the product of one or more of the government-failure conditions and is thereby a force for decreased efficiency; evasive transactions abroad are thus a proefficiency response (albeit an unnecessarily costly one) to the regulation; harmonization (to the extent it succeeds) would only buttress the national effort at inefficiency; by contrast, international competition of regulatory regimes would reduce the likelihood that the inefficient regulation could persist and would thereby increase efficiency. (2) The forced uniformity that harmonization would bring would mean too great a loss of diversity and of valuable adaptations to local (national) conditions; also, even if uniformity at the proper regulatory standard would be better (e.g., because of cost savings) than local diversity, the risk that a forced harmonization would occur at an inappropriate regulatory standard (because of the foibles of government failure) is too great.

36. A somewhat similar framework was adopted by White (1986) in addressing the question of competition among states to attract industry and by Bebchuk (1992) to address and review the literature on the competition among states to be the state of incorporation for U.S. companies. See also Steil (1992, 1993); Key and Scott (1991, 1992); and Benston (1992a, 1992b).

In my judgment, competition—whether among firms, among markets and exchanges, or among national regulatory regimes—ought to be the "default option"; that is, in the absence of a strong showing that there is a substantial market failure and that the problems of government failure can be overcome so as to create a reasonable likelihood that government intervention will improve outcomes, the competitive outcome should prevail. For the harmonization-versus-competition controversy, this position would imply that those who favor the international harmonization of specific national regulatory provisions should bear a substantial burden of making a convincing case. As is discussed below, there do seem to be specific instances where international harmonization may well be desirable; but the presumption should be in favor of competition, and a strong affirmative case for harmonization must be made in these specific instances.

7.4.3 Some Specific Examples

Most of the discussions of international harmonization of national regulation have been at a very broad level of generality and vagueness, and it is often difficult to determine exactly what regulatory provisions are candidates for harmonization. No one seems to be suggesting that the entire multifoot pile of U.S. laws and regulations that are the province of the SEC and the CFTC should be subject to international harmonization. But the specific regulatory provisions that might be the subject of harmonization are often unstated. Accordingly, the use of the regulatory classification system of section 7.2 is a reasonable way to proceed in examining some specific areas where harmonization might be worthwhile and others where harmonization is likely instead to be yet another instance of government failure dominating and worsening the market outcome.

Economic Regulation

As was discussed in section 7.3, economic regulation in principle can be a means of correcting the problems of market power. Where it is doing so effectively, the process of harmonization seems unnecessary; indeed, the widening of markets and of competition is likely to aid the process of limiting market power. But, as was also discussed in section 7.3, economic regulation in practice has frequently been the means by which market power has been protected and enhanced, often in the service of cross-subsidy. In this context, international competition is a threat to national regulation, and harmonization could be a vehicle for buttressing these anticompetitive national regulatory provisions and worsening market outcomes. There are at least two examples outside the field of financial services where an international coordinating and harmonizing organization has substantially reinforced market power and restricted competition: the International Air Transport Association (IATA) in the field of airlines (see Kasper 1988) and the United Nations Conference on Trade and Development (UNCTAD) for ocean shipping (see White 1988). These are cautionary counterexamples for anyone who might advocate international harmonization of national economic regulation.

Nevertheless, it is possible that harmonization could serve as a vehicle for *decreasing* the levels of national regulatory protectionism (i.e., decrease local market power) and subsidy. The General Agreement on Tariffs and Trade (GATT) is a useful example here. If the GATT, as a consequence of the Uruguay Round of negotiations, or IOSCO could be the vehicle for mutual reductions in the restrictive national regulatory treatments of nonnational financial service providers—under the guise of harmonization—the results could be beneficial indeed. There is, of course, the possibility that such efforts could be transformed into a defense and strengthening of protectionism; the IATA and UNCTAD counterexamples should constantly be remembered for their cautionary value, and the American regulatory experience has been that some regulatory bodies whose initial mandate was to limit market power were transformed over time into defenders and protectors of market power. Still, the value of harmonization here could be great, and any vehicle through which it could be pursued should be encouraged.

H-S-E Regulation

At first glance, the globalization of securities transactions would seem likely to extend to international markets the externalities and spillover effects that motivate some forms of national H-S-E securities regulation and thus would seem to justify harmonization to help control these effects. Upon closer examination, however, the argument is more complicated. I explore specifically the issues of systemic risk and price-and-market relationships.

Systemic risk. Concerns about market disruptions linked to the "systemic risk" caused by the failure of one or more financial services firms—arguably, a form of externality—is a dominant concern of national regulators. Much of the panoply of national safety-and-soundness (prudential) regulation of commercial banks (e.g., minimum capital requirements, limitations on suitable investments, extensive examination and supervision procedures) and the minimum capital requirements and other safety requirements for securities firms are motivated by this regulatory concern about the consequences of insolvency and failure.

Before asking whether these national concerns are a legitimate basis for seeking international harmonization, it is worth considering the reasons why a firm's insolvency and failure can have externality effects on financial markets. There are two alternative scenarios of systemic risk that are usually offered. The first might be termed the scenario of cascading failures: the insolvency failure of large financial firm (commercial bank or securities firm) would rapidly lead to a series of other failures, as firms that were substantial creditors of the initial firm are thereby thrown into insolvency, with consequent effects on yet more firms, and so forth.[37] This was one of the scenarios that motivated U.S. bank regulators to keep an insolvent Continental Illinois open in 1984, rather than closing and liquidating it (see Sprague 1986); and it is a scenario that is often offered in discussions surrounding the risks of the operations of the large interbank funds transfer systems, such as FedWire and the Clearing House Interbank Payment System (CHIPS).[38] It is instructive, though, that the failure of Drexel Burnham Lambert in early 1990 did not have any serious cascading consequences.

The second scenario of systemic risk could be termed one of depositor runs: the fear of an insolvency failure (real or imagined) of a large institution causes depositors to run (withdraw their deposits in the form of cash) on the institution and on other institutions that they fear might be in similar straits. The anticipation of such depositor runs, which could (at a minimum) impair an otherwise nonfearful depositor's timely access to the liquidity of his or her deposits and could even lead to the premature closing and liquidation of an otherwise solvent bank, may itself spark runs (see Diamond and Dybvig 1983).

Closer examination of the first scenario reveals the heart of that version of the problem: the asymmetric information ("moral hazard") problems related to financial institutions' extending sizable amounts of credit to each other for short-term periods, often as short as a few hours within a trading day. The primary responsibility for correction of this problem should be on the institution that is *extending* the credit. Regulatory requirements of adequate capital levels, so that the firm can better withstand loan losses of any kind, are vital, as are limits on its loan exposure to *any* borrower. Or if virtually all of a firm's exposure occurs through its transactions with other members of an exchange, the exchange may be an appropriate vehicle for ensuring payment; but the exchange similarly must be adequately capitalized and must have a mechanism for limiting exposure.

U.S. banking regulations already encompass limits on a commercial bank's exposure on commercial loans to any single borrower. The concept underlying these limits is a sensible one, and it should be broadened to include all extensions of credit for any length of time by any type of financial institution where a cascading systemic risk problem may be present. *Further, the logic of this position leads quickly and sensibly to the conclusion that minimum capital requirements for financial institutions (banks or securities firms or exchanges) should be applicable on a continuous (real-time) basis, rather than the periodic "snapshot" (e.g., end of calendar quarter) basis that currently applies.* A firm's exposure to default by others is on a continuous time basis, not just at discrete

37. The "cascading failure" scenario could be exacerbated by the "depositor run" scenario described below.
38. See Humphrey (1986); Dudley (1986); and the discussions in England (1991) and in the references cited in footnote 1.

time intervals; the minimum capital requirements that protect its liability holders should therefore be binding on a continuous time basis.

With these changes, national regulatory provisions should be adequate to prevent cascading consequences from institutional failures even in a world of major international interinstitutional financial flows. So long as national regulatory agencies can ensure that their home-country institutions have adequate capital on a continuous basis and are not unduly exposed to default by any borrower on a continuous basis, systemic risk can be contained nationally. International harmonization is not needed.

Close examination of the depositor-runs version of the systemic risk problem shows that it is a genuine externality problem (compounded by asymmetric information): each depositor's act of withdrawing cash increases the probability that other depositors will be unable to exercise their option to withdraw cash, thereby inducing the latter to move even earlier, and so forth. It is a problem of potential contagion.

At the national level for commercial banks, a combination of a lender of last resort, a deposit insurer, and a strong safety-and-soundness regulator that relies heavily on economic incentives (e.g., risk-based minimum capital requirements that are derived from a market value accounting system, the use of subordinated debt as a required component of capital, and risk-based deposit insurance premiums) should be adequate to deal with the problem (see, e.g., White 1991, 1992). There are problems of how to deal with the local subsidiary and branch operations of a bank that is headquartered abroad but that offers deposit services to local residents (see Key and Scott 1991, 1992); but these can probably be handled adequately through cooperation and information exchanges among national regulators. Similarly for securities firms, some form of insurance arrangement for customers and sensible safety-and-soundness regulation (again, encompassing economic incentives) should be adequate, with some international cooperation necessary for dealing with overseas branches, and so forth.

In principle, the problem of depositor runs could extend across national boundaries; in practice, the less sophisticated depositors or securities customers who would be the most likely "stampeders" would be unlikely to be major transactors with banks and securities firms located outside a country. The transnational transactors are likely to be more sophisticated (or have more sophisticated agents) and be more knowledgeable, and fear-driven contagion effects seem less likely. Again, it appears that national regulatory efforts should be adequate, and international harmonization is not necessary. In this respect, it is worth noting that the 1991 failure of the Bank for Credit and Commerce International (BCCI) did not exhibit significant contagion effects, nor did the 1990 failure of Drexel.

Is there any value to the harmonization achieved by the Basel Accord on minimum capital levels for commercial banks and by IOSCO's efforts for a similar agreement on capital standards for securities firms? Despite the previous conclusions, there is positive value from these harmonization efforts—but the rationale in support of these harmonization efforts is more subtle than the two systemic risk arguments that have just been rejected. *The value of these harmonization arrangements is primarily in limiting the implicit subsidy that most governments seem prepared to provide to their major financial institutions.*[39]

This rationale can be most clearly seen for the case of commercial banks. With or without the presence of explicit deposit insurance, most governments appear to be unwilling to force depositors to absorb the losses that would otherwise fall on them when major home-country banks become insolvent.[40] Though governments may be vague ex ante about their likely reactions, their ex post behavior has been consistent with this statement.[41] In essence, governments are absorbing the losses of these insolvent institutions and are thereby subsidizing risk taking by banks. International competition among banks (and their regulatory regimes) places extra pressures on the banks to reduce their direct funding costs by reducing their capital levels. Competitive regulatory regimes accede, since they are reluctant to put the banks within their jurisdiction at a cost disadvantage. But with lower capital levels, banks are more susceptible to failure and have greater incentives to engage in riskier behaviors, thereby raising the likelihood of failure and thus raising the level of subsidy.

The Basel Accord, by establishing a uniform set of minimum capital standards, makes this competitive regulatory behavior more difficult and thus serves to limit the competitive subsidy process.[42]

To the extent that governments would not be willing to have the creditors of securities firms absorb the losses from those failures, the same argument would

39. One should ask why it is in the interest of country B's residents to prevent country A's government from subsidizing A's banks. (After all, consumers in importing countries should generally applaud when the governments of exporting countries subsidize their exports.) There are two answers. First, if country B's banks are more efficient than A's banks, the subsidy will discourage B's banks from exporting their services to A and will also disadvantage them in competition in third markets; A's subsidy is inflicting genuine (Pareto-deteriorating) harm on B. Second, B's government may experience pressures (see the discussion of government failure) to respond with its own subsidies.

40. The failure of BCCI, with substantial losses to depositors, is an exception, but it is an explainable one. No country considered BCCI to be its responsibility; and the British government, which might have been the most concerned, was unlikely to be especially responsive to the political pressures of the depositor groups (immigrants from African and Asian Commonwealth countries) that were most affected.

41. For example, in late 1993 and early 1994, the governments of Spain, France, Japan, and Venezuela separately indicated that they would absorb specific bank losses in their countries, so as to avoid imposing losses on liability holders.

42. Also, the Basel Accord may have a secondary effect in reducing the problems of cascading failures or depositor runs. However, though the Basel Accord points in the right direction, it is substantially flawed: its broad risk categories have no obvious empirical foundation; they ignore portfolio considerations; they ignore interest rate risk; and they are based on a cost-based historical book value accounting framework rather than a market-value accounting framework. Also, as discussed in the text below, it may be very easy for countries to "cheat" on the accord if they choose to do so.

apply to IOSCO's efforts to develop harmonized capital standards for securities firms.

Prices and markets. A frequent concern by market makers and exchanges is that "outside" firms will free ride on the information—especially the price information—generated by the market. The outsider will thereby benefit and divert transactions away from the exchange. An additional concern is that such diversions will reduce the transaction volumes in the primary market, with consequent reductions in its liquidity and increases in its volatility. Finally, there are concerns that some market makers or exchanges may be willing to provide less transparency to transactions and will thereby attract the transactions of those who gain from reduced transparency. The competition among markets (and regulatory regimes) for this order flow may well lead to securities markets that generally have less transparency.

These concerns about the relationships among markets have been the basis for calls for greater international harmonization of regulatory provisions that would solve or ameliorate these problems. Again, though, closer examination is warranted.

It is clear that the information yielded by a market, including its level of transparency, is a public good in the sense defined in section 7.3, and public goods can generate the problems described. But there may be less drastic measures that can ameliorate the problem.

With respect to the price information provided by markets, the relevant market maker or exchange could be assigned the property rights in the market's information. This property-rights approach, which is similar to the way that other problems related to the creation and dissemination of information (intellectual property) in market-oriented economies are handled, would reduce free riding but need not unduly discourage the possible development of new forms of market making (see, e.g., Bronfman and Overdahl 1993). Further, it would be worthwhile for the exchanges themselves to investigate how their costs relate to the services that they provide and whether they are pricing those services appropriately. For example, the value of a dealer's or market maker's capital is to serve as a buffer during adverse circumstances (e.g., unexpectedly volatile conditions). During favorable times, the market maker's capital is redundant; during adverse times, it is vital. In essence, the market maker's costs of making an orderly market are lower during favorable times and higher during adverse times. The market maker's prices (e.g., spreads) for its services should reflect those differential costs. To try to maintain uniform spreads across good times and bad is to maintain a form of cross-subsidy—which, as was noted in section 7.3, will invite entry and "cherry picking."

With respect to market fragmentation, the rapid improvements in telecommunications and in data processing that have caused the apparent fragmentation of local markets have also improved the ability of transactors to arbitrage across these local markets and thus have widened and deepened the overall market. Fragmentation may well be more of an illusion than a reality.

Finally, transparency is a problem that probably has no easy solution. Though all transactors would like to be the recipients of the information that greater transparency would yield, larger transactors are reluctant to provide the necessary information about their own actions and positions. If required to do so by a market, they will try to find another forum where they are not required to do so—either another formal market or informal (and even less well reported) transactions among themselves. Paradoxically, an insistence on too great a level of transparency could reduce the actual levels of transparency achieved.

International harmonization of national transparency requirements might prevent a competitive regulatory "race to the bottom," but it might instead simply drive large transactors away from organized markets and result in even less information's being generated. The dangers of the latter outcome seem great enough that harmonization should only be attempted gingerly, or not at all.

Information Regulation

The needs of national regulators to enforce regulations that are information-intensive—for example, restrictions on insider trading or on front running—can probably be satisfied through cooperation and information exchanges among regulatory regimes. Harmonization is not necessary.

For information regulation itself, however, the issues are more complex. The SEC's dilemma with respect to non-U.S. firms, mentioned earlier in this section, is a good illustration. If U.S. investors persist in investing in the non-U.S. companies, there is little that the SEC can do. It might make the investors' efforts a bit more difficult by refusing to allow any securities firm located in the United States to act as an agent for investors in these transactions. But if the U.S. investors persist and simply transact with agents abroad, then even more financial services will have been diverted from U.S. providers.[43]

The SEC is trying another tack: it is allowing these firms' securities to be sold in the United States without a restatement of the financial results to U.S. GAAP, but limiting their purchases to institutions; in essence, these securities are being treated as private placements.[44] Does this system of dual listing mean that U.S. firms are at a disadvantage? This would be true only if U.S. investors do not find the greater information provided by U.S. GAAP to be worth the extra costs to the U.S. firms of conforming to GAAP, or if the SEC's reporting requirements are largely designed to remedy the "widows and orphans" type of market failure discussed in section 7.3.

Ultimately, though, because other countries are unlikely to harmonize their accounting systems to U.S. GAAP (just so the U.S. markets could gain more

---

43. In principle, the SEC could go even farther and try to forbid U.S. investors from even owning the securities of firms that do not report according to U.S. GAAP. In practice, this would be a system of capital controls that is unlikely to be politically acceptable in the United States or in other countries.

44. See Seidman (1991); Doty (1992); Kokkalenios (1992); Schimkat (1992); and Torres (1993).

listings?), the SEC may have to ask difficult questions as to whether its stringent reporting requirements for U.S. firms are necessary—especially in light of the evidence offered in a recent study that indicates that the lesser reporting requirements of other countries' securities regulators may be adequate to prevent small investors from being at a disadvantage vis-à-vis larger (and possibly more knowledgeable) investors (Baumol and Malkiel 1992).

The eventual harmonization of reporting requirements across the countries with major financial markets could well be worthwhile. The major advantage would be a savings in transaction costs, since investors (and accountants) would need to learn and become familiar with only one set of accounting rules and their applications. (As a thought experiment, it is intriguing to imagine the transaction costs that would be present if each state in the United States had its own version of GAAP and required companies operating in that state to report their financial results in terms of that state's GAAP.) In essence, the accounting frameworks of these countries would become fully compatible with each other.[45] There are, however, potential costs. One danger is that diversity and the suitability of local accounting frameworks to local circumstances, and the opportunities for local experimentation within those frameworks, would be lost. Further, even though harmonization on a single accounting system might be worthwhile if the "right" system were chosen, the process of harmonization might result in the choice of some other framework, yielding a worse outcome than the current (albeit imperfect) pattern of diversity.

An analogy may prove useful here. A compatible nationwide system of railroads with a uniform rail gauge has great value in reducing the transaction costs that would otherwise occur in transloading freight between incompatible rail systems. But different rail gauges might be best suited to different geographic terrain or different types of freight, and the advantages of this diversity are lost when uniformity is achieved. Also, if uniformity were somehow achieved with only a very narrow or a very broad gauge, the outcome of uniformity (in terms of the costs of hauling freight) might be worse than the nonuniform system.

There is no automatic answer to the question of whether the uniformity of a single accounting framework across all countries would be superior to the current pattern of different national systems.[46] But the possibility that harmonization could yield gains is real and is worth further exploration.

7.4.4   Is Harmonization Feasible?

A final question worth considering is whether agreements among countries to harmonize and limit competition among their regulatory regimes are fea-

45. For discussions of compatibility, see Braunstein and White (1985); and Economides and White (1993) and the references cited therein.
46. In essence, the choice between a single system and the current diverse system is similar to asking whether a system of monopolistic competition in equilibrium provides too many or too few varieties. The answer, as shown by Spence (1976) and Dixit and Stiglitz (1977), is "it all depends."

sible; or whether the perceived private advantages of competition and the competitive instincts of the countries would be too strong. In the latter case, they would be tempted to "cheat" on any harmonization agreement, and such agreements might soon unravel.

Any harmonization arrangement is likely to have multiple facets and multiple unspecified details that could leave plenty of room for competitive maneuvering. For example, the Basel Accord on minimum capital levels for commercial banks specifies only the broad categories and risk weights but leaves many definitions and details unspecified; most important, it is silent on the details of the accounting system that should be the basis for the calculation of capital levels. This flexibility gives national regulatory regimes wide room for competitive manipulation, and over time the erosion of the accord could become substantial.

In sum, any international harmonization arrangement that is designed to dampen competition among national regulatory regimes must face the same problem that confronts all cartel arrangements: how to prevent "cheating" by cartel members, which can cause the arrangement to unravel. Strong economic, political, and moral commitments by member countries will be necessary to make these arrangements work.

7.5 Conclusion

The question of whether the national regulation of near-globalized securities markets should be subjected to international harmonization or international competition does not have an easy or simple answer. In this paper, I have used the concepts of market failure and government failure to provide a framework for considering the alternatives. Though international competition has a great deal of appeal and a strong presumption favoring it, there are some limited circumstances where harmonization could yield significant benefits. Refining these possibilities and ensuring that any harmonization does indeed yield net benefits for the efficiency of securities markets will be a major task for public policy—national and international—in the coming decade.

References

Arrow, Kenneth J. 1985. The Economics of Agency. In John W. Pratt and Richard J. Zeckhauser, eds., *Principals and Agents: The Structure of Business,* 37–51. Boston: Harvard Business School Press.

Baron, David P. 1989. Design of Regulatory Mechanisms and Institutions. In Richard Schmalensee and Robert D. Willig, eds., *Handbook of Industrial Organization,* 2:1347–1447. Amsterdam: North Holland.

Baumol, William J., and Alvin K. Klevorick. 1970. Input Choices and Rate-of-Return

Regulation: An Overview of the Discussion. *Bell Journal of Economics and Management Science* 1 (Autumn): 162–90.

Baumol, William J., and Burton G. Malkiel. 1992. Redundant Regulation of Foreign Security Trading and U.S. Competitiveness. In Kenneth Lehn and Robert W. Kamphius, Jr., eds., *Modernizing U.S. Securities Regulation: Economic and Legal Perspectives,* 39–55. Homewood, Ill.: Business One Irwin.

Bebchuk, Lucian Ayre. 1992. Federalism and the Corporation: The Desirable Limits on State Competition in Corporate Law. *Harvard Law Review* 105:1473–1510.

Benston, George J. 1992a. Competition versus Competitive Equality in International Financial Markets. In Franklin R. Edwards and Hugh T. Patrick, eds., *Regulating International Financial Markets: Issues and Policies,* 277–90. Boston: Kluwer.

———. 1992b. International Regulatory Coordination of Banking. In John Fingleton, ed., *The Internationalization of Capital Markets and the Regulatory Response,* 197–210. London: Graham and Trotman.

Bloch, Ernest. 1985. Multiple Regulators: Their Constituencies and Policies. In Yakov Amihud, Thomas S. Y. Ho, and Robert A. Schwartz, eds., *Market Making and the Changing Structure of the Securities Industry,* 155–82. Lexington, Mass.: Heath.

Bodner, David E. 1990. The Global Markets: Where Do We Stand? In Hans R. Stoll, ed., *International Finance and Financial Policy,* 201–6. New York: Quorum.

Bradley, Caroline. 1992. The Market for Markets: Competition between Investment Exchanges. In John Fingleton, ed., *The Internationalization of Capital Markets and the Regulatory Response,* 183–96. London: Graham and Trotman.

Braunstein, Yale, and Lawrence J. White. 1985. Setting Technical Compatibility Standards: An Economic Analysis. *Antitrust Bulletin* 30 (Summer): 337–55.

Breeden, Richard C. 1992. Reconciling National and International Concerns in the Regulation of Global Capital Markets. In John Fingleton, ed., *The Internationalization of Capital Markets and the Regulatory Response,* 27–32. London: Graham and Trotman.

Breutigam, Ronald R. 1989. Optimal Policies for Natural Monopolies. In Richard Schmalensee and Robert D. Willig, eds., *Handbook of Industrial Organization,* 2:1289–1346. Amsterdam: North Holland.

Bronfman, Corinne, and James A. Overdahl. 1993. Would the Invisible Hand Produce Transparent Markets? Mimeo, Commodity Futures Trading Commission, Washington, DC.

Coffee, John C., Jr. 1995. Competition versus Consolidation: The Significance of Organizational Structure in Financial and Securities Regulation. *Business Lawyer* 50 (February): 1–38.

Diamond, Douglas W., and Philip H. Dybvig. 1983. Bank Runs, Deposit Insurance, and Liquidity. *Journal of Political Economy* 91 (June):401–19.

Dixit, Avinash K., and Joseph E. Stiglitz. 1977. Monopolistic Competition and Optimum Product Diversity. *American Economic Review* 67 (June): 297–308.

Doty, James R. 1992. The Role of the Securities and Exchange Commission in an International Marketplace. *Fordham Law Review* 60 (May): S77–90.

Dudley, William C. 1986. Controlling Risk in Large-Dollar Wire Transfer Systems. In Anthony Saunders and Lawrence J. White, eds., *Technology and the Regulation of Financial Markets: Securities, Futures, and Banking,* 121–36. Lexington, Mass.: Heath.

Economides, Nicholas, and Lawrence J. White. 1994. Networks and Compatibility: Implications for Antitrust. *European Economic Review* 38 (April): 651–62.

Edwards, Franklin R. 1992. Listing of Foreign Securities on U.S. Exchanges. In Kenneth Lehn and Robert W. Kamphius, Jr., eds., *Modernizing U.S. Securities Regulation: Economic and Legal Perspectives,* 57–76. Homewood, Ill.: Business One Irwin.

Edwards, Franklin R., and Hugh T. Patrick, eds. 1992. *Regulating International Finan-cial Markets: Issues and Policies.* Boston: Kluwer.
England, Catherine, ed. 1991. *Governing Banking's Future: Markets vs. Regulation.* Boston: Kluwer.
Fingleton, John, ed. 1992. *The Internationalization of Capital Markets and the Regula-tory Response.* London: Graham and Trotman.
Freund, William C. 1993. That Trade Obstacle, the SEC. *Wall Street Journal,* August 27, A6.
————. 1995. Two SEC Rules in an Era of Transnational Equities Trading. In Robert A. Schwartz, ed., *Global Equity Markets: Technological, Competitive, and Regulatory Challenges,* 371–79. Chicago: Irwin.
Gruenspecht, Howard K., and Lester B. Lave. 1989. The Economics of Health, Safety, and Environmental Regulation. In Richard Schmalensee and Robert D. Willig, eds., *Handbook of Industrial Organization,* 2:1507–50. Amsterdam: North Holland.
Grundfest, Joseph A. 1990. Internationalization of the World's Securities Markets: Eco-nomic Causes and Regulatory Consequences. *Journal of Financial Services Research* 4 (December): 349–78.
Guy, Paul. 1992. Regulatory Harmonization to Achieve Effective International Compe-tition. In Franklin R. Edwards and Hugh T. Patrick, eds., *Regulating International Financial Markets: Issues and Policies,* 291–98. Boston: Kluwer.
Humphrey, David B. 1986. Payments Finality and Risk of Settlement Failure. In An-thony Saunders and Lawrence J. White, eds., *Technology and the Regulation of Fi-nancial Markets: Securities, Futures, and Banking,* 97–120. Lexington, Mass.: Heath.
Isaac, William M. 1994. Miracle of the Marketplace Applies to Regulators, Too. *Ameri-can Banker,* December 15, 5.
Johnson, Phillip McBride. 1992. Reflections on the CFTC/SEC Jurisdictional Dispute. In Franklin R. Edwards and Hugh T. Patrick, eds., *Regulating International Financial Markets: Issues and Policies,* 143–50. Boston: Kluwer.
Joskow, Paul L., and Roger G. Noll. 1994. Economic Regulation: Deregulation and Regulatory Reform during the 1980s. In Martin Feldstein, ed., *American Economic Policy in the 1980s,* 367–440. Chicago: University of Chicago Press.
Joskow, Paul L., and Nancy L. Rose. 1989. The Effects of Economic Regulation. In Richard Schmalensee and Robert D. Willig, eds., *Handbook of Industrial Organiza-tion,* 2:1449–1506. Amsterdam: North Holland.
Kane, Edward J. 1986. Technology and the Regulation of Financial Markets. In An-thony Saunders and Lawrence J. White, eds., *Technology and the Regulation of Fi-nancial Markets: Securities, Futures, and Banking,* 187–93. Lexington, Mass.: Heath.
————. 1991. Tension between Competition and Coordination in International Finan-cial Regulation. In Catherine England, ed., *Governing Banking's Future: Markets vs. Regulation,* 33–48. Boston: Kluwer.
————. 1992. Government Officials as a Source of Systemic Risk in International Fi-nancial Markets. In Franklin R. Edwards and Hugh T. Patrick, eds., *Regulating Inter-national Financial Markets: Issues and Policies,* 257–66. Boston: Kluwer.
Karmel, Roberta S. 1993. *National Treatment, Harmonization, and Mutual Recogni-tion: The Search for Principles for the Regulation of Global Equity Markets.* Capital Markets Forum Discussion Paper no. 3. London: Capital Markets Forum.
Kasper, Daniel M. 1988. *Deregulation and Globalization: Liberalizing International Trade in Air Services.* Cambridge, Mass.: Ballinger.
Key, Sydney J., and Hal S. Scott. 1991. *Industrial Trade in Banking Services.* Group of 30 Occasional Paper no. 35. Washington, D.C.: Group of 30.
————. 1992. International Trade in Banking Services: A Conceptual Framework. In

John Fingleton, ed., *The Internationalization of Capital Markets and the Regulatory Response,* 35–68. London: Graham and Trotman.

Kokkalenios, Vickie. 1992. Increasing United States Investment in Foreign Securities: An Evaluation of SEC Rule 144A. *Fordham Law Review* 60 (May): S179–202.

Kosters, Marvin H., and Allan H. Meltzer. 1990. Special Issue: International Competitiveness in Financial Services. *Journal of Financial Services Research* 4 (December): 259–511.

Krueger, Anne O. 1974. The Political Economy of the Rent-Seeking Society. *American Economic Review* 64 (June): 291–303.

Kwoka, John E., Jr., and Lawrence J. White, eds. 1994. *The Antitrust Revolution: The Role of Economics.* 2d edition. New York: HarperCollins.

Lipsey, R. G., and K. Lancaster. 1956–57. The General Theory of the Second Best. *Review of Economic Studies* 24:11–32.

Noll, Roger G. 1989. Economic Perspectives on the Politics of Regulation. In Richard Schmalensee and Robert D. Willig, eds., *Handbook of Industrial Organization,* 2:1253–87. Amsterdam: North Holland.

Okun, Arthur. 1975. *Equality and Efficiency: The Big Tradeoff.* Washington, D.C.: Brookings.

Peltzman, Sam. 1976. Toward a More General Theory of Regulation. *Journal of Law and Economics* 19 (August): 211–40.

Phillips, Almarin, ed. 1975. *Promoting Competition in Regulated Markets.* Washington, D.C.: Brookings.

Posner, Richard A. 1971. Taxation by Regulation. *Bell Journal of Economics and Management Science* 2 (Spring): 22–50.

———. 1974. Theories of Economic Regulation. *Bell Journal of Economics and Management Science* 5 (Autumn): 335–58.

Quinn, Brian. 1992. Regulating Global Financial Markets: Problems and Solutions. In Franklin R. Edwards and Hugh T. Patrick, eds., *Regulating International Financial Markets: Issues and Policies* 299–306. Boston: Kluwer.

Schimkat, Harold. 1992. The SEC's Proposed Regulations of Foreign Securities Issued in the United States. *Fordham Law Review* 60 (May): S203–26.

Scott, Kenneth E. 1977. The Dual Banking System: A Model of Competition in Regulation. *Stanford Law Review* 30:1–50.

Seidman, Lawrence R. 1991. SEC Rule 144A: The Rule Heard round the Globe—or the Sounds of Silence? *Business Lawyer* 47 (November): 333–54.

Shapiro, Mary L. 1993. The SEC's Open Door Policy. *Wall Street Journal,* September 23, A17.

Siegel, Daniel R., ed. 1990. *Innovation and Technology in the Markets: A Reordering of the World's Capital Market System.* Chicago: Probus.

Spence, A. Michael. 1976. Product Selection, Fixed Costs, and Monopolistic Competition. *Review of Economic Studies* 43 (June): 217–35.

Sprague, Irvine H. 1986. *Bailout: An Insider's Account of Bank Failures and Rescues.* New York: Basic.

Stansell, Stanley R., ed. 1993. *International Financial Market Interaction.* Cambridge, Mass.: Blackwell.

Steil, Benn. 1992. Regulatory Foundations for Global Capital Markets. In Robert O'Brien, ed., *Finance and the International Economy,* 6:63–76. Oxford: Oxford University Press.

———. 1993. Competition, Integration, and Regulation in EC Capital Markets. Special Paper, Royal Institute of International Affairs, London.

Stigler, George J. 1971. The Theory of Regulation. *Bell Journal of Economics and Management Science* 2 (Spring): 3–21.

Stiglitz, Joseph E. 1988. Economic Organization, Information, and Development. In Hollis Chenery and T. N. Srinivasan, eds., *Handbook of Development Economics,* vol. 1, chap. 5. Amsterdam: North Holland.

———. 1989. Imperfect Information in the Product Market. In Richard Schmalensee and Robert D. Willig, eds., *Handbook of Industrial Organization,* 1:769–847. Amsterdam: North Holland.

———. 1990. Development Strategies: The Role of the State and the Private Sector. In *Proceedings of the World Bank Annual Conference on Development Economics,* 430–3. Washington, D.C.: World Bank.

Stoll, Hans R., ed. 1990. *International Finance and Financial Policy.* New York: Quorum.

Torres, Craig. 1993. Latin American Firms Break with Past, Scramble to Be Listed on U.S. Exchanges. *Wall Street Journal,* September 28, C1.

U.S. Department of Justice and Federal Trade Commission. 1992. Horizontal Merger Guidelines. Washington, D.C.: Department of Justice.

Viscusi, W. Kip. 1994. Health and Safety Regulation: The Mis-Specified Agenda: The 1980s Reform of Health, Safety, and Environmental Regulation. In Martin Feldstein, ed., *American Economic Policy in the 1980s,* 453–504. Chicago: University of Chicago Press.

Walker, David. 1992. Major Issues Relevant for Regulatory Response to the Internationalization of Capital Markets. In John Fingleton, ed., *The Internationalization of Capital Markets and the Regulatory Response,* 21–26. London: Graham and Trotman.

Weiss, Leonard W., and Michael W. Klass, eds. 1981. *Case Studies in Regulation: Revolution and Reform.* Boston: Little, Brown.

———. 1986. *Regulatory Reform: What Actually Happened.* Boston: Little, Brown.

White, Lawrence J. 1981. *Reforming Regulation: Processes and Problems.* Englewood Cliffs, N.J.: Prentice Hall.

———. 1986. Should Competition to Attract New Investment Be Restricted? *New York Affairs* 9, no. 3: 6–18.

———. 1988. *International Trade in Ocean Shipping: The U.S. and the World.* Cambridge, Mass.: Ballinger.

———. 1991. *The S&L Debacle: Public Policy Lessons for Bank and Thrift Regulation.* New York: Oxford University Press.

———. 1992. What Should Banks *Really* Do? *Contemporary Policy Issues* 10 (July): 104–12.

———. 1993. Competition Policy in the United States: An Overview. *Oxford Review of Economic Policy* 9 (Summer): 133–53.

———. N.d. Government Business Relationships in the U.S. in the 1980s. In Martin Feldstein and Yoshi Kosai, eds., *U.S.-Japan Economic Forum,* vol. 2. Chicago: University of Chicago Press, forthcoming.

Winston, Clifford. 1993. Economic Deregulation: Days of Reckoning for Microeconomists. *Journal of Economic Literature* 31 (September): 1263–89.

Wolf, Charles, Jr. 1989. *Markets or Governments: Choosing between Imperfect Alternatives.* Cambridge: MIT Press.

Worth, Nancy. 1992. Harmonization of Capital Adequacy Rules for International Banks and Securities Firms. *North Carolina Journal of International Law and Commercial Regulation* 18 (Fall): 134–71.

Comment   John Y. Campbell

Lawrence White's paper has many admirable features. Most basically, it starts
from scratch, asking what precisely are the sources of market failure that might
justify government regulation of securities markets in the first place. As a new-
comer to the study of financial regulation, I have been confused by the tendency of many commentators to presume that the rationale for regulation is
commonly understood, when to me, at least, it remains mysterious.

I also admire the paper's balanced treatment of government failure. It is one
thing to identify a market failure, quite another to argue that government intervention is the most practically effective way to address the problem. And it is
hard for any dispassionate observer of the U.S. system of banking and financial
regulation to believe that this structure is in any sense optimal or precisely
targeted at particular market failures.

Finally, with some qualifications I agree with White's view that competition
between regulators—domestically and, more importantly, internationally—is
likely to improve outcomes. The rest of this comment reviews White's taxonomy of market failures and suggests some modifications, then proposes a taxonomy of regulatory responses to international competition and discusses the
choice among these responses.

The Taxonomy of Market Failures

The early items on White's list are the "usual suspects" of microtheory: market power, economies of scale, and externalities. In unregulated financial markets, market power is usually thought to arise from economies of scale. For
example, it is sometimes argued that a securities exchange is a natural monopoly because traders can obtain greater liquidity and lower effective transaction
costs the more traders are already using a market. However, this argument
seems less compelling today in light of the evidence that different classes of
traders may prefer different types of exchange. The phenomenon of "competition for order flow" seems to belie the notion that an exchange is a natural monopoly.

There is a stronger case for the importance of externalities in financial markets. Perhaps most obviously, financial innovators, like other innovators,
provide an uncompensated benefit to their competitors who can imitate their
new products. Patent and copyright law are ineffective in limiting such imita-
tion, just as they are in the computer software industry. Some economists have
argued that lenders, be they banks or venture capitalists, provide an uncompensated benefit to their competitors who can observe the average return on their
investments (Lang and Nakamura 1989). In a rather different spirit, some argue
that financial institutions that take on risk impose uncompensated costs on

John Y. Campbell is the Otto Eckstein Professor of Applied Economics at Harvard University
and a research associate of the National Bureau of Economic Research.

other participants in the financial system by increasing the risk of a general financial crisis. It is hard to model this "systemic risk externality" formally, but many practitioners and regulators take it to be the most important justification for financial regulation. Finally, "network externalities" may be important in financial markets. Accounting conventions, for example, may be like other social conventions in that their value increases with the number of people who use them. Unregulated markets may have multiple Pareto-ranked equilibria, and there may be a case for government intervention to help society coordinate on the best equilibrium.

So far so good, but the paper's list of market failures becomes more problematic as it continues. Uncertainty and asymmetric information are certainly important in financial markets, but they do not by themselves justify regulation. Individuals who cannot act in their own best interests may need investor protection, but I am uncomfortable with this argument because it can justify almost any government action.

I am more sympathetic to some arguments for financial regulation that the paper does not mention. A sophisticated version of the *investor-protection* argument considers the ex ante consequences of ex post compensation schemes. Such schemes have the potential to create a moral hazard problem as agents who expect to be compensated for future misfortunes lose the incentive to protect themselves. One can understand a wide range of government activity in these terms. Society's unwillingness to tolerate poverty among the elderly led first to old-age relief and then to the social security system. Society's compassion for victims of natural disasters led first to disaster relief and then to building codes. In banking, the desire to protect depositors and the payments system led to the establishment of deposit insurance in the 1930s; the savings and loan debacle of the 1980s has been an expensive reminder of the fact that deposit insurance gives banks incentives to take excessive risks, which must be offset by regulation. In financial markets more generally, regulation may be necessary if small investors expect to be compensated for losses and act accordingly.[1] While the best solution may be to limit compensation and expectations of compensation, this may not always be possible.

The *revenue* argument recognizes that regulation may be necessary to maintain the government's tax base. Given that all realistically feasible taxes are distortionary, the optimal tax system may require some taxation of the financial system with accompanying regulation. Some countries raise large amounts of revenue through seigniorage, which is effectively a tax on bank reserves; this requires regulation to inhibit banks' efforts to economize on reserves and to limit competition from nonbank financial institutions.[2] Other countries have

1. A variation of this argument considers the costs imposed on society by investors' efforts to obtain compensation. Litigation over Lloyd's of London insurance losses, for example, is likely to tie up the British court system for years.
2. It has been estimated that the recent deregulation of the Spanish banking system has cost the Spanish government revenue of about 1 percent of GDP.

significant securities transaction taxes; the United Kingdom, for example, raises about $1.5 billion per year from its stamp duty on transactions in British equities. Some regulation is inevitable if such taxes are to raise any revenue.

I believe that these two arguments for financial regulation are at least as important as the standard ones cited in White's paper. In addition, one should not forget that a major motive for regulation, if not exactly an argument for it, is to protect the market power of domestic financial institutions whose interests are represented by regulators.

Alternative Regulatory Responses to International Competition

It is useful to supplement the taxonomies given in the paper with a classification of regulatory approaches to international competition. Regulators can handle international competition in four ways. First, they can deny foreign access to domestic customers, thereby restoring autarky and the market power of domestic financial institutions. Second, they can allow foreign access to domestic customers but apply domestic regulations; under this approach, foreign competition erodes the market power of domestic financial institutions but not the market power of domestic regulators. Third, regulators can allow foreign access to domestic customers subject to foreign regulations. This is the approach of the European Union's Single Market; a financial institution or product is presumed to be sound if it is approved in its home market. Finally, regulators can negotiate to harmonize regulations so that the second and third approaches become equivalent.

It is sometimes argued that international competition is so potent that regulators do not really have these choices. On this argument, only the third and fourth options are available to regulators. This ignores the fact that governments do have some control over domestic customers through their power to define which contracts are legally enforceable and which are not. U.S. states use this power to regulate insurance provided to their residents, and the United Kingdom uses this power to regulate ownership transfers in U.K. equities.

If all four approaches to international competition are feasible, how should we judge their relative merits? The first approach serves only the interests of domestic financial institutions, but there are some arguments in favor of each of the other approaches. The second approach seems appropriate where there are differences across countries in the optimal degree of financial regulation. Countries may differ, for example, in the degree to which small investors accept the principle of caveat emptor and thus in the extent of investor protection they require. Different payments systems may involve different regulations to limit systemic risk, and different tax systems may require different supporting regulations. It is often argued that regulations should be harmonized across countries to maintain a level playing field; this argument applies to regulations that discriminate between domestic and foreign *suppliers* of financial services, but may not apply to regulations that discriminate between domestic and foreign *demanders* of such services.

The third approach has the great merit, emphasized in White's paper, that it maintains competition among different national regulators. Competition serves to reduce the direct costs of regulation and the indirect costs of compliance, and it limits the tendency of regulators to stifle financial innovation. The importance of this is brought home by Franks and Schaefer's (1993) comparison of direct regulatory costs in the United States, the United Kingdom, and France. Franks and Schaefer report that direct costs of regulation of securities and options trading are 1.3 percent of noninterest expense in the United States, but only 0.5 percent in the United Kingdom. For life insurance, the differences are even more dramatic; direct regulatory costs are 0.12 percent of premium income in the United States, but only 0.04 percent in the United Kingdom and 0.03 percent in France. If the higher costs of U.S. regulation do not correspond to benefits for consumers of financial services, then they represent an inefficiency that may be reduced by international regulatory competition.

An important question is how one can reconcile regulatory competition with the desire of regulators to protect domestic investors. One approach is for regulators to draw a clear distinction between domestically regulated and guaranteed financial institutions and products and other institutions and products, which can compete on the basis of their own national regulations and guarantees. This is analogous to the "narrow banking" proposal under which deposit insurance would apply only to certain strictly regulated banks, while other banks would compete without the regulatory burden but also without the benefit of deposit insurance.

Finally, international harmonization may be useful where there are important externalities in the international financial system. International agreements establishing common accounting conventions and reporting requirements can be seen as a device for coordinating financial markets on a superior equilibrium in which information is cheaper to provide and easier to understand. Similarly, agreements to establish international netting schemes may reduce risks in the international payments system. The growth of derivatives trading makes this an increasingly important area for international cooperation.

References

Franks, Julian, and Stephen Schaefer. 1993. The Costs and Effectiveness of the U.K. Financial Regulatory System. City Research Project Report 2, London Business School.

Lang, William W., and Leonard I. Nakamura. 1989. Information Losses in a Dynamic Model of Credit. *Journal of Finance* 44:731–46.

Comment   Mary Ann Gadziala

The topic Lawrence White selected for discussion raises issues that are both intellectually stimulating and highly relevant to current international regulation. A significant challenge presented by the explosive movement toward full globalization of the securities markets is ensuring that the regulatory structure promotes efficient, competitive, stable, and safe global markets. White has posed an important question: Would capital markets benefit more from "harmonization" of rules or from "competition" among regulatory regimes? He concludes that there is a strong presumption favoring international competition and that national regulation of near-globalized securities markets should be subjected to international harmonization in only certain limited circumstances.

I agree with that specific conclusion. However, I would approach the analysis in a somewhat different manner. For purposes of my analysis, the worldwide securities markets would be viewed as the market, regulation as the product, and the various national regulators as competitors creating the product.

To parallel White's analysis, I would begin with the *theoretical* question of whether the market would be better served by harmonization, which creates monopoly regulation, or by competitive regulation. This is a theoretical question because there is no "world congress" or similar entity that might impose such monolithic harmonized regulation. In the current international securities market, any movement toward uniformity—or harmony in the broad sense—could be achieved *only through the competitive process.*

Therefore, the second and *key* question in my analysis is, In what circumstances will the competitive process among national regulators lead to diversity and in what circumstances will it lead to homogeneity of international regulation?

I would like to take a few minutes to elaborate on each of these questions.

Monopoly Harmonization versus Competition

First, let's explore the theoretical question of whether harmonization or competition in international regulation would best serve our securities markets. Preliminarily, it should be noted that mandated harmonization would be a major undertaking, since it would necessitate the creation of a mechanism to impose monopoly regulation on the world securities markets. Beyond that cost, we should analyze the costs and benefits of the respective processes: harmonization and competition.

The current debate over the structure of the bank regulatory system in the

Mary Ann Gadziala is senior adviser (market regulation) at the Securities and Exchange Commission.

The Securities and Exchange Commission, as a matter of policy, disclaims responsibility for any private publication or statement by any of its employees. The views expressed herein are those of the author and do not necessarily reflect the views of the commission or of the author's colleagues upon the staff of the commission (Conduct Rule 4-9 [b][2]).

United States offers some valuable insights. On the national level, harmonization can be real, rather than theoretical. The U.S. Treasury has proposed virtually complete mandated harmonization of U.S. federal bank regulation—one superregulator to replace the four current regulators. The Treasury argues that this would reduce costs by eliminating inconsistencies, inefficiencies, and duplication. Recognizing that these superficial benefits may be achieved, the Federal Reserve and the majority of U.S. banks have opposed the harmonization. They have argued that

> a monolithic monopoly regulator would become inflexible;

> there would be no diversity of regulatory views to eliminate bad proposals and moderate incentives for lax supervision;

> the monopoly regulator would be likely to swing from excessive toughness to ease, based upon cyclical complaints; and

> the healthy process of dynamic tension in setting balanced regulatory standards would be lost.

The elements of this debate may be an appropriate starting point for the analysis of regulatory harmonization versus competition on the international level.

The Competitive Process May Lead to "Harmonized" Rules

This brings us to the main question: In what circumstances will the competitive process among national regulators result in some form of "harmonized" international regulation? This analysis might be aided by considering some examples where the competitive process is now at work.

While the regulatory competitive process is dynamic, continually in play in the market, the process is generally widely dispersed, and convergence may occur at a slow evolutionary pace. This would make analysis difficult. Therefore, for purposes of analysis, it may be best to examine the operation of the process in an international forum—such as the Bank for International Settlements or the International Organization of Securities Commissions. These organizations were created to accelerate the competitive process in a closed setting where information is concentrated. We might look specifically at capital requirements where a minimum standard was established for bank credit risks, but no consensus was reached for securities firms. We might also look at accounting standards where agreement was finally reached on a standard cash flow statement, but work continues on further accords.

The competitive process requires the various regulators to deal with such factors as legal and market segmentation; unique market characteristics; differing developmental levels; and societal, cultural, and prudential needs. Regulatory regimes are analyzed, defended, and rethought, balancing competitive and customer protection interests. Market stability, integrity, and prudential concerns are key. It is also through this convergence process that "market and government failures"—as discussed by White—may be corrected. Examining all of these factors in situations where consensus was reached, and where it was not, should provide valuable insights for generalizing the circumstances where the competitive process leads to "harmonized" international regulation.

In the case where national regulators have competed to an equilibrium level and agreed upon a regulatory standard, it is not set in stone. It is important that the standard be appropriately implemented and enforced. However, divergence is not necessarily "cheating"; it may in fact be an appropriate continuation of the competitive process to ensure that regulation remains state-of-the-art and responsive to innovative market developments.

One additional point is worth noting—harmonization and competition are at opposite ends of a continuum of international regulation. Along that continuum, other alternatives—such as mutual recognition or bilateral accords—may maximize benefits to the market in particular circumstances.

In conclusion, there is no existing mechanism for subjecting the regulation of international securities markets to monopoly harmonization. Harmonization can be achieved only through the competitive process among national regulators. This process operates continually with the goal of creating a regulatory structure that maximizes the stability, integrity, resilience, and competitiveness of our interdependent capital markets. At times, the competitive process may lead to diversity in international regulation; at other times, it may lead to homogeneity or harmony.

As the chairman of the Securities and Exchange Commission said in a recent speech, this process must be "one that meets our common needs, without forsaking our individual mandates." Finding and maintaining the appropriate balance, through the competitive process among national regulators, is indeed a difficult challenge in the current, dynamic international securities market.

8   Institutional and Regulatory Influences on Price Discovery in Cash and Futures Bond Markets

Kenneth J. Singleton

8.1 Introduction

Compared to the U.S. Treasury bond (UST) market, the Japanese (JGB) and German (GGB) cash bond markets are illiquid, face more institutional "frictions" in the market-making process, and evidence a larger impact of accounting standards and regulatory restrictions on the trading strategies of final investors. Though the details of the corresponding bond futures contracts differ, there is at the same time notable similarity in the liquidities of these futures contracts. Indeed, all three contracts are among the most liquid financial instruments traded globally. This paper explores the implications of the differences in institutional frictions in cash bond markets for the joint distributions of futures and cash bond prices and, in particular, for the role of futures in the price discovery process for government bonds.

Institutional arrangements typically change slowly over time, so identification of the effects of particular frictions from a single time series for a given country is often tenuous. Accordingly, I examine securities prices that are stratified along several dimensions. First, I consider three countries that are at different stages of the financial liberalization process and have different market organizations. There are also substantial differences in the costs of market making, which include the costs of financing and hedging the risks of positions; in accounting practices, which in some cases induce preferences for par bonds and affect attitudes toward coupon versus capital gain income; and in the objectives of portfolio managers and the implied trading practices.

Second, the distributions of futures prices are compared with those of deliverable and nondeliverable bond prices and, within the deliverable sectors in

Kenneth J. Singleton is professor of finance at the Graduate School of Business at Stanford University.

The author is grateful for research assistance from Steve Gray and Raj Tewari, the assistance of Naho Nakajima and Yoko Matsunaga in preparing the data and figures, and the comments of participants at the NBER conference.

Germany and the United States, the prices of bonds with the same maturity but different deliverability status. These comparisons reveal insights into the nature of illiquidity in the cash markets and the role of futures as a price discovery vehicle for illiquid bonds. The differences in liquidities of government bonds across the three countries are large and certainly much greater than the differences that one typically sees within the UST market. I interpret these differences and the associated differences in the distributions of bond prices in the light of the differences in institutionalized frictions.

The nature of informational *spillovers* from futures to cash prices has been widely studied at the individual market level (see, e.g., Stoll and Whaley [1990]; Schwarz and Laatsch [1991]; and Quan [1992]). To the extent that the implications of regulatory constraints for price behavior have been examined, the focus has typically been on such "micro" factors within futures markets as margin requirements, within-day price limits, and so forth. Much less attention has been given to comparative analysis of the implications of the broader "macro" frictions outlined above for the joint distribution of cash and futures prices. Surely both types of frictions are important, though their effects may manifest themselves over different time frames. The daily and weekly data studied in this paper are well suited to investigating the effects of institutional frictions on cash and futures relations that persist over days at the expense of identification of the effects of frictions that only affect within-day cash and futures price changes.

Though institutional frictions in cash markets might be expected to affect significantly the joint distribution of cash and futures prices, the nature of these effects does not seem a priori obvious. Consider for instance the relation between the prices of a futures contract and an underlying deliverable bond. Frictions in the cash market that limit exploitation of deviations from the *cost-of-carry* relation might lead one to expect systematic violations of this "arbitrage" relation. On the other hand, the same frictions may compromise price discovery in the cash market to the extent that the market's pricing of cash instruments may be directly linked to the futures through the cost-of-carry relation. Indeed, I find that both scenarios occurred in the JGB and GGB markets during the sample period.

No attempt is made to develop a formal model of price discovery in the presence of institutional frictions. Rather, this study represents an effort to characterize the properties of the distributions of cash and futures prices in order to guide such modeling efforts in the future. In section 8.2, I begin by comparing the institutional environments in which cash trading takes place in the United States, Germany, and Japan. Then descriptive statistics for the yields on government bonds are presented and interpreted in the light of the background discussion on market structure. Comparing across the maturity spectrum within a bond market, the yield distributions are found to be notably different in Germany and Japan depending on whether the maturity of a bond meets the criteria for deliverability into a futures contract. The markets in Germany and the United States also permit comparisons of yield distributions for bonds with identical maturities but different deliverability status. Overall, the findings from this preliminary analysis suggest that the presence of a liquid futures market has a significant effect on the distributions of cash bond yields.

In section 8.3, I overview the structure of the primary bond futures markets in the three countries. Then descriptive statistics for futures prices and the prices of individual deliverable bonds are presented and compared. Cash prices for deliverable bonds appear to inherit the distributional characteristics of futures prices, especially in Germany and Japan. More direct evidence that futures are central to price discovery in the presence of illiquid cash markets is presented for Japan, where at times cash bonds throughout the deliverable sector were priced directly off futures in terms of conversion-factor adjusted prices.[1]

Concluding remarks are presented in section 8.4.

8.2   Structural Impediments to Price Discovery in Cash Bond Markets

The *price discovery process* for newly issued bonds is accomplished through an auction with a known price (par) or coupon. The resulting yields embody all of the information about bond markets used by traders in formulating investment decisions, as well as their own attitudes toward risk and the constraints they face in making portfolio allocations. The constraints include not only the limit of each trader's wealth, but also the legal and accounting regulations that might limit participation of some types of traders in the cash market or limit their ability to hedge cash positions with derivative products.

Subsequently in the secondary markets, price discovery is accomplished through organized trading in over-the-counter (OTC) markets. The markets for bonds are not all equally liquid or deep across the maturity spectrum. While many factors contribute to the liquidity of secondary markets, I focus on three: (1) issuing patterns in the primary market, (2) the costs of financing positions for dealers making markets, and (3) accounting standards that influence secondary market trading by final investors.

Regular issuance at a specific maturity in relatively large size through auctions provides a natural set of "benchmark" or reference bonds, relative to which other bonds with comparable characteristics can be valued. Moreover, dealers have an incentive to maintain an active secondary market and accurate price discovery following a new auction as they place their bonds. Subsequently, large issue sizes facilitate market participation by a wide variety of investors with different portfolio strategies and anticipated holding periods. Indeed, final investors who follow portfolio strategies with high turnover rates may prefer (collectively as an equilibrium) to trade primarily in the *on-the-run*

---

1. This characteristic of the Japanese market was noted by Kikugawa and Singleton (1994) and interpreted in terms of the relative liquidity of the cash versus futures markets in Japan.

issues because a concentration of trading in these issues allows dealers to quote at relatively narrow spreads for large size.[2]

Table 8.1 displays the maturities and frequencies of the auctions in the three countries we are considering. The United States has the largest number of maturity points at which new bonds are issued and the most regular issue calendar (at least quarterly). Newly issued, on-the-run bonds serve as pricing benchmarks. The liquidity premiums associated with the benchmark status of these bonds are typically on the order of five to eight basis points (bp).

Several different federal bonds are issued in Germany.[3] BUNDs (*Bundesanleihe*) are issued on an irregular basis with maturities of eight to thirty years. Most of the issuance has had a ten-year maturity, and issues with maturities over ten years have been rare. Historically the issue sizes of BUNDs have been quite small, ranging from DM2 to DM4 billion. However, starting in 1990, the federal issuing authorities increased the issue sizes and started augmenting existing issues rather than always opening new issues. Consequently, the issue sizes have grown substantially and now regularly exceed DM10 billion. This change in issuing policy has contributed substantially to the liquidity of the BUND markets. New issue premiums are ten to fifteen bp in the five-year sector, and have been closer to twenty bp in the ten-year sector. Irregular issuance remains a limiting factor in price discovery and liquidity, however, as the values of both the option to retrade and the delivery option associated with the futures contract may be affected by the uncertainty surrounding new issue announcements.[4]

BOBLs (*Bundesobligationen*) are issued on an irregular schedule in sizes between DM4 and DM10 billion (a minimum issue size of DM4 billion is required for the bond to satisfy the delivery criteria into the Deutsche Terminbörse [DTB] five-year futures contract). SCHATZs (*Bundesschatzanweisungen*) are issued bimonthly and may have maturities of one to seven years, though most issues are in the four- to five-year maturity sector with typical sizes of about DM5–6 billion. The reference bonds for the under-five-year maturity bonds are current or seasoned issues of these medium-term notes. There are large differences in liquidity among reference and off-the-run bonds at the short end of the German yield curve, with BUNDs under five years to maturity being particularly illiquid. Traders sometimes express the view that the liquidity of the cash market compares more favorably with the futures in the five-year than in the ten-year sector in Germany. The regular issue calendar may be a factor underlying this view.

Until recently, all of the JGB issuance with maturity less than ten years was

---

2. The notion that the right to retrade in a liquid market lowers yields relative to otherwise equivalent illiquid bonds is proposed by Amihud and Mendelson (1991), among others, as an explanation of the spreads between bill and seasoned bond yields of the same maturity in the UST market.

3. See McLean (1993) for an overview of the structure of the German bond market.

4. Since unification of East and West Germany, Unity bonds have been issued with ten-year maturities that are essentially equivalent to BUNDs. And Treuhand bonds have been issued in both the ten- and five-year sectors. Though Treuhands and TROBLs (as the five-year issues are called)

Table 8.1   **Structure of Government Bond Markets**

	Auctions		Futures		
	Maturity	Frequency	Maturity	Deliverables	Taxes
United States	2	Monthly	CBT 5 yr	5 yr	None
	3	Quarterly	CBT 10 yr	6 1/2–10 yr	
	4	Quarterly	CBT Bond	15–30 yr	
	5	Quarterly			
	7	Quarterly			
	10	Quarterly			
	30	Quarterly			
Germany	SCHATZ 1–7	Bimonthly	DTB 5 yr	3 1/2–5 yr	Withholding
			LIFFE 5 yr		
	BOBL 5	Irregular	LIFFE 10 yr	8 1/2–10 yr	
	BUND 8–30	Irregular	DTB 10 yr		
Japan	4	Monthly	JGB 10 yr	7–11 yr	Transactions
	6	Irregular			
	10	Monthly			Withholding
	20	Irregular			

Notes: CBT denotes Chicago Board of Trade futures, and *CBT Bond* is the futures on the long bond. *DTB* denotes the Deutsche Terminbörse, and *LIFFE* denotes the London International Financial Futures Exchange.

issued with an original maturity of ten years. Starting in November 1993, the Japanese Ministry of Finance has issued a four-year bond and more recently has started issuing six-year bonds. The issuing process in Japan is closely linked to the annual fiscal plans by the Ministry of Finance. Projections are made in December each year for the following fiscal year starting in March. Ten-year and four-year bonds are auctioned monthly, though the exact amount and coupon may not be known long in advance, since the Ministry of Finance adjusts issue sizes depending on its views about the impact of supply on the market at the time of issuance. The six-year issues have been on an irregular schedule.

The benchmark selection process in Japan is different. Though newly issued ten-year bonds often trade at a premium to their seasoned counterparts, these bonds are not the most liquid in their sector. Instead there is a specific bond—typically between eight and ten years to maturity—which is designated as the benchmark bond. A majority of the trading volume in all JGBs is concentrated in this one bond. As a consequence, this bond trades at a lower yield (rich) to JGBs with similar maturities, with the difference occasionally reaching more than twenty bp. This "benchmark premium" fluctuates substantially over time, so there is no simple relation between the yield on the benchmark and other

---

are guaranteed by the German government and deliverable into the associated futures contracts, they are not treated as equivalent by the market and often trade at relatively high yields (cheap) compared to their BUND or BOBL counterparts.

off-the-run bonds. Partly as a consequence, the JGB benchmark does not serve as the primary benchmark for price discovery of other JGBs.[5] Instead, the *on-the-run* ten-year and ex-benchmark bonds serve as key reference bonds for pricing. Ex-benchmarks play a key role in price discovery since they have relatively large issue sizes and, after losing their benchmark status, they maintain some of their liquidity relative to bonds that were never benchmarks. There are now ex-benchmark bonds along the entire maturity spectrum under ten years.

A tentative issuing plan for twenty-year bonds is also developed in December, but the issuing calendar is irregular, with new issues announced usually within a month of the auction. In the superlong (twenty-year) sector, certain bonds among those with the larger issue sizes have emerged as reference bonds for pricing and evaluating the shape of the yield curve. The typical issue size and the trading volumes in these bonds are small compared to the JGB benchmark, though recently the turnover in the secondary market for superlongs has at times been as high or higher than some ex-benchmarks.

Large issue sizes and regular issue calendars are not sufficient to guarantee that the market for a bond will be liquid or deep. Another important consideration is the dealers' cost of making markets. One particularly important influence on a dealer's cost structure is the inventory position that a dealer maintains for facilitating flow trading. Limited secondary trading in a bond may influence both the ability of dealers to satisfy demand for this bond and their willingness to absorb large blocks from sellers. Neither consideration would be a major issue if dealers were willing to maintain large inventories of individual bonds. However, these positions must be hedged against interest rate risk. Furthermore, large inventories tie up financing lines, lead to regulatory capital charges, and may affect the dealer's credit rating.

These costs can be largely avoided in the presence of an active bond borrowing and lending market, as dealers can efficiently carry small inventory positions. Borrowing of bonds can be effected in two ways: buy/sell agreements in which the purchase and sale prices are determined on the agreement date with a difference that reflects the borrowing rate, and a repo agreement, which is essentially a collateralized loan for which title to the bonds does not change hands. The repo market is well established in the United States and is actively used by dealers for financing their inventory positions. Bond lending is also viewed as an important source of portfolio yield enhancement by institutional investors. These borrowing markets are somewhat less developed in Germany. Both buy/sell and repo arrangements are available, with the former being the most common.

Japan has the least well developed borrowing/lending market. There is no repo market; all borrowing is based on a buy/sell arrangement. Moreover, a dealer cannot "fail"—fail to deliver bonds on the settlement date—in Japan.

5. This is not to suggest that market participants do not condition on the yield on the benchmark when setting prices of nonbenchmark bonds, but rather that other bonds are likely to serve as the primary pricing benchmarks.

While failing is a last resort and costly action, the possibility of failure facilitates a dealer's efforts at making active markets in bonds. Potential sources of bonds for borrowing are also somewhat limited by internal policies of financial institutions or regulatory considerations. For instance, banks that lend bonds must treat this activity as a risky loan with a 100 percent risk weighting under international capital standards, and, consequently, they may be reluctant to lend around fiscal year ends.

Investment practices by final investors have several additional significant effects on the liquidity of bond markets. In all three markets, there is some tendency for institutional investors to hold (with limited intentions of selling) newly acquired bonds in their portfolios. The motivations for this activity vary across countries as does their importance for the overall level of trading activity in secondary markets. In the United States, most institutional accounts must mark to market their bond portfolios on a regular basis. Therefore, buy/sell decisions are made in terms of current market values. In contrast, in both Germany and Japan, many accounts carry bonds at book value. Consequently, accepted accounting standards may discourage investors from selling bonds at below book value and, thereby, contribute to a buy and hold approach to portfolio management. Buy and hold investment strategies reduce the effective supplies of bonds into the market.

There are also institutionally induced preferences for high coupon bonds in Japan, associated in large part with the requirement that insurance companies pay most policy dividends from coupon income and not capital gain income. Similarly, tax policies in Germany induce a preference for low coupon bonds so that a larger share of a bond's total return is in the form of a capital gain. At times, these coupon effects manifest themselves as notable spreads between otherwise equivalent high and low coupon bonds.

Related accounting standards also increase the desire for par bonds. In Germany, bonds purchased above par must be booked at par, so that the capital loss implicit in the premium over par must be realized immediately for accounting purposes. A similar accounting "friction" exists in Japan: for bonds purchased at a discount, investors can include only the coupon payment in current income (they must defer accretion to par); for bonds purchased at a premium, they must amortize the premium, and this amortization overstates the economic reduction in value associated with the passage of time. Consequently, there is an accounting bias toward par bonds, with premium bonds tending to trade cheaply relative to otherwise comparable low coupon bonds when both are selling at a premium, and vice versa when both are discounted.

In summary, there are notable differences in institutional factors affecting price discovery in the United States, Germany, and Japan. Consequently, the nature of the benchmarks that market participants use for assessing value in the cash markets varies across markets. So does the quality of the benchmarks, in the sense that not all benchmarks are equally free of important institutional effects that may lead a reference bond to be valued implicitly by a different discount function than a nonbenchmark with comparable maturity.

If the institutional frictions outlined above have significant effects on the price discovery process, then, in light of the differences across countries, one might expect the distributions of bond yields also to differ. To investigate this possibility, descriptive statistics for a cross-section of bonds along the maturity spectrums were computed using daily and weekly data over the period October 1, 1991, through November 30, 1993. The characteristics of the bonds selected for the three countries are presented in table 8.2. When a choice was available, UST bonds with above-average issue sizes were selected among those with similar maturities.[6] In addition to a cross-section of bonds across the maturity spectrum, pairs of bonds with identical or nearly identical maturities, but different status regarding deliverability into the five- and ten-year futures, were examined. This comparison is possible because bonds that are deliverable into the five- and ten-year contracts must have an original issue maturity that satisfies the delivery criterion. To make this comparison, the sample periods for some bonds were shorter than the full sample, since over the two-year sample period some bonds that were deliverable lost their deliverability status. The delivery status of the bonds is indicated in the last column of table 8.2.[7] Similar criteria were used in selecting GGBs, and similar comparisons are possible. In addition, we compare the distributions of short-term BOBLs and BUNDs, none of which are deliverable into the five-year futures.

In the case of Japan, we chose ex-benchmark bonds since they serve as the local benchmark bonds along the yield curve.[8] All JGBs satisfying the maturity criterion are deliverable, so a deliverable/nondeliverable comparison is not possible.

All of the statistics are for the first differences of the logarithms of bond yields. In the cases of the United States and Japan, yields are measured on a bond equivalent yield basis, and for Germany, quoted yields were used. Results for daily and weekly data are displayed in tables 8.3 and 8.4, respectively. There is a tendency for the annualized standard deviations to decline with maturity (table 8.3). In the cases of the United States and Germany, the values of the standard deviation for daily and weekly data are comparable (compare tables 8.3 and 8.4). However, the volatilities of bond yields in Japan tend to be larger for the weekly data than for the daily. This suggests that the changes in bond yields exhibit little autocorrelation in the United States and Germany, but are positively autocorrelated in Japan.

The first-order autocorrelations of yield changes are displayed in the rows labeled ρ. In fact, in the United States and Germany, the daily autocorrelations are typically less than .1 in absolute value, though there is some evidence that

---

6. Yields for the on-the-runs were typically not selected, because of the need to have a yield history for calculating the statistics.

7. See section 8.3 for a description of the available futures contracts in each country and their delivery requirements.

8. Kikugawa and Singleton (1994) present similar descriptive statistics for the case of JGBs for an earlier sample period. They find similar patterns to those described subsequently.

Table 8.2 **Characteristics of Bonds**

Maturity	Coupon	Issue Date	Issue Size (million)	Comments[b]
		U.S. Treasury Bonds[a]		
5/15/95	5.875	5/15/92	$15,086	ND
5/15/96	7.375	5/15/86	$20,085	ND
4/30/97	6.875	4/30/92	$10,256	ND
4/30/98	5.125	4/30/93	$11,024	CBT 5 yr
4/15/98	7.875	4/15/91	$ 8,534	ND
4/15/99	7.000	4/15/92		ND
8/15/00	8.750	8/15/90	$10,503	CBT 10 yr
11/15/01	7.500	11/15/91	$12,004	CBT 10 yr
11/15/01	15.750	10/07/81	$ 1,800	ND
2/15/15	11.250	2/15/85	$12,667	CBT Bond
8/15/21	8.125	8/15/91	$12,008	CBT Bond
		German Government Bonds		
7/20/95	8.750	7/20/90	DM 8	BOBL92, ND
7/20/95	6.750	7/20/85	DM 2	BUND, ND
4/22/96	8.500	4/22/91	DM 10	BOBL96, ND
6/20/96	5.750	6/20/86	DM 3	BUND, ND
7/21/97	8.250	7/21/92	DM 10	BOBL00, DTB 5 yr
7/21/97	6.125	7/21/87	DM 4	BUND, ND
12/22/97	7.000	12/22/92	DM 10	BOBL04, DBT 5 yr
1/20/98	6.375	1/20/88	DM 4	BUND, ND
6/21/99	6.750	6/21/89	DM 4	BUND, ND
8/21/00	8.500	8/21/90	DM 8	BUND, ND
9/20/01	8.250	9/20/91	DM 18	BUND, LIFFE 10 yr
7/22/02	8.000	7/22/92	DM 15	BUND, LIFFE 10 yr
		Japanese Government Bonds		
7/20/95	6.20	8/20/85	¥1,300	#78, ND
6/20/96	5.10	4/25/86	¥2,707	#89, ND
6/20/97	4.70	4/20/87	¥1,400	#99, ND
6/22/98	4.60	4/25/88	¥2,000	#111, ND
6/21/99	4.80	3/20/89	¥1,852	#119, ND
3/20/00	6.40	3/20/90	¥2,300	#129, TSE 10 yr
6/20/01	6.60	4/22/91	¥2,400	#140, TSE 10 yr
3/20/02	5.50	1/27/92	¥3,200	#145, TSE 10 yr
3/20/07	5.70	10/20/86	¥1,008	#S02, ND
3/20/09	4.90	2/20/89	¥ 411	#S10, ND

[a]All bonds are noncallable.

[b]*ND* denotes not deliverable into a futures contract. *CBT* denotes Chicago Board of Trade futures, and *CBT Bond* is the futures on the long bond. *DTB* denotes the Deutsche Terminbörse, *LIFFE* denotes the London International Financial Futures Exchange, and *TSE* denotes the Tokyo Stock Exchange.

Table 8.3   **Descriptive Statistics for Daily Yield Changes, October 1, 1991–November 30, 1993**

	United States								
Security	5/95	5/96	4/97	4/98	4/99	8/00	11/01	2/15	8/21
Standard deviation	.22	.18	.18	.16	.16	.15	.13	.10	.09
				.16			.13		
Kurtosis	4.27	4.10	3.85	3.49	3.82	3.80	3.62	3.36	3.47
				3.76			3.58		
ρ	.06	.08*	.08*	.07	.07	.10*	.09*	.01	.03
				.11*			.09*		

	Germany							
Security	BOBL92 BUND	BOBL94 BUND	BOBL00 BUND	BOBL04 BUND	BUND	BUND	BUND	BUND
Standard deviation	.11	.11	.12	.11	.08	.07	.08	.08
	.13	.11	.10	.08				
Kurtosis	5.37	4.82	3.72	2.77	4.35	3.65	3.84	3.34
	7.32	4.62	5.34	5.43				
ρ	.01	.00	−.08	−.05	.01	.05	−.02	.02
	−.10	−.05	−.11	.09				

	Japan									
Security	78	89	99	111	119	129	140	145	S02	S10
Standard deviation	.13	.15	.15	.15	.14	.14	.13	.12	.08	.07
Kurtosis	12.33	9.83	8.04	6.59	6.70	5.51	4.86	4.24	5.26	5.02
ρ	.40**	.31**	.28**	.20**	.18**	.08	.05	.07	.19**	.26**

Notes: ρ denotes the first-order autocorrelation coefficient. * (**) denotes rejection of the null hypothesis of zero autocorrelation at the 5 percent (1 percent) level, using heteroskedastic standard errors (Hansen 1982).

the low autocorrelation in daily U.S. data is statistically significant. The autocorrelations in the short-term BUNDs are also larger in absolute value than the autocorrelations of the corresponding BOBLs, but none of these estimates is statistically significant at conventional levels. In contrast, yield changes in Japan exhibit substantial positive autocorrelation, with ρ often larger than .2. In all three countries, there is little evidence of autocorrelation in the weekly data, which suggests that the sources of persistence in Japan have effects that dissipate within a week.

The kurtoses (K) of the daily data are larger than three in all three countries, indicating that the distributions of yield changes have fatter tails than a normal.[9] The values of K for the United States are generally smaller than the corre-

9. The kurtosis measures the shape of the tail region of a distribution. A kurtosis greater than three indicates that the probability of a "tail event"—that is, a very large positive or negative yield change—is higher in the sample than in a normal distribution with the same mean and variance.

Table 8.4   **Descriptive Statistics for Weekly Yield Changes, October 4, 1991–November 26, 1993**

				United States					
Security	5/95	5/96	4/97	4/98	4/99	8/00	11/01	2/15	8/21
Standard deviation	.22	.19	.18	.18 .17	.16	.15	.14 .14	.11	.10
Kurtosis	3.40	3.32	3.11	2.92 3.01	3.41	3.45	3.32 3.39	3.06	3.09
ρ	.01	.04	−.05	.06 −.01	−.11	−.07	−.04 −.04	−.07	−.03

				Germany				
Security	BOBL92 BUND	BOBL94 BUND	BOBL00 BUND	BOBL04 BUND	BUND	BUND	BUND	BUND
Standard deviation	.12 .13	.11 .12	.11 .10	.10 .10	.09	.08	.09	.09
Kurtosis	6.41 6.16	5.29 5.68	2.80 5.71	3.15 6.15	5.71	3.89	3.74	3.44
ρ	.01 −.05	.04 −.05	−.08 .10	−.13 .10	.08	.06	.02	−.01

				Japan					
Security	78	89	99	111	119	129	140	145	S01	S10
Standard deviation	.17	.18	.18	.16	.15	.14	.12	.11	.09	.09
Kurtosis	6.76	7.32	6.17	5.50	4.66	5.80	6.31	5.90	3.68	4.47
ρ	.16	.02	−.02	−.07	−.04	−.09	−.11	.02	.16	.20*

Notes: ρ denotes the first-order autocorrelation coefficient. *denotes rejection of the null hypothesis of zero autocorrelation at the 5 percent level, using heteroskedastic standard errors (Hansen 1982).

sponding values for Germany and Japan. The smaller values of K for the weekly U.S. data compared to the daily data suggest that the daily data may be nonnormal.

The estimates of K for GGB and JGB yields are often much larger than three, especially for JGB yields. Furthermore, the sample kurtoses of the bonds with the highest values of K in the daily data also have estimated values of K much larger than three in the weekly data. Thus, the relatively high probabilities of large positive or negative yield changes in Germany and Japan seem to be associated with events that impact yields for at least a week. These comparisons are, of course, subject to the well-known caveat that kurtosis is determined by the fourth moment of a distribution, and fourth moments are difficult to estimate accurately.

Additional interesting patterns emerge when the results for different bonds with similar maturities are compared. In the United States, the pairs of bonds

Table 8.5   Futures Contract Specifications

Contract		Size	Notional Coupon (%)	Deliverable Maturities (years)	Average Volume[a] 11/93	Average Open Interest[a] 11/93
CBT	5 yr note	$100,000	8	4.25–5.25	45,188	180,630
CBT	10 yr note	$100,000	8	6.5–10.0	91,717	273,295
CBT	BOND	$100,000	8	15.0–30.0	390,114	339,690
DTB	BOBL	DM250,000	6	3.50–5.0	18,693	126,914
LIFFE	BOBL	DM250,000	6	3.50–5.0	2,850	23,239
DTB	BUND	DM250,000	6	8.50–10.0	40,076	111,871
LIFFE	BUND	DM250,000	6	8.50–10.0	100,330	176,636
TSE	10 yr	¥100 million	6	7.0–11.0	59,925	NA

[a]Average volume and open interest is a daily average for all contracts available for each futures.

with maturities April 1998 and November 2001 include one deliverable and one nondeliverable bond for the associated futures contracts.[10] The results for each pair are virtually indistinguishable using both daily and weekly data.

In the case of Germany, the first two pair of BOBLs and BUNDs have similar maturities, but neither is deliverable into a futures contract. The BOBLs in the third and fourth pairs of bonds are deliverable into a futures contract, while the associated BUNDs are not. The results for the first two pairs of bonds are largely the same in both the daily and weekly data. On the other hand, for the third and fourth pairs of bonds, the values of K for the deliverable bonds are notably smaller than those for the nondeliverable bonds, and this is true in both daily and weekly data.

The deliverable bonds in Japan were #129, #140, and #145 for a substantial part of the sample period. The values of K for these bonds are somewhat smaller than those for other JGBs in daily data, but not substantially so. Moreover, there is little difference between the sample kurtoses of these bonds and those with shorter maturities in weekly data. What is most striking about the results for JGBs is the relatively low autocorrelation in yield changes for the deliverable bonds, especially in daily data. Whereas all of the nondeliverable bonds have first-order autocorrelations that are significantly different from zero at the 1 percent level and often much larger than .2 in magnitude, the autocorrelations for the deliverable bonds are insignificantly different from zero at conventional significance levels and are less than .1 in magnitude.

Several observations emerge from these findings. First, changes in bond yields in Germany and Japan have higher kurtoses and, in the case of Japan, much higher autocorrelations, than the UST yield changes. This is consistent with there being important effects of the institutional frictions in the cash markets of Germany and Japan on the liquidity of GGBs and JGBs and hence the

10. See table 8.1 for a precise description of the bonds included.

distributions of yield changes compared to USTs.

Second, though Japan and Germany have many institutional frictions in common, the sample autocorrelation properties of the yield changes are very different. Two contributing factors to this difference may be the relatively larger number of auctions along the German yield curve facilitating price discovery, and the more well-developed repo market in Germany. A more efficient borrowing and lending market for bonds reduces the price-pressure effects of trading large blocks through the OTC dealer network and, therefore, would be expected to reduce the propensity for adjacent price changes to have the same sign.

Third, deliverability into a futures contract appears to alter the distributional properties of bond yields. Specifically, deliverable GGBs and JGBs have lower kurtoses and autocorrelations, respectively, than their nondeliverable counterparts. One explanation for this finding is that price discovery is more effective in the futures markets in Japan and Germany, so the relatively illiquid deliverable bonds are priced in terms of the associated futures. The results for Germany suggest that this pricing mechanism affects primarily the deliverable bonds for which the cost-of-carry relation provides potential arbitrage opportunities. The relatively illiquid, nondeliverable BUNDs of comparable maturity to the BOBL00 and BOBL04 have much larger kurtoses, which suggests that price setting in the BUND market is not as closely tied to price formation in the futures market as price setting for BOBLs.

Even if largely true, my interpretation of the markets' pricing rules is not complete, as the effects of delivery status on the distributions of bond yields differ across markets. With these differences in mind, I next describe briefly the characteristics of the primary futures markets in the United States, Germany, and Japan, and then examine in more depth the role of futures in the price discovery process.

8.3   Futures and Price Discovery in Cash Markets

If futures are central to the pricing of illiquid, deliverable cash instruments, the distributions of cash and futures prices should exhibit similar characteristics. In general, they would not be identical, of course, because futures serve at least two additional roles besides signaling value: bond futures are a key tool for managing interest rate risk associated with cash positions, and they provide a venue for investors to express views about the direction of interest rates. After briefly reviewing the contractual specifications of some of the key futures markets in the three countries being examined, I present preliminary results on the distributions of futures prices and their relations to cash prices.

Table 8.5 displays the deliverability criteria for several bond futures markets. In the United States, there are three actively traded futures markets for Treasury notes and bonds. In the cases of the five- and ten-year note contracts, the original maturities of the notes must satisfy the maturity criterion for delivery to be deliverable. The trading activity in these futures increases with maturity, as is illustrated by the average daily volumes and open interest levels for November 1993.

The London International Financial Futures Exchange (LIFFE) introduced the first BUND futures contract in 1988. Contractual obligations may be satisfied by physical delivery of any BUNDs, Unity bonds, or Treuhands with maturities between 8.5 and 10 years. In 1990, the German DTB launched an identical contract. The average daily trading volumes and open interest levels are higher on the LIFFE than on the DTB. Furthermore, the ratio of trading volume to open interest is higher at the LIFFE than at the DTB, suggesting that intraday trading is also more pronounced at the LIFFE.

A five-year futures contract was introduced by the DTB in 1991, and recently the LIFFE introduced a similar five-year contract. BOBLs, SCHATZs, and TROBLs are deliverable into these contracts if their maturity is between 3.5 and 5 years. Seasoned BUNDs are not deliverable. Among the two contracts, the DTB is clearly the more liquid (table 8.5), so price discovery within the five-year futures markets is likely to be primarily at the DTB. Also, comparing the BUND and BOBL futures for November 1993, the ten-year contract had nearly seven times the trading volume and about twice the open interest as the five-year contracts combined.

For the JGB contract, bonds with maturities between seven and eleven years are deliverable, though there are currently no deliverable bonds with maturities between ten and eleven years. Thus, bonds issued with original maturities of twenty years do not currently satisfy the deliverability requirements.

The specific terms of these futures contracts differ in regard to the treatment of margin, the nature of "delivery" and "wild card" options, the conventions for computing conversion factors, the accounting treatment of gains and losses, and so forth. Moreover, whereas the Chicago Board of Trade (CBT) and Tokyo Stock Exchange (TSE) impose daily price limits, there are no daily limits on the DTB or the LIFFE. These considerations are clearly significant from the point of view of an individual investor computing the cost of a futures position and in assessing the likely effectiveness of a hedge. To the extent that these costs affect participation, the liquidities and depths of the futures markets may be enhanced or limited by their presence. An equally important determinant of the levels of trading activities in futures markets is the *relative* cost of trading in cash compared to futures markets. The presence of the institutional frictions in the cash markets outlined in section 8.2, combined with the high degree of leverage achievable in the futures markets, suggest that the relative costs of transacting in the futures market are at times much lower than in the cash market. This may explain the relative liquidity of the futures markets, especially in Japan and Germany. The higher costs of regulatory frictions in the cash markets may also increase the weight on futures prices in the price discovery process for cash instruments.

The notion that futures contracts are central to the pricing of cash instruments can be made precise through the standard cost-of-carry relation. Let $P^N(t_c)$ and $P^N(t_M)$ denote the prices of a cash bond at the futures contracting and maturity dates, respectively. Suppose this bond pays c per year for each 100 of face value. Also, let i denote the annualized borrowing rate the investor must pay to finance the bond between t_c and t_M. Let τ denote the fraction $(t_M - t_c)/365$ of a year that the futures contract is active, and $f^\tau(t_c)$ denote the futures price at date t_c and CF the conversion factor for the Nth bond. Then the cost-of-carry relation for this market is

(1) $$CF \times f^\tau(t_c) = P^N(t_c) \times [1 + (i - c/P^N(t_c)) \times \tau].$$

The right side of equation (1) gives the "theoretical" forward price implied by the cash price at the contract date and the terms for financing the investment, and the left side is the invoice price for delivery of the bond into the futures contract. Equivalently, for a given futures price and conversion factor, (1) implies that the present value of the adjusted futures price gives the current cash price:

(2) $$P^N(t_c) = CF \times f^\tau(t_3)/[1 + (i - c/P^N(t_c)) \times \tau].$$

For at least two reasons, (2) will typically not hold for all deliverable bonds. First, there are biases inherent in using conversion factors to determine invoice prices for delivery. These biases will generally lead one bond to be cheapest-to-deliver (CTD; have the highest implied repo rate), which the futures price will tend to track over time. Second, as the shape of the yield curve changes during the futures contract period, so might the CTD bond. Since the futures track the price of the CTD bond, a potential change in the CTD bond adds an additional source of risk beyond the usual price risk of being long a futures contract. The difference between the left and right sides of (2) in the UST markets is often interpreted as the value of this delivery option implicit in the conversion factor system. In Germany and Japan, there seems to be little value to the delivery option. This may partly be a consequence of the narrower range of deliverable maturities compared to the UST contract, and to the recent slopes of the deliverable yield curves.

In its strongest form, pricing off futures can be formalized by viewing (2) as a pricing rule the market uses to price the deliverable bonds: cash prices are set approximately to the discounted values of the associated conversion-factor-adjusted futures prices. A weaker interpretation is that there may be systematic deviations from the cost-of-carry relation, especially for non-CTD bonds, but the shape of the distribution of the futures largely determines the characteristics of the distributions of cash prices in the deliverable sectors.[11] I examine each of these in turn, starting with the weaker notion.

---

11. In some markets at some times, one need not restrict attention to deliverable bonds only. For example, for an extended period of time in Japan during 1992, the superlong bonds were

Descriptive statistics for daily changes in the logarithms of futures prices on the ten-year contracts and associated deliverable bond prices are presented in the last three columns of table 8.6. The bonds chosen were the 11/15/01 7.5% UST, the 9/20/01 8.25% BUND, and the 6/20/01 6.6% JGB #140 (see table 8.2 for the characteristics of these bonds). Pairwise comparisons of the sample statistics show that the distributional characteristics of the cash and futures prices are very similar, with the only exception being the pair of kurtoses for the UST cash and futures prices.

Further insights about the nature of both the volatilities and kurtoses of futures and cash prices are obtained from estimating first-order generalized autoregressive conditional heteroskedasticity (GARCH; Bollerslev 1986) models for the daily changes in prices. More precisely, changes in the logarithms of prices, Δp_t, were assumed to be described by a normal distribution conditional on information available at date $t-1$ with conditional mean $\beta_0 + \beta_1 \Delta p_{t-1}$ and conditional variance h_t given by[12]

$$(3) \qquad h_t = \alpha_0 + \alpha_1 u_{t-1}^2 + \alpha_2 h_{t-1},$$

where $u_t \equiv (\Delta p_t - \beta_0 - \beta_1 \Delta p_{t-1})$. As noted by Bollerslev (1986) and others, (3) is a parsimonious statistical representation that accommodates persistent conditional variances ($\alpha_1 + \alpha_2 \neq 0$) and the possibility that the marginal distribution of Δp_t is fat-tailed relative to a normal distribution. The excess kurtosis (relative to normal) in the context of a GARCH model can be expressed as $6\alpha_1^2(1 - \alpha_2^2 - 2\alpha_1\alpha_2 - 3\alpha_1^2)^{-1}$. Thus, the excess kurtosis is increasing in α_1 if $\alpha_1 > 0$ and $(1 - \alpha_2^2 - \alpha_1\alpha_2) > 0$, and is increasing in α_2 if $(\alpha_2 + \alpha_1) > 0$.

Table 8.6 displays the maximum likelihood estimates of the GARCH parameters for cash and futures prices under the assumption that the conditional distribution of u_t is normal. The GARCH parameters α_1 and α_2 of the CBT T-note contract and the associated UST prices are insignificantly different from zero at conventional significance levels. That the implied excess kurtosis is near zero was anticipated by the results in table 8.3. The new information in table 8.6 is the evidence of weak temporal dependence in the conditional variances of both UST cash and futures prices.

There is much stronger evidence of conditional heteroskedasticity in the prices for the German and Japanese markets, and, within each market, the structures of the conditional variances of cash and futures prices are strikingly similar. The autocovariances of the squared disturbances, u_t^2, $\gamma_n \equiv Cov[u_t^2, u_{t-n}^2]$, are given by

$$(4) \qquad \gamma_n = (\alpha_1 + \alpha_2)\gamma_{n-1},$$

---

priced off the futures in the sense that price changes on twenty-year bonds moved one-to-one with changes in the JGB futures price.

12. Without exception, the estimate of β_1 was insignificantly different from zero, so estimates of the parameters of the conditional mean are not reported subsequently.

Table 8.6   **Descriptive Statistics for Futures and Individual Bond Prices: Daily Changes, October 1, 1991–November 30, 1993**

Security	α_0	α_1	α_2	K	σ	ρ
CBT T-note 10 yr	1.16×10^{-5}	$-.019$	.287	4.40	.0039	.01
	(2.0×10^{-5})	$(.030)$	(1.30)			
UST 11/15/01	4.63×10^{-6}	-2.95×10^{-4}	.643	3.53	.0036	.07
	(7.30×10^{-6})	(3.38×10^{-2})	$(.565)$			
LIFFE BUND 10 yr	$1.20 \times 10^{-6*}$	$.006*$	$.732*$	3.73	.0024	$-.05$
	(3.68×10^{-7})	$(.002)$	$(.007)$			
BUND 9/20/01	$3.98 \times 10^{-7**}$	.003	$.886*$	3.49	.0021	$-.02$
	(2.05×10^{-7})	$(.002)$	$(.005)$			
TSE JGB 10 yr	$2.41 \times 10^{-6*}$	$.260*$	$.428*$	4.64	.0027	.02
	(6.66×10^{-7})	$(.053)$	$(.110)$			
JGB #140	$1.06 \times 10^{-6*}$	$.198*$	$.650*$	4.46	.0025	.05
	(2.41×10^{-7})	$(.041)$	$(.054)$			

Notes: Standard errors of the estimates are in parentheses. *(**) indicates that the estimate is significantly different from zero at the 1% (5%) significance level. K = kurtosis; σ = standard deviation; ρ = first-order autocorrelation of the changes in the bond or futures prices. *CBT* denotes Chicago Board of Trade futures, *LIFFE* denotes the London International Financial Futures Exchange, and *TSE* denotes the Tokyo Stock Exchange.

where $\gamma_0 = \sigma_u^2$, the variance of u_t. It follows that the rates at which the autocovariances of squared residuals decay in Germany and Japan are very similar. Nevertheless, the distributions of the conditional variances are notably different. Compared with the German LIFFE contract, a given percentage change in the TSE futures price at date $t - 1$, u_{t-1}, has a much larger impact effect on the conditional variance, and the effects of shocks dissipate more rapidly in Japan than in Germany. Consequently, the mean lag in the conditional variance equation (expressed as a function of past squared shocks) is about 3.7 days for the LIFFE BUND future and 1.7 days for the TSE JGB future.[13]

All of these findings are consistent with the view that deliverable, cash instruments inherit the distributional properties of futures. Changes in futures prices exhibit little autocorrelation, and this may explain the low autocorrelation of changes in JGB prices for deliverable bonds (table 8.3) compared to nondeliverable bonds. Moreover, the high kurtoses of all cash bonds in Japan is consistent with the high kurtosis of the JGB futures price (the highest among the securities considered). Similarly, the relatively low kurtoses for deliverable German bonds compared to nondeliverable bonds can be explained by the low kurtosis of the LIFFE BUND futures contract and the relative liquidity and depth of the futures compared to the cash market.

While these pairwise, cash-futures comparisons are suggestive of a key role for futures in price discovery, I have not documented a close linkage for the entire deliverable sector. Such evidence is presented in Kikugawa and Single-

13. See Bollerslev (1986) for the formula for the mean lag.

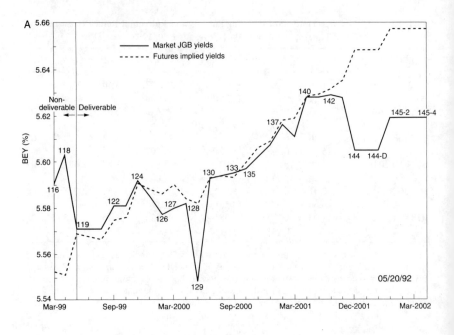

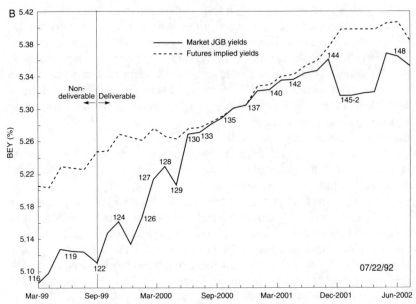

Fig. 8.1   Deliverable yield curves, Japan
Source: Data provided by Goldman Sachs and Co.

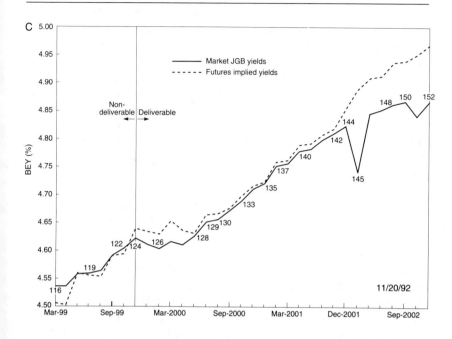

ton (1994), where it is shown that the deliverable sector in Japan was essentially priced directly off futures during much of 1992. Figure 8.1A displays the actual bond equivalent yields (BEYs; dark squares, labeled with bond numbers) of the JGBs in the deliverable sector on May 20, 1992, and the BEYs implied by the conversion-factor-adjusted futures prices discounted by the common implied repo rate on the CTD bond (i.e., BEYs implied by equation [3] with i set at the implied repo rate of the CTD bond). Consistent with pricing off futures, the two lines are virtually identical. The exceptions are #129, which was the benchmark at the time, and #144 and #145. The richness of the latter two bonds probably reflected the market's assessment of their potential benchmark status in the future; #145 became the subsequent benchmark.

Figure 8.1B displays the comparable yield curves for July 22, 1992. The shortest-maturity deliverable bond on this date was #122. Furthermore, the coupon rates on #127 and below are under 6 percent, while the coupon rates for #128–#144 are equal to or greater than 6 percent. For several months prior to April 1992, the low coupon, intermediate-maturity bonds were trading at relatively high yields and with light trading volumes, and there was a pronounced hump in the yield curve over the five- to seven-year sector. Between May and July 1992, the JGB market experienced a strong rally, especially in the five- to seven-year maturity sector of the yield curve. As trading activity increased in the low coupon nondeliverable bonds, the price discovery process changed for the similar low coupon deliverable bonds. Instead of being based on the bond future, which was tracking the longer-maturity higher coupon bond prices (#130–#144), the prices of #122 to #128 were set in relation to the more comparable low coupon (nondeliverable) #105, #111, and #119.

There are two complementary interpretations of this change in cash/futures price relations. First, the increased trading activity during July in the nondeliverable sector provided cash market benchmarks for pricing the short-maturity, deliverable bonds with comparable durations. Less weight was therefore given to the futures. A second, related consideration was that a market rally lead to the complete disappearance of a pronounced hump in the five- to seven-year sector of the JGB yield curve and a substantial steepening of the curve. Exact pricing off futures constrains the shape of the yield curve in the deliverable sector. Although the futures-implied yield curve steepens in a rally, the actual yield curve became much steeper than the futures-implied yield curve. Concurrently, the market priced in the shape of the curve. Thus, as yield curves steepen or flatten to the point that pricing off futures would create substantial arbitrage opportunities at the boundaries of the deliverable sector, market pricing reflects the importance of curve steepness.[14] Notice, however, that pricing cash bonds in terms of the futures is not a phenomenon that occurs only when market yields are near the notional yield on the futures. In late fall of 1992, there was a sell-off in the intermediate JGBs, and on November 20, 1992, for instance, the futures and implied yield curves were once again virtually indistinguishable (fig. 8.1C), with market yields well below 5 percent.[15]

Though the close relation between the cash and futures prices in figure 8.1 is striking, it is important to recognize that these patterns can exist yet there can be significant departures from the cost-of-carry relation for all bonds. The curves in figure 8.1 were derived by using the implied repo rate on the then current CTD in the right-hand side of (2) to compute implied cash prices. If the futures become very cheap (for instance) relative to cash, then this will be "absorbed" into the implied repo rate for the CTD. What figure 8.1 demonstrates is that the same implied repo rate priced all deliverable bonds during extended periods in 1992.

The absence of a well-developed repo market and the consequent high costs of shorting cash bonds mean that many market participants rely on the futures market for short selling. The consequent selling pressure on the futures mar-

14. In Japan, there were times during late 1991 and early 1992 when the gap between the yields on the shortest-maturity deliverable bond and the longest-maturity nondeliverable bond was over fifteen bp just before the expiration of the futures contract. Initially this gap represented a near-riskless trade opportunity in that, once the deliverable bond lost its delivery status (after expiration of the futures contract), it cheapened up to a comparable yield as other nearby nondeliverable bonds. Once this opportunity was recognized by most market participants, however, the gap was not tradable. TSE closing prices at times showed a yield gap, but no trades were being executed at TSE prices. As the intermediate sector rallied in mid-1992, such gaps largely disappeared.

15. Similar pricing in terms of futures has been observed in Germany. The recent steepening of the German yield curve has similarly led to discrepancies between the futures-implied and actual yield curves.

kets leads at times to the futures price in fact being very cheap relative to the cash market. The effects of these frictions can be seen graphically in figure 8.2, which displays the time series of implied repo rates on the CTDs (which change across contracts) relative to the short-term London interbank offer rate (LIBOR) for yen. Notice that for most of the first half of 1992, when there was pricing off futures in Japan, the differences between the implied repo (*CRPO*) and LIBOR (*R*) were relatively small. Thus, pricing off futures was approximately based on the cost-of-carry relation. Subsequently, LIBOR and the implied repo rate on the CTD bond have differed by up to one hundred bp. Thus, pricing of the cash market reflected the markets' assessment of an appropriate spread between the implied repo rates and LIBOR given the forces of supply and demand and the costs preventing attempts to arbitrage this gap.

8.4   Concluding Remarks

I have argued that there are important links between the institutional settings within which investors perform price discovery and the resulting distributions

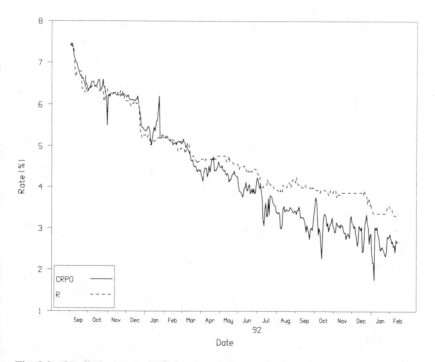

Fig. 8.2   Implied repo on CTD bond and short-term rate, Japan, September 2, 1991–November 15, 1993
Source: Data provided by Goldman Sachs and Co.
Note: R = LIBOR; *CRPO* = implied repo from the CTD bond.

of prices of fixed-income instruments. In environments like the United States, liquid UST markets are facilitated by regular auctions of new bonds of various maturities, "market-to-market" accounting, electronic settlement, a competitive dealer market with low transaction costs, and an active borrowing and lending market that makes selling short a low-cost endeavor. The institutional settings in Germany and Japan involve many more frictions, which inhibit price discovery in the cash markets. The empirical evidence suggests that these institutional factors are reflected in fatter-tailed distributions and, in the case of Japan, substantial autocorrelation of yield changes.

In the presence of institutional frictions in the cash markets, the relatively frictionless and liquid futures markets play more central roles in the price discovery process. This was reflected in the distributions of yields for cash bonds having notably different characteristics depending on whether the bonds were deliverable into a futures contract or nondeliverable. Moreover, the distributions of the cash and futures prices within the deliverable sectors were very similar. More direct evidence of the importance of futures for price discovery was presented for Japan, where the cash prices of all deliverable bonds were shown to have been, at times, set approximately to their associated conversion-factor-adjusted futures prices.

The evidence presented for Japan on pricing off futures is an extreme case. Indeed, the results suggest that nearly exact pricing off futures persisted for several months, but recently the prices in the cash market and those implied by the futures have differed by amounts that are more typical of markets in the United States. The recent patterns are consistent with the increased trading activity along the JGB yield curve, which would facilitate price discovery in the cash market. Also, though the focus has been on deliverable versus nondeliverable bonds, the thesis that cash and futures prices may be closely related during periods of low volume in the cash market suggests that under some circumstances pricing off futures might extend to bonds outside the deliverable sector. This was in fact the case in Japan during some periods in the past. Specifically, the superlong (twenty-year) bonds were for a while priced in terms of the futures.

Many questions remain for future study. In particular, why is the distribution of futures prices in Japan fat-tailed relative to the futures prices for the United States and Germany? I conjecture that the high borrowing and lending costs in the cash market, which contribute to the systematic violations in the cost-of-carry relation for the CTD bond, at least partially explain this result. If futures are the primary vehicle for shorting bonds, then the effects of institutional frictions in the cash market will spill over and help shape the distribution of the futures prices. Also, are the joint distributions of the cash and futures prices different for the five- and ten-year futures in Germany? These markets differ in their organizational design. Equally, if not more, important, the relative liquidities of the cash and futures markets appear to be different across the two sectors of the yield curve. A more thorough analysis of these differences using a bivariate model may be enlightening. In the cases of both Japan and Germany, establishing a tighter link between trading activity in the cash market and the correlation between cash and futures prices would be useful for verifying the conjectured links between these features of the markets. Addressing these issues requires the development of a much richer database of volume data and time series on the implied forward prices for individual bonds using equation (2). In future research, I plan to develop such databases for Japan and Germany and examine spillovers between cash and futures markets.

References

Amihud, Y., and H. Mendelson. 1991. Liquidity, Maturity, and Yields on U.S. Treasury Securities. *Journal of Finance* 46, no. 4: 1411–25.
Bollerslev, T. 1986. Generalized Autoregressive Conditional Heteroskedasticity. *Journal of Econometrics* 31:307–27.
Hansen, L. 1982. Large Sample Properties of Generalized Method of Moments Estimators. *Econometrics* 50:1029–56.
Kikugawa, T., and K. Singleton. 1994. Modeling the Term Structure of Interest Rates in Japan. *Journal of Fixed Income* 4 (September): 6–16.
McLean, S., ed. 1993. *The European Bond Markets.* Cambridge: Probus.
Quan, J. 1992. Two-Step Testing Procedure for Price Discovery Role of Futures Prices. *Journal of Futures Markets* 12:139–49.
Schwarz, T. V., and F. Laatsch. 1991. Price Discovery and Risk Transfer in Stock Index Cash and Futures Markets. *Journal of Futures Markets* 11:669–83.
Stoll, H., and R. Whaley. 1990. The Dynamics of Stock Index and Stock Index Futures Returns. *Journal of Financial and Quantitative Analysis* 25:411–68.

Comment   William P. Albrecht

In this paper Kenneth Singleton approaches the question of what might cause a market to be efficient (or inefficient) from a broader perspective than the typical market microstructure paper. He examines how what he calls macroinstitutional arrangements can affect price discovery and the relationship between cash and futures markets. The purpose of the paper, therefore, is not to debate whether the cash or futures market is more efficient or whether the cash market drives the futures market or vice versa. Singleton does not attempt to show that one market is necessarily more or less efficient than the other. Rather, he demonstrates that a market with fewer impediments to using it is more efficient than one with more impediments to using it.

It would be very comforting if the political discussion about the relationship

William P. Albrecht is professor of economics at the University of Iowa.

between cash and derivative markets would adopt this perspective more often. If this were to occur, governmental agencies that are concerned about why a market is not working well would spend more time looking for restrictions on voluntary exchange that may be responsible for the poor performance. This, in turn, would lead them to devote more resources to the task of eliminating such restrictions. The result would be a better balance in the types of activities engaged in by many governmental agencies. That is, they would spend more time looking for ways to remove restrictions on voluntary exchange and less time looking for ways to impose additional restrictions.

The basic structure and approach of this paper are quite sound. Singleton's macroapproach is appropriate. The purpose of this paper is set out quite clearly in the introduction, and the main conclusions appear to be consistent with the data and the statistical analysis. There are, however, a number of questions raised by Singleton that are not fully answered. The explanations of his results are not as well tied together as they might be, and there is an ad hoc nature to some of the explanations of the statistical results. This reader was left with the feeling that there is more to the story than is presented in the paper. There is, of course, always more to the story, but in this case telling a somewhat fuller story would be very helpful.

First, a number of statements about the markets in Germany and Japan raise interesting questions. Why, for example, are Treuhand and TROBLs not treated by the market as equivalent to their BOBL and BUND counterparts? Another example concerns the benchmark bonds. We learn that these bonds are designated in Japan, but it would be interesting to know more about how and why bonds are so designated. Not only would at least some readers be interested in the answers to these questions, but they might have some relevance for the analysis in the paper.

For the same reasons, I would like to know more about why the benchmark premium in Japan fluctuates and why certain ex-benchmark bonds often serve as key reference points for pricing. One reason cited is that they have large issue sizes, but surely that is why they were benchmarks. Are there other reasons? Or do all ex-benchmarks serve this function? A fuller discussion of how the lack of a repo market in Japan affects price discovery would also be useful. Singleton says that the absence of a well-developed repo market means that many market participants rely on futures markets for short selling, thereby putting downward pressure on futures prices. This, he says, causes a substantial bias toward futures' being cheap relative to cash bonds. Since the use of futures for price discovery is a central theme of the paper, this issue would seem to merit more examination.

There also appear to be some problems with identifying and explaining cause and effect. The paper states, for example, that increased trading in July 1992 in the nondeliverable sector provided cash market alternative benchmarks for price discovery. This is cited as an illustration of the prevalent phenomenon of benchmarks changing as the liquidities of candidate instruments change over time. But what causes these liquidities to change? Or is the point simply that, when volume is high in the cash market, it is used for price discovery?

Some further discussion of autocorrelation and kurtosis would also help. Why, for example, do changes in bond yields in Japan show positive autocorrelation for daily but not for weekly data? On the kurtosis issue, all three countries have fatter tails than normal for changes in yield, but the values of K are smaller for the United States. The paper also reports that there are smaller values of K for weekly data but it does not make clear exactly where these values are smaller. Nor does it explain the significance of this finding.

Finally, some of the explanations of the results that are offered in the paper are tentative or incomplete. For example, "two contributing factors to this difference may be the relatively larger number of auctions along the German yield curve facilitating price discovery, and the more well-developed repo market in Germany." And "even if largely true, my interpretation of the markets' pricing rules is not complete, as the effects of delivery status on the distributions of bond yields differ across markets."

A paper that presents as much information and analysis as this is bound to leave a number of unanswered and partially answered questions. Singleton cannot possibly address all the issues raised. These comments, in fact, point out the hazards of presenting so much information and raising so many issues. On the one hand, I have suggested that he try to provide answers to questions suggested but not explicitly addressed by the paper. On the other hand, I have complained about the tentative nature of the explanations when they are offered. Moreover, I undoubtedly would have complained if Singleton had been less tentative, on the grounds that his analysis does not support stronger answers. But, as I said earlier, there is more to the story than is presented in the paper. It would benefit from a concerted effort to tie up as many loose ends as possible.

Some of the aforementioned task could be accomplished by fuller explanations of some of the characteristics of the markets in Japan and Germany. Some of it could be accomplished by a section near the end of the paper that summarizes the major unanswered or partially answered questions and that discusses their significance for the paper's conclusions. These steps would improve what is already a solid paper—one that adds to our understanding of how the markets under discussion work.

Comment   T. Eric Kilcollin

I found it very difficult to review this paper since there's not much here you can really sink your teeth into: There is no well-defined hypothesis to be tested;

T. Eric Kilcollin is managing director of Wells Fargo Nikko Investment Advisors and chief operating officer of Wells Fargo Institutional Trust Company.

rather, as Singleton says in the paper, he's trying to characterize the properties of the joint distribution of cash and futures prices in order to guide modeling efforts in the future. He provides some institutional details about government securities and futures markets, but it is by no means a definitive treatment of these issues. He provides some data; but they, too, are certainly not exhaustive. Finally, he provides some statistics; but they, too, could certainly be expanded upon.

Fundamentally, the story line of the paper is that a host of largely unspecified accounting, regulatory, and cultural differences somehow aggregate to produce a Japanese government bond market that is less efficient than that of Germany, which, in turn, is less efficient than that of the United States. Somehow the futures markets escape these differences and are efficient in all three countries, and this relative efficiency spills over into the cash markets for deliverable securities in Germany and Japan.

The principal hypothesis is that, where cash markets don't work well, futures markets improve or at least affect cash market pricing. But we only have three data points (United States, Germany, and Japan) to test this hypothesis.

Clearly there are lots of holes in this study: for example, I did a paper on the various schemes for making a variety of bond issues deliverable against futures contracts (Kilcollin 1982). In that paper, I showed that, with the factor pricing scheme that these futures contracts use, the relation between the futures price and the prices of the various deliverable bonds is a complicated function that depends on the term structure of interest rates, the coupon structure of interest rates, and the general level of interest rates in relation to the par delivery instrument. It also depends on the volatility of these parameters. The JGB yield curve in Singleton's figure 8.1 may well be simply a reflection of these factors at work, rather than any tendency to price some cash bonds off futures prices.

As another example, Singleton notes that the JGB bonds that are deliverable against the futures contract have low autocorrelations. But these bonds also happen to be the highest-coupon, longest-maturity, and largest-issue bonds in his sample. How do we know it is deliverability against futures instead of these other factors that account for the autocorrelation numbers?

As a final example, Singleton asserts that the futures markets are largely free of the accounting, regulatory, and cultural influences he postulates for the cash markets. In the United States this is certainly not the case. U.S. futures markets have more regulation and are subject to more accounting anomalies than is the government securities market. The futures markets in Germany and Japan are also subjected to heavy regulation.

Notwithstanding these criticisms, there is an intuitive appeal to Singleton's findings—they just need more work. Longer time series covering more market conditions would bolster confidence that these results are real. Also, I'd like to see the factor-pricing issue investigated more fully. Some bonds, while *legally* deliverable, will turn out not to be *economically* deliverable. Why should their behavior be influenced by futures prices? Can other factors that might generate these results be ruled out? Ultimately, I don't think the "macro" relations of concern in this paper can be convincingly tested using a single set of data. Rather, it will be scraps of evidence from a variety of sources that together will support or reject Singleton's hypothesis.

I would suggest Singleton expand the range of his data. Certainly, France, the United Kingdom, and Australia could be included. Italy and Spain also have newer futures markets that might shed light on his hypothesis. I would also suggest looking at agricultural markets. There is a great variety of regulatory and "cultural" differences in these markets, and it is usual in agricultural markets for futures to be the main price discovery mechanism.

Finally, I would like to venture into the normative economics that Martin Feldstein warned us against. Suppose we find that futures markets do influence the distribution of cash market prices. Is this good or bad? Low autocorrelations seem desirable, but how about fat-tailed distributions? The Brady commission seemed convinced that futures cause fat-tails in equity market prices and that this is bad. Singleton finds the opposite and seems to believe that this is good. I'd like to see some discussion in future versions of this paper of what Singleton's work implies about economic efficiency.

Reference

Kilcollin, Thomas Eric. 1982. Difference Systems in Financial Futures Markets. *Journal of Finance* 37, no. 5: 1183–97.

Author's Reply

Let me begin by taking a broader perspective on the research agenda for which this paper represents an early progress report. Virtually all models of the term structure of interest rates that are studied in the finance literature or used in practice by the investment community assume the absence of arbitrage opportunities and frictionless markets. Though there are in fact many institutional and regulatory restrictions on trading practices, these models have proven to be useful abstractions for the U.S. Treasury bond markets. For other government bond markets, bond swaps along the maturity spectrum, short selling, and other trade strategies that potentially bring market prices approximately in line with the implications of models assuming frictionless markets may be significantly limited. This has been the case for Japan and Germany. Bonds of nearly identical maturities are priced to reflect accounting standards and transaction costs that impinge on these bonds in substantially different ways. In other words, the market effectively uses different discount functions to value the cash flows of these bonds. These observations have important implications for both valuation and risk management.

Consider for instance the problem of risk management. Typically, the primary objective is to find the portfolio of securities that matches the price movements of the target security. Clearly, whether prices track each other depends fundamentally on how the market sets prices. And price discovery is not independent of the institutional frictions faced by investors. This paper represents the first step of a longer-term research agenda attempting to expand our understanding of the relations between price discovery and the institutional/regulatory environment in which trades are undertaken. What surprised me, and may surprise others, is the extent to which the distributions of bond yields differ with maturity in Japan and Germany, and how they differ across markets. These differences represent in my view serious challenges for existing valuation models as well as for the design of effective hedging strategies.

The comparison across the bond markets of the United States, Germany, and Japan suggests that some of these differences can be explained by differences in the cost structures of market making, institutional frictions that affect liquidity, and the issuing practices of federal authorities. To draw out the relations between market structure and the distributions of yields and to gain some insight into how price discovery is accomplished in the presence of significant frictions, I explored the linkages between cash and futures prices. Regulatory guidelines and accounting standards appear to have contributed significantly to illiquidity in the cash market and a consequent greater reliance on the relatively liquid futures for price discovery in cash markets. This in turn can explain the substantial differences in distributions of bond yields along the yield curves and across countries.

Popular and political debates about the economic consequences of financial regulation often focus on specific aspects of contract design for derivative instruments. In particular, the focus is often on how regulatory change (e.g., margin requirements or circuit breakers) affects the costs of the economic insurance that a security provides. These issues are clearly important for determining competitive advantage among providers of insurance (the exchanges) and influencing risk management strategies of investors.

More fundamentally, regulation may affect the nature of the insurance provided by the security (i.e., its payoff distribution conditional on the state of the economy). In Japan and perhaps Germany, the steps being contemplated toward liberalization of bond markets are as much of the latter variety as the former, in part because these countries are at earlier stages of the liberalization process. For this reason, I believe that the more "macro" costs associated with market access, settlement, legality and costs of certain collateralized loans, and so forth, are much more significant for understanding price discovery in these markets than changes in the remaining regulations related to the design of futures contracts. In this regard, Kilcollin's comments suggest that he is fixated on regulations in the futures market that may be of second-order importance for price discovery rather than the more important issues facing countries that are behind the United States in liberalizing their cash markets.

I now turn to the specific comments of the discussants. Albrecht raises several interesting issues that were not fully addressed, and, as he suggests might be the case, the answers provide further support for the thesis of this paper. Addressing them in order, let me begin with the apparent differential treatment of Treuhands and BUNDs by the market. Treuhand will continue issuing until 1995, at which time it will become part of the Bundespost system. Bonds issued by the latter institution have recently been trading at about a thirty-basis-point spread to BUNDs, so investors are unsure how Treuhands will be priced in the market after they lose their deliverability status in the ten-year sector. Consequently, they trade cheap to BUNDs and are typically cheapest to deliver. In contrast, in the five-year sector, when TROBLs lose their deliverability status and Treuhand joins the Bundespost system, TROBLs will have about two years remaining until maturity, and most two-year bonds have been liquid and have little credit risk. Therefore the spreads of TROBLs to BOBLs have been much smaller.

Next Albrecht wonders about the benchmark selection process in Japan. The benchmark bond must have a large enough issue size to accommodate the high volume of trading and trade near par so that accounting considerations will not render the bond unattractive to many investors. At times the change in benchmark is perfectly predictable. This was the case, for example, with #157. The change date was the first trading date of the new settlement period after the first coupon payment. The coupon date is significant, because this is when the various tranches of the #157 merged into one tranche, and hence all of the tranches traded as the same bond. A new benchmark was expected because the market had rallied, making #145 a premium bond. On the other hand, as figure 8.1 suggests, there was considerable uncertainty about which bond would follow #129 as the benchmark. Again issue size[1] and coupon were important factors, as were the changes in market prices before the tranches were combined. However, there are no explicitly stated criteria for selecting the new benchmark. Rather, the largest securities companies in Japan seem to have selected both the bond and the change over date.

As for the role of ex-benchmark bonds serving as reference bonds for pricing, yes, it is the case that all ex-benchmark bonds have tended to play this role. In addition, there are a few bonds that were never benchmarks that have also at times served as pricing reference points. Examples include #99 and #140.

Albrecht's concern that the absence of a well-developed repo market in Japan may compromise price discovery based on futures is well taken. This issue is addressed at the end of section 8.3. To reiterate, during the period that there was evidently nearly exact pricing of cash bonds in terms of futures through the cost-of-carry relation, the implied repo rate on the cheapest-to-deliver

---

1. Bear in mind that between 60 and 90 percent of the trading volume in all Japanese government bonds has been in the single benchmark issue since the mid-1980s.

(CTD) bond and LIBOR were very close to each other.[2] In other words, there was essentially no bias in the pricing of futures. At other times, however, this bias has been substantial, as is evidenced in figure 8.2. To the extent that a subset of the deliverable yield curve was priced off futures during periods when the implied repo rate of the CTD and LIBOR differed, the market was basing pricing on both futures and a perceived reasonable spread between the two short-term rates, given supply and demand factors and the cost of shorting bonds. The periods during which the gaps between LIBOR and the implied repo rates on the CTD were largest correspond to periods during which cash and implied prices from futures evidenced the largest differences.

The high costs of market making in Japan open the possibility that large blocks of bonds will move though the dealer network slowly relative to a comparable block in the United States. Also, accounting factors, for example, may lead many domestic institutional accounts to be on the same side of the market at the same time. For example, if bonds were bought and booked at par and the market subsequently sold off, then there would be tendency for these bonds to be held in portfolios, thereby reducing the effective supply to the market. On the other hand, as the price of these bonds approaches par in a subsequent rally, trading activity may pick up as accounting constraints become less important for these bonds in portfolio rebalancings. In this manner, institutional and accounting factors can lead to large and persistent moves in Japanese government bond (JGB) yields that manifest themselves in large kurtoses and high autocorrelations.[3]

Many of Kilcollin's remarks are factually wrong and his proposed reinterpretations of the evidence suggest that he failed to grasp the meaning of the economic concept of price discovery. The suggestion that the conversion factor system itself can explain the patterns in figure 8.1 and in Kikugawa and Singleton (1994) is completely unsubstantiated. Indeed, the biases inherent in the conversion factor system are well known to induce a single CTD bond, and not the documented pattern of many deliverable bonds being nearly equally CTD for a period of months.

Kilcollin's remarks about autocorrelation and the assertion that I claim futures markets are largely free of regulation show that he did not carefully read the paper. Many of the specific accounting and regulatory factors discussed pertain to the cash markets; as noted in the introduction, the regulations related

2. Even though there was nearly exact pricing of the deliverable sector in terms of the futures price, a cheapest to deliver still existed, because the institutional and accounting factors usually implied that one bond would be slightly cheaper to deliver than all other candidate bonds. The differences in implied repo rates were small, however.

3. Some of the autocorrelation may also be due to the price quotation system for JGBs. The prices are Tokyo Stock Exchange (TSE) closing prices, which may not be exactly equal to transaction prices. This problem is more severe than an infrequent trading problem, since the TSE prices are set by one of the big four securities firms and need not be exactly equal to a recent market trade. Nevertheless, the TSE prices are usually within a few basis points of transaction prices.

to margin and contract design for futures are not the focus of this paper. Additionally, some of the *relative* advantages of executing certain trades in futures markets brought about by these cash market frictions are spelled out in the paper.

As for his remarks about autocorrelation, contrary to his claim, the deliverable bonds are not the longest-maturity bonds examined for Japan. The twenty-year bonds are not deliverable and evidenced high autocorrelations. Similar autocorrelations and kurtoses are obtained in studies of yields for high coupon superlong bonds. Also, compared to say #140, there are other, nondeliverable bonds with higher coupons and larger issue sizes. This is clearly displayed in table 8.2. Moreover, for an earlier sample period Kikugawa and Singleton (1994) found that #111 and #119 bonds also exhibited relatively low autocorrelations compared to nondeliverable bonds. Table 8.3 shows that market conditions changed in such a way that these bonds became significantly autocorrelated.

Finally, I agree with both discussants that more analysis is needed to link more tightly the empirical evidence to the institutional frictions emphasized. This will be the focus of future research. Rather than expanding the scope of the analysis by considering more countries, I am expanding the set of variables used in the empirical analysis in an attempt to better understand the three markets considered in this paper.

Reference

Kikugawa, T., and K. Singleton. 1994. Modeling the Term Structure of Interest Rates in Japan. *Journal of Fixed Income* 2 (September): 6–16.

9   Market Structure and Liquidity on the Tokyo Stock Exchange

Bruce N. Lehmann and David M. Modest

Common sense and conventional economic reasoning suggest that liquid secondary markets facilitate lower-cost capital formation than would otherwise occur. Broad common sense does not, however, provide a reliable guide to the specific market mechanisms—the nitty-gritty details of market microstructure—that would produce the most desirable economic outcomes.

The demand for and supply of liquidity devolves from the willingness, indeed the demand, of public investors to trade. However, their demands are seldom coordinated except by particular trading mechanisms, causing transient fluctuations in the demand for liquidity services and resulting in the fragmentation of order flow over time. In most organized secondary markets, designated market makers like dealers and specialists serve as intermediaries between buyers and sellers who provide liquidity over short time intervals as part of their provision of intermediation services. Liquidity may ultimately be provided by the willingness of investors to trade with one another, but designated market makers typically bridge temporal gaps in investor demands in most markets.[1]

Bruce N. Lehmann is professor of economics and finance at the Graduate School of International Relations and Pacific Studies at the University of California, San Diego. David M. Modest is associate professor of finance at the Walter A. Haas School of Business Administration at the University of California, Berkeley.

The authors thank Kazuhisa Okamoto of Wells Fargo Nikko Investment Advisors, Pete Kyle of Duke University, and participants at the NBER conference for helpful comments and suggestions. They are grateful to Nikko Securities, the Nikko Research Center, and the Institute of Investment Technology for providing them with the data and with help in all phases of this investigation. The authors have achieved their present level of understanding of Tokyo Stock Exchange mechanisms through the patience of Yutaka Fujii, Takeshi Hirano, and Shunzo Kayanuma of the TSE, all of whom endured many persistent questions with unfailing good cheer. Tony Azuma and Hiroshi Koizumi helped the authors throughout the project, both by inquiring about the TSE mechanisms and by performing the calculations. The authors remain guilty of any remaining errors.

1. The former is commonly termed natural liquidity and the latter bridge liquidity.

This is not the case on one of the largest and most active stock markets in the world: the Tokyo Stock Exchange (TSE). The designated intermediaries of the TSE are merely order clerks called *saitori*.[2] The saitori clerks log limit orders in a public limit order book and match incoming market orders to the limit orders or to each other in accordance with strict rules based on price, time, and size priority. On the TSE, orders from the investor public, not from designated market makers, bridge temporal fluctuations in the demand for liquidity services.

All continuous market mechanisms cope with temporary order imbalances that outstrip their capacity to supply liquidity, essentially by throwing sand in the gears. Since no designated market maker stands ready to absorb transient order flow variation on the TSE, its procedures provide for flagging possible occurrences of transient order imbalances and for routinely halting trade to attract orders when particular kinds of order imbalances occur. Such mechanisms always trade the benefits of attracting more liquidity to the marketplace against the cost of impeding the price discovery process and the immediacy of execution.

The Securities and Exchange Commission (SEC 1992) noted that it proposed the addition of a consolidated limit order book to the National Market System (NMS) in 1976. It went on to record that "commentators [like the exchanges] asserted that a time and price preference for public limit orders would provide a major trading advantage for those orders, thereby creating a disincentive for the commitment of market making capital by dealers, and might eventually force all trading into a fully automated trading system" (3). By contrast, many academics and practitioners believe that market structures should resemble such consolidated public limit order books because they produce low-cost liquidity, essentially by providing open and equal access to market making. The TSE has many of these features, making it an interesting subject for a comparative study.

Financial economists, practitioners, and regulators are at present evaluating the relative fairness and efficiency of alternative market structures.[3] An empirical appraisal of the TSE's mechanisms would appear to be a useful contribution at this time. In this paper, we study the procedures designed to warn of and cope with transient order imbalances and their impact on the price discovery process.[4]

---

2. The order book officials (OBOs) of the Chicago Board Options Exchange play a similar role in that market.

3. The Market 2000 study is one major focus of this effort.

4. We also devote a little attention to the division of the trading day into two trading sessions and the large tick sizes for some stocks. We ignore two important frictions: fixed commissions and the stamp tax. Commissions are sizable, just below 1 percent for one to five round lots and somewhat above 0.5 percent for ten to thirty round lots of a stock selling for ¥1,000. The stamp tax is 0.30 percent for customers and 0.12 percent for member firms. In so doing, we take the order placement strategies of investors as given and measure their impact given the constraints imposed by the market mechanism.

The paper is laid out as follows. Section 9.1 describes the market-making mechanism, and section 9.2 provides an analytical description of the data. Section 9.3 reports on the efficacy of the TSE trading mechanisms. A brief conclusion rounds out the paper.

9.1   An Analytic Description of the Tokyo Stock Exchange

In this section, we first contrast the salient qualities of the TSE with those of exchanges in the United States like the New York Stock Exchange (NYSE). We then describe the structure of the market and its trading mechanisms in some detail.[5]

9.1.1   Fragmentation and Transparency in U.S. and Japanese Equity Markets

One useful way to contrast equity trading mechanisms is in terms of fragmentation and transparency. Fragmentation has two dimensions: time and space. We discussed temporal fragmentation in the introduction—the unexpected variation in order flow over time. Spatial fragmentation refers to competing market mechanisms that might differ in trading opportunities, participants, or the method of participation. Transparency refers to the extent to which the information disseminated by a trading venue provides a clear ex ante picture of trading opportunities and a clear ex post picture of comparative trading performance. In order to contrast trading mechanisms in these dimensions, we must examine the particulars of order submission, exposure, execution, and reporting as well as those of competing mechanisms in the same securities.

Like the TSE, the NYSE is an order-driven market. However, it is not *purely* order-driven: specialists act both as designated intermediaries and as designated market makers who often supply liquidity when public orders are not available. Like the saitori, the specialist logs limit orders and either crosses incoming market orders, exposes them to the crowd, or marries them to public limit orders when possible. When order imbalances remain, specialists generally first fill any such orders out of inventory. If order imbalances are unusually large, the specialist can temporarily halt trading with the approval of a floor official of the NYSE.[6]

The TSE mechanism presupposes that order imbalances might be transient or might signal the discovery of a new "equilibrium" price. Accordingly, it advertises the presence of imbalances through indicative quote dissemination and temporarily halts trade to expose pending orders to the public when the immediate execution of one or more orders would move prices "too much."

---

5. The basic structure of the TSE has been described well by others, including Amihud and Mendelson (1989), Lindsey and Schaede (1992), Hamao and Hasbrouck (1993), and Tokyo Stock Exchange (1989).

6. See Hasbrouck, Sofianos, and Sosebee (1993) for a recent detailed discussion of NYSE halt procedures. The TSE has similar provisions for halting trade when news has been released or is pending. Such halts occur infrequently, and trade is reopened by a single-price auction.

Finding out whether such mechanisms are efficacious is one major motivation for this paper.

Spatial fragmentation is an important feature of equity trading in the United States. Numerous trading venues now provide different investors with different kinds of trading opportunities. Specialized venues exist for trading large blocks of stock on the upstairs market of the NYSE and for small retail orders through order flow purchases by third-market dealers like Madoff Securities. Several regional markets compete for order flow as third-market dealers by guaranteeing execution at or inside the NYSE spread. Several fourth-market mechanisms compete with the NYSE by letting institutions trade directly with one another without the intermediation services of an organized market or market makers. Examples include public single-price auctions like the Arizona Stock Exchange and crossing networks that use different NYSE prices or quotes during hours when the NYSE is open, like Posit and Instinet, or when it is closed, like Reuters' Crossing network.[7]

The TSE differs in this dimension as well. The vast majority of trading in equities listed on the TSE takes place on its physical or its electronic trading floor. Slightly fewer than one thousand stocks listed on the TSE are listed on regional exchanges in Japan, but volume off the TSE is small, and these exchanges cannot engage in third-market-style competition because they have very similar trading structures.[8] There is no separate structure for large and small, retail and institutional, or any other differentiation of order by size of trade, type of investor, or form of trading venue. The TSE is the largest highly consolidated equity trading mechanism in the world.[9]

Securities markets also differ in their levels of transparency. U.S. auction markets like the NYSE have routine trade reporting and dissemination procedures to ensure that trading results are broadcast widely. The TSE audit and reporting procedures resemble those of American exchanges; hence, the TSE differs little in ex post transparency.[10] As for ex ante transparency, American

---

7. Whether such fragmentation impairs liquidity and the process of price discovery or improves performance through competition remains an open question. Many of the underlying issues are complicated, including violation of price, size, and time priority across markets and the anonymity of trading on many trading venues.

8. The regional exchanges have nearly identical order-driven limit order books maintained by order clerks who do not act as market makers. Osaka is the largest regional exchange by far, largely because of its active index futures and options markets. The others are Fukuoka, Hiroshima, Kyoto, Nagoya, Niigata, and Sapporo.

9. Other markets with comparable levels of automation like the Toronto Stock Exchange and the Paris Bourse have separate block trading facilities. The TSE does have a limited public block trading facility, which accounts for only a small fraction of trading. See section 9.1.2.

10. Major differences in ex post transparency exist between order-driven markets like the NYSE and the TSE and dealer markets like the Stock Exchange Automated Quotations (SEAQ) system in London, which does not enforce last-sale reporting. Ex post transparency is a public good, and the property rights to the information that a trade has occurred (and any associated informational externalities) are assigned to the trader in many dealer markets, including SEAQ. Traders seem to value anonymity—much of the volume of the Madrid Stock Exchange and Paris Bourse (both very transparent markets) has moved to SEAQ, particularly large block trades.

exchanges and the TSE both widely disseminate the best bid and offer in a stock. However, the TSE is less transparent than its American counterparts in the dissemination of quote depth, which is broadcast widely in the United States but not in Japan.[11]

However, the TSE provides for high levels of transparency in the head offices of its member firms. Every member has a small number of terminals (based loosely on annual trading volume) on which the consolidated limit order book of any listed stock can be viewed at any time. It lists the extant bids and offers and their aggregate size at each price, but this information can be neither stored nor rebroadcast. All traders can supply liquidity in the face of fragmentation of trades over time, since the TSE routinely flags potential order imbalances. However, only head-office traders of member firms (and others who talk to them) have this special access to the limit order book, and head-office brokers can and do routinely examine the limit order book when buying or selling stock for customers, particularly for large institutions.

To some extent, then, we can think of the TSE mechanism as approximating the information content of a consolidated electronic limit order book, at least from the viewpoint of member firms.[12] In addition, the TSE mechanism advertises both potential order imbalances and temporary trading halts through the dissemination of indicative quotes as discussed below. Taken together, these features may be a close substitute for widespread dissemination of the electronic book.[13]

9.1.2 The Structure of the Tokyo Stock Exchange

There are 1,661 stocks listed on the TSE. Of these, 1,232 are in the so-called First Section, and 429 less active stocks are in the Second Section. The 151 most active First Section stocks are still traded on the trading floor.[14] The remaining First Section and all of the Second Section stocks are traded electroni-

---

11. The information content of quote depth in the United States is not clear, since quotes are often only for nominal sizes. Member firms can broadcast the best bid and offer to their branches, but not all firms do so. Outside investors can generally get only more limited data like the high, low, open, and closing prices as well as the five most recent trade prices directly from vendors like Nihon Keizai Shimbun (Nikkei).

12. The conditional statement "to some extent" is critical here—a whole host of agency problems are associated with interpreting broker-dealer observation of the limit order book as close to widespread dissemination of and open access to the book. This interpretation would surely be questioned by academics like Glosten (1994) and Black (1993) and practitioners, particularly fourth-market advocates like Steve Wunsch and the Arizona Stock Exchange.

13. Prior to the electronic book, the saitori would provide ready access to the limit order book to all trading clerks on the floor. While it is perhaps easy to understand why the TSE does not widely disseminate the electronic limit order book, the restriction of the number of screens at the head office is harder to understand. The TSE apparently views the current system as facilitating order processing and execution only and that widespread dissemination would facilitate market making by member firms, an undesirable outcome from the TSE's viewpoint.

14. New Japan Railway Company was recently added to the list of floor-traded stocks.

cally on the Computer-Assisted Order Routing and Execution System (CORES).[15]

The trading rules for floor- and system-traded stocks are identical. Orders for less than three thousand shares for floor-traded stocks are usually submitted electronically, while larger orders are brought to saitori posts manually.[16] Order entry is electronic for system-traded stocks. There is no odd-lot trading, and one thousand shares is a round lot for most stocks.[17]

The TSE has two trading sessions per day. The morning session begins at 9:00 A.M. and ends at 11:00 A.M. Trading resumes at 12:30 P.M. and ends at 3:00 P.M. Most continuous trading markets begin trading sessions with a single-price auction. The TSE is no exception, starting each session with an auction called the *itayose*. Continuous trading follows until the close of the session.

The itayose is based on standard auction market principles. Public market and limit orders are submitted in the twenty-five minutes before the open. The saitori clerks essentially search for a price that executes all market-on-open orders and roughly matches the residual supplies and demands expressed as limit orders.[18] The itayose is also used to reopen trade after a suspension by the president of the TSE.

Failure to meet these conditions results in a delayed open. In the event of a delayed open, the saitori issues a special quote (the *tokubetsu kehai*, described extensively below).[19] Briefly, the purpose of this indicative quote is to attract sufficient orders from the public until the conditions required to open the stocks are met. The special quote adjustment process used in delayed opens is identical to the one described below (which is used in the continuous market), except that the saitori cumulates orders until the itayose requirements are met.

The TSE also permits market-on-close orders to be executed in a batch auction. For such auctions, the requirement that at least one round lot of each limit

15. CORES is based on the Computer Assisted Trading System (CATS) of the Toronto Stock Exchange (a different TSE) but is operated somewhat differently. For example, the Toronto Stock Exchange has designated market makers.

16. These orders arrive via the Floor Order Routing and Execution System (FORES).

17. A round lot is one thousand shares for a stock with a par value of ¥50 and one hundred shares for the small number of stocks with a par value of ¥500 and for selected high-priced stocks. About one hundred securities fall into this latter category. Odd lots are traded off the exchange, but round lots must be traded on an exchange.

18. In order to open a stock, the saitori must execute (1) all market orders, (2) at least one limit order, (3) all limit orders that better the itayose price, (4) all limit orders on one side of the market at the itayose price, and (5) at least one round lot of each limit order on the other side of the market at the itayose price. Amihud and Mendelson (1989), Hasbrouck, Sofianos, and Sosebee (1993), and Lindsey and Schaede (1992) provide examples of the opening process. One difference between the TSE and the NYSE is that the specialist may participate in the open, but there is no designated market maker available to do so on the TSE. The requirement that a limit order participates in the TSE open replaces the possibility of specialist participation in the NYSE open.

19. The initial special quote is set equal to the prior close plus or minus the maximum price variation (see table 9.1) in the direction of the order imbalance. The initial order imbalance at that price is calculated from the demand and supply curves based on the market and limit orders submitted prior to the itayose. This order imbalance is reported as the size of the special quote on broker screens.

order on one side of the market must be executed at the itayose price is weakened. It is often difficult to execute market-on-close orders using this revised itayose mechanism because prices that would clear the market often exceed the maximum price variation between trades, and so such orders often go unexecuted. As a consequence, market-on-close orders are used much less frequently in Tokyo than in the United States.[20]

Following the itayose, the continuous auction market called the *zaraba* begins operation. The best unexecuted limit orders become the opening bid and offer. Limit orders remain on the book until they are executed or canceled or until the afternoon session ends. After the open, the saitori maintains the limit order book and marries incoming market orders with either limit orders or other incoming market orders.[21] This process continues until a temporary trading halt results from an order imbalance, the trading session ends, the president of the exchange suspends trading, or the daily price limit is hit. The latter two possibilities are extremely rare.

Virtually all trades are executed during the itayose and the zaraba. There is a very limited block trading facility and an unusual method for crossing trades. There are electronic bulletin boards on the floor on which member firms can publicly advertise large orders to potential counterparties. This limited form of sunshine trading essentially constitutes the public block trading mechanism of the TSE.[22] Crossing trades can occur only if the same member firm represents both sides of the trade.[23] Virtually all crossing trades are made with a corporate equity holder being both the buyer and the seller, and the member firm essentially serves as a dealer to facilitate the trade. The purpose of these trades is to change the book value of an equity position owned by that corporation on its balance sheet at fiscal year end.[24]

20. The TSE says there is relatively little demand for this service, an unsurprising outcome given the difficulties with the mechanism.

21. Saitori clerks also monitor the limit order book and control the execution process for system-traded stocks.

22. These advertisements are posted on the display above the trading floor and are not broadcast, although the floor brokers of member firms rapidly transmit this information to their home offices. Their use is sufficiently rare that all successful trades result in loud and widespread applause on the trading floor.

23. Strictly speaking, one customer cannot be both buyer and seller in the same transaction because of the portion of the Securities and Exchange Law that defines manipulative activity to be trading without an intent to transfer possession. Consequently, the member firm acts like a dealer and essentially executes two trades when crossing on the TSE. Since these trades must go through the limit order book, the member firm cannot cross the trade at the single market price if there are other orders on the book. Accordingly, member firms frequently cross trades on regional exchanges since their limit order books are often empty because most trading is consolidated on the TSE. In order to forestall manipulation (such as the illegal trading done in 1990 and 1991 to compensate customers for losses they incurred), large transactions in which one member firm acts as both buyer and seller must be executed at a price within a fixed limit of the last trade price on the TSE, irrespective of where the trade is executed. In addition, the member firm must report the purpose of the trade and the kind of customer to the exchange.

24. Lindsey and Schaede (1992) discuss the private crossings called *onna-hen no baikai*. Baikai do not pass through the saitori's order book but instead are treated as if they are matched by the

Trading during the day is subject to a variety of price limits that are given in table 9.1. The maximum price variation and the daily price limit are both upper bounds on price changes. The daily price limit is the maximum amount that a price can change on a trading day relative to the closing price on the prior day. Trade is suspended whenever the daily price limits are hit, but trade can resume again by the submission of limit orders at admissible prices. These limits are wide; hence, trading is rarely suspended because of them. The maximum price variation describes the maximum price change from the previous trade that a single order is permitted to cause by executing it against limit orders on the book. Much of this paper is devoted to an analysis of the role played by the maximum price variation.

A neglected institutional feature of the TSE is the tick size or minimum price variation of stocks.[25] In U.S. markets, the tick size is usually fixed at an eighth, although traders can split ticks in some circumstances. In contrast, tick sizes on the TSE depend on stock prices, as shown in table 9.1. A particularly interesting break point occurs at ¥1,000: a ¥1 minimum tick for stocks selling below ¥1,000 and a ¥10 minimum tick for stocks selling above ¥1,000.[26] Since roughly one-third of the stocks on the TSE sell for more than ¥1,000, the tick size is nearly 1 percent for many stocks, making stepping across the spread to buy immediacy quite expensive.[27]

9.1.3 Order Imbalances and the Trading Mechanisms of the Tokyo Stock Exchange

The TSE needs a mechanism to deal with temporary order imbalances because no designated market maker stands ready to meet fluctuations in the demand for liquidity. There are three components of the TSE system for coping with potential order imbalances: (1) advertising the possibility of a transient order imbalance; (2) halting trade when immediate execution of one order would move prices "too much"; and (3) providing for orderly quote changes on the path to a new "equilibrium" price when an order imbalance is created by more than one order. We devote the rest of this section to a comprehensive

---

customers themselves, with the member firm acting as consultant and certifying that the trade was consummated within exchange rules. Neither member firms nor their subsidiaries can be a buyer or seller in *baikai*. The price setting and reporting requirements resemble those for regular crossing trades.

25. Angel (1993) also notes the extreme tick-size change in percentage terms at ¥1,000.

26. Few stocks sell above ¥10,000 and only Nippon Telephone and Telegraph sells for more than ¥30,000.

27. We account for tick-size effects in much of our work by sorting stocks into price categories. We report in passing that we have observed the standard trade-off between tick size and market depth. For example, average trade size is much larger in stocks with large tick sizes, reflecting the greater protection from informed traders afforded by larger spreads. See Lehmann and Modest (1994) for more details.

Table 9.1   Tick Size, Maximum Price Variation, and Daily Price Limits on the Tokyo Stock Exchange

Price Range	Tick Size	Maximum Price Variation	Daily Price Limit
0 < ¥100	¥1	¥5	¥30
¥101 to ¥200	¥1	¥5	¥50
¥201 to ¥500	¥1	¥5	¥80
¥501 to ¥1,000	¥1	¥10	¥100
¥1,001 to ¥1,500	¥10	¥20	¥200
¥1,501 to ¥2,000	¥10	¥30	¥300
¥2,001 to ¥3,000	¥10	¥40	¥400
¥3,001 to ¥5,000	¥10	¥50	¥500
¥5,001 to ¥10,000	¥10	¥100	¥1,000
¥10,001 to ¥30,000	¥100	¥200	¥2,000

Source: Tokyo Stock Exchange, International Affairs Department, *Tokyo Stock Exchange Fact Book 1994.*

description of these procedures: the *chui* and *tokubetsu kehai* (warning and special quote) mechanisms.[28]

Figure 9.1 describes the possible chain of events following the arrival of a market order. There are numerous eventualities given in figure 9.1, but the main possibilities are numbered (1) a regular trade occurs; (2) trading occurs at several prices at which warning quotes (chui kehai) are generally issued (i.e., the order walks up or down the book), but no trading halt occurs; (3) a warning quote trading halt occurs since the maximum price variation is exceeded; and (4) a special quote (tokubetsu kehai) trading halt occurs because another order arrived on the same side of the market as the pending order. The latter three possibilities are what we mean by advertising a potential imbalance, halting a trade because of one large order, and providing for discovery of a new "equilibrium" price when a trading halt is caused by more than one large order. Note that it is usually possible to determine from the regular quotation screen which of these eventualities transpired.

When a market order arrives at the TSE, the basic initial outcomes are no trade and a regular trade. Two points of reference govern execution: the best limit orders on the book and the base price (i.e., the price of the most recent transaction). A regular trade occurs if all or part of the order can be filled at the current bid or offer.[29] No trade occurs if (1) the difference between the best quote and the prior day's closing price exceeds the daily price limit, an

28. Lindsey and Schaede (1992) describe the tokubetsu kehai mechanism in some detail. Hamao and Hasbrouck (1993) provide the most detailed account of both mechanisms we have seen, but the example they give of warning quote behavior in their table 1 seems incorrect.

29. The saitori could even issue a warning quote and halt trade if prices change only by bouncing between the bid and offer inside the maximum price variation bounds.

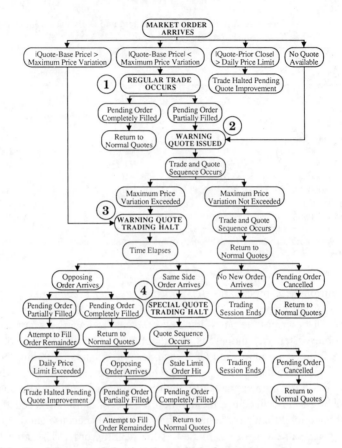

Fig. 9.1   Possible events following the arrival of a market order

uncommon event due to the price limits shown in table 9.1; or (2) there is no quote available or the difference between the base price and the available quote exceeds the maximum price variation, in which case the saitori issues a warning quote at the base price (or one tick above or below it).

The warning quote process generally follows a regular trade in two circumstances. The first case arises if the size of the market order exceeds the depth at the quote so that continued execution of the order would cause the price to change from the base price. The second case occurs if there is no quote available (that is, either there is no limit order on the books or one that, if executed, would cause the maximum variation to be exceeded). In both cases, the normal quotation screen indicates that a warning quote is pending, so that this information is widely available. Note that warning quotes do not give the size of the pending order.[30]

---

30. The size of the pending order is displayed on the electronic limit order book.

Figure 9.2 traces the sequence of events following the issuance of a warning quote. It is useful to distinguish two cases: either there are or are not limit orders on the book large enough to fill the rest of the pending order without exceeding the maximum price variation. All or part of the pending order is usually executed at different prices against limit orders on the book if the maximum price variation is not exceeded. In this case, warning quotes are generally issued as each new price is hit, as a sequence of trades and warning quotes appears on the normal quotation screen. The word "generally" covers two exceptions: the saitori may exercise his discretion (1) to execute such trades without issuing warning quotes or (2) to delay execution. Nevertheless, the saitori usually permits semiautomatic execution and warning quote issuance within the maximum price variation limits.[31]

There are two primary ways in which the nonhalt portion of the warning quote process usually ends. The pending order is either completely or only partially filled. If the pending order is completely filled, the base price is changed to the last execution price, and the trading screen will register a return to normal quotes. If it is only partially filled, a warning quote is issued at the limit set by the maximum price variation, and trade is temporarily halted. There is no formal announcement of a temporary halt; the warning quote just sits on the normal quotation screen without being altered. Hence, this occurrence can be discerned by many market participants.

There are other, less likely outcomes. An opposing order might arrive, triggering a normal conclusion of the warning quote process; an order from another member firm on the same side of the market might arrive, triggering a special quote; the pending order might be canceled, triggering a return to normal quotes; or the trading session might end. These possibilities are much less likely because the saitori usually concludes the nonhalt portion of the warning quote process quickly.

If trade is halted, all or part of the pending order is available at the warning quote. The saitori rarely changes a warning quote at the maximum price variation limit without the arrival of additional orders. Put differently, the TSE mechanism implicitly assumes that *one* order that may move prices substantially might well signify only a temporary order imbalance. Accordingly, the warning quote mechanism stops the price discovery process when the maximum price variation limit is reached, inviting potential counterparties to hit the warning quote.

Consequently, large orders have something of sunshine flavor. Since the limit order book *can* be viewed at the head office of a member firm, traders placing large orders are likely to look at it beforehand. Submitting an order large enough to cause a warning quote trading halt guarantees partial execution

31. As is evident in the results given below, saitori clerks do not issue warning quotes in these circumstances a nontrivial fraction of the time. The word "semiautomatic" means that saitori clerks choose to do so most of the time, not that this procedure is programmed into CORES.

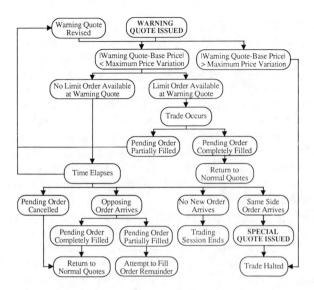

Fig. 9.2   Warning quote behavior prior to reaching maximum price variation

of the order at predetermined prices and effectively holds an auction for any part of the remainder.

Figure 9.3 delimits the ways in which warning quote trading halts can end. The auction of the pending order concludes successfully if an opposing order arrives. All or part of the pending order is then filled, the base price changes, and the quotation screen returns to normal quotes. Any unfilled portion of either the pending market order or the opposing order if it was a market order is then treated as though it were a new market order, and the process begins anew.[32] The market returns to normal quotes if the pending order is canceled, and the pending order is suspended if the trading session ends.[33]

Finally, the warning quote is converted into the other indicative quote—the special quote or tokubetsu kehai—if a market order arrives from another member firm on the same side of the market as the pending order. The issuance of a special quote is also widely disseminated on the regular quotation screen. As with the warning quote, a special quote can end if an opposing order arrives, the pending orders are canceled, or the trading session ends.

However, the mechanism provides for gradual quote adjustment past the

32. Note that a partial fill of the pending order still results in a return to normal quotes. The TSE mechanism presumes that the warning quote is a reasonable candidate for the "equilibrium price" if someone is willing to trade at that price, not requiring that trader to fill the entire pending order at that price.

33. The pending order is canceled if the afternoon session ends, and the last transaction price becomes the base price for the purpose of computing the daily price limit for the next day. The order becomes part of the afternoon itayose if it is pending at the conclusion of the morning session and is not subsequently canceled.

Fig. 9.3   Warning quote trading halts

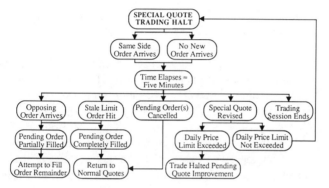

Fig. 9.4   Special quote trading halts

limit set by the maximum price variation even if no additional orders arrive. Put differently, the TSE special quote mechanism implicitly assumes that *two* orders on the same side of the market that might move prices substantially may well signal a change in the equilibrium price. Accordingly, the special quote mechanism permits the price discovery process to continue without the arrival of opposing orders.

Figure 9.4 describes this process. In the absence of opposing orders, the norm is to revise the special quote every five minutes, although the saitori may choose to revise it less frequently. The saitori seldom permits pending orders to be canceled and logs additional orders on the same side of the market for possible execution on the basis of time priority.[34] If the market remains quiescent, the saitori revises the special quote until the pending orders are eventually executed against the best limit order on the book—termed the stale limit order

---

34. There are informal rules that virtually prohibit pending-order cancellation. For example, special quote trading halts ended with order cancellation in fewer than 0.25 percent of the observations (7 out of 2,893) in our twenty-six-month sample.

in figure 9.4—if there is one.[35] An exception occurs when special quote revision would penetrate the daily price limit barrier, in which case trading is suspended pending the arrival of an order that can be executed inside the daily price limit.

Otherwise, a special quote trading halt ends in the same ways as a warning quote trading halt. If an opposing order arrives, all or part of the pending orders are filled, the base price changes, and the quotation screen returns to normal quotes. Any unfilled portion of either the pending orders or the opposing order, if it was a market order, is then treated as if it were a new market order, and the process begins anew.[36] The market returns to normal quotes if the pending orders are canceled, and the pending orders are suspended if the trading session ends.[37]

As noted earlier, the TSE does not widely disseminate information about trading opportunities beyond the current best bid and offer to most participants. Instead, it disseminates two indicative quotes when market conditions suggest either an order imbalance or a change in the equilibrium price: the warning quote (chui kehai) and the special quote (tokubetsu kehai). The saitori temporarily halts trade if continued execution of a single order would cause the price change to exceed the maximum price variation relative to the initial base price. A warning quote is converted to a special quote if an order from another member firm arrives on the same side of the market as the order that generated the warning quote. If no opposing orders arrive, the special quote is gradually revised until a new price is established by a completed transaction, which may be only a partial fill.

Finally, these procedures may not impede the trading process too much for two reasons. First, the maximum price variation bands for most stocks are between 1 and 2 percent. Second, both chui and tokubetsu kehai trading halts end if an opposing order only partially fills any pending orders, even an order for only one round lot. Accordingly, prices can move substantially on relatively small volume despite these limitations on trading.

9.2   The TSE Data and Some Limitations on What Can Be Learned from It

Our data were compiled by the TSE and provided to us by Nikko Securities. We have twenty-six months of data: January 1, 1991, through November 30,

---

35. Note that the stale limit order can be canceled by the order submitter any time during the warning and special quote process until it is executed. Once again, the stale limit order need not completely fill the pending orders.

36. Execution of the pending orders proceeds according to time and size priority. Once again, the opposing order need not completely fill the pending orders.

37. In contrast with warning quotes, the prevailing special quote becomes the base price for the purpose of computing the daily price limit for the next day if a special quote is pending at the conclusion of the afternoon session.

1991, and February 1, 1992, through April 30, 1993.[38] We have records of all (25,863,725) completed transactions on all TSE stocks and all quotes (including indicative quotes) for all system-traded stocks. We confine our attention to stocks traded on CORES since we are interested in quote behavior. We also limit our investigation to First Section stocks on the TSE, since Second Section stocks are much less actively traded, and, hence, the market for liquidity in these stocks is likely to differ substantially from that of the more active First Section stocks.

Our data on system-traded stocks are those that are widely available to market participants from member firms—that is, the data are in their broadcast form. Each record gives the best bid and offer if available, an indication of whether either quote was a warning or special quote, the trade size if a transaction took place, and a time stamp that records the time to the nearest minute.[39] Buy and sell transactions are easily distinguished—virtually all trades take place at either the bid or offer.

From these data, we identified all trades that generated warning quotes. We consolidated these data into warning and special quote events—trade and quote sequences that can show how these mechanisms work in actual practice from the time a large order triggered indicative quote dissemination to the time of the return to normal quotes. We identified 722,217 such events in our twenty-six-month sample, an average of slightly less than 1.25 times per stock per day.

This procedure omits a large class of similar events—those in which saitori clerks permit a large trade to walk up or down the limit order book without issuing a warning quote. We call these regular multiple price change events because they appear as regular trades at different prices on the transaction record. Accordingly, we searched for sequences of trades satisfying three criteria: all trades in the sequence were executed within the same minute at a monotone sequence of different prices on the same side of the market. We identified 154,582 such events that proved to be virtually identical to non–trading halt warning quote events in all details save for the lack of warning quote issuance.[40] Such events occur at an average rate of roughly 0.25 times per stock per day, making the overall occurrence of multiple price change events roughly 1.5 times per stock per day.

We are like most public investors—we do not have access to the limit order

---

38. The data for December 1991 and January 1992 were inexplicably lost.

39. Trades are time-stamped to the nearest second internally, but the broadcast data have this coarser time stamp, making it hard to detect violations of time priority. The codes are 80 for a regular quote, 81 for a warning quote, 20 for a special quote, and 00 for no quote. The no-quote indicator implies that either there is no quote available or that any available quote is very far from the executable range.

40. For example, the saitori clerks let prices exceed the maximum price variation limit in 1.83 percent (13,208 out of 722,217) non–trading halt warning quote events. In regular multiple price change events, the saitori clerks permitted this limit to be exceeded in only 0.39 percent (601 out of 154,582) of the regular events in our twenty-six-month sample.

book—and this limits what we can learn. We can only learn reduced-form facts from completed transactions, not structural observations on order-placement strategies and the supply of liquidity. Large orders may be placed only when the book indicates the market can absorb them, and small ones may be larger orders that are broken up. This observation has particular force here because we know that orders are systematically broken up and executed over time on the TSE, due to the absence of separate markets for large and small trades.[41]

One cannot be much more certain about the interpretation of completed transactions that end chui and tokubetsu kehai trading halts. Traders at member-firm head offices who end halts by hitting the warning or special quote know the pending order size(s) if they first consult the electronic limit order book.[42] Their order-placement strategies presumably take this possibility into account. For example, suppose that such traders are risk neutral and that they play competitively.[43] Then the order size they choose—the size of the completed transaction—is set so that the warning or special quote is the expected value of the asset, given current information and the size of the pending order. One cannot simply assume that the warning or special quote measures the perceived marginal value of the stock, given a trade that size, because the order submitter might know the size of the pending order too, data we do not possess.[44]

What is at issue here is the interpretation of the results of completed transactions caused by market orders hitting regular and indicative quotes. We cannot hope to learn too much about the demand for immediacy in the form of market orders without observing the supply of liquidity in the form of limit orders.[45] Accordingly, we confine our attention to unconditional moments that could reasonably be measured by investors who had access only to the widely broadcast information contained in our data. Even from this limited perspective, we can learn much about the TSE mechanisms.

41. Brokerage firms execute trades for large customers on an agency basis, and their traders routinely look at the limit order book when proceeding with trade execution. The absence of a block trading market means that we can draw no firm conclusions about how the TSE might function if such a market were introduced.

42. This is not merely an academic possibility—the TSE reports that proprietary trading by members firms accounts for 25 percent of all trading.

43. That is, they act like the limit order traders in Glosten's (1994) electronic limit order book.

44. Remember that warning and special quote trading halts end with the partial fill of any pending orders. Hence, letting Q_p denote the size of the pending order, Q_s the size of the order that hit the indicative quote, P_s the price of the order that hit the indicative quote, and P_f the price at some future point, a risk-neutral order submitter would choose Q_s so that $P_s = E[P_f \mid Q_p, Q_s] \neq E[P_f \mid Q_s]$. We might be able to make some progress by assuming that the pending order followed some sort of trading strategy whose properties we can infer from completed transactions, but such a model lies in the domain of future research.

45. We will try to obtain limit order data but are not hopeful that the TSE will permit such access.

9.3   The Efficacy of the TSE Market Mechanisms

In this section, we first provide an overview of some of the unconditional regularities in our data. We then describe our main results—trade and quote behavior before, during, and after multiple price change events, particularly those during which warning and/or special quotes were issued.

It is useful to first report some of the gross characteristics of our multiple price change events from the data. Table 9.2 foreshadows several of the conclusions that we draw from the more detailed results that follow. Nearly 85 percent of multiple price change events do not result in a trading halt. Of those that result in a trading halt, the vast majority end in a trade hitting the warning quote. Almost 80 percent of the multiple price change events and almost 90 percent of the trading halts take place in stocks selling below ¥1,000 (i.e., stocks with the small ¥1 tick size) even though only two-thirds of stocks sell for less than ¥1,000.[46] Almost one-third of the multiple price change events take place within half an hour of the open of a stock (including delayed opens), a large number given that 15 percent to 20 percent of trade volume is typically at the open. We are unsurprised by the direction of these effects but find it striking that the percentages of total events in each of these categories is so large.

To conclude this brief detour, table 9.3 reports on a distinctive feature of the TSE: the division of the trading day into two trading sessions. Roughly a third of the multiple price change events in our sample occurred during the first half hour after trade in a stock opened. The majority of such events take place after the morning open, following the longer period of market closure.[47] Delayed opens account for about half of these events.

Call markets trade off the benefits of order consolidation against the costs of fragmented price discovery during the prior period of market closure. As Amihud and Mendelson (1989) have suggested, the long period of closure prior to the morning open (save for overnight trading in foreign markets) generates subsequent order imbalances because of the absence of recent price discovery. However, the afternoon itayose follows the ninety-minute lunch break, a call market that benefits from the comparatively recent price discovery during the morning session.[48] Afternoon order consolidation in a single-price auction is followed by low-cost trading (i.e., low bid-ask spreads) because subsequent

---

46. We surmise that this occurs because (1) ¥1 is a smaller fraction of the price (i.e., it is a smaller friction) and (2) ¥10 stocks have greater quote depth because of the greater protection from informed traders (i.e., it is a larger friction).

47. There are 1,287 more multiple price change events following delayed morning opens compared with delayed afternoon opens. The largest component of this difference is that there are 1,207 more regular multiple price change events.

48. Amihud and Mendelson (1989) find evidence of excess volatility in their examination of open to open and close to close returns.

Table 9.2   How Multiple Price Change Events End

	Total	Regular Multiple Price Change Events	Warning Quote Events Ending		Special Quote Trading Halts
			Without a Trading Halt	With a Trading Halt	
All multiple price change events	876,799 100%	154,582 17.63%	579,958 66.14%	139,366 15.89%	2,893 0.33%
Multiple price change events ending in a trade	870,208 99.25%	154,582 17.76%	579,958 66.65%	133,135 15.30%	2,532 0.29%
Multiple price change events in stocks selling for <¥1,000	696,716 79.46%	100,829 14.47%	471,214 67.63%	122,121 17.53%	2,552 0.37%
Multiple price change events occurring within 30 minutes of the morning or afternoon open (including delayed opens)	282,411 32.21%	59,084 29.92%	172,847 61.20%	49,076 17.38%	1,404 0.50%

Note: The last three fractions in column 1 are percentages of the total number of events (i.e., 876,799), and the last four columns are percentages of the row totals.

order imbalances are typically more modest.[49] Similarly, it is also unsurprising that delayed opens precede many of our multiple price change events.

Before proceeding, note one final idiosyncrasy of our presentation of these results: we did not report standard errors or other indicators of the precision of the estimates. As is readily apparent, the number of occurrences in each cell is so large that the computed standard errors are extremely small. Accordingly, we omitted standard errors and will report them only when we think there is any ambiguity.

9.3.1   The State of the Market before Multiple Price Change Events

The warning and special quote mechanisms were designed to cope with order imbalances, and so we first describe the state of the market prior to multiple price change events. The figures that follow compare volume and order imbalances in the thirty minutes prior to the event as well as the average size of the ten trades prior to the event with unconditional means for all trades in the twenty-six-month sample. We also reverse the question and employ logit mod-

49. See Lehmann and Modest (1994) for additional evidence on this point. More definitive observations require a model of the motives for trade to explain why demanders of immediacy in the morning session don't shift their trades to the afternoon to exploit such cost differentials. Informed traders probably would not shift trades in this fashion in a model where private information depreciates over time (i.e., becomes public) and does not vary too much over clock time.

Table 9.3   **How Multiple Price Change Events around the Morning and Afternoon Opens End**

| | Total | Regular Multiple Price Change Events | Warning Quote Events Ending | | Special Quote Trading Halts |
			Without a Trading Halt	With a Trading Halt	
Multiple price change events occurring within 30 minutes of the morning or afternoon open (including delayed opens)	282,411 32.21%	59,084 20.92%	172,847 61.20%	49,076 17.38%	1,404 0.50%
Multiple price change events occurring within 30 minutes of the morning open (excluding delayed opens)	86,613 30.67%	19,780 22.84%	51,374 59.31%	15,014 17.33%	445 0.51%
Multiple price change events occurring within 30 minutes of the afternoon open (excluding delayed opens)	56,517 20.01%	10,819 19.14%	36,511 64.60%	8,973 15.88%	214 0.38%
Multiple price change events occurring in stocks with morning opens delayed < 30 minutes	63,481 22.48%	14,793 23.30%	36,730 57.86%	11,596 18.27%	362 0.68%
Multiple price change events occurring in stocks with afternoon opens delayed <30 minutes	38,931 13.79%	7,337 18.85%	25,115 64.51%	6,335 16.27%	144 0.37%
Multiple price change events in stocks with morning and afternoon opens delayed >30 minutes	36,869 13.06%	6,355 17.24%	23,117 62.70%	7,158 19.41%	239 0.65%

Note: The last three fractions in column 1 are percentages of the total number of events (i.e., 876,799), and the last four columns are percentages of the row totals.

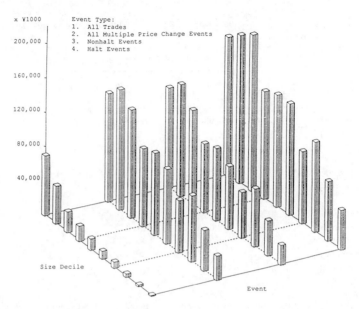

Fig. 9.5   Average volume in yen in the half hour prior to multiple price change events

els to see if trading halts are more likely in markets with greater prior order flow and order flow volatility.

Figures 9.5–9.7 describe the average state of the market prior to multiple price change events. Figure 9.5 presents average yen volume in the thirty prior minutes, figure 9.6 shows mean absolute yen order imbalance in the thirty prior minutes, and figure 9.7 shows the average size of the prior ten trades. Each figure sorts these variables into ten size deciles.[50] The first row of each picture gives the mean value of these variables for all trades in our twenty-six month sample. The second, third, and fourth rows give the means for all multiple price change events, events that ended without a trading halt, and those that resulted in a trading halt, respectively.

Not surprisingly, traders submitting market orders that initiate multiple price change events do so when the market for liquidity in a stock is volatile or, put differently, when there is considerable uncertainty about the "equilibrium"

50. We divided stocks into size deciles only once, at the close of the last day of trade prior to our twenty-six-month sample. We did not do so periodically both because it would have been sometimes difficult (because timely data on the number of shares outstanding was in another data set) and because we thought that extensive sensitivity checking of the re-sorting procedure would have been exceedingly time consuming. We thought that our approach would sort stocks into reasonably homogeneous groups. We also produced figures that sorted on both size and price. The magnitudes differed (i.e., there were larger trades and volumes in high-priced stocks), but the shape of the pattern across size deciles was quite similar in these and the other figures, so we reported these simpler pictures to conserve space.

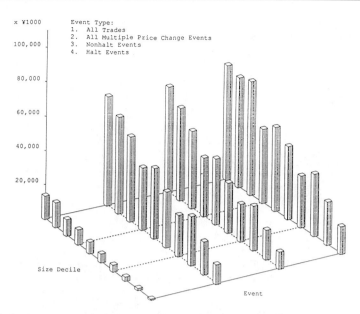

Fig. 9.6   Average absolute order imbalance in yen in the half hour prior to multiple price change events

price. Total volume and order imbalance in the half hour prior to these events are much larger than the corresponding unconditional means, especially in the medium and smaller size deciles. Figure 9.7 suggests that this is an increase in the number of trades, since traders tend to submit only slightly larger orders at these times.

In addition, larger volume, order imbalances, and trade sizes typically precede events that end in trading halts. This effect is largest in the midrange of the size deciles. However, this contrast is not nearly as sharp as that between multiple price change events and regular trades.

We sharpened the focus on this contrast by fitting a binary logit model to predict whether a multiple price change event ends in a trading halt. We report results for a logit model below but also fitted normit and gompit models (i.e., those assuming cumulative normal and Gompertz distributions for the response probabilities, respectively). Fortunately, we found that the standardized coefficient estimates for each model were very similar.[51] We estimated these models only for events that took place more than thirty minutes after the itayose.[52]

---

51. For example, the ratios of probit to logit coefficients were very close to the usual empirical value of 1.6. We had planned to employ nonparametric estimators of the response probabilities had the logit models failed this robustness check.

52. We also fit logit and duration models to the subsample of events following delayed opens or in the first half hour after the morning or afternoon open. We do not include them because the

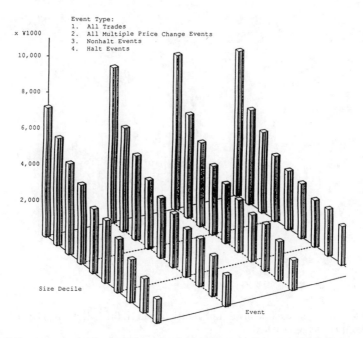

Fig. 9.7   Average trade size in yen in the half hour prior to multiple price change events

We used the same sets of variables as indicators of the state of the market before the event in all cases.[53] We employed the total yen volume of trade in each of eight time intervals: each of the first five minutes before the event and minutes six through ten, eleven through twenty, and twenty through thirty prior to the event.[54] We also utilized measures of order imbalance over these same eight time intervals. The particular form these variables took was the logarithm of the absolute value of the ratio of signed volume to total volume over the relevant interval. Finally, we added eight size/price dummies.[55]

paper is already too long. Briefly, the logit models for this subset of trading halt versus nonhalt events have coefficients of the same sign and similar magnitude, save for some of the order imbalance coefficients. The logit models for chui kehai versus tokubetsu kehai trading halts generally failed to converge.

53. This list of variables is the one with which we started. We did some search to see if the data overwhelmingly supported more parsimonious models but abandoned the search for fear of data mining.

54. Volume for some time intervals was occasionally zero, particularly for one-minute intervals. If a variable was zero, we set its logarithm to zero (recall that volume is on the order of millions of yen per trade). We also ran most models in levels instead of logs and got very similar results. We reported the log models because of their relative scale independence.

55. We divided stocks into three price categories: under ¥1,000, ¥1,000 to ¥2,000, and over ¥2,000. We divided stocks into three size groups: deciles one through three, four through seven, and eight through ten. We obtained nine size/price dummies as the product of these three price

Table 9.4 reports on the model for trading halts versus non–trading halts where an "event" is the occurrence of a trading halt. It provides the logit model coefficient estimates, their large sample standard errors, and the marginal significance level of the Wald χ^2 statistic (i.e., the square of the ratio of the coefficient estimate to the large sample standard error). We also report scaled versions of the coefficients to provide clearer indicators of the marginal effects of these variables. These marginal effects are given by the coefficients times the ratio of the average value of the logistic density to the standard deviation of the corresponding explanatory variable.[56] We also report several measures of model fit: the rank correlation of the model predictions and outcomes, the raw scores for these variables, and a likelihood ratio test for the exclusion of the volume and imbalance variables from the model.[57]

Trading halts generated by large market orders appear to be more common in two circumstances. First, halts occur more frequently if the large order was preceded by a period of relatively large order flow and low order flow volatility. The marginal order flow effects are consistent with the average effects recorded in figures 9.5 through 9.7, but the marginal order imbalance effects differ from the unconditional means displayed in the figures. Second, halts are more common if order imbalances were a large fraction of volume on relatively low volume in the last five minutes before the submission of the large order.

The conditional and unconditional observations generally accord well with a simple intuition: traders have reason to fear the information content of large trades, particularly if they are primarily on one side of the market and represent a large fraction of recent volume. The behavior of traders submitting orders that cause trading halts is more difficult to characterize because we do not know from the trading record what fraction of the original order remained after the nonhalt portion of the trade was completed. We return to this issue below.

Finally, table 9.5 reveals that it is hard to predict whether a warning quote trading halt will be converted into a special quote trading halt by the arrival of an order on the same side of the market. In part, the estimates, particularly on prior volume, are more imprecise as reflected by the large standard errors: there are fewer events in the trading halt subsample, and special quote trading

---

and size dummies. We then omitted the dummy for the largest firms selling for below ¥1,000 so that the remaining eight size/price dummies were not collinear with the intercept. We estimated some models over finer size/price partitions and obtained qualitatively similar results.

56. The marginal effect of independent variable i on the probability of a positive outcome in event j in the logit model is $\Lambda(x_j{'}\beta)(1 - \Lambda(x_j{'}\beta))\,\beta_i$ where $\Lambda(\cdot)$ is the cumulative logistic distribution function $\exp\{\cdot\}/(1 + \exp\{\cdot\})$, x_j is the vector of observed independent variables prior to event j, β is the corresponding coefficient vector, and β_i is its ith element. For the logistic distribution, $\Lambda(x_j{'}\beta)(1 - \Lambda(x_j{'}\beta))$ is the density evaluated for event j. We standardized by its average value.

57. An additional perspective on the fit of the model arises from consideration of how well the model with just an intercept and size/price dummies predicts trading halts. In the comparison of predicted probability and observed response, 43.5 percent of the pairs were concordant, 28.8 percent were discordant, and 27.7 percent were tied.

Table 9.4   **Logit Analysis for Halt versus Nonhalt Events**

A. Slope Coefficients

Variable for Minute(s)	Logarithm of ¥ Volume		Logarithm of Absolute Scaled Order Imbalance	
	Coefficient (scaled coefficient)	Standard Error (χ^2 probability)	Coefficient (scaled coefficient)	Standard Error (χ^2 probability)
1	−0.0069	0.0005	0.0288	0.0043
	(−0.0294)	(<0.0001)	(0.0114)	(<0.0001)
2	−0.0050	0.0005	0.0383	0.0049
	(−0.0208)	(<0.0001)	(0.0130)	(<0.0001)
3	−0.0037	0.0005	0.0293	0.0050
	(−0.0152)	(<0.0001)	(0.0098)	(<0.0001)
4	−0.0022	0.0005	0.0231	0.0052
	(−0.0090)	(<0.0001)	(0.0077)	(<0.0001)
5	−0.0001	0.0005	0.0224	0.0052
	(−0.0004)	(0.8484)	(0.0074)	(<0.0001)
6–10	0.0014	0.0006	−0.0217	0.0032
	(0.0056)	(0.0126)	(−0.0120)	(<0.0001)
11–20	0.0055	0.0006	−0.0118	0.0030
	(0.0197)	(<0.0001)	(−0.0072)	(<0.0001)
21–30	0.0059	0.0006	−0.0105	0.0030
	(0.0217)	(<0.0001)	(−0.0063)	(<0.0001)

B. Intercept and Size/Price Dummy Variable

Size/Price Category	Coefficient	Scaled Coefficient	Standard Error	Probability of Wald χ^2
Intercept	1.408	●	0.0102	<0.0001
Size 1/price 2	0.764	0.0577	0.0287	<0.0001
Size 1/price 3	0.737	0.0166	0.0903	<0.0001
Size 2/price 1	0.092	0.0251	0.0089	<0.0001
Size 2/price 2	0.890	0.1026	0.0204	<0.0001
Size 2/price 3	0.395	0.0315	0.0242	<0.0001
Size 3/price 1	0.378	0.0847	0.0106	<0.0001
Size 3/price 2	1.258	0.1612	0.0212	<0.0001
Size 3/price 3	0.642	0.0882	0.0162	<0.0001

C. Other Statistics

Observations			Probability/Response Correlation[a]		
Total	Halt	Nonhalt	Concordant	Discordant	Tied
737,517	116,425	621,092	58.0%	40.3%	1.7%

Rank correlation 0.589
LRT for model 1,459 ~ $\chi^2(25)$; $p < 0.0001$

[a]Correlation between predicted probabilities from the model and observed responses in the data.

Table 9.5   **Logit Analysis for Warning versus Special Quote Trading Halts**

A. Slope Coefficients

Variable for Minute(s)	Logarithm of ¥ Volume		Logarithm of Absolute Scaled Order Imbalance	
	Coefficient (scaled coefficient)	Standard Error (χ^2 probability)	Coefficient (scaled coefficient)	Standard Error (χ^2 probability)
1	−0.0036	0.0034	−0.0154	0.0313
	(−0.0153)	(0.2874)	(−0.0065)	(0.6222)
2	−0.0160	0.0035	−0.0099	0.0321
	(−0.0666)	(<0.0001)	(−0.0037)	(0.7582)
3	−0.0051	0.0036	−0.0737	0.0412
	(−0.0212)	(0.1535)	(−0.0270)	(0.0734)
4	−0.0095	0.0036	−0.1166	0.0469
	(−0.0393)	(0.0084)	(−0.0415)	(0.0130)
5	−0.0027	0.0037	−0.1411	0.0515
	(−0.0109)	(0.4664)	(−0.0500)	(0.0062)
6–10	0.0077	0.0037	−0.0820	0.0268
	(0.0310)	(0.0402)	(−0.0468)	(0.0022)
11–20	0.0000	0.0040	−0.0736	0.0240
	(0.0001)	(0.9946)	(−0.0455)	(0.0022)
21–30	0.0197	0.0036	−0.0701	0.0245
	(0.0733)	(<0.0001)	(−0.0430)	(0.0043)

B. Intercept and Size/Price Dummy Variable

Size/Price Category	Coefficient	Scaled Coefficient	Standard Error	Probability of Wald χ^2
Intercept	3.6016	●	0.0627	<0.0001
Size 1/price 2	0.2420	0.0148	0.1928	0.2094
Size 1/price 3	1.2395	0.0237	1.0048	0.2174
Size 2/price 1	0.2916	0.0804	0.0542	<0.0001
Size 2/price 2	0.1611	0.0142	0.1330	0.2257
Size 2/price 3	0.2750	0.0206	0.1638	0.0932
Size 3/price 1	0.5930	0.1283	0.0734	<0.0001
Size 3/price 2	0.2330	0.0195	0.1434	0.1041
Size 3/price 3	0.5403	0.0634	0.1219	<0.0001

C. Other Statistics

Observations			Probability/Response Correlations[a]		
Total	Special Quote	Warning Quote	Concordant	Discordant	Tied
116,425	2,148	114,277	53.6%	36.7%	9.7%

Rank correlation 0.585
LRT for model 127 ~ $\chi^2(25)$; $p < 0.0001$

[a]Correlation between predicted probabilities from the model and observed responses in the data.

halts (a "positive" occurrence in this model) are a very small fraction of trading halts. Nevertheless, several coefficients are significant at conventional levels and generally suggest somewhat counterintuitively that special quote trading halts are more common when prior volume and order imbalances in the last ten minutes were small. We return to this observation again below.[58]

9.3.2   Trade and Quote Behavior during Multiple Price Change Events

We ask three questions of our data regarding trades and quotes during multiple price change events. First, do traders submit different-size market orders when they generate warning and special quote trading halts than when they generate multiple price change events that result in no stoppage of trade? In addition, we measure how long warning and special quote trading halts last, both unconditionally and conditionally on the state of the market prior to the halt. Finally, we also ask whether trades of comparable size end warning quote and special quote trading halts. We answer these questions in turn.

Figure 9.8 compares the average size of all trades with the average volume of trade during nonhalt warning quote events and the nonhalt portion of warning quote trading halts. As before, the data are sorted into size deciles. The first row gives the mean size of all trades in our twenty-six-month sample, and the second, third, and fourth rows display the average volume of trade concluded without a trading halt in all multiple price change events, all events that did not result in a trading halt, and those that did result in a trading halt, respectively. As expected, the volume of trade is large for both halt and nonhalt events as the market order walks up or down the limit order book.

Of substantial economic interest is the role played by the maximum price variation in the volume of trade completed in both halt and nonhalt events. The average size of trade completed prior to a trading halt is only slightly smaller than the mean for nonhalt events. This would appear to be a direct consequence of the structure of the TSE warning quote trading mechanism.

Two features of the trading mechanism make the equality of trade size in halt and nonhalt events a natural economic outcome. As we have emphasized, the maximum price variation sets a bound beyond which trade is halted. Second, an order large enough to generate a trading halt can be canceled at any time prior to conversion to a special quote. Hence, market orders large enough to cause a trading halt are identical ex ante to those that would not because of the possibility of order cancellation. Traders exposing limit orders inside the bounds set by the maximum price variation would naturally take this possibility into account and, hence, would place orders equally attractive to those who would and those who would not place orders large enough to cause a trading

---

58. Once again, we consider the fit of a model with just an intercept and size/price dummies. In the comparison of predicted probability and observed response, 36.5 percent of the pairs were concordant, 26.3 percent were discordant, and 37.2 percent were tied.

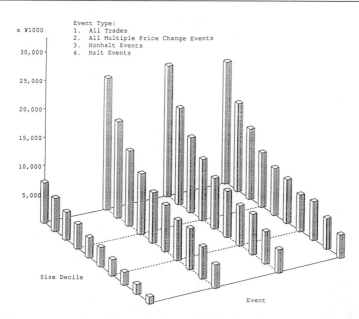

Fig. 9.8   Average volume in yen during multiple price change events prior to any trading halts

halt. Since liquidity inside the maximum price variation is identical ex ante, it should also be identical ex post.

How long do warning quote trading halts last? Unconditionally, figure 9.9 suggests the answer is, not very long. One-third of the warning quote trading halts last less than a minute, while almost half last between one and two minutes, so that more than 80 percent of warning quote trading halts last less than two minutes. The brevity of these trading halts reflects success in attracting liquidity: 94 percent of the warning quote trading halts lasting less than two minutes ended with a trade.[59]

Figure 9.10 suggests that the special quote mechanism is subject to long and variable lags. Special quote trading halts last longer than warning quote trading halts—fewer than 5 percent last less than a minute and nearly a third last longer than fifteen minutes, an outcome one would expect, given the price discovery function of the special quote mechanism. This distinction also shows up below in the size of orders that end the two kinds of trading halts.

We are also interested in how long trading halts last as a function of the

59. When warning quotes are converted to special quotes by order arrival, the order generally arrives early in the warning quote trading halt—56.95 percent arrive within the first minute and an additional 25.59 percent between the first and second minute of the initiation of a warning quote trading halt.

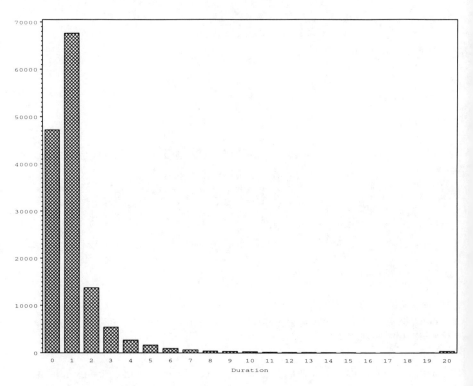

Fig. 9.9   **Average duration of warning quote trading halts**

prior state of the market, and thus we fit duration models to our trading halt data. As with the logit models, we fit a number of parametric survival models under different distributional assumptions: exponential, Weibull, gamma, logistic, and lognormal. Once again, the results were reasonably insensitive to the distributional specification. We report the results for the logistic model because this distribution is robust to large residuals, which arise in this application because of long thin tails in the distribution of warning and special quote trading halt durations.[60]

We chose the same indicators of the prior state of market liquidity as in the logit analysis—total yen volume and yen order imbalance over the same eight time intervals. For the case of special quote trading halts, we added one other predetermined variable: the duration of the prior warning quote trading halt. We reasoned that there would typically be much uncertainty as to whether the order generating the special quote represented transient liquidity demand or a transition to a new equilibrium price after a long warning quote trading halt.

---

60. Some distributions fit poorly because they could not track the asymmetry of the empirical survival distribution. The logistic model fit both this asymmetry and the long right tail reasonably well, so we chose not to fit nonparametric models.

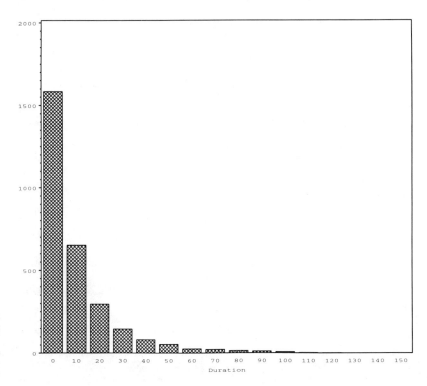

Fig. 9.10   Average duration of special quote trading halts

In the duration analysis of warning quotes, we treated three events as censor-ing normal "failures" (i.e., trades hitting the warning quote): conversion from a warning quote to a special quote, cancellation of the pending order, and the end of the trading session. Technically, it would be more appropriate to use a competing risks formulation of survival analysis to account for these distinct possible outcomes. However, the proportion of warning quote trading halts ending in a trade is so large (93.59 percent) that it seemed sensible to pool the three censoring variables into one composite indicator.[61] We had no such prob-lem with special quote trading halts: 87.52 percent end in a normal "failure" (i.e., trades hitting the special quote), and the trading session ended almost all of the remaining halts (12.24 percent).[62]

Table 9.6 reports on the duration of warning quote trading halts as a function of prior volume and order imbalances. Warning quote trading halts last longer

---

61. Pending-order cancellations total 3.15 percent, conversion of the warning quote to a special quote accounts for 2.03 percent, and the end of the session represents 1.23 percent of warning quote trading halt conclusions.

62. As we noted earlier, order cancellation concluded fewer than 0.25 percent of the special quote trading halts in our sample.

Table 9.6 **Logistic Duration Analysis for Warning Quote Trading Halts**

A. Slope Coefficients

Variable for Minute(s)	Logarithm of ¥ Volume		Logarithm of Absolute Scaled Order Imbalance	
	Coefficient	Standard Error (χ^2 probability)	Coefficient	Standard Error (χ^2 probability)
1	−0.0113	0.0005 (<0.0001)	0.0128	0.0042 (0.0023)
2	−0.0095	0.0005 (<0.0001)	0.0113	0.0047 (0.0164)
3	−0.0079	0.0005 (<0.0001)	0.0146	0.0048 (0.0024)
4	−0.0077	0.0005 (<0.0001)	0.0091	0.0049 (0.0650)
5	−0.0070	0.0005 (<0.0001)	0.0096	0.0049 (0.0530)
6–10	−0.0099	0.0006 (<0.0001)	0.0118	0.0032 (0.0002)
11–20	−0.0108	0.0006 (<0.0001)	0.0157	0.0030 (<0.0001)
21–30	−0.0100	0.0006 (<0.0001)	0.0141	0.0030 (<0.0001)

B. Intercept and Size/Price Dummy Variable

Size/Price Category	Coefficient	Standard Error	Probability of Wald χ^2
Intercept	1.7697	0.0111	<0.0001
Size 1/price 2	0.1770	0.0323	<0.0001
Size 1/price 3	0.0031	0.0925	0.9735
Size 2/price 1	−0.0842	0.0090	<0.0001
Size 2/price 2	0.0446	0.0223	0.0455
Size 2/price 3	0.0419	0.0259	0.1064
Size 3/price 1	−0.1384	0.0106	<0.0001
Size 3/price 2	−0.0894	0.0225	<0.0001
Size 3/price 3	−0.0745	0.0167	<0.0001

C. Other Statistics

Observations			Scale Parameter	
Total	Regular	Censored	Coefficient	Standard Error
116,424	108,856	7,568	0.6715	0.0018

LRT for model 13,151 ~ $\chi^2(16)$; $p < 0.0001$

when prior order imbalances are a large fraction of volume and prior volume is low. This observation is intuitively sensible. Potential counterparties to a warning quote are inclined to be cautious since the submitter of the pending order is willing to risk exposure to the special quote mechanism. The fear of the information content of the pending order is likely to be greater when it is difficult to discern whether prior trades were information or liquidity motivated (i.e., small prior volume amid large relative order imbalances). That is, warning quote trading halts last longer when prior trades are less informative about the underlying "equilibrium" price.

Table 9.7 reports the corresponding results for the duration of special quote trading halts as a function of prior volume and order imbalances. As with the logit model for warning quote versus special quote trading halts, the coefficient estimates are more imprecise in large part because special quote trading halts are so uncommon. Nevertheless, like warning quote trading halts, special quote trading halts tend to last longer when prior volume is low and prior order imbalances are a large fraction of volume. An additional result is the expected one that special quote trading halts tend to last longer following long prior warning quote trading halts. We hesitate to interpret these results further in the absence of a model for the response of traders to the quote-revision process built into the tokubetsu kehai mechanism.[63]

Sharper insights arise from the examination of the size of orders that end warning and special quote trading halts, displayed in figure 9.11. Orders that hit warning quotes are somewhat larger than regular trades but are dwarfed by the trades that hit special quotes. It is hard to provide a precise interpretation of this finding because we do not know the size of the orders pending at the end of trading halts; we only know that the volume of pending orders was at least as large as the trade quantity, but we do not know how much larger it might have been.

A trader who submits an order that generates a trading halt and leaves it pending risks losing control of order execution. If an order arrives on the same side of the market, that trader will almost certainly be unable to cancel the pending order. Other traders determine whether the pending order will be executed at the warning quote or whether the warning quote will be converted into a special quote, permitting continued price discovery. A trader who leaves an order pending at the warning quote presumably takes into account both this possibility and the possibility that some part of the order will be executed at the warning quote.

Accordingly, the small size of trades hitting warning quotes makes some economic sense. Warning quote trading halts stop the price discovery process, and thus traders hitting warning quotes should choose a trade size reflecting

---

63. By contrast, the model of Easley and O'Hara (1992) suggests that traders ought to be more confident that pending orders are not motivated by private information when they are pending for a long time. This loose reading of their model suggests that this coefficient ought to be negative.

Table 9.7 **Logistic Duration Analysis for Special Quote Trading Halts**

A. Slope Coefficients

Variable for Minute(s)	Logarithm of ¥ Volume		Logarithm of Absolute Scaled Order Imbalance	
	Coefficient	Standard Error (χ^2 probability)	Coefficient	Standard Error (χ^2 probability)
1	−0.0569	0.0405 (0.1549)	−0.0348	0.3962 (0.9307)
2	−0.0077	0.0403 (0.8435)	0.6814	0.3467 (0.0494)
3	−0.0743	0.0414 (0.0724)	0.1140	0.4852 (0.8142)
4	−0.0442	0.0419 (0.2915)	−0.0620	0.5357 (0.9089)
5	−0.0724	0.0426 (0.0893)	−0.0099	0.6010 (0.9869)
6–10	−0.0794	0.0449 (0.0772)	0.1883	0.2690 (0.4898)
11–20	−0.0688	0.0502 (0.1697)	0.3929	0.2485 (0.1233)
21–30	−0.0291	0.0446 (0.5142)	0.2223	0.2500 (0.3737)

B. Intercept and Size/Price Dummy Variable

Size/Price Category	Coefficient	Standard Error	Probability of Wald χ^2
Intercept	16.8071	0.9096	<0.0001
Size 1/price 2	−0.8036	2.4719	0.7451
Size 1/price 3	−12.7857	10.1927	0.2097
Size 2/price 1	−1.3438	0.6823	0.0489
Size 2/price 2	−3.4204	1.6065	0.0332
Size 2/price 3	−2.6898	1.9561	0.1691
Size 3/price 1	−2.7005	0.8952	0.0021
Size 3/price 2	1.9280	1.8532	0.2982
Size 3/price 3	−1.7964	1.5017	0.2448

C. Other Statistics

Observations			Warning Quote Trading Halt Duration		
Total	Regular	Censored	Coefficient	Standard Error	Probability
2,147	1,823	324	0.2457	0.0799	0.0022

LRT for model 115 ~ $\chi^2(16)$; $p < 0.0001$
Scale parameter 7.1639
Standard error 0.1435

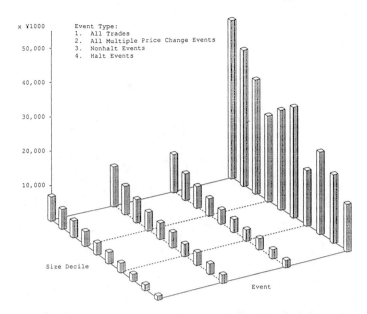

Fig. 9.11   Average size of trades in yen that end warning and special quote trading halts

their valuation of the stock, given the pending-order submitter's willingness to risk conversion to a special quote. This order size would tend to be decreasing in the size of the pending order. If the large size of orders ending special quotes is a reliable guide to the size of pending orders at warning quotes (an eventuality that we can only verify by studying the limit order book), traders hitting warning quotes would tend to submit small orders.

On this view, the large trades ending special quotes reflect the marginal decisions of traders who risk the price discovery process inherent in the special quote mechanism. Such traders lose control over the order and, in particular, the prices at which their orders will be executed. Moreover, traders initiating special quotes by joining pending orders choose to lose control over execution price. Hence, such traders are likely to be uninformed, and the confidence of potential counterparties is increasing in the size of the pending order. An uninformed trader submitting a large order in this fashion will tend to pay a smaller adverse selection cost as a consequence. Put differently, this evidence is consistent with the pending orders during special quotes being somewhat like sunshine trades.

9.3.3   The State of the Market after Multiple Price Change Events

Figures 9.12–9.14 describe the average state of the market following multiple price change events. Figure 9.12 presents average yen volume in the subsequent thirty minutes, figure 9.13 shows mean absolute yen order imbalance

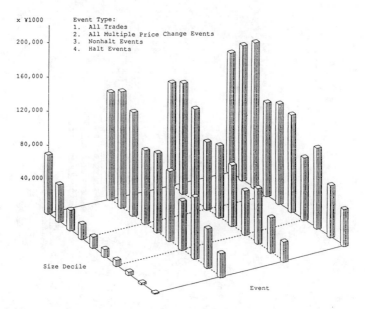

Fig. 9.12 Average volume in yen in the half hour following multiple price change events

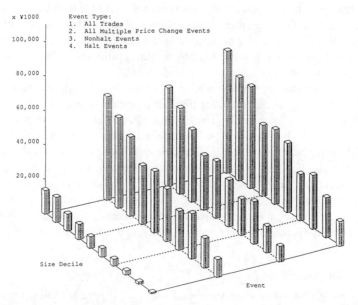

Fig. 9.13 Average absolute order imbalance in yen in the half hour following multiple price change events

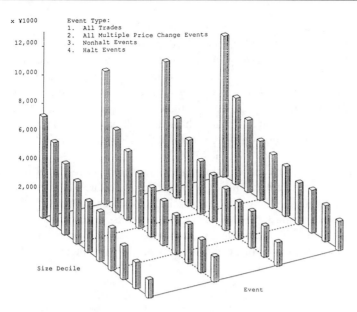

Fig. 9.14   Average yen trade size in yen in the half hour following multiple price change events

for the same period, and figure 9.14 shows the average size of the subsequent ten trades. As before, each figure sorts these variables into ten size deciles. The first row of each picture gives the mean value of these variables for all trades in our twenty-six-month sample. The second, third, and fourth rows give the means for all multiple price change events, all events that ended with no stoppage of trade, and those that did result in a trading halt, respectively.

These figures look remarkably similar to the corresponding pictures describing the prior state of the market (i.e., figures 9.5–9.7). Multiple price change events take place during periods of volatility in the market for liquidity in a stock. As before, total volume and order imbalance in the thirty minutes following these events are substantially larger than the corresponding unconditional means, especially in the medium and smaller size deciles. Figure 9.12 suggests that this is an increase in the number of trades, since traders tend to submit only slightly larger orders at these times. These effects are somewhat larger for events that resulted in trading halts, but the magnitude of this effect is small.

9.4   Conclusion

We have established several facts in these pages. Investors seldom trip the trading halt mechanisms of the TSE, and, when they do, they usually execute all or part of their pending order at the warning quote, a price they know in advance. Traders are more likely to trigger indicative quote dissemination and temporary trading halts when the market for liquidity is relatively volatile, particularly around the morning open and after delayed opens. The volume of trading during nonhalt events is very similar to that during events that result in trading halts, a result that accords with similar economic intuition. Similarly, the trades that end warning quote trading halts are generally much smaller than those that end special quote trading halts, a result that is also intuitively plausible. What is perhaps surprising is not that these results accord with intuition, but rather that they conform to it so well.

Unfortunately, we can say little from a policy perspective. Order-placement strategies and the demand and supply of liquidity are surely endogenous to the trading mechanism. We simply cannot tell if these mechanisms perform as they do because they fulfill their intended roles or because investors have learned to put up with their idiosyncrasies. We can draw one firm conclusion—the TSE is a large market whose mechanisms rarely result in the interruption of trade.

References

Amihud, Yakov, and Haim Mendelson. 1989. Market Microstructure and Price Discovery of the Tokyo Stock Exchange. *Japan and the World Economy* 1:341–70.
Angel, James J. 1993. Factors Affecting the Decision between Limit and Market Orders on the Tokyo Stock Exchange. Georgetown University.
Black, Fischer. 1993. Equilibrium Exchanges. Manuscript, Goldman, Sachs, and Co.
Easley, David, and Maureen O'Hara. 1992. Time and the Process of Security Price Adjustment. *Journal of Finance* 47:577–605.
Glosten, Lawrence R. 1994. Is the Electronic Open Limit Order Book Inevitable? *Journal of Finance* 49:1127–61.
Hamao, Yasushi, and Joel Hasbrouck. 1993. Securities Trading in the Absence of Dealers: Trades and Quotes on the Tokyo Stock Exchange. Manuscript, Graduate School of Business, Columbia University.
Hasbrouck, Joel, George Sofianos, and Deborah Sosebee. 1993. New York Stock Exchange Systems and Trading Procedures. New York Stock Exchange Working Paper 93-01.
Lehmann, Bruce N., and David M. Modest. 1994. Trading and Liquidity on the Tokyo Stock Exchange: A Bird's-Eye View. *Journal of Finance* 49:951–84.
Lindsey, Richard R., and Ulrike Schaede. 1992. Specialist vs. Saitori: Market Making in New York and Tokyo. *Financial Analysts Journal* 48:48–57.
Securities and Exchange Commission. 1992. U.S. Equity Market Structure Study. Securities and Exchange Commission, 1524 SEC Docket, vol. 51, no. 18.
Tokyo Stock Exchange. 1989. The "Saitori" System of the Tokyo Stock Exchange. Manuscript.

Comment   Kazuhisa Okamoto

The TSE implicitly assumes that numerous incoming orders in small lots are all scattered on the limit order book. This assumption is probably related to the fact that this mechanism was established in 1949, when about 70 percent of outstanding shares were owned by individual investors and only 10 percent and 5 percent were owned by financial institutions and corporations, respectively.

Current shareholder distribution looks very different; namely, individuals own only 24 percent, financial institutions own 41 percent, and corporations own 24 percent of outstanding shares. The 46 percent reduction in the share of individuals was absorbed by a combined increase in the share of financial institutions and corporations. In other words, mutual cross-holding of stocks among corporations and financial institutions has taken over holdings of individuals over the last forty-four years.

During this period, buying and selling by investors have been orchestrated by large securities companies. Individuals bought and sold based on brokers' recommendations. Investment trusts were generally owned by securities firms. With respect to cross-holdings, buyers and sellers agreed on the transaction in advance, and securities firms belonging to the same *zaibatsu* group crossed the transaction on the exchange. In the second half of the 1980s, there was a "bubble market" in which corporations and financial institutions traded stocks for realized profits with a very short-term investment horizon. Once again, large securities firms led the market, picking low-priced, large-capitalization issues for dealing purposes.

Until very recently, brokerage companies were the conductor of the market orchestra. Now that the bubble has burst, the market leaders are changing from cross-holdings and *zaitech* speculations to pension funds. The size of Japanese pension funds, which is already $1.6 trillion, is likely to double in the next ten years. Until only four years ago, the industry had been monopolized by commingled funds of life insurance companies and trust banks, and the assets were often used for cross-holding of friendly corporations. Investment advisory companies have been deregulated to manage pension funds only since 1990, but their proportion to the total is still a mere 2 percent. I think this is likely to change.

As market leaders change, characteristics of the need for liquidity in the market are likely to change. Previously, cross-holders looked for a total of investment returns and business returns, with more emphasis on the latter. Individuals tend to look at individual stocks and not at a portfolio. Zaitech speculators aimed at realizing gains in a year to boost operating earnings. Pension funds, of course, are different. They assume a longer investment horizon, con-

Kazuhisa Okamoto is managing director in charge of Japan/Asia operations of Wells Fargo Nikko Investment Advisors.

sider risks and returns, and seek diversification. They regard "investment value" to be the most important criteria for stock selection. With these changes evolving now, the question is, Is the current market mechanism good enough to support new liquidity needs?

I would like to point out a couple of barriers that institutional investors like ourselves are facing day to day. First of all, in Japan, all trades have to occur on the floor—there are no OTC crossings, no crossing networks, no upstairs, no internal crossings, and so forth. All trades are basically monopolized by the exchange. Second, important trade information is available only to stock exchange members and not to investors. Limit order book situation is available only at the headquarters of member brokers. Even while using the same Quick price-quotation systems, terminals at brokerage offices have ask and bid quotes but not the terminal at investors' offices. Exchange members are monopolizing important trade information.

It is very difficult to get a membership on the stock exchange in Japan. Only securities companies, not individuals, are qualified to be a member, and corporations must have a license from the Ministry of Finance to be a broker. The fact that the seat is so expensive is a good indication that there are some excess profits to be gained on the floor. Brokers often use monopolized information of the market to solicit orders from institutional investors. Whoever provides the most such information the fastest will get the deal. It can be considered as a tool to support fixed commissions.

These social costs reduce investment returns. Until recently, cross-holders, a dominant power in the market, did not consider investment return to be the most important criteria. Now, as pension funds gain importance in the market, investment return becomes significant. I think it is natural to assume that a mechanism closer to that of the United States will be developed as demand mounts. How fast may be a question, since the existing powers, who have been benefiting from the old regime, will try to slow the process as much as possible. However, it is impossible to stop or reverse the trend for rationality. Sooner or later, a "soft bang" is due. Furthermore, having such a rational trading mechanism, which functions better in the institutionalized market, is a prerequisite for a truly strong recovery of the Japanese stock market.

Authors' Reply

As we noted at several points in the paper, we measured the performance of the warning and special quote mechanisms of the Tokyo Stock Exchange, taking the order-placement strategies of investors as given. We realized that we could not measure the interaction between the trading mechanism and structural characteristics of both the demand for liquidity in the form of market orders and the supply of liquidity in the form of limit orders without considerably more information than that contained in the trade and quote record. We remained content to report reduced-form regularities.

As is commonplace, Kazuhisa Okamoto, along with Pete Kyle in his oral remarks at the conference, wished we had written a different paper. Okamoto asked, "What changes in the restrictions on investor access both to the trading mechanism and to information like the limit order book are appropriate in the new market for liquidity in common stocks on the TSE arising from the growth of institutional investors like pension funds?" Kyle asked, "What interests are served by the existing market structure?"

Both discussants arrived at related conclusions—the existing market structure serves the brokerage industry well by maintaining a profitable cartel, but future changes in the structure of the TSE are likely to parallel those that occurred in the United States during the last two decades, resulting in spatial fragmentation of the Japanese equity market. Both discussants thought that such changes were desirable, as they would reduce both the price of immediacy and the cost of equity capital.

We thought we would take this opportunity to speculate about these issues, to write, as it were, part of the introduction to the paper we did not prepare for this conference. In so doing, we find it useful to make distinctions that are somewhat different from those drawn by the discussants. In particular, we ask three related questions: how would the market for liquidity on the TSE change

1. if brokerage commissions were deregulated (as was done in the "May day" reform in the United States in 1975), leaving the remainder of the TSE structure intact?
2. if, in addition, investors were given direct access to the limit order books of the TSE both by becoming exchange members and through an analog of the DOT and SuperDOT systems of the NYSE (again leaving the remainder of the TSE structure intact)? and
3. if, in addition, the Ministry of Finance permitted widespread spatial fragmentation to arise in the form of separate markets for large and small orders (like the upstairs market on the NYSE), of third-market-style competition by the regional exchanges with the TSE, and of the establishment of fourth-market venues like crossing networks?

We address each of these questions in turn.

The answer to the first question seems surprisingly simple: from the perspective of institutional investors like pension funds, the answer is, not much. The commission structure already makes large orders substantially less expensive than small orders, and brokers already engage in widespread nonprice competition by aggressively "working" large orders. Brokers engage in proprietary trading in ways that give the orders of large customers favorable exposure in TSE limit order books. Small investors would be the primary beneficiaries of commission deregulation by itself. It is likely that institutional investor costs would fall substantially only if the other large explicit trading cost, the stamp tax on transactions, were reduced for nonbroker trades.[1]

The second question is considerably more complicated. In this hypothetical environment, the TSE would become a set of consolidated public limit order books. Market participants who incurred the costs of direct participation could then compete in the production of low-cost liquidity, since there would be open and equal access to market making.[2] This market structure would resemble the open electronic limit order books studied in Glosten (1994) and might well have the twin virtues they possessed in his model—they represent the lowest-cost market structures that remain viable in the face of differentially informed traders.

Nevertheless, there is reason to think that large investors like pension funds would not reap substantial benefits from a thoroughgoing change along these lines.[3] In such an environment, large passively managed pools like index funds and the passive portion of pension funds typically reduce the price of immediacy through securities lending and patient trading. However, the current system has a substitute for these low-cost suppliers of liquidity: proprietary trading by member firms on the TSE. Proprietary traders at the head offices of member firms have approximately open and equal access to the information in the limit order book. The price paid to finance proprietary trading by member firms is roughly equal to the repo rate, the marginal price that would be charged in securities lending. We certainly cannot tell if member firms supply the same quantity of liquidity services at these prices as would be supplied by potential market participants in a future consolidated public limit order book environment, but this observation is surely suggestive.

In fact, proprietary trading by member firms accounts for 25 percent of trading on the TSE, suggesting the supply of liquidity services to large customers might well be substantial to the extent that member firms do not simply front-run their customers. Member firms appear to do the opposite on the TSE—traders place orders that clear out existing orders ahead of their customer's order in the limit order book in order to make the customer order the best bid or offer. If the supply of proprietary trading for these purposes is sufficiently elastic at the present time, institutional customers would probably see only modest changes in trading costs following such a reform. Put differently, it is far from obvious that brokers in the current market system break up orders and

---

1. Currently, securities companies pay a transaction tax of 0.12 percent while all other traders pay 0.30 percent.
2. Different investors would still confront different costs, if only in the differential stamp-tax levy referred to above.
3. Institutional investors would probably place some different trades in the new environment because they would then have direct access to the same trade information as brokers currently receive. In the present environment, investors can get information like the current best bid and offer or the contents of the limit order book only from brokers.

work trades any differently from the ways in which the customers would choose to do so if they had direct access to the limit order books on the TSE.[4]

At this time, the only clear answer to the third question is that it is hard to tell. That is, the jury is still out on the costs and benefits of spatial fragmentation in American and European secondary markets. Widespread spatial fragmentation reduces costs for some traders and increases costs for others in both direct and indirect ways.[5] For example, index funds like those run by Okamoto at Wells Fargo Nikko Investment Advisors would probably experience a substantial reduction in trading costs as they would exploit opportunities to trade both in different venues and differently in existing trading venues as identifiable informationless traders. Small traders would probably benefit as well for similar reasons.

By contrast, informed traders might well experience increased price impact costs to the extent that some uninformed traders can credibly identify themselves and trade in separate markets. The associated reduction in the incentive to acquire and trade on private information might well diminish the equilibrium efficiency of the price discovery process. Strategies to reduce the price impact of large block trades, such as the delay of last-sale reporting on SEAQ International, also lessen the short-run efficiency of the price discovery process. That is, consolidation of orders on one trading venue with widespread broadcasts of trading opportunities and ex post transparency in the form of immediate last-sale reporting clearly has some benefits, too.

Since we cannot predict the consequences of possible spatial fragmentation in Japanese markets, we consider the implications of the first two scenarios outlined above for the conclusions we drew in the paper. That is, suppose that the Ministry of Finance allowed both the initiation of the free commission era and widespread public access to the limit order books of the TSE. How would the chui and tokubetsu kehai mechanisms perform under this new market structure?

It is likely that *all* of our main conclusions would survive such substantial reforms. Brokers already aggressively work institutional orders in the existing environment, and institutional investors would probably find it optimal to follow similar order-placement strategies after the reforms. Accordingly, it is likely that the warning and special quote mechanisms would be tripped infrequently by traders in the new environment and, when tripped, that the mechanisms would usually result in temporary trading halts.[6] In the new environ-

---

4. That is, existing member firms may already compete away most of the rents associated with restrictions on free entry into the market-making business. To be sure, the price of seats on the TSE is sufficiently high as to suggest that not all rents are competed away.

5. Another distinction between fragmented and consolidated markets is the elimination of time priority for limit orders across markets.

6. Similarly, the order-placement strategies followed by institutional investors in the new market environment would probably have most of the same characteristics as those documented in figures 9.5–9.14 and tables 9.2–9.7. Parenthetically, changing the tick size of stocks that sell for more

ment, orders from the broader investor public would still bridge temporal fluctuations in the demand for liquidity services much as they do on the TSE at present. That is, these mechanisms would still serve their intended purpose of organizing liquidity in the presence of the temporal fragmentation of order flow.

Reference

Glosten, Lawrence R. 1994. Is the Electronic Open Limit Order Book Inevitable? *Journal of Finance* 49:1127–61.

---

than ¥1,000 to a smaller number than its current high level of ¥10 would probably eliminate many of the differences we observed in the behavior of stocks selling above and below the ¥1,000 barrier.

10   The Price, Volatility, Volume, and Liquidity Effects of Changes in Federal Reserve Margin Requirements on Both Marginable and Nonmarginable OTC Stocks

Stephen W. Pruitt and K. S. Maurice Tse

10.1   Introduction

In a recent article, Hsieh and Miller (1990) analyze the relationship between official Federal Reserve margin requirements and the variability of the market factor over the time period from October 1934 to December 1987. While detecting the expected negative relation between changing margin levels and the total amount of outstanding margin credit, the authors conclude that the earlier findings of Hardouvelis (1988, 1990)—findings purporting to document a definite negative correlation between margin levels and stock price volatility—are the result of substantial autocorrelation problems inherent in Hardouvelis's tests. Following correction of these problems, Hsieh and Miller state that "[t]he data thus offer no support for the view . . . that Federal Reserve margin requirements are an effective tool for dampening stock market volatility" (28).

While the findings of Hsieh and Miller (1990) provide definitive answers to many questions concerning the magnitude and direction of changes in Federal Reserve margin levels and stock market linkages for *marginable* equity securities, the extent to which changes in margin levels affect marginable stocks *relative to their nonmarginable counterparts* remains unknown. Clearly, the S&P Composite index represents the only well-diversified daily market proxy available for the study of all twenty-one changes in Federal Reserve margin levels mandated since the passage of the Securities Exchange Act of 1934. Unfortunately, since all the securities included in this index over the 1937 to 1974 interval were listed on either the New York or American Stock Ex-

Stephen W. Pruitt is associate professor of finance at the Fogelman College of Business and Economics at the University of Memphis. K. S. Maurice Tse is assistant professor of finance and insurance at the Graduate School of Business at Indiana University.

Both authors would like to thank Paul Seguin, Gailen Hite, John Wei, James Largay, and Robert Conn for helpful comments on earlier drafts.

changes, they were also all subject to the full range of margin borrowing constraints imposed by changes in margin levels. Thus, index-based margin studies such as those of Hsieh and Miller (1990) and others have *necessarily compared the performance of the same market index over two different intervals of calendar time.* Given the precepts of market efficiency and the consequent poor forecasting performance of state-of-the-art return generating models, it is clear that the most appropriate test of the effectiveness of changes in stock market margin requirements at reducing "undesirable" security market perturbations would be between *otherwise identical securities* differing only with respect to the presence or absence of Federal Reserve margin requirements. Indeed, in the absence of such a test, it is virtually impossible to distinguish, at the time of the announcement of a change in Federal Reserve margin levels, those adjustments in security market behavior resulting from *information effects only* from those changes resulting from shifts in *binding borrowing constraints* on equity investors. Fortunately, a 1969 amendment to the Securities Exchange Act of 1934 allows for the development of margin-change tests that, while failing to meet the strictest requirements of a pure empirical duality, are based on pairs of over-the-counter (OTC) firms similar in many important respects while differing in marginability status. Accordingly, this study presents the results of tests of the price, volatility, volume, and liquidity differences registered by both marginable and nonmarginable OTC stocks in response to the 1970, 1971, 1972, and 1974 changes in Federal Reserve margin requirements.

10.2 Margin Requirements and OTC Firms

The Securities Exchange Act of 1934 completely prohibited securities brokers and dealers from extending margin credit for the purchase of OTC stocks. The apparent purpose of this restriction was to eliminate the possibility that unsophisticated investors could become too deeply entangled in margin borrowing on smaller, potentially lower quality securities. Interestingly, although brokers and dealers were prohibited from extending margin loans on OTC stocks, commercial banks were not subject to margin restrictions. Rather, these institutions could freely lend against OTC equities to any levels they chose.

In July 1969, the Securities Exchange Act of 1934 was amended to allow, for the first time, securities dealers and brokers to extend margin credit on certain unlisted (OTC) equity securities. According to official Federal Reserve memorandums, the change in the law was effected at the request of numerous security dealers in an attempt to provide a more level playing field for the merging OTC equity market and to help improve the efficiency of the market. In addition to allowing brokers and dealers the ability to extend margin credit, the amendment (P.L. 90-437) also limited the margin lending powers of commercial banks to levels identical to those granted brokers and dealers. The regulatory requirements of both sets of changes are embodied in regulations T and U (as amended) of the Securities Exchange Act of 1934.

The actual criteria for determining exactly which, if any, OTC securities could be margined was left to the discretion of the Federal Reserve. Initial margin eligibility requirements consisted of ten factors, including criteria concerning corporate age (three years) and time of public trading (six months), market value ($10,000,000), capital surplus ($5,000,000), average share price ($10.00), and the number of active market makers (five).[1] Although the margin-list requirements remained largely unchanged over the years encompassing the current study's tests (1970–74), several changes since that time have occurred, the most important of which automatically extends margin status to any firm listed on the National Association of Securities Dealers' (NASD) National Market System.[2] Maintenance criteria separate and distinct from the requirements established for initial marginability were first established in 1972. Although, currently, notification of margin status occurs at the time of publication of the Federal Reserve's *Official List of OTC Margin Stocks* in the *Federal Register,* in the early years of the OTC margin program, stocks were added to the list (or deleted) in the interim between publications as deemed appropriate by the board.[3] Over the 1970–74 time period, a total of seven separate OTC margin lists were released by the Federal Reserve. Given its importance in the development of the data employed in the empirical tests, the chronology of changes in both the Federal Reserve's margin requirements and the date of first publication of the Federal Reserve's OTC margin lists from July 8, 1969, to September 29, 1975, is summarized in table 10.1.

10.3 Previous Results

As noted in the introduction, previous empirical literature on the efficacy of Federal Reserve margin regulation has typically been conducted by comparing the price and volatility changes of a general market index (such as the S&P Composite index) concomitant with changes in margin levels. While differing in their various methodologies, studies by Hsieh and Miller (1990), Ferris and Chance (1988), and Hardouvelis (1988, 1990) all follow this general procedure, albeit with occasionally divergent results. While both Hsieh and Miller and Ferris and Chance join earlier researchers such as Largay and West (1973), Grube, Joy, and Panton (1979), and the Board of Governors of the Federal

---

1. Board of Governors of the Federal Reserve System, Official Office Correspondence, March 1, 1976.

2. All OTC firms traded on the NASD's National Market System became eligible for margin lending on March 2, 1984 (Board of Governors of the Federal Reserve System, Official Office Correspondence, March 2, 1984).

3. Board of Governors of the Federal Reserve System, *Official List of OTC Margin Stocks,* various issues.

Table 10.1   Chronology of Margin Changes and the Release Dates of the Federal
                    Reserve Board's Official List of Marginable OTC Equities

Date	Item
7/8/69	First Federal Reserve OTC margin list released
5/6/70	Federal Reserve reduces margin requirement by 15%
7/20/70	Second Federal Reserve OTC margin list released
7/12/71	Third Federal Reserve OTC margin list released
12/6/71	Federal Reserve reduces margin requirement by 10%
5/15/72	Fourth Federal Reserve OTC margin list released
11/24/72	Federal Reserve increases margin requirement by 10%
9/4/73	Fifth Federal Reserve OTC margin list released
1/3/74	Federal Reserve reduces margin requirement by 15%
7/29/74	Sixth Federal Reserve OTC margin list released
9/29/75	Seventh Federal Reserve OTC margin list released

Reserve System's own staff analysis (1984) in maintaining that changes in margin levels are associated with only trivial changes in security market behavior, Hardouvelis's investigation, as noted in the introduction, suggests otherwise.[4]

In work more closely related to the present study, researchers such as Grube, Joy, and Howe (1987), Grube and Joy (1988), Seguin (1990), and Wolfe, Klein, and Bowyer (1992) examine the price, volume, volatility, and liquidity effects of additions to and deletions from the Federal Reserve's list of marginable OTC securities following passage of the 1969 amendment to the Securities Exchange Act of 1934. The findings of each of these studies are summarized below.

Grube, Joy, and Howe (1987) perform an event-time analysis of the price impact of additions and deletions of selected OTC firms to the Federal Reserve Board's *Official List of OTC Margin Stocks.* Using ninety firms collected from three listing dates, weekly data, and two separate return generating models, the authors identify significant price increases in the week of margin eligibility but not in the week of delisting. Taken separately, the positive price listing results point toward either an implied Federal Reserve "endorsement" effect or a credit convenience effect, while the delisting results seemingly indicate no effect at all. However, as Grube, Joy, and Howe note, when the two sets of results are integrated and the regulation T "grandfather clause" is acknowledged, the

4. Additional empirical work on the effectiveness of Federal Reserve margin requirements has been conducted by Moore (1966), Friend (1976), Officer (1973), Luckett (1982), and Pruitt (1993). In general, both Moore and Officer suggest "that not one of the aims of the legislation establishing margin requirements has been accomplished" (Moore 1966, 158), while Friend, Luckett, and Pruitt conclude that "the margin requirement is an effective regulatory tool" (Luckett 1982, 783). Studies of exchange-specific 100 percent margins by Largay (1973) and Eckardt and Rogoff (1976) have generally concluded that the banning of credit transactions in individual security issues is associated with a moderation of "speculative" activity in these stocks.

empirical results indicate that significant short-term stock price changes accompany Fed credit regulatory activities.[5]

In a companion study, Grube and Joy (1988) analyze the volatility effects of additions to the OTC margin list. Again using ninety firms and weekly price data, Grube and Joy fail to support the hypothesis that additions to the OTC margin list result in reductions in overall return volatility. Rather, the authors note that the Federal Reserve appears to select OTC stocks for inclusion on the broker loan list after they experience a decline in relative return variance.

Seguin (1990) employs daily return data for approximately 2,400 firms added to the OTC margin list from 1976 to 1987 to test the hypothesis that margin trading leads to destabilizing price and volatility effects. Noting that stock trading volumes increase by about 15 percent, overall price volatility declines by about 2 percent and stock prices increase by about 2 percent upon margin listing. Seguin concludes that, if there is an OTC margin effect, "it is value" (120).

Wolfe, Klein, and Bowyer (1992) perform an analysis similar to that conducted by Seguin (1990), with the exception that Wolfe, Klein, and Bowyer examine price effects across firms of differing market value. Those authors interpret that their findings of no excess returns upon listing for stocks in the largest market value portfolio, but highly significant abnormal returns for smaller firms, are consistent with "the Federal Reserve endorsement theory since, under the credit convenience theory, positive excess returns should be realized without regard to the market value of the [listed] company" (94). This hypothesis is also consistent with the lack of any price effects at the time of delisting, since the process employed by the Federal Reserve for deleting a stock from the list is quite protracted.[6] In contrast to the findings of Seguin (1990), Wolfe, Klein, and Bowyer are unable to document any statistically significant volume changes in the newly marginable firms. In addition, no statistically significant net changes in the average bid-ask spread are observed following margin listing.

While the studies of Grube, Joy, and Howe (1987), Grube and Joy (1988), Seguin (1990), and Wolfe, Klein, and Bowyer (1992) represent important con-

5. The regulation T "grandfather clause" states that any security removed from the OTC margin list can, at the discretion of the broker, continue to qualify for preexisting broker loans. This fact suggests that strong credit-motivated selling pressure need not arise for newly delisted OTC stocks.

6. The process involved in removing a stock from the OTC margin list begins when the Federal Reserve sends a registered letter to the firm stating that the firm is under review. This letter must be sent at least one month, and usually is sent more than one month, before the effective date of delisting. Since the *Federal Register* is the official organ employed in the notification of delisting, and since, over the time period encompassed by the Wolfe, Klein, and Bowyer (1992) study (1985–87), changes to the margin list were published once per quarter, the notification letter could be out as long as three months before official publication in the *Federal Register*. Not surprisingly, firms subject to delisting also have the right to appeal the Federal Reserve's ruling, a process that, if followed, further increases the lag from first notification to final delisting.

tributions to the literature, none of these efforts deals directly with the impact of *changes* in margin levels on OTC firms. In fact, being concerned solely with the valuation effects of additions to (and deletions from) the Federal Reserve's OTC margin lists, these studies are inherently incapable of differentiating between those security market responses resulting from the information effects associated with margin listing (e.g., the Federal Reserve "endorsement effect") and those effects resulting from changes in binding borrowing constraints on equity investors due to changes in margin.

10.4 Data and Empirical Methodology

10.4.1 Data

As stated above, the purpose of this study is to establish a controlled experiment capable of distinguishing between adjustments in security-market behavior resulting from *information effects only* and those changes due to *shifts in margin-imposed binding constraints* on equity investors. As such, all of the tests presented in section 10.5 are based upon specially matched OTC security pairs constructed from the seven OTC margin lists noted in table 10.1. The purpose of the matched pairings is to create the most homogeneous samples possible for study of the effects of changes in Federal Reserve margin levels on both marginable (experiment) and nonmarginable (control) OTC firms. Since over the 1970–74 time interval each of these listings warn that "[s]tocks will be added to the List, or deleted, in the interim between publications as deemed appropriate by the Board," extreme care is taken to ensure that firms placed in either the marginable or nonmarginable portfolios for each margin change are categorized properly. Thus, a stock is considered for inclusion in the marginable firm portfolio for a given margin change only if it appeared on those OTC margin listings published both before and after the change.[7] Similarly, a stock is considered for inclusion in the nonmarginable portfolio only when its first appearance on the OTC margin list occurs on the second OTC firm margin listing following the margin change.

For example, firms included on *both* the OTC margin lists released on July 8, 1969, and July 20, 1970, are considered eligible for inclusion in the marginable firm portfolio for the 15 percent margin decrease announced on May 6, 1970. Similarly, firms are considered eligible for the nonmarginable portfolio only when first included on the OTC firm margin list released on July 12, 1971. In addition to ensuring that each included firm is indeed either marginable or nonmarginable as of the date of a given margin change, this procedure eliminates the possibility that a firm's margin status might have changed

7. Otherwise apparently eligible OTC firms reported in the *Federal Register* as having been removed from the Federal Reserve's *Official List of OTC Margin Stocks* are also eliminated during the construction of the marginable firm portfolios.

over the parameter estimation intervals required by the conducted tests.[8] This latter point is particularly critical, given the parameter estimation biases that might result from the price, volume, and volatility effects associated with OTC firm additions to the list of marginable securities. (See, e.g., Seguin [1990]; and Wolfe, Klein, and Bowyer [1992].)

Since the Center for Research in Security Prices (CRSP) OTC daily data tape begins in 1976, and since the last change in Federal Reserve margin levels occurred in 1974, all of the data employed in the present study are necessarily collected by hand from various quarterly issues of the *ISL OTC Stock Price Guide*.[9] Because of the desire to employ daily data in the analysis and the extremely high opportunity costs associated with hand collection, a total of 20 marginable and 20 nonmarginable firms are included in each of the OTC firm pair groupings employed in the empirical tests for each of the four post-1969 amendment margin changes. For each of these 160 firms, closing bid and ask prices are collected over event days $t = -126$ to $+25$, relative to the day 0 margin change date. Additionally, since daily trading volume data are included in the ISL OTC guides beginning in 1972, volume data for the 40 matched pairs (80 firms) employed in tests of the 1972 and 1974 margin changes also are collected over event days $t = -126$ to $+25$. Combining these two security series results in a final data set exceeding sixty thousand individually hand-collected points.

The actual mechanics for determining which firms are included in the analysis is straightforward. Following the determination of which firms are potentially available for inclusion in both the marginable and nonmarginable portfolios for each of the four margin changes, subsets of these firms are then matched on the basis of four-digit industrial SIC codes. Since the set of potential nonmarginable firms is typically much smaller than the set of available marginable firms, in approximately 70 percent of all cases more than one (and as many as six) four-digit SIC code–matched marginable firm are available for pairing with each nonmarginable firm. In these instances, additional matching criteria based on both similarities in market value and debt/equity ratios are employed to complete the margin pairings. While the market value matching criterion requires no justification here, debt/equity ratios are included in the matching process as an attempt to control for the plausible possibility that some investors might view margin and corporate borrowing as substitutes in

8. The OTC marginable/nonmarginable inclusion criteria for the 1971, 1972, and 1974 margin changes are as follows: 1971 marginable, included on the 7/20/70, 7/12/71, and 5/15/72 margin lists; 1971 nonmarginable, included on the 9/4/73 margin list, but not on the 7/12/71 or 5/15/72 list; 1972 marginable, included on the 5/15/72 and 9/4/73 margin lists; 1972, nonmarginable, included on the 1/3/74 list, but not on the 5/15/72 or 9/4/73 list; 1974 marginable, included on the 9/4/73, 7/29/74, and 9/29/75 margin lists; and 1974 nonmarginable, included on the 9/29/75 list, but not on the 9/4/73 or 7/29/74 list.

9. Unfortunately, attempts to employ an optical scanner in the collection of the data proved unsuccessful.

the sense of the "homemade leverage" arguments proposed by Modigliani and Miller (1958) and others.[10]

10.4.2 Empirical Methodology

The purpose of this study is to determine whether the security-market responses observed previously in response to changes in Federal Reserve margin requirements are due to information effects only or to changes in margin-imposed binding constraints upon investors. The information effects hypothesis suggests that security-market responses to margin changes result from innovations in expectations concerning either the condition of the stock market or the economy as a whole, and that changes in margin levels serve essentially as a signaling mechanism employed by the Federal Reserve in the dissemination of relevant information to the marketplace. In this case, most securities, regardless of their relative accessibility of margin credit, should react in roughly the same magnitude and direction to a given change in margin requirements.[11] Conversely, the binding constraint hypothesis suggests that security-market reactions to changes in margin requirements should differ across issues, particularly with respect to cross-sectional differences in the availability of margin loans, as margin traders adjust their portfolios in response to changes in the lending environment. Accordingly, the standardized abnormal returns differences methodology developed below is designed to detect deviations in *relative* price performance between the marginable and nonmarginable portfolios described above in response to a change in Federal Reserve margin requirements.

Returns for each marginable or nonmarginable firm i for each event day t, $t = -125 \ldots +25$, follow Seguin (1990) and are calculated as

$$(1) \qquad r_{it} = \ln\left(\frac{(A_{it} + B_{it})/2 + D_{it}}{(A_{it-1} + B_{it-1})/2}\right),$$

where A_{it} and A_{it-1} and B_{it} and B_{it-1} are the ask and bid prices for security i at time t and $t - 1$, respectively, and D_{it} is any cash dividend or other cash distribution accruing to stockholders of firm i at time t. All return calculations are corrected for both stock dividends and stock splits, if any.

Returns for the twenty marginable and nonmarginable firms for each margin change are combined into equally weighted portfolio indexes as

$$(2) \qquad R_{MAR,t} = (1/20)\sum_{t=1}^{20} r_{it} \quad \text{and} \quad R_{NMR,t} = (1/20)\sum_{t=1}^{20} r_{it},$$

where $R_{MAR,t}$ and $R_{NMR,t}$ are the mean returns for the marginable and nonmarginable firm OTC indexes for all 151 event days t, respectively.

Abnormal returns for each OTC index $j(j = 2)$ for each event day t are calculated via the market model and are defined as

$$(3) \qquad AR_{jt} = R_{jt} - (\hat{\alpha}_j + \hat{\beta}_j R_{mt}), \qquad t = -25 \ldots +25,$$

where R_{mt} is the daily return of the CRSP value-weighted market index and $\hat{\alpha}_j$ and $\hat{\beta}_j$ are Scholes-Williams (1977) intercept and slope coefficients estimated over event days $t = -100$ to -26, relative to the day 0 margin change announcement, and are defined as[12]

$$(4) \qquad \hat{\alpha}_j = \frac{1}{98} \sum_{t=-125}^{-26} R_{jt} - \hat{\beta}_j \frac{1}{98} \sum_{t=-125}^{-26} R_{mt}$$

and

$$(5) \qquad \hat{\beta}_j = (\beta_j^- + \beta_j + \beta_j^+)/(1 + 2\rho_m),$$

where ρ_m is the estimated first-order autocorrelation coefficient of the market index over the period $t = -125$ to -26, and the individual β terms are ordinary least squares coefficients estimated from the following three regressions:

$$(6) \qquad R_{jt} = \alpha_j^- + \beta_j^- R_{mt-1} + \varepsilon_{jt}, \qquad t = -124, \ldots, -26;$$

$$(7) \qquad R_{jt} = \alpha_j + \beta_j R_{mt} + \varepsilon_{jt}, \qquad t = -124, \ldots 26;$$

$$(8) \qquad R_{jt} = \alpha_j^+ + \beta_j^+ R_{mt+1} + \varepsilon_{jt}, \qquad t = -125, \ldots, -27.$$

The abnormal returns difference for each event day t, ARD_t, is simply the arithmetic difference between the abnormal returns for each of the two OTC indexes ($AR_{MAR,t}$ and $AR_{NMR,t}$) for each event day t and is defined as

$$(9) \qquad ARD_t = AR_{MAR,t} - AR_{NMR,t}$$

Note that, by employing a time series of paired abnormal return differences, any marketwide cross-sectional dependencies of the abnormal returns are effectively purged. The cumulative abnormal returns difference for the interval from T_1 to T_2, $CARD_{T_1 T_2}$ is defined as

$$(10) \qquad CARD_{T_1 T_2} = \sum_{t=1}^{N} ARD_t,$$

where $N = T_2 - T_1 + 1$.

Standardized abnormal return differences for each event day t, $SARD_t$, are calculated by dividing the abnormal return differences for each event day t in the event interval by the square root of the variance of the ARD_t over the 125-day estimation interval. Mathematically,

---

12. As expected, given the results of Brown and Warner (1985), alternative abnormal return calculation methods such as the ordinary least squares market model and the market-adjusted returns model produce no substantive differences in the results achieved. Further, the results prove similarly insensitive to alternative market indexes such as the CRSP value-weighted index and the S&P 500 index.

(11) $$SARD_t = ARD_t / (s^2_{ARD})^{1/2},$$

where s^2_{ARD} is defined as

(12) $$s^2_{ARD} = \frac{1}{124} \sum_{t=-125}^{-26} (AR_{MAR,t} - AR_{NMR,t} - \overline{MARD})^2,$$

and where

(13) $$\overline{MARD} = \frac{1}{125} \sum_{t=-125}^{-26} (AR_{MAR,t} - AR_{NMR,t}).$$

The cumulative standardized abnormal return difference from T_1 to T_2, $CSARD_{T_1 T_2}$, is defined as

(14) $$CSARD_{T_1 T_2} = \sum_{t=T_1}^{T_2} \frac{SARD_t}{\sqrt{T_2 - T_1 + 1}}.$$

This test statistic is assumed distributed asymptotically unit normal (t) and is employed to determine the significance of each event interval tested for each margin change pair.

10.5   Empirical Results

10.5.1   Price Tests

Tables 10.2–10.5 document the daily and cumulative abnormal return differences and their associated daily test statistics (t) between the marginable and nonmarginable OTC firm samples for the 1970, 1971, 1972, and 1974 margin changes, respectively, for event days $t = -25$ to $+25$ relative to the day 0 announcement of each Federal Reserve margin change. Recall, due to the mechanics of the abnormal portfolio return equation (9), a positive abnormal return value for a given even day indicates that the price performance of the marginable OTC firm portfolio exceeded that of the nonmarginable OTC firm portfolio after adjusting for all market movements. In addition to portfolio-specific return data, tables 10.2–10.5 also reproduce the daily and cumulative returns of the CRSP equally weighted index for each event day.

As illustrated in table 10.2, the lack of any positive, statistically significant abnormal returns around the time of the 15 percent decrease in Federal Reserve margin levels enacted on May 6, 1970, strongly suggests that the performance of the nonmarginable OTC firm portfolio mirrored its marginable OTC firm counterpart. While the abnormal return for event day $+3$ is positive and statistically significant, it seems extremely unlikely that this finding—occurring as it does a full three days after the margin change—is the result of a margin-induced change in binding borrowing constraints on OTC firm investors. The insignificant rise in the cumulative abnormal returns over event days $+1$ to $+25$ ($CARD = 3.29$ percent, $CSARD = 1.79$) further underscores the lack of

Table 10.2 **Price Differences between the Marginable and Nonmarginable OTC Firm Portfolios for the 1970 Margin Decrease**

Event Day	CRSP Index	Σ CRSP Index	MAR − NMR (ARD$_t$)	Test Statistics (SARD$_t$)	CARD$_{T_1 T_2}$
−25	−.0002420	−.0002420	−.0117487	−1.4091150	−.0117487
−15	−.0086740	−.0395400	.0071752	.8605785	−.0266280
−5	−.0144620	−.1280480	−.0128349	−1.5393910	−.0096200
−4	.0208060	−.1072420	.0074914	.8985030	−.0021286
−3	−.0034220	−.1106640	−.0183067	−2.1956680	−.0204353
−2	−.0011080	−.1117720	−.0073447	−.8809080	−.0277800
−1	−.0255220	−.1372940	.0056639	.6793163	−.0221161
0	−.0109500	−.1482440	.0066261	.7947207	−.0154900
1	.0121670	−.1360770	−.0044613	−.5350790	−.0199513
2	.0063200	−.1297570	.0044212	.5302695	−.0155301
3	−.0050870	−.1348440	.0203159	2.4366470	.0047858
4	−.0107460	−.1455900	−.0044089	−.5287942	.0003769
5	−.0089880	−.1545780	.0098005	1.1754520	.0101774
15	−.0133190	−.2794580	−.0024386	−.2924805	.0673350
25	.0003140	−.1711940	.0092849	1.1136120	.0174969

Notes: This table documents the daily (*ARD$_t$*) and cumulative (*CARD*) abnormal return differences and associated daily abnormal return test statistics (*SARD$_t$*) between a portfolio of marginable and nonmarginable OTC firms around the 15 percent decrease in Federal Reserve margin requirements enacted on May 6, 1970. Daily and cumulative changes in the CRSP equally weighted index also are presented.

Table 10.3 **Price Differences between the Marginable and Nonmarginable OTC Firm Portfolios for the 1971 Margin Decrease**

Event Day	CRSP Index	Σ CRSP Index	MAR − NMR (ARD$_t$)	Test Statistics (SARD$_t$)	CARD$_{T_1 T_2}$
−25	.0013600	.0013600	.0169072	2.1402440	.0169072
−15	−.0135690	−.0153110	.0116321	1.4724870	−.0206326
−5	.0183380	−.0195630	.0068407	.8659500	−.0095260
−4	.0181610	−.0014020	.0072385	.9163035	−.0022876
−3	.0073560	.0059540	.0207235	2.6233470	.0184359
−2	.0174890	.0234430	.0062550	.7918085	.0246909
−1	.0029870	.0264300	−.0029344	−.3714570	.0217566
0	.0119510	.0383810	−.0150132	−1.9004880	.0067434
1	−.0043440	.0340370	−.0218976	−2.7719800	−.0151543
2	.0046030	.0386400	−.0053207	−.6735385	−.0204750
3	.0016230	.0402630	−.0046687	−.5910037	−.0251437
4	.0002580	.0405210	−.0085862	−1.0869100	−.0337299
5	.0082160	.0487370	−.0024231	−.3067365	−.0361530
15	.0016790	.0805470	−.0081754	−1.0349050	−.0356022
25	−.0001820	.1094550	.0017698	.2240416	−.0159524

Notes: This table documents the daily (*ARD$_t$*) and cumulative (*CARD*) abnormal return differences and associated daily abnormal return test statistics (*SARD$_t$*) between a portfolio of marginable and nonmarginable OTC firms around the 10 percent decrease in Federal Reserve margin requirements enacted on December 6, 1971. Daily and cumulative changes in the CRSP equally weighted index also are presented.

Table 10.4   **Price Differences between the Marginable and Nonmarginable OTC Firm Portfolios for the 1972 Margin Increase**

Event Day	CRSP Index	Σ CRSP Index	MAR − NMR (ARD_t)	Test Statistics $(SARD_t)$	$CARD_{T_1 T_2}$
−25	.0059850	.0059850	.0014315	.5734817	.0014315
−15	.0087990	.0426000	.0016413	.6575332	−.0167560
−5	−.0031780	.0707950	.0022984	.9207926	−.0026486
−4	.0052010	.0759960	.0015898	.6369066	−.0010588
−3	.0033340	.0793300	−.0026210	−1.0500270	−.0036798
−2	.0002530	.0795830	.0002736	.1096371	−.0034062
−1	.0047300	.0843130	.0004294	.1720352	−.0029767
0	.0060940	.0904070	−.0010509	−.4210181	−.0040277
1	.0029690	.0933760	−.0010552	−.4227587	−.0050830
2	−.0034770	.0898990	−.0011348	−.4546217	−.0062178
3	−.0015240	.0883750	.0000427	.0171417	−.0061750
4	.0004780	.0888530	−.0012381	−.4959964	−.0074131
5	.0026640	.0915170	.0021748	.8712687	−.0052382
15	−.0030690	.1034480	−.0001277	−.0511793	−.0104012
25	.0091340	.1120880	−.0055319	−2.2161370	−.0162990

Notes: This table documents the daily (ARD_t) and cumulative ($CARD$) abnormal return differences and associated daily abnormal return test statistics ($SARD_t$) between a portfolio of marginable and nonmarginable OTC firms around the 10 percent increase in Federal Reserve margin requirements enacted on November 24, 1972. Daily and cumulative changes in the CRSP equally weighted index also are presented.

Table 10.5   **Price Differences between the Marginable and Nonmarginable OTC Firm Portfolios for the 1974 Margin Decrease**

Event Day	CRSP Index	Σ CRSP Index	MAR − NMR (ARD_t)	Test Statistics $(SARD_t)$	$CARD_{T_1 T_2}$
−25	−.0292590	−.0292590	.0156217	1.0332130	.0156217
−15	.0154200	−.0153360	.0265804	1.7580200	.0301715
−5	−.0056990	−.0691410	−.0007229	−.0478155	.0571953
−4	.0281460	−.0409950	−.0308005	−2.0371380	.0263948
−3	.0206470	−.0203480	−.0056012	−.3704586	.0207936
−2	−.0011290	−.0214770	−.0110722	−.7323141	.0097214
−1	.0019370	−.0195400	−.0072027	−.4763867	.0025187
0	.0033430	−.0161970	−.0439908	−2.9095390	−.0414721
1	.0238500	.0076530	−.0244960	−1.6201560	−.0659681
2	−.0050550	.0025980	−.0226153	−1.4957680	−.0885834
3	−.0057600	−.0031620	−.0066456	−.4395393	−.0952290
4	−.0181950	−.0213570	.0193431	1.2793460	−.0758859
5	−.0278670	−.0492240	−.0094121	−.6225135	−.0852980
15	.0054740	−.0133790	−.0074288	−.4913417	−.0909986
25	.0030280	−.0477420	.0019639	.1298889	−.1136665

Notes: This table documents the daily (ARD_t) and cumulative ($CARD$) abnormal return differences and associated daily abnormal return test statistics ($SARD_t$) between a portfolio of marginable and nonmarginable OTC firms around the 15 percent decrease in Federal Reserve margin requirements enacted on January 3, 1974. Daily and cumulative changes in the CRSP equally weighted index also are presented.

a significant margin-change differential between the marginable and nonmarginable portfolios.

Clearly, the lack of a positive, statistically significant rise in the prices of the marginable OTC firm sample relative to their nonmarginable counterparts suggests that any pricing revaluations in response to the 1970 margin change were due to *information effects only* and *not* due to changes in margin-imposed binding constraints on equity investors, at least over the short run. The consistent downward trend in the level of the CRSP index over event days $t = -25$ to -1 is consistent with the hypothesis that the Federal Reserve reduces margin requirements in response to declining equity price levels.

Table 10.3 summarizes the findings for the 10 percent decrease in margin levels announced on December 6, 1971. Whereas the test statistics for the abnormal returns associated with event days 0 and +1 indicate a definite margin-change differential between the two OTC firm portfolios, the direction of the difference (negative) is exactly the opposite of the a priori hypothesis that reductions in margin levels should result in price increases in marginable OTC firms vis-à-vis their nonmarginable counterparts. As was the case with the 1970 margin change, the cumulative abnormal return levels registered over event days $t = +1$ to $+25$ are similarly inconsistent with an identifiable margin-change performance differential between the two OTC firm portfolios ($CARD = -2.27$ percent, $CSARD = -1.57$).

The abnormal returns associated with the 10 percent increase in margin requirements mandated on November 24, 1972, are summarized in table 10.4. As before, there is absolutely no evidence presented in table 10.4 that would suggest an identifiable differential response between the marginable and nonmarginable OTC firm portfolios. Indeed, none of the eleven event days immediately surrounding the day 0 announcement of the increase even approach significance at conventional statistical levels. Again, the lack of a consistent trend in the postannouncement abnormal returns over event days $t = +1$ to $+25$ ($CARD = -1.23$ percent, $CSARD = -0.98$) underscores the inherent price performance similarity of the two portfolios. Similar to the case of the 1970 margin decrease, the substantial cumulative return increase registered by the CRSP index prior to the announcement of the 1972 margin increase is consistent with the hypothesis that changes in equity levels are an important input into the Federal Reserve's margin-change decision calculus.

In a perhaps initially surprising result, the abnormal return performance of the nonmarginable OTC firms substantially and statistically exceeded the performance of their marginable counterparts at the time of the announcement of the final change in Federal Reserve margin levels announced on January 3, 1974 (table 10.5). Indeed, given the hypothesis that changes in margin levels are associated with changes in binding constraints on equity investors, the abnormal return performance of the marginable firms would, if anything, be expected to exceed that of the nonmarginable firms. However, the fact that this margin change occurred on the second trading day of the year, combined with the fact that the average asset levels of the firms in the marginable firm portfolio exceeded that of the nonmarginable portfolio, suggests that the previously described inverse correlation between stock returns and firm size around the turn of the year (see, e.g., Keim [1983]) may well lie at the root of this empirical finding. Over the entire twenty-five-day postevent period, the cumulative abnormal return performance of the nonmarginable firm portfolio exceeded that of the marginable firms by over 7 percent ($CARD = -7.21$ percent, $CSARD = -2.96$).

Overall, the pricing results clearly refute the hypothesis that changes in margin requirements are associated with changes in binding constraints on security investors. Rather, the results for the marginable and nonmarginable firm pairs for the 1970, 1971, 1972, and 1974 margin changes provide the strongest empirical evidence to date that the pricing dynamics observed by previous researchers in response to changes in margin levels are due strictly to information effects common to all equity securities.

10.5.2 Volatility Tests

Table 10.6 presents a preliminary comparison of differences in volatilities between the marginable and nonmarginable OTC firm portfolios before and after each margin change. Comparisons of the cross-sectional variances are made between the two samples by means of an F-test. Volatility differences (at

Table 10.6   **Across-Sample Comparisons of Means and Variances for the Marginable and Nonmarginable OTC Firm Portfolios**

	1970		1971		1972		1974	
	MAR	NMR	MAR	NMR	MAR	NMR	MAR	NMR
Preannouncement Comparisons								
Mean	0.0108	−0.0098	0.0004	−0.0004	0.0022	0.0013	−0.0009	−0.0021
Variance	0.0025	0.0025	0.0003	0.0001	7.6E-5	4.6E-5	0.0005	0.0004
Observations	25	25	25	25	25	25	25	25
Degrees of freedom	24	24	24	24	24	24	24	24
F-statistic	1.0076		2.0619		1.6318		1.3967	
$p(F < f)$	0.4928		0.0413		0.1187		0.2095	
F critical	1.9838		1.9838		1.9838		1.9838	
Postannouncement Comparisons								
Mean	−0.0021	−0.0031	0.0039	0.0048	0.0022	0.0018	−0.0028	0.0017
Variance	0.0006	0.0009	0.0001	4.0E-5	7.1E-5	0.0001	0.0002	0.0002
Observations	25	25	25	25	25	25	25	25
Degrees of freedom	24	24	24	24	24	24	24	24
F-statistic	1.5933		2.9084		1.7248		1.1615	
$p(F < f)$	0.1305		0.0057		0.0945		0.3584	
F critical	1.9838		1.9838		1.9838		1.9838	

Note: This table presents preliminary comparisons of the differences in volatility for the marginable (MAR) and nonmarginable (NMR) OTC firm portfolios in the pre-margin-announcement period and the post-margin-announcement period for the 1970, 1971, 1972, and 1974 changes in Federal Reserve margin levels.

the 5 percent level) between the marginable and nonmarginable firms in the preannouncement period (event days $t = -25$ to -1) are evident only for the 1971 margin change. This result also holds for the F-tests of the differences in volatility between the two samples over the postannouncement period ($t = +1$ to $+25$ event days). While the statistically significant differences between the volatility of the marginable and nonmarginable OTC firm portfolios both before and after the 1971 margin change are interesting, far more important from a policy perspective are questions concerning changes in the variances of the marginable firms *relative to* their nonmarginable counterparts following the announcement of changes in Federal Reserve margin levels.

To investigate relative differences between the marginable and nonmarginable firm samples following the announcement of margin changes, two separate methodologies are employed. The first method, initially developed by Ohlson and Penman (1985) and later replicated by Dubofsky (1991), measures changes in volatility following a specific event via the observation that squared mean daily stock returns are approximately 0.1 percent in order of magnitude compared to expected squared returns. Thus, the null hypothesis that Federal Reserve margin changes have no effect on stock volatilities may be simply restated as $E[R_a^2] - E[R_b^2] = 0$, where R_a and R_b are the returns on security i before and after the margin change, respectively. The statistical approach employed is based on the binomial distribution and assumes simply that, if Federal Reserve margin changes have no effect on security volatility, the percentage of squared returns following a margin change exceeding those prior to the change (p_0), for each portfolio for each of the four margin changes, should be equal to the random chance probability of 0.5. Thus,

(15) $$Z = 2(p_0 - 0.5)\sqrt{n},$$

where n is the number of return pairs.[13]

The Z-test to determine the statistical significance of the difference in the proportion of the squared returns registered between the marginable and nonmarginable firms for each margin change is given by

(16) $$Z = \frac{p_1 - p_2}{\sqrt{\left(\dfrac{n_1 p_1 + n_2 p_2}{n_1 + n_2}\right)\left(1 - \dfrac{n_1 p_1 + n_2 p_2}{n_1 + n_2}\right)\left(\dfrac{1}{n_1} + \dfrac{1}{n_2}\right)}},$$

where n_1 and p_1 and n_2 and p_2 are the total sample sizes and proportions of squared returns higher following each margin change for the marginable (1) and nonmarginable (2) firm portfolios, respectively.

13. While Ohlson and Penman employ a day-of-the-week matching procedure in their volatility tests, the common events dates of the present study mitigate the need for such an adjustment. Thus, the squared return for the first trading day following the 1970 margin change is paired with the first trading day prior to the margin change for both the marginable and nonmarginable OTC firm portfolios, and so on until all twenty-five event days on each side of each margin change are included in the analysis.

Table 10.7 presents the proportion (p) of cases in which the postannounce-ment squared daily return exceeds the matched-pair preannouncement squared daily return for both the marginable (MAR) and nonmarginable (NMR) portfo-lios, respectively, as well as the Z values associated with these proportions (in parentheses). In addition, the table also reports the overall Z value for the difference in the proportions registered by each portfolio for each margin-change announcement.

As reported in table 10.7, while there are clearly significant reductions in volatility for both the marginable and nonmarginable firms in response to the 1971, 1972, and 1974 margin changes, there are no statistically significant dif-ferences between the volatility responses of the two portfolios for any of the four tested margin changes. Further, the fact that the postevent returns volatil-ity of the marginable OTC stocks actually fell following the 1971 and 1974 margin decreases further underscores the results of earlier researchers such as Ferris and Chance (1988), who suggest that changes in margin levels and stock return variability are not always inversely correlated.

In an effort to further evaluate whether there is a different margin-induced volatility relationship between the marginable and nonmarginable OTC firms around the time of changes in Federal Reserve margin levels, a two-way AN-OVA test also is performed. The model tested is

$$(17) \qquad X_{ijk} = \mu + \alpha_i + \beta_j + \gamma_{ij} + \varepsilon_{ijk},$$

where X_{ijk} is the natural log of the ratio of the postannouncement estimated variance to the preannouncement estimated variance for firm k in sample $i =$

Table 10.7   **Squared Daily Return Volatility Differences between the Marginable and Nonmarginable OTC Firm Samples around the time of Federal Reserve Margin Changes**

Margin Change	Total Firms MAR	Total Firms NMR	Matched Pairs MAR	Matched Pairs NMR	p MAR	p NMR	Z^a
1970	20	20	500	500	0.501 (0.05)	0.535 (1.51)	−1.039
1971	20	20	500	500	0.434 (−2.95)	0.378 (−5.45)	1.803
1972	20	20	500	500	0.424 (−3.40)	0.400 (−4.47)	0.771
1974	20	20	500	500	0.386 (−5.10)	0.334 (−7.42)	1.713

Notes: This table presents the proportions of cases in which the postmargin squared daily return exceeds the matched premargin squared daily return for the marginable and nonmarginable OTC firm portfolios around the times of the 1970, 1971, 1972, and 1974 margin changes. This propor-tion is denoted by p for the marginable (MAR) and nonmarginable (NMR) OTC firm samples. The individual margin-change Z-statistic (in parentheses) tests whether $p = .05$.

[a]The Z-statistic test for the difference between the proportions of the marginable and nonmar-ginable samples.

Table 10.8   **Results for the Two-Way ANOVA Model**

Source of Variation	Sum of Squares	Degrees of Freedom	Mean Squares	F Ratio	p Value	F Critical
Model	46.892	7	6.699	6.91	0.004	3.23
Error	147.420	152	0.970			
Corrected total	194.312	159				
Marginability	0.238	1	0.238	0.24	0.621	3.90
Year	44.581	3	14.860	15.32	0.000	2.66
Interaction	2.072	3	0.691	0.71	0.546	2.66
Model R^2 = 0.2413						

Notes: This table presents the results of the following two-way ANOVA model: $X_{ijk} = \mu + \alpha_i + \beta_j + \gamma_{ij} + \varepsilon_{ijk}$, where X_{ijk} is the natural log of the ratio of the postmargin announcement estimated variance to the premargin announcement variance, μ is the overall grand mean (a constant), α_i is the marginability effect, β_j is the year effect, and γ_{ij} is the interaction effect between marginability and year.

marginable, nonmarginable in year j = 1970, 1971, 1972, 1974; μ is the overall grand mean, a constant; α_i is the effect of marginability (MAR − NMR effect); β_j is the effect of year; γ_{ij} is the effect of the interaction between marginability and year; and ε_{ijk} is a normally distributed random error with mean equal to zero, and variance equal for all i, j, and k.

Table 10.8 presents the results of the ANOVA analysis. The null hypothesis of no margin effect on the volatility of the marginable firms relative to their nonmarginable counterparts is that α_i = 0. The extremely low significance level of α_i (0.62) indicates clearly the lack of a margin-induced volatility differential between the two samples. The high degree of significance of the time (year) variables underscores the results presented in table 10.7, while the highly significant $F(F = 6.91, p = 0.0045)$ and R^2 values ($R^2 = 0.2413$) confirm the general goodness of fit of the model.

Overall, the results presented in tables 10.6–10.8 offer no support for the view that changes in Federal Reserve margin levels lead to changes in the underlying return volatility of marginable OTC stocks relative to their nonmarginable counterparts. Rather, in every test scenario, the volatility results presented support the discussion of the pricing results discussed above and suggest that any changes in return volatility in response to changes in Federal Reserve margin levels are due only to information effects and *not* to shifts in binding constraints on security investors.

10.5.3   Volume Tests

While early researchers such as Grube, Joy, and Panton (1979) observed statistically significant increases in daily trading volume for the S&P Composite index around the time of announcement of Federal Reserve margin changes, the findings of more recent margin-based experiments employing OTC stocks are contradictory. Specifically, Seguin (1990) documents volume increases of about 15 percent for stocks added to the Federal Reserve's list of marginable

OTC securities. Seguin's findings suggest that in only three of the first hundred postlisting trading days is security trading volume lower than the average of the hundred days just prior to listing. Conversely, Wolfe, Klein, and Bowyer (1992) document that only 48 percent of the firms in their sample experience increases in relative *market-adjusted* trading volumes following placement on the Federal Reserve's OTC margin list.

Despite this discrepancy, given the expected positive relationship between increases in "speculative activity" and trading volume, it is reasonable to posit that, if decreases (increases) in Federal Reserve margin requirements are associated with the loosening (tightening) of a binding constraint on security investors, the average trading volumes of marginable OTC securities should be expected to rise (fall) vis-à-vis their nonmarginable counterparts.

To assess changes in the mean relative percentage trading volumes between the two samples, a paired-differences methodology is employed. In these tests, the percentage change in the mean daily trading volume for the marginable ($DTVMAR_i$) and nonmarginable ($DTVNMR_i$) firms in each OTC firm pair is calculated by taking the natural log of the ratio of the mean daily trading volume for the twenty-five event days before the margin change and the twenty-five event days following the announcement. Thus, $DTVMAR_i = \ln(TVMAR_{ia}/TVMAR_{ib})$, and $DTVNMR_i = \ln(TVNMR_{ia}/TVNMR_{ib})$, where $TVMAR_{ib}$ and $TVNMR_{ib}$ and $TVMAR_{ia}$ and $TVNMR_{ia}$ are, respectively, the mean daily trading volumes for the marginable and nonmarginable firms in each OTC firm pair before and after each margin change.

The net change in the daily percentage trading volume for each firm pair (DTV_i) is calculated by subtracting the mean percentage change in daily trading volume for the nonmarginable firm of each OTC firm pair from that of its matched marginable firm, $DTV_i = DTVMAR_i - DTVNMR_i$. Thus, if the mean daily percentage trading volume for a given marginable firm increased following a given margin change relative to its nonmarginable counterpart, this difference will be positive. The test statistic for the mean difference of the individual OTC pair differences for each of the four margin changes is then calculated via a standard paired differences t-test.

Table 10.9 reports the mean daily trading volumes (in thousands of shares) and the mean percentage change in daily trading volumes for the firms in the marginable and nonmarginable OTC portfolios both before and after the 1972 and 1974 changes in Federal Reserve margin levels. Recall, daily trading volume figures are not reported in the *ISL OTC Stock Price Guide* prior to 1972. Also reported in the table is the mean difference between the changes in percentage trading volumes, the standard error of this difference, and the associated test statistic (t).

As shown in table 10.9, there is no evidence that the 10 percent increase in Federal Reserve margin levels announced on November 24, 1972, led to decreases in the relative mean daily trading volumes for the firms included in the marginable OTC portfolio. Whereas the mean marginable firm trading volume

Table 10.9   **Mean Daily Trading Volume Differences between the Marginable and Nonmarginable OTC Firm Portfolios before and after Federal Reserve Margin Changes**

1972 margin increase	
Marginable firm mean trading volume following change	76.549
Prior to change	77.899
Mean percentage change	−1.748
Nonmarginable firm mean trading volume following change	30.785
Prior to change	33.100
Mean percentage change	−7.251
Mean percentage difference	5.503
Standard error of mean percentage difference	52.409
Test statistic (t) of mean difference	0.105
1974 margin decrease	
Marginable firm mean trading volume following change	86.850
Prior to change	76.150
Mean percentage change	13.101
Nonmarginable firm mean trading volume following change	41.252
Prior to change	48.900
Mean percentage change	−17.006
Mean percentage difference	30.107
Standard error of mean percentage difference	15.600
Test statistic (t) of mean difference	1.930

Notes: This table presents an analysis of the mean changes in daily trading volume (in thousands) for the marginable and nonmarginable OTC firms following the announcement of the 1972 and 1974 changes in Federal Reserve margin requirements. The net percentage change in mean trading volume is equal to the difference between the mean percentage post- and premargin trading volume for the marginable firms, less the difference between the mean post- and premargin percentage trading volume for the nonmarginable firms.

did decrease by just under 2 percent, the mean trading volume of the nonmarginable firms fell by over 7 percent, implying that the mean relative trading volume of the marginable firms increased by approximately 5.5 percent.

Table 10.9 reports the same statistics for the 15 percent decrease in margin levels enacted on January 3, 1974. Similar to the case of the 1972 increase, there is only weak evidence that the 1974 decrease in margin requirements led to higher trading volumes for the marginable OTC firms relative to their nonmarginable counterparts. While the mean daily percentage trading volume of the marginable OTC stocks rose by 13 percent in the postannouncement period relative to preannouncement levels, and the mean daily percentage trading volume of the nonmarginable firms fell by 17 percent over the same time period, the net difference between these two figures is only marginally significant at conventional statistical levels ($t = 1.930$).

10.5.4   Liquidity (Bid-Ask Spread) Tests

In an effort to determine whether changes in margin levels led to changes in the relative liquidity of the marginable OTC stocks vis-à-vis their nonmarginable counterparts, paired difference tests for changes in the mean daily percentage bid-ask spread also are performed via a methodology similar to the paired-volumes tests discussed above. In these tests, the differential change in the percentage bid-ask spread for the marginable and nonmarginable firms in each OTC firm pair is calculated by subtracting the mean percentage bid-ask spread figures for the twenty-five event days before the margin change from those for the twenty-five event days following. The *net* change in the percentage bid-ask spread for each firm pair is then calculated by subtracting the mean percentage change in the bid-ask spread for the nonmarginable firm of each pair from that of its matched marginable firm. As before, if the percentage bid-ask spread for a given marginable firm increased following a given margin change relative to its nonmarginable counterpart, this difference will be positive.

While the null hypothesis of no difference in the mean daily percentage bid-ask spreads between the marginable and nonmarginable OTC firm pairs seems reasonable, there are alternative hypotheses that could, under certain conditions, suggest either an increase or decrease in relative spreads or, conceivably (in the case of exactly counterbalancing effects) lead to no change at all. In a study that presents estimates of two components of the bid-ask spread, Glosten and Harris (1988) suggest that changes in the spread arise from the interplay of the transitory and adverse-selection components. Thus, by extension, the extent to which the relative bid-ask spread of marginable OTC firms is affected by a change in Federal Reserve margin levels is due in part to the degree to which the monopoly profits generated by market makers from liquidity-motivated traders are counterbalanced by the profits earned by informed traders possessing valuable asymmetric information. Since it is reasonable to posit that the quantity of both liquidity- and informationally motivated trades may increase (decrease) following the imposition of lower (higher) margin levels— the former by virtue of increased (decreased) trading activity in general, the latter due to the fact that decreases (increases) in margin levels allow informationally motivated margin traders to assume larger (smaller) positions in marginable stocks—and since changes in the relative proportions of these two types of traders cannot be determined for the sampled stocks over the time periods under study, the magnitude and direction of changes in *relative* bid-ask spreads for marginable firms in response to changes in margin levels cannot, a priori, be determined.

The results of the tests of the mean bid-ask spread differences between the marginable and nonmarginable OTC firm pairs before and after each of the four margin changes are presented in table 10.10. Similar to the price, volatility, and volume tests presented above, there is no consistent pattern evident in

Table 10.10   Bid-Ask Spread Differences between the Marginable and Nonmarginable OTC Firm Portfolios before and after Federal Reserve Margin Changes

Margin Change	Premargin Spread		Postmargin Spread		Net Change	Test Statistics
	MAR	NMR	MAR	NMR		
1970	0.05792	0.05017	0.06635	0.06868	−0.01008 (0.00540)	−1.87
1971	0.04620	0.03681	0.04526	0.03478	0.00109 (0.00274)	0.40
1972	0.03525	0.04033	0.03579	0.03816	0.00270 (0.00174)	1.55
1974	0.07389	0.07838	0.06277	0.07310	−0.00585 (0.00653)	−0.90

Notes: This table presents an analysis of the mean changes in the reported closing percentage bid-ask spreads for the marginable and nonmarginable OTC firms following the announcement of changes in Federal Reserve margin requirements. The net change in the mean percentage bid-ask spread is equal to the difference between the mean post- and premargin spreads for the marginable firms, less the difference between the mean post- and premargin spreads for the nonmarginable firms. The standard errors of these net differences are reported in parentheses.

the results. While the 1970 and 1974 margin decreases led to reductions in the bid-ask spread for marginable firms vis-à-vis their nonmarginable counterparts, the 1971 margin decrease led to an increase in the spread, as did the 1972 margin increase. The results remain inconsistent even when measured *gross* of changes in the bid-ask spread of the nonmarginable firm portfolio. In this case, the observed mean bid-ask spread rises following the 1970 and 1972 margin changes and falls after the 1971 and 1974 changes. In no case, however, are the observed differences statistically significant. Indeed, only the relative bid-ask spread reduction associated with the 1970 decrease in margin levels approaches significance at conventional levels.

10.6   Conclusions

Recent empirical work on the efficacy of Federal Reserve margin regulation typically has been conducted by comparing the price and volatility changes of the S&P Composite index concomitant with changes in margin levels. The present study represents a unique departure from this approach by exploiting a 1969 amendment to the Securities Exchange Act of 1934—an amendment that allowed brokers and dealers to extend margin credit for the purchase of selected OTC issues—to create two separate portfolios of OTC firms similar in many important respects (e.g., industry, exchange, size, debt/equity ratio) while differing with respect to the presence or absence of Federal Reserve margin requirements. Prior to this development, it was impossible to distinguish, at the time of the announcement of a change in Federal Reserve margin levels, those adjustments in security market behavior resulting from information effects only from those changes resulting from shifts in binding borrowing constraints on equity investors. The results of the conducted price, volatility, volume, and liquidity tests of these matched-pair marginable and nonmarginable OTC firms for the 1970, 1971, 1972, and 1974 Federal Reserve margin changes are summarized below.

Market-adjusted price comparisons of the marginable and nonmarginable OTC firm portfolios failed to document statistically significant differences between the two portfolios in a direction consistent with a priori expectations. Indeed, rather than the positive (negative) relative price performance for the marginable firm portfolio that would be consistent with the loosening (tightening) of a binding constraint facing investors in these securities following margin decreases (increases), no statistically significant price reactions were observed following either the 1970 margin decrease or the 1972 margin increase, while negative and statistically significant relative price performance for the marginable firm portfolio was observed following the 1971 and 1974 margin decreases. Thus, the results of the conducted price tests provide the most convincing evidence to date that the security market reactions observed in response to Federal Reserve margin changes are due to information effects only rather than due to changes in margin-imposed binding constraints on security investors.

Tests for changes in overall return variability provide no evidence of a differential effect between the marginable and nonmarginable firm portfolios following the announcement of either margin increases or decreases, rather than the increasing (decreasing) relative variability of the marginal OTC firm portfolio that would be predicted by the binding constraint hypothesis following the announcement of margin decreases (increases). Further, in findings that support the earlier results of both Hsieh and Miller (1990) and Ferris and Chance (1988), there was no consistent pattern in even the gross changes in volatility of the marginable OTC firms independent of the effect of nonmarginable firms, as the volatility of the marginable firms actually fell in the post-event period following both the 1971 and 1974 margin decreases.

Following the pattern established in the price and volatility results discussed above, tests of changes in marginable and nonmarginable OTC firm trading volume fail to yield a picture consistent with the hypothesis that decreases (increases) in Federal Reserve margin levels should be associated with increases (decreases) in trading volume for marginable equity securities. While the trading volume of the marginable firms did fall following the 1972 margin increase, the volume of the nonmarginable firms fell by an even greater amount. Unfortunately, the lack of daily trading volume figures for the 1970 and 1971 margin changes reduces the extent to which solid inferences may be made concerning the direction and magnitude of changes in marginable and nonmarginable OTC firm trading volumes in response to margin changes.

As mentioned in the discussion of the empirical results, shifts in net direction of the interplay between the transitory and adverse-selection components of the bid-ask spread make it difficult to predict, a priori, the extent to which the relative bid-ask spreads of marginable OTC firms should be affected by a change in Federal Reserve margin levels. Given this caveat, tests of the mean bid-ask spread differences between the marginable and nonmarginable OTC firm pairs before and after each of the four margin changes reveal no consistent pattern in the results. The 1970 and 1974 margin decreases led to reductions in the bid-ask spread for marginable firms vis-à-vis their nonmarginable counterparts, and the 1971 margin decrease and the 1972 margin increase led to an increase in the spread. In no instance are the observed differences statistically significant.

Taken as a whole, the empirical tests presented in this study offer *no support* for the view that Federal Reserve margin requirements function as originally conceived or that changes in margin levels are associated with changes in margin-imposed binding constraints on security investors. Rather, in every test scenario, the findings of the study are consistent with the hypothesis that the price, volatility, volume, and liquidity effects observed in equity securities in response to changes in Federal Reserve margin levels are due to information effects only. As such, the results of the study provide powerful and important new evidence that the findings of Hardouvelis (1988, 1990)—findings purporting to suggest that margin requirements "seem to be an effective regulatory tool" (1990, 736)—do indeed represent a significant overstatement of the strength of the case.

References

Board of Governors of the Federal Reserve System. 1984. A Review of Evaluation of Federal Margin Regulation, Staff Study, Washington, DC.

Brown, S., and J. Warner. 1985. Using daily stock returns: The case of event studies. *Journal of Financial Economics* 14:3–31.

Dubofsky, D. 1991. Volatility increases subsequent to NYSE and AMEX stock splits. *Journal of Finance* 46:421–32.

Eckardt, W., and D. Rogoff. 1976. 100% margins revisited. *Journal of Finance* 31:995–1001.

Ferris, S., and D. Chance. 1988. Margin requirements and stock market volatility. *Economics Letters* 28:251–54.

Friend, I. 1976. The economic consequences of the stock market. *American Economic Review* 66:25–39.

Glosten, L., and L. Harris. 1988. Estimating the components of the bid-ask spread. *Journal of Financial Economics* 21:123–42.

Grube, R., and O. Joy. 1988. Some evidence on the efficacy of security credit regulation in the OTC market. *Journal of Financial Research* 11:137–42.

Grube, R., O. Joy, and J. Howe. 1987. Some empirical evidence on stock returns and security credit regulation in the OTC equity market. *Journal of Banking and Finance* 11:17–32.

Grube, R., O. Joy, and D. Panton. 1979. Market responses to Federal Reserve changes in the initial margin requirement. *Journal of Finance* 34:659–74.

Hardouvelis, G. 1988. Margin requirements and stock market volatility. *Federal Reserve Bank of New York Quarterly Review,* 80–89.

———. 1990. Margin requirements, volatility, and the transitory component of stock prices. *American Economic Review* 80:736–62.

Hsieh, D., and M. Miller. 1990. Margin regulation and stock market volatility. *Journal of Finance* 45:3–30.

Keim, D. 1983. Size-related anomalies and stock return seasonality: Further empirical evidence. *Journal of Financial Economics* 12:13–32.

Largay, J. 1973. 100% margins: Combatting speculation in individual security issues. *Journal of Finance* 28:973–86.

Largay, J., and R. West. 1973. Margin changes and stock price behavior. *Journal of Political Economy* 81:328–39.

Luckett, D. 1982. On the effectiveness of the Federal Reserve's margin requirements. *Journal of Finance* 37:783–95.

Modigliani, F., and M. Miller. 1958. The cost of capital, corporation finance, and the theory of investment. *American Economic Review* 48:261–97.

Moore, T. 1966. Stock market margin requirements. *Journal of Political Economy* 74:158–67.

Officer, R. 1973. The variability of the market factor of the New York Stock Exchange. *Journal of Business* 46: 434–53.

Ohlson, J., and S. Penman. 1985. Volatility increases subsequent to stock splits: An empirical aberration. *Journal of Financial Economics* 14:251–66.

Pruitt, S. 1993. Small firm responses to changes in Federal Reserve margin requirements: Evidence from early data. *Economics Letters* 41:301–6.

Scholes, M., and J. Williams. 1977. Estimating betas from nonsynchronous data. *Journal of Financial Economics* 5:309–27.

Seguin, P. 1990. Stock volatility and margin trading. *Journal of Monetary Economics* 26:101–21.

Wolfe, G., D. Klein, and L. Bowyer. 1992. The impact on stock returns and liquidity for OTC equity issues added to the list of marginable OTC stocks. *Financial Review* 27:81–105.

Comment   A. Craig MacKinlay

Over the years there has been considerable debate concerning the effect of margin requirements for purchasing common equity on the volatility of the stock market. Recently, the debate has been active because of arguments that margins in the stock index futures market should be the same as margins in the cash market. (See Sofianos [1988] for details concerning the margin requirements on equity instruments.) The ultimate question from a policy point of view is whether margin requirements represent an effective tool for the Federal

A. Craig MacKinlay is professor of finance at the Wharton School of the University of Pennsylvania and a research fellow of the National Bureau of Economic Research.

The author thanks Marshall Blume, Andrew Lo, and Krishna Ramaswamy for helpful discussions.

Reserve to use to control market volatility. A recent round of the debate is between Hardouvelis (1990) and Hsieh and Miller (1990). Hardouvelis presented evidence that margin requirements influence the volatility of the market and hence can be a useful tool. However, Hsieh and Miller reexamined Hardouvelis's evidence and find that his results can be explained by statistical biases. Based on a combination of this finding and some new analysis, they reject his conclusion. In this paper, Pruitt and Tse begin at this point. They add to the body of evidence by comparing two samples of OTC stocks; one sample is marginable stock and the other sample is nonmarginable. Their results support the conclusion of Hsieh and Miller (and much previous work).

Rather than spend my discussion time on the specifics of the Pruitt and Tse paper, I thought it might be useful to step back and ask a few broad questions about the margin requirements and stock market volatility debate. These questions have not been addressed in previous work. I have divided my thoughts into two categories—theoretical questions and empirical questions, and I will deal with these in turn.

Theoretical Questions

One shortfall on the theoretical side is the apparent lack of theory with specific empirical predictions for the margins and volatility relation. Existing theory argues that low margin requirements lead to speculative excesses. These excesses can introduce the possibility of an initial price drop triggering a pyramiding effect where calls for collateral lead to forced liquidations and further price drops. (See Garbade [1982] for a review of these arguments.) Such theory appears to predict nothing more specific than that lower margin requirements will lead to higher volatility. This has left empiricists with the choice of designing tests that only assume that volatility is a decreasing function of margin requirements or of adding ad hoc structure (which is usually linear in nature—see Officer [1973] for an example). As we shall see in the section on empirical questions, this lack of specificity can make given relations difficult to detect.

Some other questions also come to mind. Why is it that the studies are concerned only with the initial margin requirements and ignore maintenance margins? If one is concerned with forced liquidations, it seems that the maintenance margin is of some relevance. However, the lack of study of the role of the maintenance margin might be explained by the fact that it has not changed in the United States over the time period researchers have drawn upon for their empirical analysis. More generally, one might ask, To what extent are margins binding at all? Potentially investors can effectively avoid any constraint that high margin requirements impose, by the use of bank lending. If this is the case, then looking for a relation is a fool's errand.

Another question is, Where does one expect the effects of margin requirements to appear in terms of volatility changes? Most studies have focused on a broad-based stock market index (often the S&P 500 index) and hence are looking for marketwide effects. However, if margin accounts are concentrated in a particular segment of the market (e.g., low-capitalization stocks), there may be more fruitful portfolios to examine. Pruitt and Tse deserve credit here. They have gone beyond a broad-based index by using a specific sample of OTC stocks. But such a choice is not without costs, as they have only one margin change to look at. Related to this is the question of how systematic the effects of margin requirements will be. There could be possible benefits from looking at the variances of individual stocks rather than the variance of a portfolio of stocks. One would like to select stocks with a high number of margin purchasers.

Empirical Questions

My empirical questions follow from the issues presented in the theoretical questions. In this section I would like to address the likelihood of statistically detecting a margin requirements and volatility relation if one did exist. While my priors are that none exists, I also suspect that, if one does exist, it will be difficult to find. The subsequent analysis draws heavily on the basic framework of Hsieh and Miller (1990). Using the history of margin changes from 1934 to the present, they consider changes both individually and in aggregate. They find that, in aggregate, the test they use to detect volatility effects has high power, given a "strong negative relation." I believe further analysis is warranted for two reasons. Most important, I find the relation they pose is so strong that it is economically unrealistic. For example, with their alternative relation, when the margin requirements are reduced from 100 percent to 75 percent, the variance of returns increases by 900 percent. Also, they present tests using individual changes and do not report on the power of such tests.

Miller and Hsieh base their analysis on the Levene test. This test is useful because it does not require strong distributional assumptions. However, there is a potential loss of power with this test because it does not incorporate the direction of the volatility change when margins change. To investigate this possibility, a one-sided F-test is also included.

In order to answer the posed question one needs to specify possible alternative margin requirements and volatility relations. This is done using the linear relation proposed by Hsieh and Miller (1990). They use standard deviation of return (σ) to measure volatility and percent initial margin (M) to measure margin requirements. The relation they consider is

$$(1) \qquad \sigma = \alpha - \beta M.$$

Hsieh and Miller calibrate their model using a monthly interval. The relation is completely specified by assigning values to α and β. Five cases are considered, the null hypothesis (alternative 0) and alternatives 1 to 4. The parameter β is selected to control the strength of the relation. It ranges from 0.000 (null hypothesis) to 0.319 (alternative 4). Alternative 4 is the alternative used by Hsieh and Miller (1990). Given β, the parameter α is selected so that the annualized standard deviation is 23.1 percent when the margin requirement is 40 percent. The range of parameters is reported in table 10C.1, and the relations are plotted in figure 10C.1. Also reported in table 10C.1 for each alternative is the standard deviation of return when M is 100 percent. This value ranges from 4.0 percent for the Hsieh-Miller alternative to 23.1 percent for the null hypothesis.

I begin with the consideration of detecting volatility effects given a single margin change. Hsieh and Miller consider this using the Levene test statistic.[1] Define r_{ij} as the jth observation of margin requirement regime i. Consider G regimes and N observations per regime.[2] To construct the statistic, we need the absolute deviations from the mean within each regime. Define z_{ij} as the mean absolute deviation for observation j, regime i. Then

$$(2) \qquad z_{ij} = |r_{ij} - \bar{r}_i|,$$

where

$$(3) \qquad \bar{r}_i = \frac{1}{N} \sum_{j=1}^{N} r_{ij}.$$

Let L be the Levene test statistic; then

$$(4) \qquad L = \left[\frac{GN(N-1)}{(G-1)} \right] \left[\frac{\sum_{i=1}^{G} (\bar{z}_i - \bar{z})^2}{\sum_{i=1}^{G} \sum_{j=1}^{N} (z_{ij} - \bar{z}_i)^2} \right],$$

where

$$(5) \qquad \bar{z}_i = \frac{1}{N} \sum_{j=1}^{N} z_{ij}$$

and

$$(6) \qquad \bar{z} = \frac{1}{G} \sum_{i=1}^{G} \bar{z}_i.$$

Under the null hypothesis that the returns are independently and identically distributed, L is distributed $F[G - 1, G(N - 1)]$ asymptotically.[3] In the case of a single change in margin requirement, $G = 2$.

For comparison, the usual F-test using the ratio of the variances of returns on each side of the margin requirements change is presented. Let Q be the test statistic. Then

---

1. Hsieh and Miller use a slight variation of the Levene test statistic because they want to allow for heteroskedasticity in the data that is unrelated to margin changes. In the analysis of this paper, because all returns are simulated to be homoskedastic except for the volatility changes due to margin changes, the usual Levene test is reported. This difference is likely to bias the results in this paper toward overstating the power relative to the test used by Hsieh and Miller.

2. Because the null distribution is known only asymptotically, for all results presented the null critical values are determined by simulation.

3. In general N can vary across regimes. See Hsieh and Miller (1990).

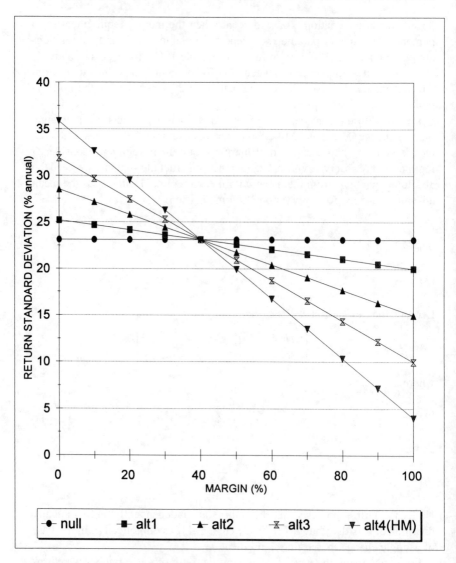

Fig. 10C.1   Margins and volatility relation

$$(7) \qquad\qquad Q = \frac{\hat\sigma_A^2}{\hat\sigma_B^2},$$

where $\hat\sigma_A^2$ and $\hat\sigma_B^2$ are the usual maximum likelihood estimators of the variance for regimes A and B, respectively. A and B are adjacent regimes, with regime A being the one with lower margins. This definition of regimes captures the one-sided nature of the hypothesis. Under the null hypothesis the distribution of Q is $F[N - 1, N - 1]$.

Table 10C.1   **Parameters for Alternative Models of Volatility and Margin Requirements**

Alternative	α	β	$\sigma[M = 100]$
0	23.1	0.000	23.1
1	25.2	0.052	20.0
2	28.6	0.136	15.0
3	31.9	0.219	10.0
4	35.9	0.319	4.0

Notes: A linear relation between annual standard deviation and margin requirements is assumed. The model is $\sigma = \alpha - \beta M$, where σ is the annual standard deviation, M is the margin requirement, and α and β are the model parameters. β is increased to strengthen the relation, and α is selected so that at $M = 40$ percent the standard deviation is 23.1 percent.

The individual change analysis is presented for the four alternatives previously described. The number of observations per regime is set to twenty-five. This roughly corresponds to the average number of months per regime since 1934. Three margin changes are considered, 45–55 percent, 50–70 percent, and 75–100 percent. These all represent changes that actually took place. Independent and identically distributed returns are simulated within each regime. The standard deviation of returns for each regime is given by the linear volatility and margins relation. In table 10C.2 the power of the two tests at the 5 percent level of significance is documented for the four alternatives. Although the power of the two tests is similar, throughout the table the (one-sided) F-test does dominate the Levene test. As expected, the power of both tests is lowest for alternative 1 and the 45–55 percent margin change and the highest for alternative 4 and the 75–100 percent margin change. The difference in magnitudes is extreme, however, with the power ranging from the size of the test to almost 1.0. This illustrates the importance of the alternative one has in mind in assessing the usefulness of the tests. The margin change being considered is also important. The power is low for all alternatives when the 45–55 percent change is considered and is only high for the extreme alternatives and extreme margin change. In summary, only when extreme changes in volatility occur would one expect these tests using individual change events to be able to statistically detect the volatility effects.

Next we address the power of the tests if the margin requirements changes are aggregated together. With the Levene statistic this is easily accomplished by setting G to the number of regimes. In the case at hand $G = 23$ since there are twenty-two margin requirements changes over the 1934-to-present sample. To aggregate the F-test, we form a new statistic based on the average of the Q statistic across regime changes. The size of the sample to be averaged is twenty-two. The null hypothesis critical values of this aggregate F-test are determined by simulation.

The power of the aggregate tests are reported in table 10C.3. Results are reported for three significance levels, 1 percent, 5 percent, and 10 percent. In terms of being able to statistically detect volatility effects, the Levene test has

Table 10C.2   **Power of Two Tests at 5 Percent Significance Level for Individual Margin Changes**

	Change A, 45–55%		Change B, 50–70%		Change C, 75–100%	
Alternative	L-test	F-test	L-test	F-test	L-test	F-test
1	0.047	0.053	0.057	0.084	0.062	0.096
2	0.060	0.080	0.102	0.117	0.145	0.277
3	0.079	0.128	0.163	0.219	0.465	0.671
4	0.094	0.179	0.380	0.403	0.999	0.999

Notes: The two tests are the Levene test (L-test) and the F-test. Four alternative hypotheses are considered. See table 10C.1 and figure 10C.1 for details of the alternatives. Each cell is based on one thousand independent replications.

Table 10C.3   **Power of Two Tests at Various Significance Levels for Twenty-three Margin Changes**

	Significance Level					
	1%		5%		10%	
Alternative	L-test	F-test	L-test	F-test	L-test	F-test
1	0.014	0.073	0.081	0.226	0.158	0.351
2	0.160	0.600	0.366	0.835	0.495	0.915
3	0.811	0.999	0.938	1.000	0.973	1.000
4	1.000	1.000	1.000	1.000	1.000	1.000

Notes: The two tests are the Levene test (L-test) and the aggregate F-test. Four alternative hypotheses are considered. See table 10C.1 and figure 10C.1 for details of the alternatives. The twenty-three margin changes are selected to match the actual margin changes that occurred from October 15, 1934, to January 3, 1974. The margin ranges from 40 percent to 100 percent. See table 1 of Hardouvelis (1990) for the margins and change dates. Each cell is based on one thousand independent replications. The finite sample critical values are determined empirically using ten thousand replications.

low power against alternative 1, moderate power against alternative 2, and high power against alternatives 3 and 4. The aggregate F-test displays a similar pattern but in many cases dominates the Levene test substantially. For example, with alternative 2 and a 5 percent significance level, the power of the aggregate F-test is 83.5 percent, whereas the power of the Levene test is only 36.6 percent. Considerable power gains can be achieved by incorporating the inverse nature of the margin change and volatility relation.

One's satisfaction with the performance of the aggregate tests depends heavily on the alternative deemed economically reasonable. If one accepts the linear relation and views alternative 1 as realistic, the tests are not very useful for detecting volatility effects. In contrast, if one deems the Hsieh and Miller (1990) alternative as realistic, the tests are very useful because they have high power.

Conclusion

To summarize, I find the issue of the relation between margin requirements and volatility in need of further theoretical modeling. The current theory lacks specific predictions. This lack of specificity leads to difficulties empirically designing an informative framework for investigation. For plausible scenarios where there is a relation between margin requirements and volatility, with commonly employed tests, one would be unlikely to find such a relation statistically. While Pruitt and Tse have made some progress, I believe there is still more to be done.

References

Garbade, Kenneth. 1982. Federal Reserve Margin Requirements: A Regulatory Initiative to Inhibit Speculative Bubbles. In Paul Wachtel, ed., *Crises in Economic and Financial Structure.* Lexington, MA: Lexington Books.

Hardouvelis, Gikas. 1990. Margin Requirements, Volatility, and the Transitory Component of Stock Prices. *American Economic Review* 80:736–62.

Hsieh, David, and Merton Miller. 1990. Margin Regulation and Stock Market Volatility. *Journal of Finance* 45:3–30.

Officer, Robert. 1973. The Variability of the Market Factor of the New York Stock Exchange. *Journal of Business* 46:434–53.

Sofianos, George. 1988. Margin Requirements on Equity Instruments. *Federal Bank of New York Quarterly Review* 13 (Summer): 47–60.

Comment   Paul H. Kupiec

In their paper, Stephen Pruitt and K. S. Maurice Tse (PT) examine the effects of changes in margin requirements on the returns of small capitalization stocks. The distinguishing feature of this study is its use of a "matched-pair" statistical design. The methodology measures the differential impact of a margin rate change on selected characteristics of two stocks that, aside from their marginability status, are close substitutes. This methodology is designed to difference out the background noise that might make an underlying margin-volatility, margin-price, or margin-liquidity effect difficult to detect. PT interpret their statistical results as strong evidence against the hypothesis that federal margin requirements impose binding constraints on investors.

Before discussing the specific methodology and results of the PT paper, I

Paul H. Kupiec is a senior economist in the Division of Research and Statistics at the Board of Governors of the Federal Reserve System.

The views, analysis, and conclusions of this paper represent those of the author and do not represent the opinions of the Federal Reserve Board or any of the Federal Reserve Banks. The author is grateful to Andrew Lo for organizing the conference and inviting the author to comment on this paper.

first consider the potential importance of these results for the conduct of federal margin policy. The literature investigating the effects of regulation T margin changes on the volatility of returns to broad stock market indexes is extensive.[1] The vast majority of margin-volatility studies conclude that there is no statistically significant relationship between changes in the Federal Reserve's regulation T margin requirement and subsequent changes in the volatility of returns to broad stock market indexes.[2]

Suppose for a moment that PT were to find that their matched-pair statistical design generated results consistent with the hypothesis that higher margins dampen stock price volatility. Would such a finding imply that margin requirements are an effective tool that can be used to control the volatility of the stock market? I would argue not. The stocks included in the PT sample design are among the smallest capitalization stocks investors can trade. If margins affect the volatility of the very smallest stocks, it need not follow that margins must also affect the aggregate volatility of the stock market. It is possible that margins could have effects on the returns of individual stocks, in this case the smallest equity issues, and yet in aggregate have no effect on overall market volatility.

The theoretical results of Kupiec and Sharpe (1991) are useful in explaining how there might be a statistical margin-volatility relationship in some individual stocks' returns and yet be no evidence of an aggregate margin-volatility relationship. Kupiec and Sharpe show that an increase in margin requirements may cause a risky asset's volatility to either increase or decrease. Margin requirements affect volatility by constraining the holdings of investors. If margin requirements keep irrationally optimistic investors from bidding a stock's price above its sustainable long-run equilibrium price, an increase in margin requirements will reduce that asset's price volatility. Alternatively, margin requirements may prohibit rational risk-tolerant investors from purchasing additional shares when new information causes a share's price to fall or prohibit these investors from short-selling sufficient shares to offset the demands of irrationally optimistic traders. In either instance, a higher margin requirement will increase an asset's price volatility by restricting the volatility-attenuating demands of rational investors. Thus, in an economy with heterogeneous investors, an increase in margin requirements might have positive effects on the return volatility of some shares, negative effects on the return volatility of other shares, and, in aggregate, no measurable effect on the return volatility of the overall stock market index.

The upshot of this argument is that the results of a study that measures the effects of margin-requirement changes on the volatility of small capitalization stocks need not have direct implications for the conduct of margin policy. From

1. See, for example, Moore (1966); Largay and West (1973); Hardouvelis (1988, 1990); Kupiec (1989); Salinger (1989); and Hsieh and Miller (1990).
2. Hardouvelis (1988, 1990) are the only studies that find a statistically significant relationship between margin requirements and the volatility of a broad index of stock returns.

an academic perspective, it might be interesting to know whether federal margin policy has an effect on the price volatility and market characteristics of small capitalization stocks, but it would not be appropriate to generalize these results into statements about the effects of margin changes on the equity market in aggregate. If small capitalization issues were affected by margin requirements, however, such a result would be evidence that small capitalization stocks have a different investor clientele than the clientele that typically invests in large capitalization issues. The finding that investors in small firm shares are somehow different from average market investors would be of interest to researchers outside the margin-volatility debate.

The methodological innovation PT bring to the margin-volatility debate is the use of the matched-pair statistical design. PT choose stocks on the Federal Reserve's OTC marginable stock list and then match each stock with a nonmarginable OTC stock in the same four-digit SIC code category. Under the null hypothesis that margin requirements have no effect on investors in these issues, the differences in price changes, volatility changes, volume changes, and bid-ask spread changes for these matched pairs of stocks on dates surrounding changes in margin requirements should not be statistically different from zero.

Notwithstanding PT's discussion of the advantages of the matched-pair design, it is doubtful that this methodology is appropriate for measuring the effects of margin changes on marginable OTC stocks. The problem in applying the matched-pair design is that it is unlikely that there exist nonmarginable OTC stocks that are close matches for stocks on the Federal Reserve's OTC marginable stock list. One firm's shares are included in the Federal Reserve's OTC margin list and another firm's shares are not marginable precisely because the characteristics of these firms are different. As discussed by PT, critical factors used by the Federal Reserve to determine margin eligibility status include minimum capitalization standards, firm age, tenure of listing, average share price, the number of active market makers, and the dispersion of share ownership. Strictly speaking, it is impossible to match a nonmarginable OTC firm with a firm eligible for margin lending unless the Federal Reserve erred in classification. Clearly one or more of the margin eligibility factors differs across the firms in each PT matched pair. The assumption that a four-digit SIC code is a sufficient statistic for the matching criterion is clearly incorrect.

Although it is possible that the differences between marginable and nonmarginable firms in a PT matched pair are minor and have little bearing on the analysis, PT do not report statistics that measure the magnitudes of these differences in firm characteristics. As a consequence, it is unclear exactly how completely the paired firms are matched. This issue is important because firm returns are almost certainly related to firm size in a systematic way, and they may be related to the other characteristics as well.[3] Without statistics that suggest otherwise, the reader must conclude that the PT matching criterion ignores

3. For example, it is well known that returns to shares in an initial public offer differ in systematic ways from the returns to shares of seasoned firms.

these potentially important factors and controls only for an industry factor (and the market-model factor) in the return generating process.

The empirical evidence reported by PT suggests that omitted factors may be compromising the integrity of their reported test statistics. Consider the margin-requirement price-effect tests reported in tables 10.2–10.5. Each table reports the standardized abnormal return estimate difference (*SARD*) and the cumulative *SARD* (*CARD*) estimates for the margin-change event beginning on event day −25.

In the four separate margin-change events examined, PT find significant evidence of a price effect in the +25 day *CARD* statistic only in the 15 percent margin-requirement decrease of January 3, 1974. For this event, PT calculate that marginable OTC firms underperformed nonmarginable firms by an average 7.21 percent in the fifty-one-day event window. PT find this negative differential return effect of a margin reduction counterintuitive and attribute the result (without statistical confirmation) to the so-called small-firm effect. If this explanation is correct, it is clear that the PT matched-pair criterion does not adequately control for a firm size factor.

Determining whether or not an omitted small-firm factor is the source of the significant *CARD* in the 1974 margin-change event is critically important. PT mistakenly assume that any potential margin-price effect is unidirectional. In their view, if investors are constrained by a margin requirement, relaxing the requirement could only lead to a higher share price. PT do not recognize that margin requirements may prohibit investors from short-selling as many shares as they otherwise might desire. Under regulation T, a short sale is treated as a loan and a share purchase. For margin purposes, the transaction is treated as if the owner of the share sells the security to the short seller and provides the short seller financing to purchase the share. Because the financing is collateralized by the share being purchased, the size of the loan to the short seller is limited by the margin requirement. Effectively, if the margin requirement is 50 percent, the short seller must post margin collateral equal to 50 percent of the value of the shares being sold short.[4] The implication is that a reduction in the margin requirement would allow investors to increase short sales that could potentially cause share price declines.

Aside from the 1974 margin-change event, there is other evidence in the individual *SARD* estimates reported in tables 10.2–10.5 that indicate problems with PT's statistical methodology. Under the null hypothesis, individual *SARD* estimates are distributed (asymptotically) as normal zero-one variables. An examination of the individual *SARD* estimates suggests that their empirical distribution does not correspond very closely with this theoretical distribution. Recall that, based upon the fifty-one-day *CARD* statistics, PT conclude that the 1970 (table 10.2) and 1971 (table 10.3) margin decreases had no measurable

---

4. Since the proceeds of the stock sale are held by the lender and unavailable to the short seller, the margin requirement is effectively 150 percent in this example.

price effect. Despite the overall insignificance of these events, the tables contain many extreme-valued *SARD* estimates. In the eleven days surrounding the 1970 event date alone, two days have *SARD* statistics that exceed the 3 percent two-tailed critical value. The surplus of extreme-valued *SARD*s is even more evident in the results reported in table 10.3. The relative abundance of extreme-valued *SARD*s reported by PT may be an an additional indication of poorly matched firms generating omitted-factor contamination in the test statistics.

After attributing the statistical significance of the 1974 margin change to an omitted small-firm factor, PT conclude, "[T]he pricing results clearly refute the hypothesis that changes in margin requirements are associated with changes in binding constraints on security investors." The methodological problems identified in this discussion suggest otherwise. If the matched-pair statistics are not biased by omitted factors, then the 1974 margin event is statistical evidence that, in some instances, margin requirements do impose binding constraints on investors. If omitted factors bias the event test results, the binding-constraint hypothesis has not been subjected to an accurate test.

Although my priors are consistent with the conclusions of PT, the methodological issues raised in this discussion reduce my confidence in the accuracy of their reported statistics. The potential statistical problems at issue are important, but they may also be relatively easy to address. I encourage the authors to consider these issues in any future revision of this paper.

References

Hardouvelis, G. 1988. Margin Requirements and Stock Market Volatility. *Federal Reserve Bank of New York Quarterly Review,* 80–89.

———. 1990. Margin Requirements, Volatility, and the Transitory Component of Stock Prices. *American Economic Review* 80:736–62.

Hsieh, D., and M. Miller. 1990. Margin Regulation and Stock Market Volatility. *Journal of Finance* 45, no. 1: 3–30.

Kupiec, P. 1989. Initial Margin Requirements and Stock Returns Volatility: Another Look. *Journal of Financial Services Research* 3, no. 2–3: 287–301.

Kupiec, P., and S. Sharpe. 1991. Animal Spirits, Margin Requirements, and Stock Price Volatility. *Journal of Finance* 46, no. 2: 717–31.

Largay, J., and R. West. 1973. Margin Changes and Stock Price Behavior. *Journal of Political Economy* 81:328–39.

Moore, T. 1966. Stock Market Margin Requirements. *Journal of Political Economy* 74:158–67.

Salinger, M. 1989. Stock Market Margin Requirements and Volatility: Implications for Regulation of Stock Index Futures. *Journal of Financial Services Research* 3, no. 2–3: 121–38.

Authors' Reply

One of the most interesting aspects of being invited to present a paper at a research conference is the generally high variability in the content of the discussants' comments. In their remarks, Paul Kupiec and Craig MacKinlay offer further empirical evidence in support of this proposition. As the present reply will show, we believe that many of Kupiec's more paper-specific comments are undeservedly critical, while MacKinlay's more generalized comments represent a considerable and insightful research advance.

The basic premise of our paper is a very simple one. Specifically, we believe that the only appropriate test of the effectiveness of changes in stock market margin requirements at reducing "undesirable" security market perturbations is between otherwise identical securities differing only with respect to the presence or absence of Federal Reserve margin requirements. Indeed, since changes in margin requirements are one of only a very few discrete policy tools that the Federal Reserve has at its disposal to influence general economic conditions, it is extremely likely that changes in margin levels will have important signaling ramifications, *independent of any changes in the overall security lending environment.* Thus, without the creation of separate "marginable" and "nonmarginable" stock portfolios, it is impossible to distinguish between those adjustments in security market behavior resulting from *information effects only* (that is, effects that are identical across *all* equity securities) from those changes resulting from *shifts in binding borrowing constraints on equity investors* (that is, effects due to changes in the overall security lending environment). Our study, by exploiting a 1969 amendment to the Securities Exchange Act of 1934—an amendment that allowed, for the first time, securities dealers and brokers to extend margin credit on *selected* (but not all) OTC equities— is the first specifically designed to effectively differentiate between these effects. Such a differential test is extremely important since there is ample evidence that both changes in Federal Reserve margin levels *and* inclusion on the Federal Reserve's OTC margin list are associated with statistically significant changes in security pricing behavior. The findings of the present study illustrate that price changes around changes in Federal Reserve margin levels are the result of information effects only and are not due to changes in binding borrowing constraints on equity investors.

Kupiec begins his comments by noting that we "examine the effects of changes in margin requirements on the returns of small capitalization stocks." Yes, the firms included in our sample are relatively small when compared with larger, listed firms. However, the purpose of the study was not to study low-capitalization stocks per se. Our concentration on OTC stocks occurred precisely because these are the only groups of stocks via which an effective control portfolio could be constructed. The fact that the majority of these issues are "small" is an important by-product of the study—not its chief contribution. Further, it should be noted that, by their very construction, marginable and nonmarginable portfolios included in the tests comprised the largest firms traded on the OTC market.

While it is clearly true that studies examining the volatility changes of the S&P Composite index in response to changes in margin levels generally find no relationship between the two, it is also true (but not generally known) that the S&P Composite index *consisted of only ninety U.S. stocks until March 1957*. The larger S&P 500 index has been employed in margin tests only over the 1957 to 1974 time interval. Almost half (ten of twenty-one) the margin changes have been tested with an index employing only ninety of the largest U.S. firms. It is, therefore, by no means surprising that previous researchers have mined so little from the margin-change vein. It would be surprising only if they hadn't.

In a *direct test* of the relationship between firm size and security responses of NYSE-listed equities to change in margin levels, Pruitt (1993) clearly documents that smaller firms respond to a statistically significantly greater degree to the announcement of margin changes than the S&P Composite index. Given the known inverse relationship between firm size and firm leverage and the "homemade leverage" arguments of Modigliani and Miller (1958), the known inverse relationship between firm size and firm-specific informational asymmetries (e.g., Barry and Brown [1984]), and the known inverse relationship between firm size and institutional ownership (e.g., Pruitt and Wei [1989]), it is clear that individual margin traders must hold a proportionally larger share of the stock of smaller firms. Thus, while it is true that most previous researchers have found no consistent relationship between changes in margin levels and stock return behavior, it is equally clear that these same researchers have examined the very index of securities least likely to illustrate a demonstrable margin effect.

Kupiec's next major point concerns the efficacy of margin changes in a broader context: "Would [finding small firms respond more to margin changes] imply that margin requirements are an effective tool that can be used to control the volatility of the stock market?" We argue that it could. Indeed, a careful reading of the Securities Exchange Act of 1934 makes it clear that one of the three important reasons for the passage of margin regulations in the first place concerned the protection of unsophisticated investors. While one could argue that margin traders are not, by definition, unsophisticated, could the same be said for the nonmargin traders investing in heavily margined securities? We believe that margin regulations were not enacted to protect margin traders. Rather, we believe that they were enacted to keep the trading activities of margin traders from adversely affecting less sophisticated nonmargin traders. To the extent that changes in margin levels are employed by the Federal Reserve to reduce the "undesirable" results of margin trading activity by margin traders in smaller firms, the Federal Reserve will have enhanced the safety of nonmargin traders in these same issues. Thus, a potential and important paradox is resolved. It is indeed quite possible for changes in margin levels to simultaneously reduce "undesirable" security return behavior in smaller issues while failing to lead to any measurable effects in a broader market index, such as the S&P Composite.

Kupiec's comments concerning our methodology are more relevant. No, the methodology is not perfect. None ever is. However, given the extremely high costs associated with the hand collection of data, we continue to believe that the methodologies employed in the empirical tests are the best that can reasonably be performed.

Kupiec states that our data-selection criteria "match[es] each [marginable] stock with a nonmarginable OTC stock in the same four-digit SIC code category." This is correct as far as it goes, but it by no means describes all the selection criteria employed. First, we don't simply grab "any" marginable firm included on the Federal Reserve's OTC margin list. Rather, all marginable firms serve as *potential* sample firms only because they are included on the OTC margin list. To actually be included in the study they must then be matched with a nonmarginable OTC firm *that itself is later added to the OTC margin list.* This latter point is especially critical. Although Kupiec is correct in that there may, in general, be quite a few differences between the firms included on the Fed's OTC list and those not included on the list, it almost certainly is true that the underlying differences between firms added to the list between, say, May and November 1972 must be very slight indeed. Again, *all of the firms included in each of the nonmarginable OTC samples as of a given margin change were themselves added to the Fed's OTC list by the time of the next margin change.*

Also ignored in Kupiec's discussion of our research design is the actual matching procedure employed. While we did match on the basis of four-digit SIC codes, this is by no means the only criterion involved in the firm matching. Rather, as is noted in the study, in addition to SIC codes, firms were also matched on the basis of debt/equity ratios as well as total sales. Thus, although it is clear that our marginable/nonmarginable firms are not in point of fact perfect substitutes, they are very closely matched indeed. We are not aware of a more careful matching procedure employed in any research endeavor employing hand-collected data.

In addition to his general and methodological concerns, Kupiec takes exception with our interpretation of the 1974 margin decrease results. In these tests we note that the price changes observed for the nonmarginable sample significantly exceed those registered by the marginable sample. Given that this particular margin change occurred on January 3, 1974, we correctly interpret this differential response as a result of the well-known small-firm effect. Kupiec, on the other hand, suggests that this result may in fact be due to the trading behavior of short sellers taking advantage of the lower margin levels. To test this hypothesis directly, we divided each firm listed on either the New York or the American Stock Exchange into ten market-value deciles as of January 3, 1974. We next calculated the abnormal returns of each of these deciles em-

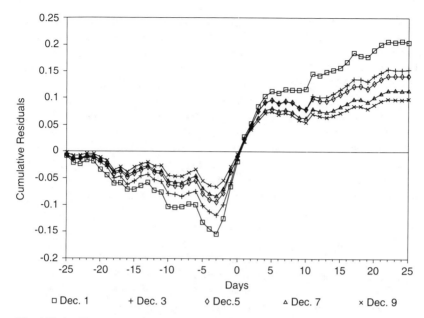

Fig. 10R.1   Unexpected decrease, 1974, deciles 1, 3, 5, 7, 9
Source: Scholes and Williams, Value-Weighted Index.

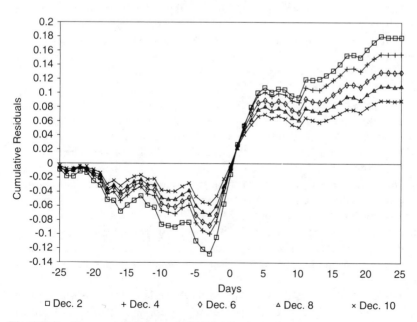

Fig. 10R.2   Unexpected decrease, 1974, deciles 2, 4, 6, 8, 10
Source: Scholes and Williams, Value-Weighted Index.

ploying a standard market-model methodology. Figure 10R.1 plots these results for deciles 1, 3, 5, 7, and 9, while figure 10R.2 provides the same results for size deciles 2, 4, 6, 8, and 10. Even the most casual observer will recognize the obvious relationship between firm size and price performance around the time of this margin change. Thus, it should be quite clear that our January 1974 margin-change results are indeed driven by the small-firm effect. The fact that such a size differential exists at all does support Kupiec's conjecture that our firm-matching procedure is not entirely capable of eliminating *all* nonmargin effects between the two sets of firms. However, the "relative abundance of extreme-valued *SARD*s reported" in our study are almost certainly the result of the fact that the hand collection of our data set limited the size of our marginable and nonmarginable firm portfolios to twenty stocks each.

In sum, we are sympathetic to the wishes of Kupiec with respect to both a larger data set and a more precise marginable/nonmarginable firm-matching criteria. Until finer work on the subject is forthcoming, however, we will continue to maintain that our study represents the best that has yet to be performed on the subject of the price, volatility, volume, and liquidity effects of changes in Federal Reserve margin requirements. But just how good is the best? It is to this issue and, more specifically, MacKinlay's insightful analysis that we address the following brief comments.

MacKinlay attacks the margin-change, security-response question in an entirely new and innovative manner. His comments concern the statistical likelihood of actually detecting a margin-change price volatility relationship should one indeed exist. Drawing heavily on the empirical results presented previously by Hsieh and Miller (1990), MacKinlay establishes numerically that the Levene test employed by these authors is almost incapable of detecting volatility effects in response to margin changes. In other words, the power of their test statistics is quite low. While noting that the F-statistics employed in the present paper are more powerful than the Levene tests, MacKinlay's simulations clearly document that "only when extreme changes in volatility occur would one expect these tests using individual change events to be able to statistically detect the volatility effects." The F-statistics employed in the present study are indeed based upon individual margin changes and, as such, strongly suggest that our failure to document a statistically significant volatility response between the marginable and the nonmarginable portfolios may be due as much (or more) to low statistical power as an inherent inability on the part of margins to influence actual return behavior. Thus, one is forced to conclude that, even if the current study is indeed the best yet performed concerning the margin-change price behavior question, it may not be good enough to finally put it to rest.

While specifically addressed only to our volatility tests, one could ask if similar things could not be said concerning our price, volume, and liquidity tests as well. We believe not. Indeed, detailed simulation studies by Brown and Warner (1985) have fully documented the statistical power of the event methodologies employed in the present (and similar) studies. While by no means all-powerful, such tests have repeatedly (and accurately) been employed to assess the valuation effects of a variety of economic phenomena. Thus, our failure to identify a statistically significant differential price response between the marginable and nonmarginable OTC stock portfolios around the time of Federal Reserve margin changes is more than likely due to a lack of such a differential effect rather than a paucity of statistical power. Given their basis in such event-type models, we believe that similar things could be said for our volume and liquidity tests as well. Unfortunately, as we note in the study, the lack of a firm unidirectional hypothesis concerning our liquidity tests renders these tests interesting, but largely meaningless.

We agree with MacKinlay that more theoretical work on the relationship between stock prices, volatility, volume, and liquidity is needed. Kupiec's own work on this area is especially interesting in this respect. We continue to believe that our study is the best yet performed. We believe that it addresses and, in some cases, answers several important questions concerning the current status of margin regulation. However, we must agree with MacKinlay when he states in his comments that "there is still more [work] to be done."

References

Barry, Christopher B., and Stephen J. Brown. 1984. Differential information and the small firm effect. *Journal of Financial Economics* 13:283–94.

Brown, Stephen J., and Jerold B. Warner. 1985. Using daily stock returns: The case of event studies. *Journal of Financial Economics* 14:3–31.

Hsieh, David A., and Merton H. Miller. 1990. Margin regulation and stock market volatility. *Journal of Finance* 45:3–30.

Kupiec, Paul, and Stephen Sharpe. 1991. Animal spirits, margin requirements, and stock price volatility. *Journal of Finance* 46:717–31.

Modigliani, Franco, and Merton H. Miller. 1958. The cost of capital, corporation finance, and the theory of investment. *American Economic Review* 48:261–97.

Pruitt, Stephen W. 1993. Small firm responses to changes in Federal Reserve margin requirements: Evidence from early data. *Economics Letters* 41:301–6.

Pruitt, Stephen W., and K. C. John Wei. 1989. Institutional ownership and changes in the S&P 500. *Journal of Finance* 44:509–13.

Contributors

William P. Albrecht
Department of Economics
University of Iowa
Iowa City, IA 52242

Bernard S. Black
School of Law
Columbia University
435 West 116th Street
New York, NY 10027

Corinne Bronfman
Department of Finance
McClelland Hall, Room 315R
University of Arizona
Tucson, AZ 85721

John Y. Campbell
Department of Economics
Littauer Center 213
Harvard University
Cambridge, MA 02138

John C. Coffee, Jr.
School of Law
Columbia University
435 West 116th Street
New York, NY 10027

Ian Domowitz
Department of Economics
Northwestern University
2003 Sheridan Road
Evanston, IL 60208

Philip H. Dybvig
Olin School of Business
Washington University
1 Brookings Drive
St. Louis, MO 63130

Edward H. Fleischman
Linklaters & Paines
885 Third Avenue, #2600
New York, NY 10022

F. Douglas Foster
College of Business Administration
Department of Finance
University of Iowa
Iowa City, IA 52242

Mary Ann Gadziala
Senior Advisor
Division of Market Regulation
Securities and Exchange Commission
Washington, DC 20549

Kathleen Hagerty
Kellogg Graduate School of Man-
   agement
Northwestern University
2001 Sheridan Road
Evanston, IL 60208-2006

Lawrence E. Harris
Department of Finance
School of Business Administration
University of Southern California
Los Angeles, CA 90089-1421

Chris A. Hynes
President
State Street Brokerage Services, Inc.
PO Box 1985
Boston, MA 02105

T. Eric Kilcollin
Managing Director and Chief Operating
    Officer
Wells Fargo Nikko Investment Advisors
45 Fremont Street
San Francisco, CA 94105

Paul H. Kupiec
Board of Governors
Federal Reserve System
Mail Stop-89
Washington, DC 20551

Bruce N. Lehmann
Graduate School of International Rela-
    tions and Pacific Studies
University of California, San Diego
1415 Robinson Building
La Jolla, CA 92093

Andrew W. Lo
Sloan School of Management
Massachusetts Institute of Technology
50 Memorial Drive
Cambridge, MA 02142

Robert L. McDonald
Kellogg Graduate School of Man-
    agement
Northwestern University
2001 Sheridan Road
Evanston, IL 60208

Thomas H. McInish
Fogelman College
Department of Finance
University of Memphis
Memphis, TN 38152

A. Craig MacKinlay
Department of Finance
The Wharton School of Management
Steinberg-Dietrich Hall
University of Pennsylvania
3620 Locust Walk
Philadelphia, PA 19104

Ananth Madhavan
FBE Department
701 Hoffman Hall
University of Southern California
Los Angeles, CA 90089

Harold C. Messenheimer
65 Rincon Loop Road
Tijeras, NM 87059

Geoffrey P. Miller
The Law School
University of Chicago
1111 East 60th Street
Chicago, IL 60637

David M. Modest
Haas School of Business
University of California
350 Barrows Hall
Berkeley, CA 94720

Harold Mulherin
Department of Finance
Pennsylvania State University
University Park, PA 16802

Robert Neal
Federal Reserve Bank of Kansas City
10th Street and Grand Avenue
Kansas City, MO 64198

Kazuhisa Okamoto
Managing Director
Wells Fargo Nikko Investment Advisors
12-7 Iidabashi 1-Chome
Chiyoda-ku, Tokyo 102
Japan

Stephen W. Pruitt
Department of Finance, Insurance, and
    Real Estate
Fogelman College of Business and Eco-
    nomics
University of Memphis
Memphis, TN 38152

David Reiffen
Bureau of Economics
Federal Trade Commission
6th & Pennsylvania NW
Washington, DC 20580

Peter C. Reiss
Graduate School of Business
Littlefield Hall
Stanford University
Stanford, CA 94305

Michael D. Robbins
40 East 88th Street, Apt. #3A
New York, NY 10128

Kenneth J. Singleton
Graduate School of Business
Stanford University
Stanford, CA 94305

K. S. Maurice Tse
Graduate School of Business
801 West Michigan Street
Indianapolis, IN 46202

Ingrid M. Werner
Graduate School of Business
Littlefield Hall
Stanford University
Stanford, CA 94305

Lawrence J. White
Stern School of Business
Management Education Center
New York University
44 West 4th Street
New York, NY 10012

Robert A. Wood
Distinguished Professor of Finance
Department of Finance
University of Memphis
Memphis, TN 38152

Participants

Preconference

Geoffrey Carliner	NBER
Richard Caves	Harvard University
James Cochrane	New York Stock Exchange
Oliver Hart	Massachusetts Institute of Technology and NBER
Joel Hasbrouck	New York University and New York Stock Exchange
Jerry Hausman	Massachusetts Institute of Technology
Paul Healy	Massachusetts Institute of Technology
Andrew W. Lo	Massachusetts Institute of Technology and NBER
Robert C. Merton	Harvard Business School and NBER
Sharon Oster	Yale University
Nancy Rose	Massachusetts Institute of Technology and NBER
James Shapiro	New York Stock Exchange

Conference

William P. Albrecht	University of Iowa
Peter Algert	Securities and Exchange Commission
Bernard S. Black	Columbia University
Marshall Blume	University of Pennsylvania
Corinne Bronfman	University of Arizona

John Y. Campbell	Harvard University and NBER
James H. Cheek, III	Bass, Berry & Sims
James Cochrane	New York Stock Exchange
John C. Coffee, Jr.	Columbia University
James D. Cox	Duke University
Ian Domowitz	Northwestern University
Michael P. Dooley	University of Virginia
Philip H. Dybvig	Washington University
Martin Feldstein	Harvard University and NBER
Edward H. Fleischman	Linklaters & Paines
F. Douglas Foster	University of Iowa
Mary Ann Gadziala	Securities and Exchange Commission
Larry Glosten	Columbia University
Joseph Grundfest	Stanford University
Kathleen Hagerty	Northwestern University
Robert W. Hamilton	University of Texas, Austin
Lawrence E. Harris	University of Southern California
Chris A. Hynes	State Street Brokerage Services, Inc.
T. Eric Kilcollin	Wells Fargo Institutional Trust Co.
Michael S. Knoll	University of Southern California
Paul H. Kupiec	Federal Reserve System
Pete Kyle	Duke University
Bruce N. Lehmann	University of California, San Diego
Andrew W. Lo	Massachusetts Institute of Technology and NBER
Robert L. McDonald	Northwestern University and NBER
Thomas H. McInish	University of Memphis
A. Craig MacKinlay	University of Pennsylvania and NBER
Ananth Madhavan	University of Southern California
Harold C. Messenheimer	Commodities Futures Trading Commission
Geoffrey P. Miller	University of Chicago
Merton Miller	University of Chicago
David M. Modest	University of California, Berkeley
Andrew G. T. Moore, II	Supreme Court of Delaware
Harold Mulherin	Pennsylvania State University
Robert Neal	Federal Reserve Bank of Kansas City
Kazuhisa Okamoto	Wells Fargo Nikko Investment Advisors
Stephen W. Pruitt	University of Memphis
David Reiffen	Federal Trade Commission

Peter C. Reiss	Stanford University and NBER
Michael D. Robbins	Independent floor broker, New York Stock Exchange
Richard Roll	University of California, Los Angeles
Stephen Ross	Yale University
James Shapiro	New York Stock Exchange
Kenneth J. Singleton	Stanford University and NBER
George Sofianos	New York Stock Exchange
Hans Stoll	Vanderbilt University
K. S. Maurice Tse	Indiana University
Ingrid M. Werner	Stanford University and NBER
Lawrence J. White	New York University
Robert A. Wood	University of Memphis
Susan Woodward	Securities and Exchange Commission

Author Index

Subject Index

Accounting standards: compatible international, 230; German and Japanese bond markets, 249. *See also* Generally accepted accounting principles (GAAP)

Arizona Stock Exchange, 96

Auctions: Arizona Stock Exchange, 96; automated single-price systems, 97; price discovery for newly issued bonds, 245; TSE batch auction, 280–81; TSE *itayose* price, 280, 291; TSE *zaraba* market, 281; Wunsch Auction System, 101, 105, 113

Automation Review Policy, Securities and Exchange Commission, 98

Basel Accord, 226–28

Benchmark selection: bond markets in Japan, Germany, and United States, 249; German cash bond market, 246; Japanese cash bond market, 247–48

Best bid-ask spreads. *See* Touch (best bid-ask spread)

Best interest justification for regulation, 214, 237

Bid-ask spreads: comparison of quoted and touch spreads on SEAQ and Nasdaq, 129–45; derivative pricing from, 82; differences in SEAQ and Nasdaq transaction spreads, 133; effect of trading fragmentation on, 71–72; with increased competition, 63–64; marginable and nonmarginable OTC firm portfolios, 336–37; in market with competitive broker, 48; in measurement of portfolio trading quality, 67, 76; monopolist broker, 42–43; SEAQ

distribution quoted and touch spreads, 146–50; SEAQ quotation system, 126–27; touch or best, 4, 132–45; in trade execution, 178–79; variation in SEAQ apparent quote and touch spreads, 150–63. *See also* Touch (best bid-ask spread)

Bids: automated continuous markets, 97; single-price auction systems, 97

Binding constraint hypothesis, 324

Board of Trade of the City of Chicago v. Securities and Exchange Commisson (SEC) (1991), 100n24, 102n33

Bond characteristics, German, Japanese, and U.S., 250–51

Bond markets: auctions and futures of German, Japanese, and U.S., 246–47; factors contributing to liquidity in secondary, 245–46; price discovery in secondary, 245

Bond markets, cash: impediments to price discovery in, 245–55; role of futures in price discovery on, 255–63

Brokers: actions in securities market model, 39–41; comparison of monopolist and competitive, 36–37; competitive market, 43–49; incentives to acquire specialist unit, 199; as market makers, 50; monopoly market, 41–43; regulation of, 98; in risky asset model, 39

Broker-dealers: acquisition of specialist units, 177–78, 181–84; exchange rules related to relations with specialists, 180–84; regulation of, 98; on SEAQ system, 125